FREUD AND ORIGINAL SIN

FREUD
AND ORIGINAL SIN

Sharon MacIsaac

PAULIST PRESS
New York / Paramus / Toronto

Library of Congress
Catalog Card Number: 73-92232

ISBN: 0-8091-1822-X

Published by Paulist Press
Editorial Office: 1865 Broadway, N.Y., N.Y. 10023
Business Office: 400 Sette Drive, Paramus, N.J. 07652

Printed and bound in the
United States of America

ACKNOWLEDGMENTS

I wish to thank Sigmund Freud Copyrights, Ltd., The Institute of Psycho-Analysis,
The Hogarth Press, Ltd., Basic Books, Inc., Liveright and Co., W. W. Norton and
Co., G. Allen and Unwin, Ltd., and Routledge and Kegan Paul, Ltd., for permission
to publish material quoted from the *Standard Edition of the Complete Psychological
Works of Sigmund Freud* (revised and edited by James Strachey). Acknowledgments
are made also to The Hogarth Press, Ltd. for quotations from Ernest Jones' *Sigmund
Freud: Life and Work*, Vol. I; and to Basic Books, Inc. for material from Sigmund
Freud, *The Origins of Psycho-Analysis* (edited by M. Bonaparte, A. Freud and E. Kris).
Finally, thanks are extended to McMaster University for a Summer Research
Stipend that facilitated the preparation of this manuscript for publication.

CONTENTS

vii

PART TWO

ORIGINAL SIN

To
Lea Hindley-Smith

INTRODUCTION

Biblical scholars have concluded that the starting point for the Genesis narrative of the fall was an existential realization rather than a tradition handed down from the beginnings of the race. The starting point was a recognition of the human condition as deeply vitiated. In other words, the reality confronting the sacred author was the sin of the world. The conviction that framed the story of the first man and woman was that the destructive influences had to be of human origin; they were not of God the Creator. They were introduced by a human option in the remote past [1]—an option which the author ascribes to the primal ancestral couple, thereby underlining its nature as a universal negative dispensation over all their progeny.[2] Thus the vitiating influences in the very tissue of human existence took on the added meaning of *peccatum originale originatum*.

It is important for a profound and substantial theology of original sin that the experiential starting point be the focus. That theology has been weakened and even trivialized by over-speculation, by a shift of emphasis onto hypothetical and deductive elements on the periphery of the central message. The mention of original sin conjures up debates on original justice, polygenism, the state of limbo, etc., while the phenomenological starting point—the human condition as diseased by a cumulative, pre-deliberate perversity—has been probed only too little.

In the words of a Catholic reference text, *peccatum originale originatum* is "a condition of guilt, weakness or debility found in

1

human beings historically (or in which they are personally situated), prior to their own free option for good or evil. . . . This
is a state of being rather than a human act or its consequence." ³
This definition is a shorthand account of an experience portrayed
by virtually every great writer and artist. Within the Judaeo-
Christian tradition, it is a constant theme throughout Scriptures,
finding definitive expression in St. Paul's Epistle to the Romans.
Especially since the time of St. Augustine, it has received specific
(if not isolated) attention, and at certain periods in history,
notably at the time of Pelagius, the Reformers, and the present
day, crisis has brought a fresh appreciation of its centrality. The
Church declared the Catholic consensus on its meaning at the
Council of Trent.

From these varied modes of expression a common message
emerges. There are deep-seated, destructive influences at work
in human behavior. These are experienced as in some real sense
autonomous, removed from conscious control. Herein is perhaps
the most characteristic aspect of *peccatum originale originatum,*
this failure of integration which results in the painful sense
of self-alienation. They are specified by the term concupiscence,
which is the materiality of original sin.⁴ The sinfulness is experienced as collective. That is, not only is it experienced by
every human being, but human beings as a group and as a
race affect one another at a level below conscious awareness,
helping to form in one another the nature and strength of the
non-integrated forces. There is a continuous subliminal interaction in the present and from one generation to the next, so that
the consequences of moral victory or defeat are never just personal; they are always collective. We merely state this factor
from a slightly different viewpoint when we say that sinfulness
has an historical dimension. Certain ancient myths express the
feeling that there was a primordial time when man was at harmony with himself, with nature and with other men. He destroyed that harmony himself, and successive generations have
intensified the estrangement. Our present condition has a history
determined in very complex ways by men's choices. Finally, there
is a more or less vague but persistent linking of sinfulness and
the body. Our bodies are still so amazingly little known to us,

with their strange, unruly, tenacious impulses. Transparent in so many of the descriptions of sin is the sense of the body as unchartered and inimical territory.

The phenomenology of the human condition, specifically its pathological features, can be enormously enlightened by the contributions of the modern social sciences. This book stems from the conviction that the discipline initiated by Sigmund Freud can *N.B.* greatly enrich the understanding of original sin and the sin of the world.

There are certain features of psychic life which make predicament inevitable. Delicate, complex, a tension of powerful forces, it is peculiarly vulnerable to disorientation. Freud exposed the psychic dialectic and its pathologies with singular perspicacity. His exposition speaks to virtually every aspect of the theology of *peccatum originale originatum:* the universal phenomenon of non-integration, the experience of dissociated or quasi-autonomous psychic activity; the formative influence exercised by the environment; the psyche as a function of the race's history; and the dialectic with the instincts, which are both psychic and somatic.

The theology of cumulative, antecedent sinfulness is in need of empirical amplification. While Christian teachers from the earliest centuries to the present day have made impressive use of various philosophies to understand the conscious, discrete actions of the individual, an equally fundamental reality—the unconscious, collective and pre-deliberate factors from which every act issues—has been strikingly neglected. Literature on original sin abounds. But it seems justified to say that in general, consideration of the phenomenological aspect is limited to brief descriptions of the characteristic elements or to lamentations; its relationship to other doctrines seems to dominate. Historically, the theology of original sin suffers from over-speculation, and at worst, from obscurantism and a kind of pseudo-mysticism. It is rarified because the sinful conditioning of man—as distinct from his conscious, moral struggle in discrete acts—has received so little hardheaded, inquisitive and resourceful attention.

I feel that this neglect is integrally related to a wider exclusion: to the obscurity and superstition in which men have been content to leave the reality of unconscious mental activity. Not until the end of the 19th century did a scientific, systematic investigation of the unconscious begin to gather momentum. And though Freud is one of the great modern revolutionaries, it can hardly be said that a common, enlightened seriousness about the unconscious now exists. It is still an area of illiteracy. This book is rooted in the conviction that the kind of sinful reality referred to by the terms *peccatum originale originatum* and the sin of the world bears primarily on man as unconscious.

N.B.

The above remarks are made specifically of theological reflection on original sin. They must be complemented, however, by a recognition of the growing influence of psychoanalysis on writings in moral theology. That relatively new discipline has had a profound influence on the awareness of Western man, and its influence is naturally perceptible in the works of contemporary theologians. What is more, there is a considerable quantity of literature dealing explicitly with the encounter of psychoanalysis and the faith. Nevertheless, the resources which I found most helpful in the preparation of this work were either psychoanalytic works or theological re-examinations of original sin. Works of synthesis were not constitutive of the theological perspectives I have suggested.

The reasons for this pertain to the genesis and methodology of this book. It grew out of the promise I sensed of a concurrence between certain emerging directions in the theology of original sin and some of Freud's insights. The former beg for development through intensive studies in the social sciences. After satisfying myself that no examination of Freud in this light had been undertaken, I moved directly from a study of the theology of original sin into the reading of the Freudian corpus. A second and more thorough reading of the literature on psychoanalysis and the faith was taken up after this book was virtually completed. It has confirmed the impression that this work, in its method and content, not only is not a duplication of previous efforts, but has gained from plunging first into the primary sources. There is no substitute for that experience. An extension of the discussion here does readily suggest itself, namely to develop it with respect to the work being done on moral theology and the psychoanalytic contribution. Reference will be made to some of these writings in the footnotes. However, since in general the subject of original sin is referred to there only in passing, that development seems to me to extend to another volume.

The prevailing literature on psychoanalysis and the faith seems on the whole to have arisen from a different starting point. Insofar as the distinction is meaningful, it is pastoral rather than speculative. In general, this literature is a response to the challenge, and, at first, the threat which psychoanalysis presented to the believer. Some of it is rather banal and even poor; some of it is excellent. The concern has been first of all to clear the authentic tradition from the aspersions which Freud cast upon it. Then, as the contributions of the new discipline have been increasingly appreciated, has come the concern to demonstrate that Freud's assessment of Christianity, its faith and morals, is not integral to his extraordinary insight into the human psyche, that it can be ascribed to him as an individual and as a child of the 19th century. There is great care, therefore, to clarify for a confused, reserved or intimidated public what might be called the formal object of psychoanalysis, in order to show that it does not supersede the faith, whatever its enthusiasts may claim. At the same time, there is a solid appreciation of the challenge of psychoanalysis to believers, and an overall sense that it, in fact, confronts them afresh with the authenticity and profundity of their faith. In the more advanced works, there is a concerted effort to integrate psychoanalytic insight into the pastoral ministry.

The questions posed in this encounter already seem well established. A few may be listed here. Religion, according to Freud, was an obsessional neurosis, or, alternately, an infantile projection onto, a creation of, a father image. Freud seems in many of his formulations to equate the superego with the conscience, with the result that all morality becomes pseudo-morality. His exposition of the unconscious determinants of human acts challenges former assumptions regarding moral freedom. What is the place of asceticism, of celibacy, given Freud's contention of the sexual etiology of psychic dispositions? Is the neurotic capable of a truly Christian disposition and life? What is the relationship between psychic health and holiness? Does the sacrament of penance have any place in the world of the psychoanalytic session? These questions have spurred a wholesome and perspicacious re-examination of the teachings of the faith, and most conspicuously, of the pastoral ministry.[5]

The aim of this book is to provide a richer phenomenological basis for theological reflection on original sin. The heart of the work is, therefore, Part One. Its preparation involved reading Freud's collected works in their entirety and ordering their elements into a synthesis that would be meaningful and clear to the non-psychoanalytic theologian. Secondary sources were avoided until the work had assumed definitive form. The proportions alone of Freud's work are, generally speaking, prohibitive to the theologian, and there are the added difficulties involved in embarking independently on a rather technical discipline. This synthesis is offered to the reader for his own reflection and development, and as an introduction to the reading of Freud himself and to such successors as Wilhelm Reich, Erich Fromm, Erik Erikson and R. D. Laing. Theological remarks, therefore, have been kept to a minimum in the first part; they serve only to give a sense of direction to the exposition. Nevertheless, the entire work is theological: the *lumen sub quo* of the reading, selection and synthesis was theological. As far as I know, this is the only work of its kind and certainly of its extent in the area of original sin—though the comparison so naturally suggests itself.

In Part Two, I have expressed my reflections on the relationship between a relatively new discipline and an ancient doctrine. It is done in broad, indicative lines, and speaks primarily to new directions in the theology of original sin which seem so akin to Freud's architectonic insights. Their questions converge on the necessity for a more searching anthropology. An exhaustive treatment is not attempted; that would be the work of several volumes and is of a different modality than this more introductory work. If this effort is successful, the reader, after completing it, will return to a more meaningful reading of Part One, and thence to Freud and the leading figures in the tradition he founded.

This study would seem to be within the stream which Gregory Baum has recently described as "prospective" theology. He compares it to normative theology, which "focuses on God's self-communication in Israel and Jesus Christ, as handed on by the Church, and therefore looks to the normative revelation of the past". It "deals with the *special* salvation history that constitutes the Christian Church". Prospective theology "is the discernment of, and the systematic reflection on God's ongoing self-communication in history and the cosmos".[6] It deals with the *universal* salvation history that constitutes the human race. "Specifically Christian in prospective theology are as *lumen sub quo* the question asked and hence the orientation of research as well as the sensitivity with which the material is examined and organized: question and sensitivity are taken from personal faith experienced in the Church." Father Baum adds, "While prospective theology is non-ecclesiastical in the sense that it does not study doctrine, sacraments, and ministry, it is nonetheless dependent on the Church's faith and the normative theology which interprets and elucidates the faith."[7]

It seems to me that the literature briefly reviewed above is predominantly normative. It is valuable, often brilliant, and an indispensable groundwork. If uncomplemented by this prospective approach, however, it risks being subtly out of step with the disposition of what might be called the "secular" Christian. In the present day, Catholics with sound theological backgrounds are entering into the social and political sciences—theory and praxis—with an involvement as unreserved and critical as their peers. The theology which issues from that involvement is distinctive. It fears apologetics or premature attempts at synthesis with the traditional, the fruit of a too secure or too exclusively specialized immersion in traditional theology. The challenge to the secular Christian is not only that he integrate the new with the old, but that he also be on the cutting-edge of his own disciplinary effort towards humanization. That kind of Christian involvement in psychoanalysis—one that is second to none in perspicacity, initiative and courage—has, I think, yet to be felt theologically.

Finally, discussion of fine points, inconsistencies, controverted elements and criticisms of Freud's statements have been omitted. The accuracy of the exposition has, I hope, been insured by discussions in the footnotes. They were prepared for the additional purpose of indicating where further reading could be done on issues raised in the text. I have avoided developing Freud's later and more advanced theory of the ego because its bearing on cumulative, antecedent sin is less direct. There is one theme, however, whose relevance is more promising: that is, the dynamic called masochism, the self-destructive tendency present in every human being. I have omitted it because Freud's mature interpretation of it was integrally bound up with his theory of a primal death instinct. In that theory, he radicalized the self-destructive, regressive tendencies in the psyche to the level of primal instinct. That move, whose rather insubstantial grounds he himself admitted, has always been a controverted issue among his successors. The psychic phenomena—self-destruction, a regressive trend apparently towards ultimate inertia, the compulsion to repeat even harmful experiences—which occasioned the theory have been more incisively analyzed by Wilhelm Reich, and there, paradoxically, in closer accord with Freud's foundational insights. The relationship between those tendencies and original sin could be very fruitfully investigated through the study of Reich.

This study is a slightly revised version of a doctoral thesis completed at the Institute of Christian Thought in the University of St. Michael's College, Toronto, where it was written under the direction of Gregory Baum. The graduate student who makes it across the great doctoral divide knows how many people were integrally involved on the way. I want to thank all of these: my family, the Sisters of Sion who made my theological studies possible, the fine and generous scholars in the Institute of Christian Thought, and Therafields, the therapeutic community which has so grounded and vivified the whole learning experience.

PART ONE

FREUD

1. MAN'S CONSTITUTIVE SELF-ALIENATION:
Freud's Theory of the Unconscious

It would be peripheral and somehow dishonest to begin our study anywhere else but with Freud's understanding of the unconscious mind of man. Too many select his later more sociological works such as *Civilization and its Discontents* or *The Future of An Illusion,* publications from the last years of Freud's life, and feel confident that they have acquainted themselves with this modern giant. According to Freud himself, however, such writings emanate from a period in which he turned from his life's work proper to questions of a social nature that had preoccupied him years before.[1] They are valuable expressions of a brilliant individual's reflections on human society, but they are to a certain extent only extrapolations from the intense research into the workings of the psyche which occupied most of his life. This latter is the real core of his genius and his contribution, and it is there that I prefer to concentrate. In fact, he repeatedly emphasized that his exposition of the unconscious was at the heart of all his writings and was absolutely pivotal.[2]

There are reasons more proper to the subject of this work for beginning with Freud's understanding of the unconscious. Three aspects in this exposition move us directly into traditional reflections on original sin. In the first place, the unconscious by definition describes those forces not fully integrated by the ego

11

or "I". A more contemporary term for original sin, all distinctions guarded, might be self-alienation, or the experience of the divided self. Secondly, for Freud, the unconscious was the seat of the deepest influences of the race upon the individual. Now a characteristic of original sin is that it is "communicated to all men . . . by propagation." Thirdly, the unconscious evolves from and around the nucleus of the instincts, those forces at the threshold of mind and body. St. Paul speaks of "the sin living in my members" or "in my body" (Rom. 7:23), but his is only one expression of the traditional conviction that original sin has to do with a profound disorder at the level of instinctual life. Speaking formally, the Church refers to that sin as concupiscence, which is by definition such a disorder. These three aspects will define the three major directions of this work.

The Freudian insistence on the unconscious is a stumbling block for many, not only for those engaged in the various disciplines subsumed under psychology, but also for the layman. It is necessary at the outset, therefore, to gain as clear an understanding as possible of precisely what phenomena Freud indicated by this term. The best way of gaining it is to study Freud's own itinerary of discovery: his first encounters with non-conscious mental activity and the reasons that moved him to draw the conclusions he did.

The Path from Symptoms to the Unconscious

> Ladies and Gentlemen,—I know you are aware in regard to your own relations, whether with people or with things, of the importance of your starting point. This was also the case with psychoanalysis. . . . It began its work on what is, of all the contents of the mind, most foreign to the ego—on symptoms. Symptoms are derived from the repressed, they are, as it were, its representatives before the ego, but the repressed is foreign territory to the ego—internal foreign territory—just as reality (if you will forgive the unusual expression) is external foreign territory. The path led from symptoms to the unconscious, to the life of the instincts, to sexuality.[3]

Freud wrote the above passage in 1932, describing a series of events which had been set in motion almost exactly one-half a century earlier. The genesis of psychoanalysis, he stated, lay in the encounter with symptoms. What he was referring to are the symptoms found in the emotional disorder termed hysteria, the first disorder Freud was to work with and which served as his introduction to the life of the unconscious.

Hysteria was a more comprehensive diagnosis in the 19th century than it is today. Those suffering from it displayed a wide variety of symptoms including chronic nausea, blindness, paralysis, deafness and speech disturbances. What was peculiar to all of them was that though they revealed evident suffering, no physical explanation was discoverable. The medical profession, therefore, tended to regard hysterics as malingerers and as morally degenerate. In earlier times they were thought to be possessed.[4]

Freud's first significant encounter with hysteria was through an older friend and eminent physician, Josef Breuer. One evening in 1880, when Freud was still a medical student preparing for his final examinations, Breuer was called to the sick bed of a young woman of twenty-one years. Her name was Bertha Pappenheim, and her case was later recorded under the pseudonym of Anna O.

Anna O. was richly gifted intellectually and imaginatively, but like so many girls of her social status and time, she lived a monotonous life in the bosom of her family, spending long hours in mindless, "womanly" occupations. She developed the habit of daydreaming, and would lose herself for hours on end in what she called her "private theatre". In short, there were few opportunities for emotional and intellectual outlets. When she was twenty-one, her father, of whom she was passionately fond, fell ill of a peripleuritic abscess that eventually proved fatal. Anna devoted all her energies to nursing him, a task that meant long hours sitting at his bedside and watching him gradually succumb. After a few months, she fell ill herself and developed a series of strange symptoms.

> She suffered from a rigid paralysis, accompanied by loss of sensation, of both extremities on the right side of her body; and the same trouble from time to time affected her on the left side. Her eye movements were disturbed and her power of vision was subject to numerous restrictions. She had difficulties over the posture of her head; she had a severe ner-

vous cough. She had an aversion to taking nourishment, and on one occasion she was for several weeks unable to drink in spite of a tormenting thirst. Her powers of speech were reduced, even to the point of her being unable to speak or understand her native language. Finally, she was subject to conditions of *"absence"*, of confusion, of delirium, and of alteration of her whole personality.[5]

Breuer was very much interested in the girl, but felt helpless in the beginning as to how to proceed. In retrospect, there seemed to be a series of chance events which suddenly lighted up the way. And these small indications were not lost to his acute observation. When Anna was in a state of confusion or absence, she was given to muttering phrases to herself. Breuer noted what she said, and when she was herself again, put her into a state of hypnosis where he would repeat these phrases to her. She began to describe in detail their context: daydreams and painful memories of her father's illness. It became clear that this highly emotional content was the cause of her strange states. As the "talking cure" or "chimney-sweeping", as Anna called it, proceeded, her condition improved.

The real turning point in the case came with the revelation that talking could bring more important results than temporary relief. Breuer was using hypnosis so that Anna could relax deeply and speak without inhibition. While under hypnosis one evening, she muttered about a scene which had disgusted her, became very angry (she hadn't at the time of its occurrence), and then promptly drank a glass of water. Now a glass of water had figured prominently in the remembered scene, and since then, the girl, even when tormented by thirst, had been unable to bring herself to drink. Breuer was astonished:

> Never before had anyone removed a hysterical symptom by such a method or had thus gained so deep an insight into its causation. It could not fail to prove a momentous discovery if the expectation were confirmed that others of the patient's symptoms—perhaps the majority of them—had arisen and could be removed in the same manner. Breuer spared himself no pains in convincing himself that this was so, and he proceeded to a systematic investigation of the pathogenesis of the other and more serious symptoms of the patient's illness. And it really *was* so. Almost all the symptoms had arisen in this way as residues—"precipi-

tates"—they might be called—of emotional experiences. To these experiences we later gave the name of "psychical traumas", while the particular nature of the symptoms was explained by their relation to the traumatic scenes which were their cause.[6]

The discovery was fashioned into a therapeutic tool called the cathartic method.

All the hysterical phenomena, it was discovered, had been produced from the events of the six months in which Anna had nursed her father. The symptoms described earlier disappeared one by one as Anna was able to remember—and release—the emotions surrounding the scenes which had caused them. The most dramatic and well known scene is the following:

> She once woke up during the night in great anxiety about the patient, who was in a high fever; and she was under the strain of expecting the arrival of a surgeon from Vienna who was to operate. Her mother had gone away for a short time and Anna was sitting at the bedside with her arm over the back of the chair. She fell into a waking dream and saw a black snake coming towards the sick man from the wall to bite him. (It is most likely that there were in fact snakes in the field behind the house and that these had previously given the girl a fright; they would thus have provided the material for her hallucination.) She tried to keep the snake off, but it was as though she was paralysed. Her right arm, over the back of the chair, had gone to sleep and had become anesthetic and paretic; and when she looked at it the fingers turned into little snakes with death's heads (the nails). (It seems probable that she had tried to use her paralysed right arm to drive off the snake and that its anaesthesia and paralysis had consequently become associated with the hallucination of the snake.) When the snake vanished, in her terror she tried to pray. But language failed her: she could find no tongue in which to speak, till at last she thought of some children's verses in English and then found herself able to think and pray in that language. The whistle of the train that was bringing the doctor whom she expected broke the spell.[7]

When Anna had recollected these scenes under hypnosis and began to vent the powerful emotions she'd striven to hide from the sick man, the symptoms disappeared. Yet in a normal state, she was no more able to remember the causative events or to make any more sense of her varied symptoms than could those around her. In her normal moments she was even annoyed with herself and thought it all simulated.[8]

The student Freud was greatly interested in the now famous case, and Breuer, who was completely absorbed in it, was glad to discuss it with him. "He repeatedly read me pieces of the case history, and I had an impression that it accomplished more towards an understanding of neurosis than any previous observation." [9] In 1885, Freud went to Paris to study under one of Europe's most famous neurologists, Jean Charcot. Charcot was the first to take hysteria seriously from a medical viewpoint, to study its laws and to teach it systematically. He lectured at the Salpêtrière, Paris' famous asylum for the insane.

> I was determined to inform Charcot of these discoveries when I reached Paris, and I actually did so. But the great man showed no interest in my first outline of the subject, so that I never returned to it and allowed it to pass from my mind. When I was back in Vienna I turned once more to Breuer's observation and made him tell me more about it. . . . The immediate question, however, was whether it was possible to generalize from what he had found in a single case. The state of things he had discovered seemed to me to be of so fundamental a nature that I could not believe it could fail to be present in any case of hysteria if it had been proved to occur in a single one. But the question could only be answered by experience. I therefore began to repeat Breuer's investigations with my own patients and eventually . . . I worked at nothing else.[10]

Seven years later, Freud and Breuer published the results of their work in a "Preliminary Communication" (1893), which was followed in 1895 by the book *Studies on Hysteria*.

Studies On Hysteria is generally regarded as the starting point of psychoanalysis.[11] The case of Anna O. had fortuitously brought to light the existence of amnesia in hysterical illness. With that discovery and the again almost fortuitous lifting of the amnesia came an immediate realization. There exists a mental and emotional life which is not accessible to conscious awareness, but which nevertheless operates as a powerful agent in conscious life. The authors began referring to it as "the unconscious" (*"das Unbewusste"*).[12]

What was their conception of the unconscious at this early

stage? Their language shows them conceiving of it as a kind of province of the mind. Thus Breuer spoke of Anna O.'s disturbing ideas "acting as a stimulus 'in the unconscious' "; [13] and Freud of perceptions "in the unconscious" beginning to show through indistinctly.[14] In fact, Freud's language outstripped his intellectual resolution of the data. It was only a few years later, as late as *The Interpretation of Dreams* (1899), that he clearly had accepted a second truly mental province of the psyche.[15]

Writing years later, Freud described the intellectual stage to which his early research had brought him:

> The oldest and best meaning of the word "unconscious" is the descriptive one; we call a psychical process unconscious whose existence we are obliged to assume—for some such reason as that we infer it from its effects—, but of which we know nothing. In that case we have the same relation to it as we have to a psychical process in another person, except that it is in fact one of our own. If we want to be still more correct, we shall modify our assertion by saying that we call a process unconscious if we are obliged to assume that it is being activated *at the moment,* though at the moment we know nothing about it.[16]

He went on to describe an uncertainty with which he had wrestled in the years following the *Studies:*

> This qualification makes us reflect that the majority of conscious processes are conscious only for a short time; very soon they become *latent,* but can easily become conscious again. We might also say that they had become unconscious, if it were at all certain that in the condition of latency they are still something psychical. So far we should have learnt nothing new; nor should we have acquired the right to introduce the concept of an unconscious into psychology.[17]

In terms of hysterical phenomena, the problem was whether the forces behind the symptoms could truly be called mental when they were not active, when their subject was in a more normal state. If these forces were not mental, then in what condition were they? And not only they, but the vast majority of our thoughts, feelings and memories, for they are actually conscious only episodically. To assert that the state of latency is not a mental one is to be forced to posit an unacceptable discontinuity in mental processes. On the other hand, that continuity is retained if mental events, when latent, remain in a psychic state but lack only the quality of consciousness. This was the conclusion Freud finally reached,[18] but his first response was to ignore the quality of consciousness and to try to account for the whole range of psychic behavior in a purely neurological manner. He framed his theory around the conditions of two material entities: the neurone and a chemical or physical energy which was kinetic or in a state of flow.

A circumstance from Freud's life explains his theoretical move. At this point in his life, Freud was still pursuing the neurological work for which he had been trained, as well as the new avenues of discovery which his "nervous" patients were opening up for him. His intense preoccupation with formulating a physical theory of psychical behavior was like working a neurological dream out of his system. He called it a "Project for a Scientific Psychology". Once it was drafted and sent to his close friend Wilhelm Fliess, however, he repudiated it and entered decisively upon a psychoanalytic approach to clinical phenomena, an approach which as a natural scientist he had been resisting.[19] Only the language of mental processes could account for the intricacies which his practice was increasingly forcing upon his attention.

Two clinical phenomena in particular demanded the existence of processes which were both unconscious and mental. These were the phenomena of repression and resistance. The more dramatic moments in the therapy of hysterics revealed not only the presence of "forgotten" but powerfully charged memories; they also revealed that hitherto a positive force had been at work to prevent them from coming to full attention. This quality of aversion to exposure was given the name resistance. Repression is a type of resistance: it refers to the act of denying certain memories or ideas access to conscious attention.

As long as the principal therapeutic method was the hypercompliant state of hypnosis, the patient's resistance was not so evident. It came into greater prominence as the result of a technical expediency. Freud found real difficulties in the use of hypnosis: only a fraction of his patients could enter it in any depth.

Some resisted any attempts at it. Its results could be soon shattered. He therefore tried to work out other methods which would achieve the same extension of consciousness. At first, he would simply place his hand on the patient's forehead and say with unshakeable conviction that a thought or image which was significantly related to his distress would occur to him. He would insist further that the patient voice the thought whether or not it seemed important or admissible. The change in technique brought fresh insight:

> Since this insistence involved effort on my part and so suggested the idea that I had to overcome a resistance, the situation led me at once to the theory that *by means of my psychical work I had to overcome a psychical force in the patient which was opposed to the pathogenic ideas becoming conscious (being remembered)*. A new understanding seemed to open before my eyes when it occurred to me that this must no doubt be the same psychical force that had played a part in the generating of the hysterical symptom and had at that time prevented the pathogenic idea from becoming conscious.[20]

Freud asked himself why he kept encountering an inner resistance, and upon considering his clinical experience, found an answer ready to hand:

> I recognized a universal characteristic of such pathogenic ideas: they were all of a distressing nature, calculated to arouse the effects of shame, of self-reproach and of psychical pain, and the feeling of being harmed; they were all of a kind that one would prefer not to have experienced, that one would rather forget. From all this there arose, as it were automatically, the thought of *defence*. . . . Thus a psychical force, aversion on the part of the ego, had originally driven the pathogenic idea out of association and was now opposing its return to memory.[21]

Freud was justly excited by the twin discovery of mental resistance and repression (or defence). He described it as "the cornerstone on which the whole structure of psycho-analysis rests",[22] for it constituted the advance from a purely descriptive understanding of unconsciousness to a sense of the dynamic etiology behind it. A cohesive, psychical explanation for the gaps in consciousness was now emerging.

Freud felt, moreover, that the phenomenon of defence and the mechanisms peculiar to hysteria had to be expressions of a more radical psychic principle. He formulated that principle in the so-called law of constancy: "The mental apparatus endeavours to keep the quantity of excitation present in it as low as possible or at least to keep it constant." [23] Repression operates in the service of this principle, but it is inevitably shortsighted, for distress cannot be obviated by the tactic of conscious evasion. According to the same law of constancy, the repressed responses must find some release, for they are nonetheless real. In the case of Anna O., they found outlet in physical symptoms. That release was pathological because veiled, and so, contorted and inadequate. Anxiety, spite, nightmares, depressions, psychotic episodes, obsession—all these were seen as delayed and distorted ways in which the psyche seeks to unburden itself of stimulation. In a healthy situation, strong emotion will be discharged more immediately and straightforwardly, in crying, shouting, talking, pacing, or even "thinking things through". With such discharge comes a return to equilibrium and the prevention of pathological distortions. It might be noted that in this same context of the principle of constancy came a forecast of a later and most unpopular Freudian emphasis: "The sexual instinct is undoubtedly the most powerful source of persisting increases of excitation (and consequently of neuroses)".[24]

The Importance of Dreams

The next major event in Freud's research into the unconscious came with his discovery of the importance of dreams. The correspondence with Wilhelm Fliess is our best source for his gradual insight into their logic. He realized first that every dream is a fictitious attempt to fulfil a wish—herein lay what he called "the Secret of Dreams".[25] Out of this realization came a rush of fresh insight into the inner dynamics of the mind. He found no dream an exception to this rule, whether it be the patent wish-fulfilments found in children's dreams or the terrifying nightmare. The latter, he showed, betrays a longing which powerfully threatens the ego and causes the dreamer acute anxiety.[26] He concluded that the conditions of sleep are such that unconscious activity can be permitted a freer rein. The real world is withdrawn from in sleep; there is no fear of expressing forbidden wishes in speech or motor expression, so the vigilance of repression, of the mind over itself, can be relaxed. The dream is a compromise, therefore, a fact further attested by the inability of the dreamer to make sense out of his wishes upon waking. In this way, the conditions of unconscious freedom are limited to the innocuous state of sleep.[27]

The wishes embodied in dreams have a peculiar characteristic. On the surface are wishes originating out of the contemporary experiences of the dreamer. But as the mind allows the memory of the dream to take over, a series of associations results, and almost invariably these associations reach further into the dreamer's past. "We find the child and the child's impulses still living on in the dream." [28]

Dreams revealed the foundational importance of childhood, the period of life when impressions go deepest and where the basic paths of self-direction are set down. A realization already forming itself in the work with hysterics was soundly confirmed: the experiences of the past are the source of unconscious activity.[29]

If dreams afford an opportunity to see the unconscious mind in a uniquely uninhibited state, then Freud's exultation can be full appreciated. He called them "the royal road to a knowledge of the unconscious activities of the mind".[30] He recognized, but through a much more ample and communicative medium, the mental dynamics that produced neurotic symptoms.[31] *The Interpretation of Dreams,* Freud wrote some thirty years after its publication, "contains, even according to my present-day judgement, the most valuable of all the discoveries it has been my good fortune to make. Insight such as this falls to one's lot but once in a lifetime".[32]

The understanding of dreams was a critical turning point in psychoanalysis for another reason. Unlike severely neurotic and psychotic symptoms, they form a part of normal human life; virtually everyone dreams. With dreams, then, came the crucial link between the normal and the pathological, and therefore the possibility of formulating sound general principles and foundations.[33]

With dreams, the laws and dynamics of the obscure unconscious came into fuller view. Though capable of producing complex mental products, unconscious activity, i.e., the mental activity in dreams, is not governed by the same laws of logic prevailing in conscious thought. In fact, it "might be called the Realm of the Illogical".[34] For example, unconscious thought shows a marked tendency to condensation: a single person, thing or word will be divested with very diverse meanings. The dream images are " 'nodal points' on which a great number of dream-thoughts converge".[35] Images are chosen for their rich associative possibilities. Thus the use of collective and composite figures is very common in dreams. Symbolism, which is at once rich and economical, is characteristically preferred. Emotions, moreover, are displaced with astonishing motility. Thus strong animosity or affection may be dislodged from their real objects and directed onto a person only slightly known to the dreamer.

Thus it can be said that dreams have an internal logic. Their logic derives from the wishes (the latent dream thought) which they more or less enigmatically express, and in these terms, from the distinctive patterns—condensation, symbolism, displacement —through which they allow unconscious wishes expression (the dream work).[36]

It would be suspicious, however, if the mental activity characteristic of dreams were apparent only there. In fact, it is not. These same processes are operative in the defence mechanisms (to be discussed later) of the average person. They are more clearly evident in the expressions of the psychotic and neurotic. Thus Anna O.'s strange symptoms constituted a kind of language: her paralyzed right arm, her inability to speak in her native tongue. More positively, these same modalities give a richness and profundity to human life. Poetry, literature, the arts, mythology and lore—the best of these are masterful instances of condensing, displacing, symbolizing thought and emotion. ("All my pictures are dreams", Ingmar Bergman has said. "Films go straight to the emotions, to the subconscious, and that is the secret of their strange language" [37]). The empathetic and mu-tually enlightening relationship between psychoanalysis and the arts and between psychoanalysis and lore is a recurrent theme in the Freudian corpus.[38]

Like the neurotic and the psychotic, like the artist, the dreamer creates works whose meaning he cannot articulate. The absurdity of dreams is not only a function of less orderly thought-proc-esses, however; it is absurd by inner design. The dream is like Lear's fool, who was emboldened to speak directly and pro-foundly because of his pose as fool. It is characteristic of the dream that it communicates in a disguised fashion; this is the proviso under which unacceptable thoughts find expression. Freud recognized that part of the dream work was a secondary revision, to blunt those fictions that were too telling. Censor-ship, then, is also operative in dreams, though less actively than in the waking state. The very common forgetting of dreams serves the same purpose of obscuring them from the dreamer's view.[39]

In the dream, we see the mind divided against itself. It repudiates a whole level of its activity, allowing that activity expression only under the strictest conditions. And the condition underlying all others is that the left hand, so to speak, not know what the right hand is doing. The discovery of repression renders this self-division comprehensible, for the unconscious is in part constituted by ideas and emotions which the subject re-fuses to acknowledge because he has found them repugnant or dangerous to his self-direction. They have accrued from the earli-est years of life. All of these find expression when vigilance is relaxed in the state of sleep. Thus if we consider our dreams, we find an unrecognizable self: one who kills or is killed—or less bluntly, who imagines his loved ones dead—who indulges in sexual excesses indiscriminantly, who lampoons those he re-spects, and is indifferent or cruel to those he loves. All of it is expressed so bizarrely, that one can describe one's dreams with amused detachment upon waking.

With the writing of *The Interpretation of Dreams,* the foun-dations of psychoanalysis were laid. Freud could now not only vindicate the existence of unconscious mental activity; he was able to describe extensively something of its logic, content and relation to the conscious mind. Limited no longer to discrete unconscious phenomena, he could now frame the essentials of a more systematic approach. This he described as the topographical or spatial approach to the psyche. His language, even as early as the *Studies on Hysteria,* had foreshadowed this intellectual position.

Before outlining a systematic exposition of his research, however, Freud had recognized a distinction within unconscious manifestations. "The majority of conscious processes are conscious only for a short time; very soon they became *latent,* but can easily become conscious again." [40] In the moments preceding sleep, for example, a series of thoughts flits through one's mind. One becomes aware of the feelings and impressions which were elicited by the events of the day, but which were insufficiently acknowledged because one's attention was elsewhere engaged. Or perhaps, one was fully conscious of them at one point and they return to conscious purview. One experiences the same phenomenon during a quiet break in the day, in meditation and at other moments of fuller consciousness, or again when the solution to a difficult intellectual problem with which one has been struggling suddenly comes to one "out of nowhere". Such thoughts, impressions and emotions which are latent, but which become conscious with relative ease, Freud termed "preconscious"; they are, so to speak, at the tip of consciousness. [41]

If this were all that unconsciousness involved, there would be no depth psychology. The ideas and emotions which eventually found expression in Anna O.'s symptoms could hardly be described as easily capable of becoming conscious. Anna O. was unable to reclaim them by her own efforts; they were as inaccessible to her as the experiences of another person. They were unconscious not because "consciousness is in general a highly fugitive state", [42] but unconscious by powerful inner design. The precise purpose of the repressive mechanism is to disavow certain of one's experiences, to cut off their access to conscious possession. Freud referred to such ideas, emotions and memories as "dynamically unconscious". [43] Henceforth, when he spoke of the unconscious, he generally meant the dynamic unconscious. Otherwise he used the term preconscious.

By 1900, with *The Interpretation of Dreams,* Freud's understanding had advanced from the descriptive to a systematic level.

> Under the new and powerful impression of there being an extensive and important field of mental life which is normally withdrawn from the ego's knowledge so that the processes occurring in it have to be regarded as unconscious in the truly dynamic sense, we have come to understand the term "unconscious" in a topographical or systematic sense as well; we have come to speak of a "system" of the unconscious, of a conflict between the ego and the system *Ucs.,* and have used the word more and more to denote a mental province rather than a quality of what is mental.[44]

Whatever the more philosophical nature of his later writings, Freud eschewed indulging his own philosophical bent by working over the results of his research. The existence of an unconscious mind was a practical and necessary assumption forced upon him by the experiences of his practice. With this assumption, not only could he make sense of hitherto incomprehensible human activity, he could also undertake therapeutic methods which were unmistakably effective. As far as Freud was concerned, psychoanalysis grew on the model of the natural sciences, with their reciprocal relations between observable facts, theories, hypotheses, laws and practical application.[45]

Freud did not stop with the conception of an area of the mind that has inner coherence and intelligibility but is unconscious. His experiences pushed him to a more radical position: "In psycho-analysis there is no choice for us but to assert that mental processes are in themselves unconscious, and to liken the perception of them by means of consciousness to the perception of the external world by means of the sense-organs." [46] Except for the latter kind of perception, "everything mental . . . is in the first instance unconscious; the further quality of 'consciousness' might also be present, or again it might be absent." [47]

Freud rightly assessed this statement as revolutionary. He compared it to two other revolutions in the history of Western civilization:

> Do not suppose that the resistance to us rests only on the understandable difficulty of the unconscious or the relative inaccessibility of the experi-

ences which provide evidence of it. Its source, I think, lies deeper. In the course of centuries the *naïve* self-love of men has had to submit to two major blows at the hands of science. The first was when they learnt that our earth was not the centre of the universe but only a tiny fragment of a cosmic system of scarcely imaginable vastness. This is associated in our minds with the name of Copernicus, though something similar had already been asserted by Alexandrian science. The second blow fell when biological research destroyed man's supposedly privileged place in creation and proved his descent from the animal kingdom and his ineradicable animal nature. This revolution has been accomplished in our own days by Darwin, Wallace and their predecessors, though not without the most violent contemporary opposition. But human megalomania will have suffered its third and most wounding blow from the psychological research of the present time which seeks to prove to the ego that it is not even master in its own house, but must content itself with scanty information of what is going on unconsciously in its mind. We psychoanalysts were not the first and not the only ones to utter this call to introspection; but it seems to be our fate to give it its most forcible expression and to support it with empirical material which affects every individual.[48]

Whatever his insistence on the scope of unconscious mental activity, it must not be assumed that Freud suffered from some mystical infatuation with it. The whole thrust of his therapeutic and intellectual effort was to render the unconscious conscious, to engender in Western man a more ample consciousness of himself and so of his world.

At first we are inclined greatly to reduce the value of the criterion of being conscious since it has shown itself so untrustworthy. But we should be doing it an injustice. As may be said of our life, it is not worth much, but it is all we have. Without the illumination thrown by the quality of consciousness, we should be lost in the obscurity of depth psychology.[49]

Or again, "The property of being conscious or not is in the last resort our one beacon light in the darkness of depth-psychology".[50]

The Primary and Secondary Processes

At the time of the *Project for a Scientific Psychology,* Freud was already convinced that part of the reason why the unconscious is in fact unconscious is that as a method of mental functioning it has been found inadequate and has been overlaid by a secondary method of mental adjustment to the life struggle. Unconscious mental activity, as he had glimpsed it, showed a powerful inclination towards discharge of excitation without regard to the conditions erected by experience in a real external world. Its law, in other words, was satisfaction of instinctual impulses. Mental activity itself, in many instances, showed servitude to this law of desire rather than to the discernment of reality. This thrust of the psyche was what Freud called the primary mode of mental functioning, primary in the sense that it is the mode in which we begin life, and therefore also primary in that it underlies our subsequent psychic development.

The secondary process is that of psychic maturation, of dialectic between the life of our instincts and the realities of our environment. In it is the genesis of the ego and of conscious mental economy.

The isolation of a primary mode of mental functioning represents Freud's efforts to systematize the principles that seem to govern unconscious activity.[51] He proceeded from the evidence afforded by the mental disturbances of neuroses and psychoses, and from dreams and other lapses in the rationality of normal men, to work out the description outlined in the next few pages.

Initially and basically, the mental processes are reflexive; that is, the mind seeks to discharge excitation immediately, through speech and movement, in order to achieve satisfaction or to flee from unpleasant stimuli.[52] Stimuli may originate from outside the body (exogenous) or from within the body (endogenous), perhaps in the forms of hunger, pain or sexual desire. Pleasure results from the discharge of mounting excitation (which, however, is also felt as pleasurable when a favorable outcome seems likely). Unpleasure is the accumulation of stimuli without apparent or immediate possibility of release.

> In the theory of psycho-analysis we have no hesitation in assuming that the course taken by mental events is automatically regulated by the pleasure principle. We believe, that is to say, that the course of those

events is invariably set in motion by an unpleasurable tension, and that
it takes a direction such that its final outcome coincides with a lowering
of that tension—that is, with an avoidance of unpleasure or a production
of pleasure.[53]

This is the foundational state of affairs. The reflex response
describes the economy of the lowest forms of life and clearly
underlies the more complex development of the higher forms.

Freud's contribution lay in revealing the extent to which the
primary drive towards satisfaction can structure even the most
redoubtable processes of thought, and how common yet subtle
that domination can be.

In children we see the mind in what we consider to be its
undeveloped state. We speak of their "growing minds", by which
we signify that the power to comprehend reality and its mutual
relations is still only developing. We also mean, and the two are
integrally related, that children are less willing to accept the
exigencies posed by reality and much more likely, left alone,
to be governed by their desires. For these reasons, childhood and,
a fortiori, infancy must be a time of dependency. During childhood, to express these observations in Freudian terminology, a
secondary mode of mental functioning is slowly gaining ground.

Freud extrapolated from his experience with children and
adults to the experiences of the infant. He considered the case
of the very young infant in the grip of an instinctual demand,
for example, hunger. It experiences a rising excitation which
is felt as distressful or unpleasurable. Freud conjectured that a
characteristic response of the infant to such demands is to hallucinate the experience which brings satisfaction. It already
possesses a body memory of the satisfaction, in this case, of the
breast. That experience is associated with a certain touch, smell,
warmth and image. The infant knows that this sensory experience is also associated with the release of its strident needs. Its
first response, then, to the recurrence of hunger is to recall to
itself the elements of the breast experience. At this early stage,
there is not yet a division between its memory and objective
existence, so that infantile memory is more in the nature of
hallucination.[54]

Whether the infant hallucinates satisfaction or not cannot be confidently stated. Whether or not the very young child does can be: the mental life of the child is extensively and characteristically one of phantasy, and the child often shows a marked inability to distinguish between phantasy and reality. The infantile mind clearly exemplifies the use of mental activity to satisfy instinctual need, an activity whose reference to reality is not so much one of verification but in order to gather the elements of its fictions.

What is apparent in this type of mental activity is the attempt at self-sufficiency, the attempt to form a closed system. In this respect, too, it resembles the lower forms of life with their extremely limited concern with external realities. More importantly, it resembles the intra-uterine condition which is our primary experience of life. Although that period is shrouded in unassailable mystery, this much is true, that the infant experiences something close to an immediate satisfaction of its bodily needs, whatever the trauma, tension and anxiety it may also experience through its mother's body. Its first life experience, therefore, is a self-sufficient one, of an environment organized around itself. Because it is so almost totally organized, that environment becomes an object of no importance. It is only when the environment in some way fails the infant, as it inevitably will after birth, that it is forced to contend with it. This reckoning with the environment happens as a more or less distressing expedient.

At this point some crucial qualifications—which Freud too much neglected in this context—must be stated. In the first place, there is the positive aspect under which the environment confronts the infant. All is not brute expediency. The youngest infant is fascinated with those external realities that impinge upon its developing senses: sounds and moving objects, forms. There is also its expansive response to song, speech, laughter—in a word, to communication. An infant of only a few weeks literally drinks in its surroundings, and when it is mobile, it has continually to be "kept out of things". This fascination with reality is far more than one of expediency; it is one of the strongest thirsts of the human psyche. Nevertheless, at this fundamental theoretical level, namely in the analysis of primary and secondary mental processes, there is minimal attention to the curiosity drive. It is the more surprising in that curiosity was so powerful in Freud's own personality. In his work on Leonardo da Vinci, he does speak of it:

> Investigating has taken the place of acting and creating as well. A man who has begun to have an inkling of the grandeur of the universe with all its complexities and its laws readily forgets his own insignificant self. Lost in admiration and filled with true humility, he all too easily forgets that he himself is a part of those active forces and that in accordance with the scale of his personal strength the way is open for him to try and alter a small portion of the destined course of the world—a world in which the small is still no less wonderful and significant than the great.[55]

(He also acknowledged the centrality of the curiosity drive in his remarks on the sexual researches of children, which will be discussed in Chapter Three).

The second qualification is intimately related. The infant's relationship with the mother is a veritable life-line. She is more than the provider of emotional security and physical needs. There is a powerful movement on the infant's part towards her love, warmth, speech and song, a truly expansive movement that is the very matrix of self-transcending response to reality. It is at least as powerful as necessity.[56]

At the same time, it must be remembered that Freud's primary referent is the environment as immediately post-uterine, as "primordial", as it confronts the neonate. The following weeks and months of life—when curiosity and the bond with the mother are growing in strength—bear out Freud's contention that even then primary megalomania is abandoned only under considerable duress.

To return to the hypothesis of infantile hallucination: tension may be released in the initial enjoyment of the chimeric satisfaction, but the hunger persists, and the outcome is only exacerbated distress; disappointment is added to hunger. Part of the early experience is a first and crucial distrust of proceeding along reflexive pathways.

At the same time, the sensory apparatus of the infant becomes increasingly acute. The frustration of its megalomania strengthens the natural tendency to a keener sensory awareness. This orientation is at the basis of a secondary mode of mental functioning. In this secondary mode, the infant "waits" for certain indications proceeding from the senses, for definite images, odors, sounds and tactile sensations. These must be present, it learns, before the release which comes from satisfaction can be allowed. Moreover, a certain number of them must be present in recognized conjunction, or the same overwhelming disappointment will be experienced.

In Freud's view, the primitive form of thought is hallucination. In this rudimentary thought form, mnemonic residues are utilized to provide self-satisfaction. The elementary act of judgement described in the previous paragraph is a momentous advance, because it demands that such mental activity be inhibited, held until there is adequate sensory information. The pleasure principle cannot be allowed to make thought its creature in the same simplistic fashion. What is called into play in the elementary act of judgement is truly a different mode of mental functioning.

Freud stressed the impressive advance involved in the ability to judge. It requires a store of remembered impressions which must be consulted. But more than that, it requires growing detachment from the affect with which these memories are charged. Among the memories, there will be unpleasant ones. Despite the primary impulse to flight from anything unpleasurable, if the process of judgement is not to be arrested and overwhelmed, the mind must be increasingly capable of revitalizing its memories in order to make decisions in their light. The power of judgement, as we know only too well, is not always equal to its task.[57]

The development sketched above shows an increasing strength in the judging and self-directing agency, or the ego. It is tantamount to a higher level of energy, energy with the power of containment. "We recognize in human beings a mental organization which is interpolated between their sensory stimuli and the perception of their somatic needs on the one hand and their motor acts on the other, and which mediates between them for a particular purpose. We call this organization their ego [lit.

'*Ich*' or 'I']." [58] The ego is the agent of the rational and conscious life. The more developed the ego, the more it is governed
by what Freud called the reality principle. Precisely the same
statement may be made of the development of the secondary
process in respect of the reality principle.

The reality principle clearly develops out of the pleasure principle; it represents the pleasure principle in the context of external reality. It might be called enlightened self-interest. "Reality—wish-fulfilment: it is from this contrasting pair that our
mental life springs." [59]

Freud's description of another mode of mental functioning,
the primary, is a description of the unconscious activity which
his research disclosed. It is primary in that it is the archaic or
infantile form of thought, which nevertheless remains active
throughout adulthood. Its infantile nature is signalled by the
reversion to sensory images, by the re-emergence of infantile
experiences and phantasies, and by the very tactic of hallu-
cinating satisfaction. The dream is the favored vehicle of this
modality: "Dreaming is a piece of infantile mental life that has
been superseded".[60] And it is in the state of sleep that adults
regress most completely to the infantile condition. The relationship with the external world is withdrawn; the senses are
dimmed. The demands out of which the secondary mode originates are almost extinguished. Under these conditions, the mind
continues to operate, but in decidedly different patterns.

The most striking characteristic of the mind in the state of
sleep is its entire disregard for "reality-testing".[61] There is no
distinction between the wish and its actual fulfilment. Thus we
may waken in the grip of a dream so "real" that it is some moments before we can regain our orientation. Moreover, there is no
sense of contradiction, so that we find ourselves loving and hating
the same person in the same dream; or the most important
features may be reversed: a large man—very significant to the
dreamer—may be depicted as a very slight stranger.[62] Emotions
are displaced from one object to another with astonishing freedom: we are being pursued by a strange person who might be X,
but is also like Y. Suddenly he changes to Z. There is no sense
of time in dreams; elements from various periods in our lives are

mingled. Thus we may find ourselves with present-day friends but in a childhood setting. The recurrent dream shows the same timelessness. In short, if the dreamer were to speak and act, he would be indistinguishable from the psychotic. We dream under an arrangement of *lèse majesté,* because sleep, as such, can insure immunity from consequence.

The reason for the riotous and bizarre nature of dreams lies in the fact that they are products of another mental function than the one with which we are most familiar. The thought processes of sleep are designed to discharge emotion. They are, in other words, at the service of the pleasure principle. Shreds of memories, images, and ideas are juxtaposed into one shifting constellation after another, in order to provide vehicles for gratifying wishes. The gains of our perceptual life are ripped from their contexts and put to this use. "To sum up: exemption from mutual contradiction, primary process (mobility of cathexes [excitations]), timelessness, and replacement of external by psychical reality—these are the characteristics which we may expect to find in processes belonging to the system Ucs." [63] The dream is nevertheless a mental product; there is a definite and fully intelligent train of thought beneath the juxtapositions. It is always in the form of a desire. In the words of Ricoeur, "Displacement, condensation, pictorial representation, secondary revision, these well-defined procedures open the way to new structural analogies. If dream interpretation can stand as the paradigm for all interpretation it is because dreams are in fact the paradigm of all the stratagems of desire".[64]

The primary mode, in other words, also operates extensively in waking life. To take more dramatic instances first, the psychotic is one at the mercy of powerful emotions. They are invariably rooted in his childhood. He shows an almost complete inability to recognize the present and unique nature of the reality surrounding him. It is twisted into old shapes, so that he is terrified of, or violent, or tender towards complete strangers. Men who are unquestionably sane will speak of times when in the grip of powerful emotion they have had momentary hallucinations. On a more everyday level there is the mechanism so aptly called "rationalization", where thought serves desire (sometimes to such an extent that only an objective person can discern the subservience). Daydreaming, in which virtually everyone indulges, is a thought form designed to modify real conditions. The entertainment arts create worlds which like daydreams are mental creations designed to yield pleasure. In both of the latter examples, the sense of reality, though held in abeyance, is retained.

> Every desire takes before long the form of picturing its own fulfillment; there is no doubt that dwelling upon imaginary wish-fulfillments brings satisfaction with it, although it does not interfere with a knowledge that what is concerned is not real. Thus in the activity of phantasy human beings continue to enjoy the freedom from external compulsion which they have long since renounced in reality. They have contrived to alternate between remaining an animal of pleasure and being once more a creature of reason. Indeed, they cannot subsist on the scanty satisfaction which they can extort from reality. . . . The creation of the mental realm of phantasy finds a perfect parallel in the establishment of "reservations" or "nature reserves" in places where the requirements of agriculture, communications and industry threaten to bring about changes in the original face of the earth which will quickly make it unrecognizable. A nature reserve preserves its original state which everywhere else has to our regret been sacrificed to necessity. Everything, including what is useless and even what is noxious, can grow and proliferate there as it pleases. The mental realm of phantasy is just such a reservation withdrawn from the reality principle.[65]

The primary mode is much more observable or conscious in the early years of childhood. The challenge facing the child is enormous. Dependent, vulnerable, endowed with inchoate ego and intelligence, he is introduced to more in a shorter period of time than at any other period in life. In dealing with the world outside himself, the child fills out his understanding with a degree of conjecture and phantasy which would astonish most adults. He ascribes surprising motives, intentions and threats of punishment to the adults and other children in his ambit. Very little of this is verbalized.[66]

It is rare that the adult can reclaim these moments of his childhood. Freud found such infantile conjecture and fantasy to be unconsciously formative, nevertheless, of the emotional disposition of the adult, of his relations to the people and things around him. They are formative, in other words, of the character structure peculiar to each individual.

The most profoundly therapeutic moments in Freud's work occurred, therefore, when infantile thought returned to consciousness. This happens only when a present-day situation revives memories of a more remote one. If the response is irrational, then the remote situation must have overwhelmed the subject, either because of the strength of his own inner impulses or for reasons intrinsic to the nature of the event (such as cases of parental brutality, premature sexual experiences, or the death of a family member). For whatever reason, he had been too immature to deal with it at the time and had repressed it unresolved.

Freud's fascination with the continuity of psychic experience soon gave way, however, to a bewilderment that challenged all of his gains. He realized that many of these powerfully charged memories were of events that had never happened. He could attest to that from other sources. At the point when everything was thrown into confusion, it dawned on him that the memories were not only childish chronologically; they were childish as well in that they showed the same lack of a sense of reality. The memories were riddled with childish misconstruction and straightforward phantasy. Because they had been repressed or driven into the unconscious, they had been immunized from the normal processes of maturation. "There was the definite realization that there is no indication of reality in the unconscious, so that it is impossible to distinguish between truth and emotionally-charged fiction." [67]

Moments of recollection such as these are powerful and unforgettable. They are powerful because the individual experiences a degree of self-possession which can only be called privileged. His personal history is telescoped, for to some extent he resumes a childhood stance, this time with the powers of mature integration.

To state the experience in Freud's theoretical terms, these are moments when the primary or infantile mode is fully accepted, understood and revised by the secondary. They undo the pattern of self-alienation which describes so extensively individual human development. For the more prevalent pattern is that the secondary mode of mental functioning overlays rather than integrates the primary. The child abandons certain modes under the stress of fear and confusion and "learns" a more successful though less personal adaptation. There is always a certain degree of irresolution and simple inhibition due to the inadequacy of the child's ego.[68] What the mind will permit external expression becomes more selective, and the terms of selection are dependent on the external conditions of the environment as their complexity is increasingly grasped. In other words, it is the secondary mode which gains control over speech and movement and over the thoughts and impulses which are anterior to them. These constitute consciousness. The only times when this control is reclaimed by the unconscious are in psychotic breakdown, sometimes in sleep and in artificial states such as hypnosis. In the normal situation, the direct expression of the unconscious is curtailed.[69] The primary mode of immediate discharge, of mental fictions that disregard reality becomes more remote from consciousness, until it is unrecoverable. Thus we regard as normal the striking phenomenon of circumscribed amnesia which characterizes human life: though as children we are highly impressionable and gifted with lively memories, the years of childhood are largely lost to adult memory. We become alienated from an earlier mode of perception and response.[70]

Nevertheless, the primary mode of archaic is not moribund. The instinctual impulses which are the sources of activity remain, and so does the tension between the modes of permitting them expression. Our language reveals this human predicament. We speak of certain gestures as "inadvertent", or we say that X "betrayed" his real feelings on a particular issue, or that Y was caught "off guard". Such impulses reveal an overweening thrust towards external expression (characteristic of the primary mode); and when they succeed in slipping through the secondary control over conscious deportment, they always evoke at least momentary chagrin and defensiveness on the part of the subject. The same dynamic is operative in the so-called parapraxes: slips of the tongue, of the pen, idle but revealing gestures, acts of forgetting.[71]

In his formulation of two laws of mental functioning, Freud provided a more comprehensive picture of the ways of the mind. It is safe to say that under the power of the rationalistic and conscious bias which has prevailed in Western culture, the nature of the mind is generally described only partially. Thus we would tend to describe it as the agency directed towards an understanding of reality and, within these terms, as directive of our behavior. All else is more or less pathological, or at least in the category of exceptions. According to Freud, this exposes only one mental mode. His contribution was to study as scientifically as possible a wider array of mental manifestations, and to insist on the necessity for taking them seriously. In these manifestations, he discovered another purpose of the mind, but one which strikes us as repugnant, as an aberration of the truly mental, and scarcely deserving of the adjective. Nevertheless, Freud's massive research revealed the mind at work in these ways, revealed it as intent upon discharging impulses to the extent of being flippant and callous about the sacred laws of logic and reality. Yet this too is a function descriptive of the mind. It is too extensively exercised, too intricate, too constitutive of our very perceptions to warrant oversight. Freud demanded that it be accorded a proportionate position in any theory of the mind.

In fact, the bias against admitting *all* mental activity to scientific examination was in Freud's view identical to the bias according to which the mind represses and denies a good deal of its own activity. The secondary mode is, after all, of relatively belated appearance. Its domination is at times a shaky one, uneasy to the degree that it assumes control through repressive measures. The primitive mental impulses with which it has to contend are powerful indeed. Yet the self-deception with which our mental activity is always threatened proceeds not only from the unruly, self-satisfying trend of the primary mode. It proceeds as well from the timorousness of the secondary mode, whereby it builds on the shifting sands of denial and repression, of self-alienation. It thereby leaves itself open to compromise, ruse and masking of real intent, for strong impulses will have their way in some fashion. On the other hand, the secondary process always at least pretends to reconciliation with real external conditions. Deceitfulness enters with maturing years because the claim to that reconciliation, which is not made by the small child, is increasingly professed. The examples cited above of persons caught "off guard" and of their defensiveness at the breakdown of control are vignettes of the faultiness of such a resolution.

Freud was graphic not only on the blindness and unruliness of the drive towards instinctual satisfaction, but also on the deceitful and compromising measures to which the ego, the agent of the secondary mode, has resort. In the later years of his practice, Freud's attention turned increasingly to the ego, and as part of that preoccupation, to defence.

Defence Mechanisms: The Ego and the Id

The topic of defence was raised earlier in the brief discussion of resistance and repression, which Freud deemed to be the cornerstone of psychoanalysis. For most of his writing career Freud used the terms repression and defence almost interchangeably, at an earlier period preferring to use the latter, then abandoning it for the former. In 1926, he wrote: "It will be an undoubted advantage, I think, to revert to the old concept of 'defence', provided we employ it explicitly as a general designation for all the techniques which the ego makes use of in conflicts which may lead to a neurosis, while we retain the word 'repression' for a special method of defence." [72] It is in this sense that the word is used here. With the topic of defence, we tap one of the richest veins in Freud's research. In a sense, that topic is the burden of the entire Freudian corpus. One has to delve into it personally to appreciate the subtlety and resourcefulness of mental dynamics.

The dynamics which Freud detected beneath the elaborate symptoms of his disturbed patients were, in fact, common mechanisms, which in these instances had gone to very self-destructive extremes. "A normal ego . . . is, like normality in general, an ideal fiction. . . . Every normal person, in fact, is only normal on the average. His ego approximates to that of the psychotic in some part or other and to a greater or lesser extent." [73] The ego mediates between instinctual demands and the demands of the external world, with a view to protecting the former. Because the two frequently conflict, it is common for the ego to regard instinctual demands as dangers. Under the influence of education, it grows accustomed "to mastering the *internal* danger before it has become an *external* one".[74] In the effort to circumscribe stress, it makes use of procedures known as mechanisms of defence.

One of the most common of these is repression. Repression is an attempt to deny the very existence of a memory, idea or feeling. Eventually, these will be lost to the powers of recollection as, for example, are the years of childhood. For this reason, memory can be treacherously selective.[75] An arbiter in a dispute is there because he will be inclined to acknowledge all the elements of the situation. Yet disputants very frequently cannot be faulted with conscious dishonesty. They are victimized by a mental grip so powerful that it amounts to an inability to see obvious facts, or to remember pertinent details. The mind is being used to protect the self. Thus repression can extend to a denial of perception as well as of memory. If the denial is extensive, the subject is termed psychotic. Such a person, for example, may continue to speak to or prepare meals for a loved one who has died. This is the most extreme measure to which the ego resorts in the face of intolerable stress.[76]

What the ego is frequently protecting itself against in the tactic of repression is intense self-reproach. Few experiences are more painful than that of guilt. The ego attempts to hold it in abeyance by warding off the event in question. Hence the household in which no one speaks of a suicided member. The ego may also attempt to escape self-reproach by reconstructing a situation in which it was aroused. Thus an individual will dilate on the aspects of an experience which serve to justify his part in it, and forget or override the others. The party to whom he speaks will frequently betray his own accurate assessment, for we are often anxious to spare each other, and so ourselves, the pains of honesty. The same selective acknowledgement is evidenced in carrying grudges or collecting injustices. They provide a focus for intense preoccupation, so that more distressing perceptions are held at bay.

Another common measure aimed at deflecting self-reproach is to project reproach onto others. This is the mechanism which characterizes paranoia.[77] The reproaches may be identical. Thus the man who grows pathologically suspicious of his wife is himself tempted to infidelity. The individual who is convinced that others look down on him holds them in secret contempt. The major part of one's mental energies may be deflected onto the flaws in one's ambit. The paranoid is acutely perceptive, and this is a source of considerable self-flattery. But the individual whose criterion for others is perfection itself is staving off an inner agony of shameful impulses and corresponding self-hatred. Freud discovered, for example, that paranoia invariably covered homosexual urges.[78] The same individual can show astonishing credulity when it suits some inner purpose.

> Thus his critical faculty is not an independent function, to be respected as such, it is the tool of his emotional attitudes and is directed by his resistance. If there is something he does not like, he can put up a shrewd fight against it and appear highly critical; but if something suits his book, he can, on the contrary, show himself most credulous.[79]

Closely related to projection is the tactic of pleading guilt for the lesser crime. The scrupulous person is also afflicted with perfectionism, but he makes his own demeanor its victim. However, his absurd anxiety over minutiae covers a profound sense of guilt. The guilty deeds, feelings or memories have been repressed, and the guilt, now generalized, places its crucifying grip on more indifferent matters. Such a person strains the gnat and swallows the camel. Though one of the ego's less successful strategies, it does protect the subject from acknowledging the power of his cruder impulses, such as revenge and sexual desire. It also creates a situation of almost invincible self-involvement. The refinement of his moral sense is a source of self-esteem and a continual protestation of his ethical sensitivity. The mechanism here is one of substitution or displacement, one referred to earlier in connection with dreams. It characterizes the obsessive and compulsive individual, whose actions—for example, the compulsive washing of hands—are designed to placate self-reproach or to ward off repetition of a misfortune.[80] Displacement is also operative in phobias, which disguise the real objects of fear.[81]

By the mechanism of "reaction-formation", the ego attempts to dilute the power of certain impulses, by developing their opposites to an exaggerated degree. Thus the hopeless misanthrope devotes himself to a general humanitarian issue or becomes a fanatical lover of animals. The moralism and idealism of the adolescent is, in part, a reaction to the instinctual upheaval of puberty. Maudlin pity covers sadism; fastidiousness an earlier fascination with excreta; exaggerated and anxious affection, hostility. Reaction-formation is a frequent escape from the tension of ambivalence which marks the infantile response to significant persons. Exaggerated hostility or affection frequently testify to an attempt to blot out their opposites.[82]

As destructive to self-interest as these adjustments are, the subject shows an astonishing tenacity to them. There is a "compulsion to repeat".[83] Defensive response becomes automatic in situations where the matured ego no longer has anything to fear. What has been established through repression is extremely difficult to undo because it has become unconscious. And every deceitful tactic is debilitating to the ego because it compromises its sources in reality. The weakened ego shows a characteristic resistance to change, for change is taxing.[84] Moreover, the individual has accrued certain "secondary gains" from his unwholesome resolutions. Some of these have already been mentioned: pride in one's lynx-like shrewdness with respect to others, the conviction of a rarified moral sense, or the attention from others and surrender of responsibility for self-preoccupation which the hysteric or hypochondriac gains. "In this way the symptom gradually comes to be the representative of important interests; it is found to be useful in asserting the position of the self and becomes more and more closely merged with the ego and more and more indispensable to it." [85]

All of these constitute reasons for the resistance which the individual experiences towards change, intolerable as his situation may be. The phenomenon of resistance led Freud to clearer insight. He worked with patients who were initially eager and

cooperative. It was clear from their symptoms that certain unconscious drives were striving mightily to break through to conscious expression. Whence came the powerful check on their
revelation? Why did the disposition of the patient change to one
of mental reservation, distrust, obtuseness? [86] Experience revealed that the suppression of the unconscious forces had been
the result of an earlier, almost reflexive inhibition that was still
at work. The inhibition had been in the interests of self-preservation, a judgement of the inexpediency of releasing certain
impulses, based on reality as the subject then perceived it. Now,
such a judgement is a function of the ego. In other words, much
of the drama between the forces of instinctual release and those
of self-preservation proceed unconsciously. The orientations of
the ego itself are in large part unconscious.

It was no longer precise, therefore, to speak of a struggle between the ego and the unconscious. The greater extent of our
mental activities proceed unconsciously. They are not all psychic
activity of the primary mode, but also according to the secondary
mode, though not conscious to us. To specify those unconscious
forces antithetical to the ego, Freud introduced the term the
id—literally "the it". "This impersonal pronoun seems particularly well suited for expressing the main characteristic of this
province of the mind—the fact of its being alien to the ego [I]." [87]
"Instinctual cathexes seeking discharge—that in our view is all
that there is in the id." [88]

The infant is all id. The ego develops, therefore, out of the id;
it is the instinctual life as progressively modified by the perceptual processes.[89] The ego serves the id as a protective shield;
yet fearful of its instinctual power, it also pits its resources against
the id.[90] Here in theoretical terms is a general explanation of the
defence mechanisms discussed above. It is also a more advanced restatement of Freud's principle that a secondary mode of
mental functioning overlays a primary one in human psychic
development.[91]

> The relation to the external world has become the decisive factor for the
> ego; it has taken on the task of representing the external world to the
> id—fortunately for the id, which could not escape destruction if, in its

blind efforts for the satisfaction of its instincts, it disregarded that supreme external power. In accomplishing this function, the ego must observe the external world, must lay down an accurate picture of it in the memory-traces of its perceptions, and by its exercise of the function of "reality-testing" must put aside whatever in this picture of the external world is an addition derived from internal sources of excitation. The ego controls the approaches to motility under the id's orders, but between a need and an action it has interposed a postponement in the form of the activity of thought, during which it makes use of the mnemonic residues of experience. In that way it has dethroned the pleasure principle which dominates the course of events in the id without any restriction and has replaced it by the reality principle, which promises more certainty and greater success.[92]

It is the ego, because of its grounding in the perceptual system, which provides the sense of time entirely lacking on the instinctual level. What especially distinguishes the ego from the id is the tendency to synthesis, to higher organization. Its only means of controlling instinctual impulses is to give them a place relative to the whole, to deal with them within a coherent context. The ego, therefore, grows in strength as the secondary mental function of inhibiting impulses by waiting, testing through thought processes that consult memory and fresh perception, grows in strength. "To adopt a popular mode of speaking, we might say that the ego stands for reason and good sense while the id stands for untamed passions." [93]

The ego is strong insofar as its original identity with the id is operative. "If a real split has occurred between the two, the weakness of the ego becomes apparent." [94] Such a split is effected through a conflict of interests, and too often gives rise to defence mechanisms rather than true ego decision. On the one hand, measures such as repression and reaction-formation witness to the superior strength of the ego over impulses from the id, a strength which derives from the decisive fact "that the ego is an organization and the id is not".[95] Its strength, surprising in view of its original identity with the id, derives too from its constitutive proximity to the perceptual processes. By reason of that association, it can forbid instinctual release which would compromise the well-being of the psyche as a whole. Therefore, it still attains "its object with the aid of that almost omnipotent institution, the pleasure principle",[96] only now in terms of external as well as internal conditions.

On the other hand, the same defence mechanisms and their extensive role in psychic life betray the fact that the dominance of the ego and secondary process is too often one of uneasy tyranny rather than comprehension and reason. Those mechanisms betray, in a word, the limitations of the ego.

> The ego is after all only a portion of the id, a portion that has been expediently modified by the proximity of the external world with its threat of danger. From a dynamic point of view it is weak, it has borrowed its energies from the id. . . . The ego must on the whole carry out the id's intentions; it fulfills its task by finding out the circumstances in which those intentions can best be achieved. The ego's relation to the id might be compared with that of a rider to his horse. The horse supplies the locomotive energy, while the rider has the privilege of deciding on the goal and of guiding the powerful animal's movements. But only too often there arises between the ego and the id the not precisely ideal situation of the rider being obliged to guide the horse along the path by which it itself wants to go.
>
> There is one portion of the id from which the ego has separated itself by resistances due to repression. But the repression is not carried over into the id: the repressed merges into the remainder of the id.[97]

And to the extent that the ego relinquishes control over aspects of mental experience, it is at their mercy.

> We are warned by a proverb against serving two masters at the same time. The poor ego has things even worse: it serves three severe masters and does what it can to bring their claims and demands into harmony with one another. These claims are always divergent and often seem incompatible. No wonder that the ego so often fails at its task. Its three tyrannical masters are the external world, the super-ego [the primitive conscience] and the id. When we follow the ego's efforts to satisfy them simultaneously—or rather to obey them simultaneously—we cannot feel regret at having personified this ego and having set it up as a separate organism. It feels hemmed in on three sides, threatened by three kinds of danger, to which, if it is hard pressed, it reacts by generating anxiety. Owing to its origins from the experiences of the perceptual system, it is earmarked for representing the demands of the external world, but it strives too to be a loyal servant of the id, to be on good terms with it, to recommend itself to it as an object and to attract its libido [love] to

itself. In its attempts to mediate between the id and reality, it is often obliged to cloak the *Ucs.* demands of the id with its own *Pcs.* rationalizations, to conceal the id's conflicts with reality, to profess, with diplomatic disingenuousness to be taking notice of reality even when the id has remained rigid and unyielding. On the other hand it is observed at every step it takes by the strict super-ego, which lays down definite standards for its conduct, without taking any account of its difficulties from the direction of the id and the external world, and which, if those standards are not obeyed, punishes it with intense feelings of inferiority and guilt. Thus the ego, driven by the id, confined by the super-ego, repulsed by reality, struggles to master its economic task of bringing about harmony among the forces working in and upon it; and we can understand how it is that so often we cannot suppress a cry: "Life is not easy!" If the ego is obliged to admit its weakness, it breaks out in anxiety—realistic anxiety regarding the external world, moral anxiety regarding the super-ego and neurotic anxiety regarding the strength of the passions in the id.[98]

In the Freudian view, then, the genetic nucleus of mental life, but more precisely of unconscious mental activity, is the instincts seeking discharge. "All instinctual impulses have the unconscious systems as their point of impact".[99] The primary mode of mental functioning exploits all the capacities and gains of intelligence in order to provide instinctual release. The secondary mode husbands this release in terms of the conditions of the external world. Mental activity is an infinitely complex intermingling of the two modes. That activity may be conscious or easily capable of becoming so, or it may be unconscious by more or less powerful intent. In fact, as Freud's understanding of psychic dynamisms grew, the importance of conscious and unconscious as categorical distinctions lessened. He spoke more in terms of a dialectic between ego, id and super-ego, and referred to conscious and unconscious as the "psychical qualities" within that dialectic.[100]

The nucleus of mental life referred to in the preceding paragraph is, in other terms, the id, the archaic form of the mind. In the id is to be glimpsed the complete and unchallenged dominance of the primary process.

You will not expect me to have much to tell you that is new about the id apart from its name. It is the dark inaccessible part of our personality; what little we know of it we have learnt from our study of the dream-work and of the construction of neurotic symptoms, and most of that is of a negative character and can be described only as a contrast to the ego. We approach the id with analogies: we call it a chaos, a cauldron full of seething excitations. We picture it as being open at its end to somatic influences, and as there taking into itself instinctual needs which find their psychic expression in it, but we cannot say in what substratum. It is filled with energy reaching it from the instincts, but it has no organization, produces no collective will, but only a striving to bring about the instinctual needs subject to the observation of the pleasure principle. The logical laws of thought do not apply in the id, and this is true above all of the law of contradiction. Contrary impulses exist side by side, without cancelling each other: at most they may converge to form compromises under the dominating economic pressure towards the discharge of energy. There is nothing in the id that can be compared with negation; and we perceive with surprise an exception to the philosophical theorem that space and time are necessary forms of our mental acts. There is nothing in the id that corresponds to the idea of time; there is no recognition of the passage of time, and—a thing that is most remarkable and awaits consideration in philosophical thought—no alteration in its mental processes is produced by the passage of time. Wishful impulses which have never passed beyond the id, but impressions too, which have been sunk into the id by repression, are virtually immortal; after the passage of decades they behave as though they had just occurred. They can only be recognized as belonging to the past, can only lose their importance and be deprived of their cathexis of energy, when they have been made conscious by the work of analysis, and it is on this that the therapeutic effect of analytic treatment rests to no small extent.[101]

In this and the following paragraph is condensed much of what was said earlier, but less precisely, of the "unconscious".

The id of course knows of no judgements of value: no good and evil, no morality. The economic or, if you prefer, the quantitative factor, which is intimately linked to the pleasure principle dominates all its processes. Instinctual cathexes seeking discharge—that in our view is all that there is in the id. It even seems that the energy of these instinctual impulses is in a state different from that in the other regions of the mind, far more mobile and capable of discharge; otherwise the displacements and condensations would not occur which are characteristic of the id and which so completely disregard the *quality* of what is cathected—what in the ego we should call an idea. We would give much to understand more about these things! You can see, incidentally, that we are in a position to attribute to the id characteristics other than that of its being unconscious, and you can recognize the possibility of portions of the ego and super-ego being unconscious without possessing the same primitive and irrational characteristics.[102]

"Id" indicates what in common parlance is described as the "lower" side of man, his "animal" nature. An explicit discussion of the instincts and the evolutionary origins of man is in order.

2. THE INSTINCTS AS PREDICAMENT

Freud's General Theory of the Instincts

The id, according to Freud, "is filled with energy reaching it from the instincts". And again, "Instinctual cathexes seeking discharge—that in our view is all that there is in the id." The primitive mind is seen as growing out of instinctual energy: "We picture it as being open at its end to somatic influences, and as there taking into itself instinctual needs which find their psychic expression in it." [1] In this sense, the nucleus of the mind is the instinctual energies. All mental activity proceeds in dialectic with them: in order to satisfy them directly, to provide modified forms of satisfaction, or to quell them. Without the energy of the instincts, there would be no mental activity.

It must frankly be acknowledged that in discussing the instincts, we are on dim and controverted ground. Freud described them as "at once the most important and the most obscure element of psychological research." [2] He lamented the "total absence of any theory of the instincts which would help us find our bearings". [3] What he wrote in 1932 remains true of the contemporary controversy on the nature of the instincts:

The theory of the instincts is so to say our mythology. Instincts are mythical entities, magnificent in their indefiniteness. In our work we cannot for a moment disregard them, yet we are never sure that we are seeing them clearly. You know how popular thinking deals with the instincts. People assume as many and as various instincts as they happen to need at the moment—a self-assertive instinct, an imitative instinct, an instinct of play, a gregarious instinct and many others like them. People take them up, as it were, make each of them do its particular job, and then drop them again. We have always been moved by a suspicion that behind all these little *ad hoc* instincts there lay concealed something serious and powerful which we should like to approach cautiously.[4]

The obscurity which will always surround the instincts derives from the fact that the instinct "appears to us as a concept on the frontier between the mental and the somatic, as the psychical representative of the stimuli originating from within the organism and reaching the mind". [5] Though they are the sources of mental activity they are as such (as somatic) inaccessible to it.

An instinct can never become an object of consciousness—only the idea that represents the instinct can. Even in the unconscious, moreover, an instinct cannot be represented otherwise than by an idea. If the instinct did not attach itself to an idea or manifest itself as an affective state, we could know nothing about it. When we nevertheless speak of an unconscious instinctual impulse or of a repressed instinctual impulse, the looseness of phraseology is a harmless one. We can only mean an instinctual impulse the ideational representative of which is unconscious, for nothing else comes into consideration.[6]

If an organic process stimulates the mind, that stimulus must take on a mental quality or "representative". This latter constitutes the limits of subjective intelligibility. It is with the representative, therefore, that psychoanalysis begins its discussion.[7]

The subjective experience of the instinct is that of a pressure. "The characteristic of exercising pressure is common to all the instincts; it is in fact their very essence".[8] Thus the instinct is "a measure of the demand made upon the mind for work in consequence of its connection with the body".[9] Unlike an external stimulus, it is a constant pressure from which there is no escape save through some form of satisfaction.

The instinctual pressure has intelligibility, though at first only rudimentary, in that it is a desire for something to alleviate the

demand. Freud saw psychic development as an increasing remoteness from these primal representatives of the instincts, to the
point, in fact, of inaccessibility. The first forms of psychic representation are extremely simplistic. With the developing sense of
an external world, the demands are represented with increasing
complexity. A fundamental tenet of Freud's understanding of
the instincts must be noted at the outset if the psychical methods
of dealing with them are to be appreciated. What is more radical
in the functioning of the instincts is not their objects, but their
aims, which is in every case satisfaction. It is the aim which over-
rides all else, so that if one object does not bring satisfaction,
another or a combination of others will be marshalled into service by the mind. This feature explains the marked freedom and
mobility characteristic of unconscious processes. The mechanisms
of displacement and condensation are cases in point.[10] From this
relationship between instinctual aim and object derives the flexi-
bility and complexity of mental life.

From it also derive what Freud called the vicissitudes which the
instincts undergo during their existence. These are actually
modes of defence "against an instinct's being carried through in
an unmodified form".[11] An instinctual demand may be met by
simple repression, that is, by denying it access to consciousness.
Thus a man may be in the grip of a rage of which he is unaware.
His exterior expression may be only a rigid smile, a forced affection, or a sense of remoteness. An instinctual demand may be
changed into its opposite, as in the single case of love and hate.
Hell hath no fury to equal that of the woman scorned. The fanatical adherent, if converted to another ideology, becomes the fearful adversary. An intense and very preoccupying hatred always, in
fact, betrays the power of attraction which the object still wields
—to the fury of the subject involved. The tendency to deny powerful attraction is very common; it is an attempt to evade stimulation and its challenge to the mind. An instinctual pressure may
be turned round onto the subject's own self. A child, for example,
may break into a tantrum where, fearing to damage the people
and objects around him, he will slap or beat his own head. Adults
have more sophisticated forms of self-punishment for their rages.

Fourthly, the instinct may be sublimated: "This enables excessively strong excitations from particular sources of sexuality to find an outlet and use in other fields, so that a not inconsiderable increase in psychical efficiency results from a disposition which is in itself perilous." [12] Thus the instincts may find sublimated expression in altruism or artistic and intellectual creativity. In any case, except that of repression, yet there too in distorted ways, the instinctual energy finds release. This is possible because of the dominance of aim over object.

Psychoanalytic research revealed the remoteness of consciousness from the primal instincts. Freud was convinced that the instinctual demands of which we are aware have already undergone considerable modification. He appears to have concluded that the earliest psychic representatives which instinctual pressures assume are to a greater or lesser degree repressed during the years of childhood. Their representatives are, of course, some form of infantile desire: to suck, smell, tear, bite and so on. Those primitive representatives are in time deeply repressed. Because repressed, they are fixated at that level, or unaltered as an expression of the instinct.[13] A sense of disgust, which is a stratagem for denying what previously gave pleasure and is often an express part of the civilizing process, cannot as such shake that fixation.[14] Desires or ideas in any way associated with the primitive representative—so-called unconscious "derivatives" [15]—must also threaten the ego and be kept from exposure. In fact, the repression and anxiety which is encountered in clinical work is of this derivative sort; it is the most accessible outcome of a series of censorships.[16]

The fear of the instincts which is so characteristic of human life, individual and collective, finds at least partial explanation in the inaccessibility of this "primal repression". A certain degree of repression is inevitable; it is the simplest mechanism available to the undeveloped ego. The fantasies of children are primitive and highly exaggerated. Their anger, for example, is translated into flashing images of tearing, biting and eating, or cutting off members. Their fears are translated into threats of the same inflicted upon themselves. Their erotic desires are expressed in images which in adulthood are felt to be disgusting. Instinctual impulses so represented, once repressed, are tied to those representatives, or "fixated". To repress means not only to deny access to the subject's conscious awareness, but also to the modifications and versatility which his growing maturity could bring to bear on them. We are inclined

> to forget too readily that repression does not hinder the instinctual representative from continuing to exist in the unconscious, from organizing itself further, putting out derivatives [17] and establishing connections. Repression in fact interferes only with the relation of the instinctual representative to *one* psychical system, namely, to that of the conscious.
>
> Psycho-analysis is able to show us other things as well which are important for understanding the effects of repression in the psychoneuroses. It shows us, for instance, that the instinctual representative develops with less interference and more profusely if it is withdrawn by repression from conscious influence. It proliferates in the dark, as it were, and takes on extreme forms of expression, which when they are translated and presented to the neurotic are not only bound to seem alien to him, but frighten him by giving him the picture of an extraordinary and dangerous strength of instinct. This deceptive strength of instinct is the result of an uninhibited development in phantasy and of the damming-up consequent on frustrated satisfaction.[18]

The modifications to which instinctual impulses are subjected in mental processes remain bound about with obscurities. Freud himself felt relatively knowledgeable only with regard to the sexual instincts, for their manifestations, even in convoluted forms, appear more clearly. It was the mentally disturbed who afforded the best opportunity for studying the instincts, since these individuals have failed to integrate and to modify their impulses in the manner demanded by successful societal adjustment. Freud was confident that a deeper understanding of what he called the ego or self-preservative instincts would result from psychoanalytic work with severe psychoses, with schizophrenia and paranoia. (His own experience excluded institutionalized patients.) In the "return of the repressed", which is what constitutes disturbance, these impulses could be seen more distinctly.

We may say, then, that the process of repression proper consists in a detachment of the libido (love) from people—and things—that were previously loved. It happens silently; we receive no intelligence of it, but can only infer it from subsequent events. What forces itself so noisily upon our attention is the process of recovery, which undoes the work of repression and brings back the libido again on to the people it has abandoned. In paranoia this process is carried out by the method of projection.[19]

Freud's understanding of the instincts underwent significant changes in his long career, most notably with respect to their kinds and groupings. By 1915, for example, he proposed two groups of primal instincts: the ego or self-preservative instincts and the sexual instincts, which correspond roughly to hunger and love respectively. He regarded this proposal, however, as "merely a working hypothesis, to be retained only so long as it proves useful, and it will make little difference to the results of our work of description and classification if it is replaced by another".[20] By 1920, he was inclined to associate these two within one major group, the instincts of "*Eros*", and to distinguish them from a death instinct ("*Thanatos*"). With respect to the existence of a primal death instinct, he was avowedly less certain.[21] What he did regard as a necessary postulate was the principle of constancy: "The nervous system is an apparatus which has the function of getting rid of the stimuli that reach it, or of reducing them to the lowest possible level; or which, if it were feasible, would maintain itself in an altogether unstimulated condition." [22]

Much of Freud's later explicit discussions on the instincts are rather speculative, an attempt to review them in terms of his theory of a primal death instinct. They are less valuable for the purposes of this thesis than his more clinically orientated expositions, most notably of the sexual instinct. This latter will be discussed in the following chapter, and will provide exemplification for the schematic treatment above.

To recapitulate, the primary mode of mental activity is, in other terms, mentality dominated by instinct. This mode, because primary, is extremely tenacious. It is in fact indestructible, for it has been precluded from the rational powers of consciousness.

Human development consists in claiming from it one enclave after another of psychic life, and this for as long as one lives.[23] The mind lapses into it in sleep, and the lesions in waking life are numerous and continual: psychotic periods, neuroses, commonplace parapraxes and commonplace phantasies. The fact that such reversions to primary functioning are necessary, or that they will unfailingly occur with the relaxation of the "higher" mental faculties shows the inadequacy of the secondary-preconscious and conscious systems for coming to terms with the whole of psychic life, or more specifically, for coming to terms with instinctual forces. Every human being labors under a failure of integration. The repressive measures by which he to some extent adjusts stifle the vitality of the instinctual impulses which are the sources of life. They are denied their rightful place and, therefore, the benefits of increasing psychic competence. On the other hand, his perceptual and reasoning powers are debilitated by their chosen partiality. It goes without saying that this state of affairs is more or less pronounced in different individuals and at different moments. Nevertheless, <u>self-alienation is an integral feature of human life as such.</u>

This self-division, at least in part, results from the peculiar nature of the evolution of the human psyche. Freud, from the outset, proposed that it had a more basic explanation still in the evolution of the human race itself. His statements were, on his own admission, conjectural, but they are suggestive to a theology which is more and more locating the discussion of original sin within an evolutionary context.

The Evolutionary Dimension of the Struggle with the Instincts

Even in his very early writings, Freud spoke of the fear of evolutionary regression, and of a corresponding aversion for the more recent stages through which we have passed. The virtually ubiquitous repression of certain desires, most especially sexual ones, cries out for a radical explanation. The primitive and erotic pleasures deriving from the sense of smell, for example, are widely suppressed. Freud suggested that when man assumed an erect posture, his sense of smell dwindled in importance. This diminishing was not simply an incidental by-product; it was also a definite devaluation, which Freud called "organ repression", or "the organic defence of the new form of life achieved with man's erect gait against his earlier animal existence".[24] As part of the distance which man put between himself and his former keenness of smell, he increasingly repressed olfactory pleasures or found revolting what he once found—and what children and animals still find—pleasurable or attractive. The "civilized" are repelled by the odors of excreta and of the genitals. (Significantly enough, a frequent characteristic of the psychotic is his uncanny sense of smell).

Freud's theory of the repression of the primary as an evolutionary exigency finds the most remarkable reinforcement in a recent work entitled *Man's Presumptuous Brain,* by A. T. W. Simeons.[25] In a chapter entitled "The Evolution of the Human Psyche", Simeons points out that man's brain has evolved by way of addition to the brain stem of premammalian vertebrates, first by the burgeoning of the cerebral hemispheres, and then by the vast increase in the area of their cortical covering. However, each stage of development was facilitated by the censorship of an agency which had previously served the organism well. The cortex was the seat of such censorship. The first agency he specifies is the sense of smell. Life in the trees demanded a keener visual than olfactory sense. An automatic response to olfactory stimuli was arrested by the cortex in order to allow for a greater variety of responses. Memory and learning from experience were necessary concomitants of this inhibition, so that the cerebral hemispheres grew to accommodate this more perspicacious adjustment. Gradually, one after another of the senses were subjected to cortical censorship, "to suppress useless incoming messages to which the brain would otherwise have been bound to react in the old way".[26]

The most important part of the brain stem is the diencephalon. There the instincts of fear, rage, hunger and sex are translated into physiological changes, such as preparation for flight, attack, etc. These changes are initiated in response to hormonal and sensory stimuli; they are initiated automatically. But as man evolved, they no longer proceeded to full term automatically. They were inhibited at the level of the cortex, which had also taken over control of movement from the brain stem.

At this stage of prehistoric development, there was already a certain lack of integration. The diencephalic instincts continued to be expressed automatically in a fashion which had previously saved man from extinction. But their full expression, that is, into sound and movement, was frequently thwarted by a more re-fined cortical assessment of the external situation.

The gap between the old brain stem and the relatively new cerebral development was to increase enormously as man began more and more to make use of artifacts. Artifacts such as fire, weapons and secure shelters made man safe in the face of dangers from which previously he would have had to take early flight. The instinct of fear was nevertheless evoked, and the dien-cephalon continued to mobilize the body for flight by such measures as evacuating the bowels and bladder, raising pulse and blood pressure, and tensing the muscles. A more extensive censorship was required. Now man excluded such bodily changes from his *conscious awareness*: he gradually ceased to acknowl-edge that his body was gripped by fear, because fear was no longer rational and therefore not deserving of the same mental resourcefulness.[27] Other instinctual pressures such as rage, hun-ger, sleep and sex were similarly censored. Without cortical ap-proval, they could not become conscious. This latter censorship at the level of consciousness was and is a product of civilization.

The brain stem and diencephalon continue to function in old ways. Because they are unaware of the demands of civilization, of an external world of artifacts and *mores,* they are out of harmony with the conscious mind. Many of their responses, such as anxiety in its forms of high blood pressure, indigestion, in-somnia and sexual impotence are a source of alarm and of be-wilderment to modern man. He is similarly disconcerted by his raw sexual responses. In many cases, he is actually unaware of the real nature of either sexual, angry or fearful bodily responses. Simeons sees a direct connection between this split and the high incidence of psychosomatic illness in our complex modern society.[28]

The parallels between Simeons' description of psychic development and Freud's are striking. In the first place, they concur in their paradigmatic explanation of the evolutionary process: automatic, reflexive response is inhibited in the interests of development. Physiologically speaking, instinctual response was inhibited by the developing cortex for the purpose of gaining a more detailed and associative understanding of external reality. Psychologically speaking, primary thought—thought in the grip of instinct—was inhibited by the ego, and for the same reason. It is interesting that when Freud spoke of psychic development on an individual level, though he explicitly excluded any anatomical specifications, he did speak of the ego as the cortex of the id.[29] Freud's description of the ego within psychic functioning is strikingly analogous to that of the development of the brain into a human form. The necessity for an increasingly sensitive grasp of reality, for a more ample memory, the postponement interposed between impulse and action in order to exploit the memory, the giving over of access to motility to conscious control; these adjustments are closely paralleled in the psychic development of the individual and the anatomical development over centuries of the race.

Both authors, moreover, have pointed out that cortical development on the one hand and the development of the secondary process on the other have tended to err by excess, and have done violence to the more primitive processes out of which they evolved.[30] The point at which that happens is when instinctual responses such as fear, rage and sex are ignored at the conscious level. Such censorship or simple withdrawal of attention is an expedient aimed at functioning more smoothly in society. But it easily becomes a two-edged sword.

Finally, proceeding from different data, both authors have concluded that man has evolved to the point of a strong cortical bias, at the expense of his instinctual life. His evolutionary course has incidentally been in the direction of self-alienation. Let no one think it is an easy process to undo! The struggle with which each individual in his society is faced—the dialectic between ego and id, between primary and secondary—has the fierce power of the evolutionary struggle for survival behind it. Freud maintained that the personal struggle is thus intensified: the opposing forces in it draw on a power which is not adequately explained by the factors of personal life.

Simeons points to a record of the history of human evolution in the very structure of the brain. Freud postulated a similar record in the deepest reaches of the unconscious mind; he considered the individual's psychic development to be a recapitulation of the evolutionary struggle.

This is a rich theme in Freud's writing and one that he approached from several angles, including that of "organic defence". Two facts must be stated by way of preliminary. In the first place, the limited environment into which the infant is born has remained unaltered in its essentials throughout the millennia. The all-important, primordial relationship of child to mother or mother-surrogate remains. Gradually, and in terms of that relationship, others enter the emotional sphere of the child: father, siblings and perhaps other close associates of the family. The child will work out a place for himself in this nuclear society. If one or another of these members is not present, then their very absence will also be a formative factor, and sooner or later, the individual will have to come to terms with their analogues. Secondly, the infant enters life with the same basic human resources. For these reasons, the child will find himself within the same basic emotional constellations as the children of past ages. He will be faced, therefore, with the same emotional options.

Some of these options have been discovered to be unwise, certain of them disastrously so. The options of murder, incest, and sexual perversions are of this kind. In the history of civilization, they have been ruled out as acceptable possibilities.[31] They are self-destructive, both intrinsically and because the weight of the societal consensus is against them. Nevertheless, impulses in these directions are felt by every individual. Incestuous impulses, for example, are a simple inevitability. The earliest erotic stirrings of the child are bound to be directed towards the persons most important in his life, namely the members of his own family. There is a powerful environmental fear surrounding the ex-

pression of such impulses; they are "taboo" to quote, with
Freud, a primitive term. It does not seem common, for instance,
that frankly incestuous or perverse tendencies in small children
are treated with equanimity and a certain humorous wisdom
about the stages of growth. They seem frequently to be met with
an emotional climate of obscurantism, titillation, or severe or
anxious disapproval. These dispositions, even when subtle, do not
escape the keen sensitivity of children, who in turn incorporate
the attitudes of their environment.

In the ideal situation, the short-sighted options mentioned
above will quite naturally give way to others that are more satisfying. At the far end of the spectrum from that of the severely
repressed are society's outcasts who cannot resist these instinctual attractions. The unconscious phantasies of the former "show
precisely the same content as the documentarily recorded *actions*
of perverts . . . psycho-neuroses are, so to speak, the *negative* of
perversions". More basically, perversions "are a development of
germs all of which are contained in the undifferentiated sexual
disposition of the child." [32] In between the extremely repressed
and the perverse lie the multitude in whom these impulses are
more or less repressed. In other words, such impulses commonly
live on in unenlightened fashion in the unconscious, both individually and collectively. The fascination and apprehension which
they evoke is uncanny.[33]

Freud was excited by the similarities between the psychic life
of children, neurotics and primitive societies still in existence.[34]
The sources of mental disturbance lie in impulses which have
remained infantile and archaic, impulses overt in children and
more primitive cultures. "I have repeatedly been led to suspect",
he wrote, "that the psychology of the neuroses has stored up
in it more of the antiquities of human development than any
other source." [35] In another passage, he included dreams along
with neurotic phenomena as preservers of "mental antiquities".[36]
But the neurotic harbors no impulses unfamiliar to his more
balanced brethren, as the psychology of dreams will bear out. It
is the unconscious mind which is the bearer of the archaic, therefore, since it is at once the oldest form of mental life and the place

of mental events denied access to consciousness and maturation.

So far, the recapitulation of the racial past in each individual has been demonstrated on the grounds of the identity through time of innate human resources and the emotional situation into which each human being is born. Relatively late in his writings, Freud began to propose the possibility that actual ancestral experiences could be transmitted through remote memory traces to succeeding generations.[37] Though his suggestion is highly conjectural, the clinical phenomena on which he based it are intriguing and merit attention here. Freud coined the term "archaic heritage" for the hypothesized memory traces.[38] He seems to have reached this conclusion on the basis of what he called "primal phantasies" and of the nature of symbolism.

Folklore, fairy tales, dreams, humor, myths and linguistic usage show a striking and undeniable identity in their use of symbolism. Moreover, children use this same "language" in their play, speech, and phantasies. There is no evidence in most cases that they have been taught a symbolic connection between two entities. "These comparisons are not freshly made on each occasion; they lie ready to hand and are complete, once and for all. This is implied by the fact of their agreeing in the case of different individuals—possibly, indeed, agreeing in spite of differences of language." [39] The use of symbols is a main characteristic of the unconscious mode of thinking. In other words, it is an archaic mode. Dreams, therefore, are a construction of symbols, some very personal, but others universally used. The dreamer, Freud regularly found, was ignorant of the meaning of the latter sort. Dreams do not use the conscious, contrived symbols of everyday life, such as flags or signs. The dreamer draws on an ancient source also exemplified in the forms noted above: fairy tales, folklore, and so on.

A few examples will make his thinking clearer. Birth is regularly symbolized in dreams by some connection with water. One falls into the water or comes out of it. Now a predominant feature in the births of heroes is their rescue from the water. With regard to this symbol, Freud made explicit allusions to an evolutionary context:

We must not forget that this symbol is able to appeal in two ways to evolutionary truth. Not only are all terrestrial mammals, including man's ancestors, descended from aquatic creatures (this is the more remote of the two facts), but every individual mammal, every human being, spent the first phase of its existence in water—namely as an embryo in the amniotic fluid in its mother's uterus, and came out of that water when it was born.[40]

Death is frequently symbolized by a long journey—in common parlance, rituals ancient and modern, and in dreams.

The body, and particularly its sexual activity, abound in symbolic expressions. A very common symbol for the woman is a room, or a house, an oven, a box, a landscape. The common use of a landscape to represent the woman recalls the fertility cults of antiquity, as well as the expression "Mother Earth." The male genitalia are regularly symbolized by weapons such as knives and firearms, trees, triform objects and a variety of instruments. These dream symbols are reiterated in humor and in poetry. Sexual intercourse is frequently symbolized by actions of climbing, an allusion reflected in the sexual connotations of the word "to mount", both in German and English. "One gets an impression that what we are faced with here is an ancient but extinct mode of expression, of which different pieces have survived in different fields",[41] a sort of "primal language".[42] Another area in which it finds expression is in neurotic symptoms. There appears to be no satisfactory explanation for its transmission through the generations. Linguistic usage can account for only a part of it.[43] "It seems to me", Freud concluded, "that symbolic connections, which the individual has never acquired by learning may justly claim to be regarded as a phylogenetic heritage." These connections occur "in so far as each individual somehow recapitulates in an abbreviated form the entire development of the human race".[44]

The concurrence in the use of symbolism may find adequate explanation in the closeness to the elemental which is characteristic of the unconscious mind and of simple and creative persons. Whether it also embodies rudimentary memory remains unanswered by the above considerations alone.

In any case, Freud's hypothesis of an archaic or phylogenetic heritage seems to have been precipitated more by the phenomenon of what he called "primal phantasies".[45] He was impressed by the recurrence of certain sets of memories among his patients: memories of having been seduced in childhood by an adult, of observing parental intercourse, of being threatened with castration by a parent or nurse. In his very early experience, Freud accepted the seduction memories as objectively true, and as for threats of castration, the child-rearing notions in Central Europe at the time could offer many confirmations. He began to realize, however, that in many instances, such memories were not of objective events, but of fictions of the infantile mind. "There was the definite realization that there is no 'indication of reality' in the unconscious, so that it is impossible to distinguish between truth and emotionally-charged fiction." [46]

The subjective origins as well as the basic similarity underlying these infantile phantasies forced Freud to question their source:

> Whence comes the need for these phantasies and the material for them? There can be no doubt that their sources lie in the instincts; but it has still to be explained why the same phantasies with the same content are created on every occasion. I am prepared with an answer which I know will seem daring to you. I believe these *primal phantasies,* as I should like to call them, and no doubt a few others as well, are a phylogenetic endowment. In them the individual reaches beyond his own experience into primaeval experience at points where his own experience has been too rudimentary. It seems to me that all the things that are told to us today in analysis as phantasy—the seduction of children, the inflaming of sexual excitement by observing parental intercourse, the threat of castration (or rather castration itself)—were once real occurrences in the primaeval times of the human family, and that children in their phantasies are simply filling in the gaps in individual truth with prehistoric truth.[47]

One set of phantasies in particular interested Freud; those surrounding the so-called Oedipus complex. The Oedipus complex refers to that stage of development in which the child begins to relate to his parents as male and female, and to work out his own place in terms of this new understanding. This is the stage at which he begins to recognize a particular relationship existing not only between each parent and himself, but also, alas, between his parents quite apart from himself. Every child comes to terms with these realities in his own peculiar fashion. His readiness to do so marks the climax of early childhood.[48]

Freud found this stage easier to understand in the male child than in the female.[49] With regard to the male child, he uncovered a consistent set of emotions and, of course, phantasies. Along with the development of a tender, young masculine love for the mother was an attitude of rivalry and fear towards the father. Freud found this complex to be so universal and critical, and in many cases so bound about with an anxiety not warranted by the actual situation, that he argued for an archaic upheaval whose disastrous elements were, in some remote fashion, being remembered. He argued this, too, from the persistence with which the same complex of emotions was expressed in the classics through the ages—most clearly in the drama which gave the complex its name—and the power which they perennially exercised over their audiences.[50] He made bold to sketch that remote event: it consisted of the murder of a primaeval patriarch by his grown sons. Presumably, that patriarch, as in the case of some animal species, had sole sexual rights within the group. The chief motive for the parricide was the right to sexual relations with the female(s), who were in fact their own mother(s). Once they had come to their senses, the sons recoiled in horror and dreadful guilt from their crime and took powerful measures to prevent its recurrence. Freud regarded those measures as the primaeval foundations of human society, so foundational as to inculcate an innate sense of boundary or of taboo in all succeeding generations.[51] That ancient parricide was the original sin.[52]

Freud's hypothesis of the primal horde probably has few literal adherents. It was too confidently elaborated in its details, too bound up with a single event. This is especially true of the confident manner in which he used the hypothesis in writing after *Totem and Taboo*. In that work, though, he met the objection: "The lack of precision in what I have written in the text above, its abbreviation of the time factor and its compression of the whole subject-matter, may be attributed to the reserve necessitated by the nature of the topic. It would be as foolish to aim at exactitude in such questions as it would be unfair to insist upon certainty".[53] However, the unconscious *is* redolent of the primitive and archaic, and nowhere is this more striking than in its proclivity for symbolism and elemental phantasies. The connection with ancient myth and lore, with the customs of primitive peoples, is not only natural for the person in any way familiar with them; indeed, it forces itself upon him.[54] The conjectures outlined above are personal formulations of that unmistakeable impression. It is significant that Freud crowned his extraordinary insight into the ways of the mind with the postulate of an original sin.

The basic question here regards the nature of historical influence on the individual; whether the cumulative modifications exerted by events in the history of the race can be transmitted at the level of nature itself, or whether they are exerted only after conception. Freud's explanation of primal phantasies shows him inclined to opt for the former position, at least in part.

He expressed the same option in another passage. It may be recalled, by way of preface, that to speak in Freudian terms of the level of nature itself, of innate resources, is to speak of the id. For the id, organized around the nucleus of the primal instincts, is the origin of the psyche. "The content of the *Ucs.* [used here in the more precise sense of the id] may be compared with an aboriginal population in the mind. If inherited mental formations exist in the human being—something analogous to instinct in animals— these constitute the nucleus of the *Ucs.*" [55] If racial memory is involved in that inheritance, then the id would be its bearer in the individual. The ego is the agency of self-direction which evolves out of the peculiar circumstances of individual life. On the face of it, therefore, it cannot be inherited. However, at this point Freud cautioned against a too rigid isolation of psychic faculties. The ego is, after all, the id as modified by the dialectic with external reality. Freud went on to reiterate his acceptance of the transmission of experience.

When we speak of an "archaic heritage", we are usually thinking of the id and we seem to assume that at the beginning of the individual's life no ego is as yet in existence. But we shall not overlook the fact that id and ego are originally one; nor does it imply any mystical overevaluation of heredity if we think it credible that even before the ego has come into existence, the lines of development, trends and reactions which it will later exhibit are already laid down for it. The psychological peculiarities of families, races and nations, even in their attitude to analysis, allow of no other explanation.[56]

Nevertheless, another explanation for the latter characteristic, that of very early environmental influence does occur to one. In another passage, he said:

The experiences of the ego seem at first to be lost for inheritance; but, when they have been repeated often enough and with sufficient strength in many individuals in successive generations, they transform themselves, so to say, into experiences of the id, the impressions of which are preserved by heredity. Thus in the id, which is capable of being inherited, are harboured residues of the existences of countless egos.[57]

Freud, then, viewed the ego-choices of countless generations, when crystallized into what some would call an option, as eventually constitutive of psychic inheritance. These are definite analogies on the level of physical evolution. (Freud mentions "instinct" in animals, meaning presumably, those peculiar to the species or sub-species.) This is the most radical statement of environmental influence on the self.

In the last analysis, there is no certainty in this matter. It must suffice to expose the material which moved Freud to the conclusions he drew. When it came to persuading others of the weight of his theoretical positions, he sometimes declared that only if these others entered into the ways of the psyche with the same laborious care as he did, could he argue with them the merits of one or another conclusion. This would seem to be one such case. It would also seem to be an area more vulnerable to subjective inclination. One student of human nature will seem more inclined to accept the reality of inherited influences, another to be impressed anew by the almost osmotic influence of the early environment.

The sense of the environmental context of individual psychic development pervades all of Freud's writings. In his correspondence with Fliess, for example, he was already preoccupied with the familial contexts from which his patients came to him.[58] And towards the end of his life, he turned increasingly to a study of civilization and the dialectic between the collective forces of society and the instinctual demands in its members.[59]

He felt that the most important messages from one generation to the next were conveyed subliminally, as it were.

> We may safely assume that no generation is able to conceal any of its more important mental processes from its successor. For psycho-analysis has shown us that everyone possesses in his unconscious mental activity an apparatus which enables him to interpret other people's reactions, that is, to undo the distortions which other people have imposed on the expression of their feelings.[60]

Basic psychic dispositions, such as warmth, expansiveness, benignity, solidity—or fear, rigidity, distrust, self-isolation and despair, form the emotional matrix in which the infant and child come to the most elementary resolutions. These dispositions are most often not verbalized or consciously inculcated. Much of this is conveyed at a physical level, is an organic communication. This is most clear with respect to emotions such as anxiety, coldness, depression, anger, or states of positive emotional vibrancy such as warmth and enthusiasm.[61]

In one context, Freud was particularly elaborate on the transmission of values through the generations. That was in speaking of the super-ego or primitive conscience. In childhood, instinctual impulses are most simplistic and ungoverned; or from another point of view, they are initially the sole governing influences. The id "knows of no judgements of value: no good and evil, no morality".[62] Its only law is the economic drive towards release. Only when the instinctual forces run up against disagreeable consequences, or the threat of them, does an internal faculty of criticism, of objectivity and self-limitation begin to emerge in the child. Insofar as the consequences are grasped and reckoned with by the child's intelligence, they are formative of the ego. But to a considerable degree, the curbing of impulse originates only from parental strictures and occurs for reasons he cannot understand. The child will nevertheless internalize these norms because of his own inadequacy, his desire for acceptance and security, and his blind fear of punishment. They provide an additional source of self-criticism, though a less organic, truly personal and enlightened one. They constitute what Freud called the super-ego, an internalized authority which stands "above" or over against the ego. The super-ego is the agent of childhood "morality": this action must or must not be done because the parents or teachers would have one do or not do it. It is also the agent of much of what passes for morality in adults.

The super-ego will be discussed again in the following chapter. What is important here is the nature of this psychic stance towards the instincts. It is an unenlightened and fearful one. The child internalizes parental attitudes towards instinctual impulses as he perceives them. His adaptations will necessarily therefore be distorted; good parents cannot be assured of untroubled children. The formation of a superego is inescapable; it is a function of the long period of dependence in man.[63] Yet along with distortion, there is an element of unerring accuracy, for with the sensitivity peculiar to the child, he will discern the unspoken fears and personal irresolutions of his elders, and internalize these. Thus in the formation of the super-ego, the child falls heir to the cultural values of his predecessors.

The details of the relation between the ego and the super-ego become completely intelligible when they are traced back to the child's attitude to its parents. This parental influence of course includes in its operation not only the personalities of the actual parents but also the family, racial and national traditions handed on through them, as well as the demands of the immediate social *milieu* which they represent. In the same way, the super-ego, in the course of the individual's development, receives contributions from later successors and substitutes of his parents, such as teachers and models in public life of admired social ideals. It will be observed that, for all their fundamental difference, the id and the super-ego have one thing in common: they both represent the influences of the past—the id the influence of heredity, the super-ego the influence, essentially, of what is taken over from other people—whereas the ego is principally determined by the individual's own experience, that is by accidental and contemporary events.[64]

With this fear-ridden and unenlightened surrogate for ego and true conscience, this agency in large part relegated to the unconscious because infantile, men individually and collectively face the enormous challenge posed by the instincts—or at least they do so to a considerable degree. It is a rule all too immune to reflection and development, and therefore a powerful source of blind conservatism.

3. THE CENTRALITY
OF THE SEXUAL INSTINCT
IN THE HUMAN CONDITION

Introduction

The sexual instinct is the most familiar and obstreperous of the instincts for Western man; here he experiences instinct as such. The experience of the instincts of hunger or self-preservation in their raw and simple forms, as distinct from their elaborations, can hardly be called familiar to those living in a functioning society. The rationale behind society is, after all, to provide against that experience. Not so with the sexual instinct; the normal and abnormal human being of the 20th century still experiences the urge for sexual gratification in its powerful and primitive instinctual form, however inimical his society is to its acceptance. Of all the instincts, therefore, the sexual one epitomizes for modern man the struggle between the ego and the instinctual life outlined in the first and second chapters: "Sexual life is especially well suited to provide the content [of early traumas later repressed] owing to the very great contrast it presents to the rest of the personality and to its ideas being impossible to react to." [1]

Freud's insistence upon the importance of sexuality in the whole of psychic life, including its phases in infancy and childhood, condemned him to unpopularity from the beginning. His position was caricatured, trivialized, met with righteous indigna-

71

tion, olympian indifference, or mindless application. Freud admitted that he had to overcome his own "personal disinclination" to probe evidence, which, had it involved any other dimension, he would have pursued more readily.[2] Colleagues who had voiced their own views in private about a sexual psychogenesis of certain disorders disassociated themselves from his attempts to put the matter on the level of scientific research.[3] Moreover, the psychoanalytic movement itself in the later years of his life showed a definite tendency to ease off the sexual emphasis.[4] In a word, the issue was fraught from the outset with striking resistance—certain evidence that it was touching upon something very close to the marrow of the human struggle.

The tradition of original sin has always included a sexual dimension, though it has perhaps been more frequently implicit. The Genesis narrative speaks of the freedom the man and woman felt in their nakedness, and of their discomfiture after the sin. With the sin came divisiveness between the man and the woman. St. Paul's lament in Romans 7 speaks of the sin living in his members, of his body following a different law than the law of his reason. The Council of Trent speaks of concupiscence, the tendency which inclines to sin and comes from sin. Both the Pauline and Tridentine passages refer to an instinctual unruliness which undoubtedly includes the sexual instinct. Certain Christian authors throughout the ages have been more explicit: for example, in speculations concerning the nature of the first sin, and in the theory that original sin is transmitted in the act of coitus. It is safe to say that concupiscence has had a definite sexual connotation on the popular level, which until very recently was formed by the theology manual tradition. In short, the theology of original sin has always included a sense that the sexual instinct is in some way integrally involved in man's alienation from God and himself.

Freud strove for a lifetime to understand more accurately the role of the sexual instinct in the whole of psychic life. Certain characteristics of the sexual instinct as he explained them go far in explaining the integral yet problematic part it plays in human development. This chapter will be devoted to a discussion of these characteristics, with a view to gaining a more complete picture of the human predicament.

What Freud thrust into the forefront was how integral sexuality is to the intellectual, moral and emotional evolution of the human being. He came to it negatively, in that he gradually discovered that in every psychic disturbance without exception, the sexual instinct was causally involved. This could be true of psychic pathology only if the sexual instinct was integral to normal development; if, that is to say, the capacity to love and to understand things truly is in part a function of sexual development. Secondly, he showed that of all the instincts, the sexual instinct alone undergoes a significant development. The fact that it must do so is the reason for its important place in overall psychic development. It can be either a catalyst for change or a powerful factor in regression. Thirdly, the sexual instinct is more refractory to tutelage by reality factors than the instincts of hunger and self-preservation. To refuse the demands of reality has only brutal consequences in the last two instances. The sexual instinct, however, has open to it the option of auto-satisfaction, and this characteristic is extremely consequential. An individual can, in this respect, resist reality and still survive. Finally, the sexual instinct, or libido, is at the beginning of life entirely bound up with self-interest. The infant is born in a state which Freud described as primary narcissism. In a healthy situation, that self-interest develops to include others in what is essentially the same dynamic. This change is what Freud described as the transformation of ego-libido into object-libido. It cannot take place, however, unless there is love surrounding the child, and only to that extent. Failures constitute a withdrawal of the interest back into the self; these are the source of the narcissistic elements in the adult. Love and narcissism are opposite polarities. Both, however, have their origins in the same instinct: the one being its fixated expression, and the other the outcome of its healthy development. The biblical image of sin as a turning in on the self and the Freudian term narcissism describe the same reality.

Freud's Introduction to the Importance of Sexuality

"Freud's *Three Essays on the Theory of Sexuality* stand, there can be no doubt, beside his

Interpretation of Dreams as his most momentous and original contributions to human knowledge." [5] They were Freud's own favorites and the two which he kept constantly revised as they appeared in successive editions. He once remarked to Ernest Jones, "It seems to be my fate to discover only the obvious: that children have sexual feelings, which every nursemaid knows; and that night dreams are just as much wish-fulfilment as day dreams." [6]

The correspondence with Wilhelm Fliess is the best source for Freud's first inklings of the importance of the sexual factor. Among his patients were several suffering from anxiety and neurasthenia, a rather general term which described conditions of chronic headache, fatigue, lethargy, digestive disturbances, and so on. He discovered the methods of treatment then in use to have only temporary effect. Further, he was gradually struck by the fact that unhealthy sexual conditions were concurrently always present. [7] He concluded that a physiological disturbance was inevitable, for he was already convinced of the presence of a chemical factor in sexuality. Though personally unable to explain its nature, he declared it to be an urgent area for further research. [8]

From the mid-90's until the end of the 19th century, he tested the validity of his observations and partly formed conclusions in his letters to Fliess. He noted, for example, that there are areas in the child's body which are peculiarly sensitive to stimulation, but whose erotic interest is suppressed in later childhood. He proposed that the sources of both neurotic "morality" and sexual perversion were to be found in this dual situation. [9] He was aware of the severe sexual agitation in every case of hysteria. It was precisely that agitation which found indirect expression in bizarre physical symptoms which were at once painful and a powerful source of preoccupation. The case of Anna O. had revealed events of her recent past as the source of her symptoms, but Freud was convinced that a more satisfying explanation for hysteria had to be sought in the events of childhood. At the time of the *Project for a Scientific Psychology*, he saw sexuality as a dormant force in childhood, one which could only be prematurely and disastrously aroused by an adult or older child. He had concluded that hysteria was one of the results of this sort of seduction.[10]

All of these issues which he was later to expand upon were at this time probings and suggestions based on his neurological practice. The keystone to his understanding of the sexual factor in psychic life was discovered in his self-analysis, which he undertook after the death of his father, and which centered chiefly on the interpretation of his own dreams.[11] At this time, his traumatic theory of the neuroses (namely, that hysteria as well as other mental disturbances were the eventual result of premature, or childish, sexual traumata) [12] suffered its first blow. In the summer of 1897, he wrote to Fliess:

> I no longer believe in my *neurotica* [theory of the neuroses]. That is hardly intelligible without an explanation; you yourself found what I told you credible. So I shall start at the beginning and tell you the whole story of how the reasons for rejecting it arose. The first group of factors were the continual disappointment of my attempts to bring my analyses to a real conclusion, the running away of people who for a time had seemed my most favourably inclined patients, the lack of the complete success on which I had counted, and the possibility of explaining my partial successes in other, familiar ways. Then there was the astonishing thing that in every case the father, not excluding my own, had to be blamed as a pervert—the realization of the unexpected frequency of hysteria, in every case of which the same thing applied, though it is hardly credible that perverted acts against children are so general. (Perversion would have to be immeasurably more frequent than hysteria, as the illness can only arise where the events have accumulated and one of the factors which weaken defence is present). Thirdly, there was the definite realization that there is no "indication of reality" in the unconscious, so that it is impossible to distinguish between truth and emotionally charged fiction. (This leaves open the possible explanation that sexual phantasy regularly makes use of the theme of the parents). . . . So far was I influenced by these considerations that I was ready to abandon two things—the complete solution of a neurosis and sure reliance on its aetiology in infancy. Now I do not know where I am.[13]

His uncertainty regarding the sexually traumatic origins of mental disturbance was not resolved until the results of other observations had received clearer formulation. Another such formulation was emerging at the same time:

Being entirely honest with oneself is a good exercise. Only one idea of general value has occurred to me. I have found love of the mother and jealousy of the father in my own case too, and now believe it to be a general phenomenon of early childhood. . . . If that is the case, the gripping power of *Oedipus Rex,* in spite of all the rational objections to the inexorable fate that the story presupposes, becomes intelligible, and one can understand why later fate dramas were such failures. Our feelings rise against any arbitrary, individual fate . . . but the Greek myth seizes on a compulsion which everyone recognizes because he has felt traces of it in himself. Every member of the audience was once a budding Oedipus in phantasy, and this dream-fulfillment played out in reality causes everyone to recoil in horror, with the full measure of repression which separates his infantile from his present state. The idea has passed through my head that the same thing may lie at the root of *Hamlet.* I am not thinking of Shakespeare's conscious intentions, but supposing rather that he was impelled to write it by a real event because his own unconscious understood that of his hero.[14]

The directions indicated in the two preceding passages soon ripened into a single conviction: much of psychic phenomena, both normal and pathological, arise from the mental life of the child. But further, since the child is drawing on his own resources in these phantasies and emotional states, then the sexual instinct is already operative in childhood though in different ways. The base of the new discipline shifted from one of trauma to one of instinctual life. Nevertheless, it was eight years before Freud placed his findings before the public in *Three Essays on the Theory of Sexuality.*

In the meantime, he began publishing his views in scientific journals. The so-called "actual neuroses" of anxiety and neurasthenia, termed "actual" because they were caused by circumstances in the present-day life of the patient, had their origins in unwise and therefore disturbing sexual practices.[15] But more deep-seated psychic disturbances (the "psychoneuroses") that resulted in hysterical, obsessional and paranoid symptoms also had a sexual etiology, in that all of them defended against incompatible sexual inclinations. The pathological power of these inclinations derived from a personal history of irresolution. Patients instinctively remembered a series of similarly disturbing occasions that reached back into childhood.[16] Freud wrote: "I can only repeat over and over again—for I never find it otherwise—that sexuality is the key to the problem of the psychoneuroses and of the neuroses in general. No one who disdains the key will ever be unable to unlock the door." [17] The sexuality of which he spoke was broadly conceived: in his view, it closely coincided with Plato's concept of *Eros*.

It is important to dwell on this point since Freud's use of "sexuality" has been so widely misunderstood. His own clarification in response to general misconception is probably the best one:

> Libido is an expression taken from the theory of the emotions. We call by that name the energy, regarded as a quantitative magnitude (though not at present actually measurable), of those instincts which have to do with all that may be comprised under the word "love". The nucleus of what we mean by love naturally consists (and this is what is commonly called love, and what the poets sing of) in sexual love with sexual union as its aim. But we do not separate from this—what in any case has a share in the name "love"—on the one hand, self-love, and on the other, love for parents and children, friendship and love for humanity in general, and also devotion to concrete objects and to abstract ideas. Our justification lies in the fact that psycho-analytic research has taught us that all these tendencies are an expression of the same instinctual impulses; in relations between the sexes these impulses force their way towards sexual union, but in other circumstances they are diverted from this aim or are prevented from reaching it, though always preserving enough of their original nature to keep their identity recognizable (as in such features as the longing for proximity, and self-sacrifice).

Psychoanalysis "has done nothing original in taking love in this 'wider' sense". "Anyone who considers sex as something mortifying and humiliating to human nature is at liberty to make use of the more genteel expressions 'Eros' and 'erotic'." In essence, "psycho-analysis, then, gives these love instincts the name of sexual instincts, *a potiori* and by reason of their origin".[18] "In thus distinguishing between libidinal and other forms of psychical energy we are giving expression to the presumption that the sexual processes occurring in the organism are distinguished from the nutritive processes by a special chemistry." [19]

If irregularities in the evolution of the sexual instinct are the key to psychic pathology, it is only because that evolution is equally cardinal in normal psychic development.

There is a dictum in general pathology, Gentlemen, which asserts that every developmental process carries with it the seed of a pathological disposition, in so far as that process may be inhibited, delayed, or may run its course incompletely. The same thing is true of the highly complicated development of the sexual function. It does not occur smoothly in every individual; and, if not, it leaves behind it either abnormalities or a predisposition to fall ill later, along the path of involution (i.e. regression).[20]

The Evolution of the Sexual Instinct

The most important section in *Three Essays on the Theory of Sexuality* is the one entitled "Infantile Sexuality". It traces sexual manifestations from the stages of infancy and childhood through to puberty. This constantly revised work was foundational to all of Freud's research and will form the basis for the following discussion.

We found it a regrettable thing that the existence of the sexual instinct in childhood has been denied and that the sexual manifestations not infrequently to be observed in childhood have been described as irregularities. It seemed to us on the contrary that children bring germs of sexual activity with them into the world, that they already enjoy sexual satisfaction when they begin to take nourishment.[21]

It is for this very reason that the infant and young child isolates the act of sucking from the total act of taking nourishment. The sensual nature of sucking is clear: the rhythmic movement, the complete absorption of attention which leads to sleep or even to a motor reaction in the nature of an orgasm.[22] The show of disgust at, and the restriction of, thumb-sucking by some parents betray their recognition of the erotic nature of the habit.

At a later period, the child shows the same sensual satisfaction in the act of defecation. He will discover, too, the pleasure associated with stimulation of the genitals. There are, then, portions of the body which are particularly susceptible to pleasure if stimulated. These Freud called "erotogenic zones"; they are chiefly the mucous membrane of the mouth and anus, and finally, in a most developed way, the genitals. In fact, generally speaking, "the skin, which in particular parts of the body has become differentiated into sense-organs or modified into mucous membrane . . . is the erotogenic zone *par excellence*".[23]

The zonal nature of sexuality has several important implications. In the first place, it will be noted that the areas of pleasure are precisely the foci of our vital functions: of nourishment, elimination and reproduction. Secondly, a definite pattern can be discerned in the functioning of the sexual instinct: one area will have heightened erotic interest at a certain period, and then cede its favored place to another, until the genital stage of adulthood. Thirdly, the experience of sensual satisfaction can assume a place apart from the vital function with which it is associated. There is an urge to isolate and repeat the pleasure, and this in a fashion which is predominantly auto-erotic. Finally, auto-erotic forms of pleasure (thumb-sucking, masturbation) clearly also provide a source of security, a kind of anchorage. Unusual or prolonged indulgence is, in fact, symptomatic of emotional stress. For this reason, auto-erotism, particularly under the stress of change, can easily reinforce regression to an earlier, more comforting emotional time. But it may also indicate an impoverishment of elements, notably love and pleasure, vital to human life.[24]

Precisely because it attempts to isolate and exploit sexual satisfaction, the phenomenon of auto-erotism brings out with peculiar clarity the role of sexuality. It also demonstrates the connection between certain forms of sexual pleasure and the phases of emotional development to which they most characteristically correspond. In a derivative and sometimes negative fashion, it emphasizes the fact that the evolution of sexual objective and the evolution of emotive-intellectual life are in a relation of mutual cause and effect.

The dominance of an erotogenic zone contributes to overall emotional and intellectual response. In the first phase of life, stimulation of the mouth is central. The act of sucking brings the infant security, a sense of well-being and of emotional grounding. But the mouth also becomes a medium for knowing the small child's environment. Each new interesting object goes into its mouth, and this is obviously an attempt to get to know something of its meaning. The stance of the infant and very young child is one of ingestion; it is absorbedly "taking in" its surroundings. The very act of seeing is one of "drinking in". The act of sucking is paradigmatic of an intellectual and emotional response to the environment. An individual may remain at this oral stage even into adulthood, so that he remains needy, insatiably feeding off others, and on a deep emotional level as incapable of giving as is an infant. Such an individual is fixated, a condition which less commonly may also take the form of sexual perversions involving the mouth.[25]

The focus of pleasure and curiosity will gradually shift from the mouth. The next area of heightened interest seems to be the anus and the excretory function. A new sense of muscular control, of autonomy, emerges. It is, of course, more general than the new measure of excretory control, but a quite distinct pleasure is associated with the latter. Furthermore, the child is more aware of his excrement. It is a source of fascination and pride to him, the first of his productions. Thus he will proudly summon adults to the scene of his creativity to rejoice with him. This phase is obviously an important period in the formation of a sense of self-worth and independence. When the emotional atmosphere is not so sensitive to the delicacy of the issues involved, or when the child comes to them already disturbed and regressive, less healthy results may occur. Stubbornness is a frequent trait in children of this age. Toilet training is often a fierce battle of wills, wherein the child at last has a completely impregnable weapon of defiance at his disposal. Just as the crucially important growth of independence may be exploited for the purposes of defiance and contention, so the growing sense of power may shade off into excessive aggressiveness and even sadism, a quality only too common in disturbed children. Avarice and reaction-formations such as excessive neatness may also develop. These traits in adults show that the challenges confronting the child of this phase have remained unresolved. If the erotic interest characteristic of this period is overt, when the fixated adult will seek for anal stimulation in sexual perversity.[26]

Before entering upon a discussion of the last discernible phase of early childhood, a word must be said about a characteristic peculiar to the sexual instinct, or libido. Libido is the name

Freud gave "to the energy of the sexual instincts and to that form of energy alone"; [27] it is "the force by which the sexual instinct is represented in the mind". [28] The characteristic is that the sexual instinct manifests itself in the activity of a number of "component instincts". The sexual instinct is initially free-floating; it makes little distinction between male and female, or even between human and animal. "It is an instructive fact that under the influence of seduction children can become polymorphously perverse, and can be led into all possible kinds of sexual irregularities. This shows that an aptitude for them is innately present in their disposition." [29] The component instincts are dependent upon erotogenic zones in the body; "they operate independently of one another in a search for pleasure, and they find their object for the most part in the subject's own body. Thus at first the sexual function is non-centralized and predominantly *auto-erotic*." [30] The phases of development under consideration represent stages of synthesis of these disparate forms of satisfaction. Something has already been said of the sexualizing or "libidinizing" of the vital functions and of the auto-erotic practices that isolate that pleasure. Other activities can also be sexualized, and characteristically are during childhood. For example, the acts of looking and of being looked at can be highly eroticized. Acts of muscular competence, or aggressiveness, or of sadism can afford what can only be described as sexual pleasure, and so too can the act of experiencing pain. This is seen most clearly in cases of outright perversion, but these are only the most overt extremes within a continuum.

In fact, Freud was convinced that any emotional constellation can be eroticized, and that this peculiarity explained the tenacity of unwholesome and self-destructive character traits. The sexual instinct epitomizes his dictum that instinctual aim (satisfaction) is more radical than instinctual object. An example may serve to clarify all this. The punishment of children is too often a sensual experience for parent and child alike. Once the child is reduced to tears and humiliation, the parent will accord it tenderness and intimacy. These latter moments have an unmistakably sensual aspect. Generally, with such parents the same sort of intimacy is not granted when the child is spirited. He is then bereft of inti-

mate acceptance by the parent; and this is a price too great for
the child to pay. Children brought up in this atmosphere will
inevitably see humiliation as more acceptable, self-lessening as
provocative of a loving response, and sturdy independence as
lonely and stoical. Thus, unhealthy constellations of feeling are
valued because they continue to be a source of sensual gratification and so of some measure of security. On the other hand, if
parents are delighted by the healthy high spirits of their children,
and if a bracing gratification comes from keeping communication
open and forward-moving, then the child too will work to have
around him the same emotional atmosphere.[31] Emotional states
are sexually energized; herein is the source of their power of
attraction both for good or ill. If those states are pathological,
they will hold the individual in their grip despite the distress
they will also bring to him. They are like so many stagnant pools
which have leaked off from the main stream. If those states are
vital and creative, they will draw their subject on to an ever
more creative and courageous response to life, a response which
seems almost superhuman to those not similarly impelled. What
the latter do not understand is that such a person is powerfully
stimulated by the quality of his life; it becomes more attractive
and desirable to him than anything else. "For the man who has
will be given more; from the man who has not, even what he has
will be taken away." [32] "Our present point of view can be
roughly expressed in the statement that libido has a share in
every instinctual manifestation, but that not everything in that
manifestation is libido." [33] What is also and incidentally illus-
trated in the above considerations is that the sexual stage of development to which the adults surrounding the child have progressed is crucial to his own development, and that that influence
is inescapable.

Sexual development is the organization of these disparate
sources of pleasure into some system of priorities, some self-
direction and choice. Ultimately, that orientation is a result of the
so-called genital phase. The course of sexual development is also
in the direction of greater personalism and away from
auto-erotism.[34]

This stage is already entered upon in childhood, in what is
termed the phallic phase. At about two to four years of age, the

child experiences an increased fascination with his genitals and a greater awareness of their pleasurable potential. "Among the erogenetic zones that form part of the child's body there is one that certainly does not play the opening part, and which cannot be the vehicle of the oldest sexual impulses, but which is destined to great things in the future." [35] This interest coincides with the child's growing sense of his parents as other persons and with an inkling of the sexual differences between them. This stage, therefore, marks the child's first attempts to grasp his own sexual identity. Child analysis has revealed that the child, particularly the boy, does in some dim way glimpse the meaning of his genital structures. It is a time of intense curiosity regarding the differences between boys and girls, and often, the origin of babies.

This point calls for an important digression. Freud frequently referred to the relationship existing between sexual vitality and intellectual vitality. "It is hardly to be believed what goes on in a child of four or five years old. Children are very active-minded at that age; their early sexual period is also a period of intellectual flowering. I have an impression that with the onset of the latency period they become mentally inhibited as well, stupider." [36] "Think of the depressing contrast between the radiant intelligence of a healthy child and the feeble intellectual powers of the average adult." [37] Negatively speaking, mental obtuseness, lethargy and falsification or mental disturbance of whatever degree are correlates of sexual repression, for repression eventuates in the alienation of the self from its own vital energies. On the other hand, sublimation or healthy diversion of sexual energy—a process impossible for the severely repressed who remain tyrannized by infantile impulses—finds one of its chief forms in a keen spirit of investigation.[38] Freud was therefore emphatic on the necessity for respecting the powerful desire to know in children, a desire which is directed onto the most elemental realities. Mental disturbances are always disturbances of the thirst for knowing things as they really are, and both result from pathological handling of the sexual instincts. If certain areas take on the nature of the forbidden to the mind of the child, then the drive to know is stifled. Knowing becomes threatening; it must be limited to areas whose acceptibility seems to be agreed upon.

Girls and boys in this phase definitely show germs of the capacity to love characteristic of women and men. The girl does so in her response to her father, the boy in his feelings towards his mother, and both in their new indifference or even frankly rivalrous feelings towards the parent of the same sex. The emotional objectives of this (Oedipus) complex are, however, doomed to failure, at least in the healthy situation. After this time of intense emotional involvement, the child will tend to turn to interests outside the home. Much of what went before is repressed. This is the period of latency, in which society begins its systematic education of the young. The emotional and erotic intensity of the earlier time will be revived at puberty. Sexual evolution in human beings is what Freud called diphasic (a fact he considered crucial for hominization—and neurosis).[39] Only with puberty does the genital phase proper begin, because the nature of female genitality is only then grasped by both sexes. The peculiar characteristics of adolescence in each individual will be profoundly structured by the nature of his or her responses to both parents in the phallic phase.

Freud considered the Oedipal phase to be the omega point of childhood, and its wholesome resolution to be a *sine qua non* of human mental health.

> It has justly been said that the Oedipus complex is the nuclear complex of the neuroses, and constitutes the essential part of their content. It represents the peak of infantile sexuality, which, through its after-effects, exercises a decisive influence on the sexuality of adults. Every new arrival on this planet is faced by the task of mastering the Oedipus complex; anyone who fails falls a victim to neurosis.[40]

There are a number of reasons for the central importance which Freud accorded to the resolution of the Oedipal challenge. In the first place, it represents the highest synthesis of sexual objectives. Only with such a synthesis can the integration, the focussing of potential and the personalism which characterizes true adulthood be achieved. Genital love, which is the ultimate expression of Oedipal resolution, subsumes the facets of earlier eroticism. These rediscover their place in it in the modified form of foreplay.[41] In genital love, the quality of the communication between the two persons involved plays a quite unique part. Any lesions or intensities in their relationship are in the most intimate tension with the physical experience of pleasure. The sensitive counterpoint to genitality—or integration of libido—is the ability to love another precisely as other. The other is not the all-providing mother, nor the one against whom one must struggle for independence and self-expression, nor the member of the opposite sex with whom full sexual expression is overwhelming or unattainable. To the extent that these elements still govern emotional response, genitality has not been achieved—or rather, it is not yet attractive. "We have learned from analytic researches how universal and how powerful the earliest allocations of libido are. In these we are concerned with infantile sexual wishes which are clung to . . . wishes which frequently enough were directed towards other things than intercourse or included it only as a dimly perceived goal." [42] Failures in genitality are, in fact, regressions to the infantile sexuality which still holds the subject's interest; they are disparate and auto-erotic. Even when two persons are involved, the tonality of their sexual satisfaction may be auto-erotic rather than mutual. Auto-erotism is always characterized by isolation and self-sufficiency (the earmarks of the primary process), or, at most, reaches the level of identification with another's pleasure (mutual masturbation). It is by no means rare that an adult finds an earlier form of erotic pleasure more satisfying, though his preference may be no more overt than a general quality of restlessness and unfulfillment. If his erotic interest is tied to earlier forms of pleasure, then his emotional development will be arrested there with it, whatever the social and intellectual achievement he may evince. A man is what he loves; this is the essence of psycho-analytic theory. He is formed for good or ill by the quality of his chosen pleasures. [43]

The Oedipal complex is critical, too, because it initiates the understanding of sexual identity. Ideally speaking, the sense of one's preciousness as male or female begins here. The child undergoes a complex set of responses to the parent of the opposite sex, but in some ways, an even more complex reckoning with the parent of the same sex. Certain negative and broadly consequential developments have their roots here: the girl's contempt for her own sex and her rivalry with the male, the boy's fear and envy of the female, the investment of erotic attraction in the members of one's own sex, the incestuous tie with either father or mother which prevents the adult from entering upon new relationships of his or her own.[44]

Finally, in Freud's view, the first inner self-criticizing agency is formed with the subsiding of the Oedipal conflict. Freud saw the super-ego as a kind of precipitate of the complex emotions of that phase.[45] At that time, the child is first confronted by a task of integration with which he will also struggle in adolescence and adulthood, but there more resourcefully. Not only are the intensity and confusion of his instinctual impulses overwhelming at times, but his desires must meet with defeat; they are a pre-science of the sexual and emotional directions which must wait for adulthood to find expression. Equipped with undeveloped ego and intelligence, the child finds the necessary self-direction by internalizing parental and environmental norms. The super-ego is the child's expedient, to free himself from confusion and anxiety, and to safeguard the satisfaction of his impulses by forcing them to respect the conditions obtaining in the home. There is considerable repression involved in this resolution.[46]

The super-ego is the early form of conscience. Yet it cannot simply be called the conscience because it is not formed by a personal judgement of reality. It is infantile, because it instantiates values insofar as the child sensed them as operative in his parents. It is the result of an often anxious sense of inadequacy and of fear regarding the consequences of instinctual impulse. These latter constitute a tyranny from which many adults never free themselves, and none do so entirely. The unmitigated control of the super-ego is always a factor in mental disturbance, in which an irrational guilt and a deep sense of personal worthlessness play an important part. The super-ego is harsh, undiscerning and threatening; it is the child's moral dogmatism and fear of punishment. The formation of true conscience is the work of a lifetime, and one of its greatest obstacles is the super-ego, whose rationale is fear of consequences, self-distrust and surrender to external norms. Thus, moral choice is often attended by disproportionate anxiety. The subject cannot explain the dread he experiences because its sources are infantile and therefore unconscious. The activity of the super-ego shares the fixated and unenlightened qualities of unconscious activity as well as its subtle and profound influence over conscious choice.[47]

It is true that the child distorts parental values in this internalization. In every psychic history there is the crucial factor of the unique manner in which the individual handles his instinctual impulses and responds to his peculiar environment. Ultimately, that is his own doing and is simply not reducible to environment. The most favorable conditions cannot obviate deeply distorted responses. On the other hand, it is also true that the child as such is peculiarly sensitive to parental fears and irresolution with regard to instinctual forces, however liberal his parents may consciously strive to be. Thus, the deepseated cultural fear of the instincts is transmitted from one generation to the next in the child's formation of a super-ego.[48] And an undeniable element in systematic education is the exploitation of super-ego morality: the subtle threats of loss of acceptance and the implication of the nameless dangers surrounding rejection of external norms.

Narcissism

The publication of *Three Essays on the Theory of Sexuality* in 1907 brought to a close the first chapter of Freud's research into the workings of the sexual instinct. In this brilliant monograph, he condensed into a systematic theory two decades of clinical observations. Two years later, a new direction in his understanding of the libido was already beginning to take shape. It was catalyzed by a new awareness of the dynamics operative chiefly in homosexuality and the severe disturbances of schizophrenia and paranoia. The psychic patterns observed in the more common states of sleep, falling in love, and organic disease reinforced his confidence that he was glimpsing there a new but basic developmental syndrome in sexual evolution.

Freud became aware first of a common pattern underlying cases of homosexuality. Complex and diverse as its instances are, he found that the strong early attachment to the mother had remained dominant in the erotic and emotional disposition, that there had been no real growth beyond it. In the early stage in question, the child occupies a central and consuming position in his mother's life. The partners in a homosexual liaison revive that situation: one is loved in this way; the other loves him in this way and, vicariously, is thereby so loved.[49] The roles will characteristically be reversed at different times. What is essential is that the homosexual regards the object of his love as another self. It is an extended infatuation, a *narcissisme à deux*. So essentially vicarious is this arrangement that the homosexual is incapable of extending himself beyond the sexual difference.[50] The successful homosexual has the resources to play one or the other role in the drama. In antiquity, men of position surrounded themselves with beautiful young boys. In the homosexual underworld of our society, men are haunted by the fear of aging, particularly if they do not have the wealth and influence to engage younger men. Homosexuality, Freud concluded, was a fixated stage in which the object of the libido is the self-image.

Freud associated the etiology of homosexuality with that of schizophrenia and paranoia. When these latter have progressed to a characteristic extreme, their subjects show at once an extraordinary megalomania and an extraordinary lack of involvement with the external world. Psychotics of this sort show no evidence of loving anyone or anything. Freud concluded, along with his colleague Karl Abraham, that the sexual instinct, the source of erotic and loving attachments, had become disengaged from external reality and centered wholly on the self. Hence the pronounced megalomania.[51]

It is axiomatic to psychoanalysis that every mental disposition instantiates one or another phase in the richly complex course of psychic development. No psychic state, however aberrant, reaches beyond the boundaries of the evolutional process. Therefore, if certain psychic states, whether normal or pathological, show a predominant investment of the sexual instinct in the self, then they must crystallize or exaggerate a disposition normal to the process. Freud concluded from his experience with homosexuality that its subjects have remained fixed in a disposition characteristic of the small child who is only beginning to develop the capacity for a first love of others. The child of this age loves his mother's love for himself. This is the love in which he loves himself, from which he derives his security and sense of worth. What the mother herself is beyond that does not yet exist for him. Freud called it the narcissistic phase.

In infancy, these characteristics are even more marked and the mother even less a person in her own right. In the discussion of auto-erotism it was noted that the vital functions are sexualized. And only in their service do other persons enter the infant's world. "The sexual instincts find their first objects by attaching themselves to the valuations made by the ego-instincts precisely in the way in which the first sexual satisfactions are experienced in attachment to the bodily functions necessary for the preservation of life." [52] So close is the integration of self-preservative and pleasure drives, they are almost indistinguishable. When so complete an identification exists, there is no libidinizing of any element broader than this total self-interest. The nascent ego, which emerges in the organizing of diffuse auto-erotic impulses, is its own first love. Such a state is primitive on the evolutionary scale, pre-personal, a state which Freud called "primary narcissism". It is to this stage, "the half-way phase between auto-erotism and object-love",[53] that the severe psychotic regresses. Narcissism Freud defined as "the libidinal complement to the egoism of the instinct of self-preservation—a measure of which," he added, "may justifiably be attributed to every living creature".[54] Egoism is the concern for one's own advantage; narcissism takes one's libidinal satisfaction into account as well. "It is possible to be absolutely egoistic and yet maintain powerful object-cathexes, insofar as libidinal satisfaction in relation to the object forms part of the ego's needs. In that case, egoism will see to it that striving for the object involves no damage to the ego." [55]

In the infant the ego is, as yet, undeveloped. It develops *pari passu* with his growing awareness of reality. The state of primary narcissism gives way as the libido extends to objects other than the vital functions. It becomes free of its service to the self-preservative instinct. Nevertheless, a child in this stage is still very narcissistic. He is the center of the universe, and others are grasped only in terms of their relationship to himself. Though almost helpless, he still experiences the omnipotence which obtained in uterine existence. This illusion is apparent indirectly in the child's inability to grasp that his thoughts and wishes may have no external objectification. The belief in magic is its prolongation.[56] This illusion also explains the guilt and fear that frequently overwhelm children; they make no distinction between erotic or destructive phantasies and actual deeds. Moreover, the child considers his own the infinite powers of his parents. Omnipotence of thought (whose prototype is the infantile hallucination discussed in Chapter One) and megalomania are concomitants of primary narcissism.

In Freud's view, it is the growing strength of the sexual instinct which progressively turns the subject's interest to a world larger than himself. If its development is untrammelled, the sexual instinct impells towards the synthesis of more and more comprehensive unities, though its first attachment is to the narrow base of the self-preservative functions. The whole available amount of libido, then, is at first stored up in the ego (is "ego-libido"), and is progressively invested in other objects (becomes "object-libido").[57]

> Here we may even venture to touch on the question of what makes it necessary at all for our mental life to pass beyond the limits of narcissism and to attach the libido to objects. The answer which would follow from our line of thought would once more be that this necessity arises when the cathexis of the ego with libido exceeds a certain amount. A strong egoism is a protection against falling ill, but in the last resort we must begin to love in order not to fall ill, and we are bound to fall ill if, in consequence of frustration, we are unable to love.[58]

Nevertheless, the process is dialectical. The investment in others can be withdrawn back into and onto the self: object-libido can revert to ego-libido. This reversal Freud called "secondary narcissism".[59] The disturbances discussed above are exemplifications, and there are instances of it as well in normal life. The state of sleep affords "a picture of the blissful isolation of intra-uterine life. In a sleeper the primal state of distribution of the libido and ego-interest, still united and indistinguishable, dwell in the self-sufficing ego." [60] The phenomena of illness and pain offer other examples:

> It is universally known, and we take it as a matter of course, that a person who is tormented by organic pain and discomfort gives up his interest in the things of the external world, insofar as they do not concern his suffering. Closer observation teaches us that he also withdraws *libidinal* interest from his love-objects: so long as he suffers, he ceases to love. The commonplace nature of this fact is no reason why we should be deterred from translating it into terms of the libido theory. We should then say: the sick man withdraws his libidinal cathexes back upon his own ego, and sends them out again when he recovers. "Concentrated is his soul", says Wilhelm Busch of the poet suffering from toothache, "in his molar's narrow hole". Here libido and ego-interest share the same fate and are once more indistinguishable from each other. The familiar egoism of the sick person covers both. We find it so natural because we are certain that in the same situation we should behave in just the same way.[61]

The severe psychotic states are extreme forms of secondary narcissism. Objects are emptied of their importance; the libido attaches itself once more to the ego, enhancing it to the heights of unreal megalomania. The psychotic believes himself to be possessed of virtual omnipotence. He can kill with his eyes, pronounce magical phrases, hate and thereby annihilate the passing objects of his hatred. The mad conviction that the end of the world has come epitomizes the withdrawal of concern: the world ceases to exist for such a one.[62]

The severe psychoses are disturbances of a developmental period that precedes that of homosexuality.[63] The adult, if he is to fall ill, regresses to the emotional stance in which he found the securest anchorage. The phases following that one have been overwhelming, have confronted him with challenges he had neither the resources nor, therefore, the desire to meet. The severity of disturbance varies with the earliness of the phase regressed to: severe cases are such precisely because the very foundations of emotional life were precarious. They always constitute a disturbance of the sexual instinct or love energy.

With the introduction of narcissism into his exposition, Freud pushed through to a more radical insight into the dynamics of loving. He saw it as a continual process of extension and withdrawal of libido from the ego and back onto or into the ego. He conjured up the image of the amoeba which pushes its proto-plasm into a pseudopod and withdraws it again into the main mass.[64] Object-love grows at the expense of narcissistic love, and conversely.

The development of the ego consists in a departure from pri-mary narcissism to external reality. But throughout life, there is a tenacious inclination to recover the elements of the narcissistic state.[65] The growth out of primary narcissism must be an organic one. In other words, it must occur within a loving environment, for only there are the laws of growth respected. In any case, it is painful. Infantile megalomania covers the dawning, overwhelm-ing recognition of helplessness; the small child teeters between one and the other extreme. (Primary narcissism "excludes the possibility of their having any primary sense of inferiority".) [66] The violence done to this megalomania by brutalizing emotional conditions is the most damaging blow possible to the psyche; the love of self is a *sine qua non* of psychic health.

The healthy person has a wholesome self-regard which derives from residual narcissism; we never transcend our beginnings. Secondly, it springs from measuring up to one's self-ideal. The self-ideal is initially imposed on the child from without and challenges the uncritical self-embracing characteristic of the nar-cissistic phase. Nevertheless, it develops organically out of his love for himself. Finally, self-regard grows out of the reciproca-tion of one's strongest loves.[67]

If one or another of these elements is inadequate, a sense of inferiority results. It can very easily be pathological; in fact, it is always a component in mental disturbance. Like the child, the psychotic pushes off a helpless and overpowering sense of worth-lessness, which verges on the fear of self-dissolution. His flight into exaggerated megalomania is a defence against that experi-ence. In less healthy development, the self- or ego-ideal merges almost completely with the super-ego, whose criticisms are es-sentially infantile. They are of untempered harshness, irrational, and born of fear. In fact, in the super-ego of the neurotic or psychotic (who has no solid self-ideal), the origins of that agency in primary narcissism are most apparent. The demands it imposes are of megalomaniacal proportions; infantile narcissism has to that extent not truly been resolved. (The impossible standards which the scrupulous person sets for himself draw no small part of their attraction from his recognition that others around him do not aspire to such heights. His disproportionate self-love has merely been displaced onto his self-ideal.) Finally, the love for others from whom there is no return of love results in a painful impoverishment of the ego, which can readily become pathological, especially in children.[68]

Self-regard and the desire to enhance it are impelling forces in the erotic life of the sexes. The psychic condition of "falling in love", like that of sleep and organic illness, shows unique characteristics which cease to surprise us because they are part of the warp and woof of life. Freud isolated what he called the "sexual over-evaluation" of the object.[69] The person in love is completely absorbed, completely focussed on his beloved, who appears to him as an impossible dream come true. It is clear that the profoundest reaches of the psyche are drawn upon in this powerful experience. In other words, the primitive experiences of childhood are revitalized, and the loved one appears as one who can satisfy impossible and rejected hopes. The person in love feels once again capable of everything in the interests of his love. According to Freud, this all-engaging experience constitutes a return of narcissism; only this time the narcissism is displaced onto the beloved. The other becomes an impossible dream come true, the satisfaction of impossible hopes, because he is invested with a narcissism which has had to be sobered and disclaimed in the process of coming to terms with a real world. Megalomania reappears in an acceptable and enhanced form: as projected onto another. If the love is mutual, the subject enjoys the same idealized and powerful investment from the other. Thus he regains in his own eyes and in those of another the perfection which has been so sadly eroded in the process of maturing.

The dynamic admits of many variations. Reciprocity may be more or less present, so that one may appear more as the beloved, the other more as the lover. That is, what Freud called respectively the narcissistic and the attachment or "anaclitic" prototypes may predominate in one or the other partner. The narcissistic prototype is so-called because in it the person loves what he himself is, or was, or would like to be, or someone who was once a part of himself. He loves himself in the eyes of another. To the degree that these components figure, the role is narcissistic. The anaclitic or attachment type of love also has an infantile prototype in which the object of love is "(a) the woman who feeds him, (b) the man who protects him, and the succession of substitutes who take their place".[70]

> We have, however, not concluded that human beings are divided into two sharply differentiated groups, according as their object-choice conforms to the anaclitic or to the narcissistic type; we assume rather that both kinds of object-choice are open to each individual, though he may show a preference for one or the other. We say that a human being has originally two sexual objects—himself and the woman who nurses him—and in doing so we are postulating a primary narcissism in everyone, which may in some cases manifest itself in a dominating fashion in his object-choice.[71]

The reappearance of narcissistic love is also evident in parental love for a child. Most parents are amusingly unobjective about the consummate perfection of their offspring. Parents who spoil their children transfer onto them their own unresolved megalomania. "Illness, death, renunciation of enjoyment, restrictions on his own will, shall not touch him; the laws of nature and of society shall be abrogated in his favour; he shall once more really be the centre and core of creation—'His Majesty the Baby', as we once fancied ourselves." [72] In the phenomenon of group loyalty, megalomania or narcissism is transferred by the adherents onto the group-image and its leader(s). Thus, they feel free to claim perfections and privileges for it to which singly they would never presume. Rationality, sobriety and respect for real conditions are frequently overridden. Its members would have the group unboundaried by criticism from within and without, by law, convention, or even decency. Freud concluded that the power of group allegiance is derived from instinctual power itself; the group and its leader are a libidinal object. Unfortunately, it often mobilizes sexual energy of the most primitive or narcissistic type.[73]

Freud's analysis of the genesis of love and hate both summarizes and throws fresh perspective on the discussion in this chapter. (The reader is reminded at this point of the neglected dimensions of curiosity and the infant-mother relationship as discussed above).

If loving can be defined as "the relation of the ego to its sources of pleasure",[74] he wrote, then its prototypical antithesis is indifference to the external world. However, since external objects will necessarily impinge on the inchoate ego, a second opposite to loving emerges, that of hating. Insofar as these objects are sources of pleasure, they are taken into or identified with the self; insofar as they are sources of unpleasure, they are expelled. The qualities of the mother which impinge on the infant's awareness are thus introjected and indistinguishable from himself until a later period of growth. Beyond what is so introjected, the external world remains an object of indifference or, when it introduces unwanted stimuli, of hate.

As the stage of primary narcissism gives way to that of first object-love, the infant more definitely reaches out to the object, is "attracted" to it. From other objects he will take flight and in time may turn his aggression onto them. In linguistic usage we do not strictly speak of "loving" objects that serve the interests of self-preservation, but rather of "needing" them. As the child develops, the distinction between love and need becomes more apparent. "Thus the word 'to love' moves further and further into the sphere of the pure pleasure-relation of the ego to the object and finally becomes fixed to sexual objects in the narrower sense and to those which satisfy the needs of sublimated sexual instincts."[75] In linguistic usage, once again, we do not speak of the sexual instinct as loving the object, but of the ego as so doing. The capacity to love is a function not only of the separation of self-preservative and sexual instincts but also of the ordering of instinctual desires. Ultimately, the word loving can be applied only "after there has been a synthesis of all the component instincts of sexuality under the primacy of the genitals and in the service of the reproductive function".[76] The use of the word hate implies no such intimate connection with the sexual instinct but rather with the ego's attempts to preserve and maintain itself.

What is hated is what is a source of unpleasure, whether that
threatens self-preservative or sexual needs.

In the following passage, Freud synthesized his earlier insights
into the evolution of sexuality and his later theory of narcissism:

> It now remains for us to put together what we know of the genesis of
> love and hate. Love is derived from the capacity of the ego to satisfy
> some of its instinctual impulses auto-erotically by obtaining organ-
> pleasure. It is originally narcissistic, then passes over on to objects, which
> have been incorporated into the extended ego, and expresses the motor
> efforts of the ego towards these objects as sources of pleasure. It becomes
> intimately linked with the activity of the later sexual instincts and, when
> these have been completely synthesized, coincides with the sexual im-
> pulsion as a whole.

What follows offers particularly rich insights into the human
dilemma of ambivalence (which is central to concupiscence, to
cite one example).

> Preliminary stages of love emerge as provisional sexual aims while the
> sexual instincts are passing through their complicated development. As
> the first of these aims we recognize the phase of incorporating or devour-
> ing—a type of love which is consistent with abolishing the object's
> separate existence and which may therefore be described as ambivalent.
> At the higher stage of the pregenital sadistic-anal organization, the striv-
> ing for the object appears in the form of an urge for mastery, to which
> injury or annihilation of the object is a matter of indifference. Love in
> this form and at this preliminary stage is hardly to be distinguished from
> hate in its attitude towards the object. Not until the genital organization
> is established does love become the opposite of hate.
>
>   Hate, as a relation to objects, is older than love. It derives from the
> narcissistic ego's primordial repudiation of the external world with its
> outpouring of stimuli. As an expression of the reaction of unpleasure
> evoked by objects, it always remains in an intimate relation with the
> self-preservative instincts; so that sexual and ego-instincts can readily
> develop an anti-thesis which repeats that of love and hate. When the
> ego-instincts dominate the sexual function, as is the case at the stage of
> the sadistic-anal organization, they impart the qualities of hate to the
> instinctual aim as well.
>
>   The history of the origins and relations of love makes us understand
> how it is that love so frequently manifests itself as "ambivalent"—i.e. as
> accompanied by impulses of hate against the same object. The hate
> which is admixed with the love is in part derived from the preliminary

stages of loving which have not been wholly surmounted; it is also in part based on reactions of repudiation by the ego-instincts, which, in view of the frequent conflicts between the interests of the ego and those of love, can find grounds in real and contemporary motives. In both cases, therefore, the admixed hate has as its source the self-preservative instinct. If a love relation with a given object is broken off, hate not infrequently emerges in its place, so that we get the impression of a transformation of love into hate. This account of what happens leads on to the view that the hate, which has its real motives, is here reinforced by a regression of the love to the sadistic preliminary stage; so that the hate acquires an erotic character and the continuity of a love-relation is ensured.[77]

The strongest love relationships must combine sensuality—for when isolated and uninhibited it becomes "extinguished when it is satisfied"[78]—and affection, which is the "older of the two. It springs from the earliest years of childhood; it is formed on the basis of the interests of the self-preservative instinct and is directed to the members of the family and those who look after the child." The eventual objects of love "will still be chosen on the model (imago) of the infantile ones, but in the course of time they will attract to themselves the affection that was tied to the earlier ones. A man shall leave his father and his mother—according to the biblical command—and shall cleave unto his wife; affection and sensuality are then united."[79]

The most fulfilling love relationship is one, then, that combines indistinguishably satisfaction of ego-libido and object-libido.[80] That is, the drives towards self-preservation and towards others are again united. Loving occupies the place in psychic economy that Revelation declares it to have in life. The growth out of the indifference, hate and egoism of narcissism is achieved. The most elemental of the instincts, the instinct of self-preservation, is broadened to include others within its dynamic; this is the love that is stronger than heaven or hell,[81] the life instinct.

The unique contribution of Freud to the understanding of love is his exposition of its developmental process; the matured capacity for which we properly reserve the term love grows directly out of rudimentary and narrow origins. Gnosticism in its multiple forms is always a contempt for origins and an attempt to negate their indestructible influence. Reductionism, on the other hand, sees only the origins and discredits any development out of them. There is no doubt that Freud was sometimes guilty of reductionism, most notably in his analysis of religious belief. Some of his remarks on love seem tinged by the same inclination.[82] It is too easy, however, to feel affronted by the developmental approach and to lose sight of its formal *ratio*. Paul Ricoeur is particularly clear on its nature:

> Everything that is "primary" in analysis—the primary process, primal repression, primary narcissism, and, later on, primary masochism—is primary in a sense that is completely different from the transcendental: it is not a question of the justification of grounds, but of what takes precedence in the order of distortion or disguise. Thus the primary process expresses the hallucinatory wish-fulfillments that precede all other fantasy formations; primal repression decides which idea will be attached to an instinct first; primary narcissism denotes the reservoir underlying all object-cathexes and the source from which all instincts proceed.[83]

Whatever the trenchant and sometimes over-enthusiastic nature of Freud's expressions, he did not pretend to an exhaustive analysis.[84] His contribution is redoubtable, not only because it introduced the developmental understanding of love with the unique solidity which an etiological approach brings to bear, but also because he emphasized an aspect too commonly neglected in overly refined expressions.

To sum up the themes of this chapter: the sexual instinct gives pleasure and energy to the basic activities of life, to nourishment, excretion, reproduction, to sight, smell, touching, hearing, knowledge, communication. It is the principle of change; the thrust forward to change, to the synthesis of unities, is impelled by the energy of attraction. These are the qualities characteristic of the human species, in which the sexual instinct is strongest and most highly developed. The role of the sexual instinct, in the comprehensive sense in which Freud exposed it, is broad and profound.

The quality peculiar to the sexual instinct is that it must evolve; the individual must relinquish certain sources of satisfaction. The only wholesome or thorough-going way in which this can occur is when he grows to prefer another satisfaction. And this, in turn, because of the risk and self-deprivation temporarily involved, will happen only if there are sources of love and security supporting him. All forms of mental disturbance are forms of attraction to satisfactions that should have been superseded. Their symptoms result from the desperate defence of the more developed self against those desires.

Of all the instincts, the sexual instinct is also the most refractory to development. It remains more closely associated with the primary process of mental functioning or, from another point of view, with the narcissistic stance because the subject's own mind and body can provide it with a variety of satisfactions. The very extensiveness of its manifestations provides the subject with pleasures in which he need take neither his environment nor other human beings into account. He can even derive pleasure from the psychic stimulation of pain. His thoughts can provide physical stimulation (witness the daydreaming that dominates adolescence). It is only because of the auto-satisfaction possible to the sexual instinct that human beings can successfully construct an emotionally closed system, that they can approximate to the self-sufficiency which is the aim of the archaic primary process.

The power of attraction is more compelling than any other. Little wonder that men fear this power in themselves. They will fear it in any case, but when one also considers the comprehensive nature of this instinctual force, the primitive nature of its early attractions, the deceitful and manipulative lengths it may impel, and its potential for evading the demands of reality, then one understands more clearly why Freud placed man's struggle with his sexuality at the heart of the human predicament.

PART TWO

ORIGINAL SIN

4. NEW PERSPECTIVES ON AN ANCIENT DOCTRINE

Introductory

The exposition of Freudian insights and theories in the first section is offered as background for a reconsideration of the reality of original sin. This material was organized around three major themes according to which, in this second section, I should like to reconsider aspects of the ancient doctrine of original sin. Chapter One dealt with the fact and nature of man's constitutive self-alienation. What implications does constitutive psychic dualism, examined more exhaustively in the 20th century than ever before, have for our theological appreciation of concupiscence? Chapter Two dealt with the instinctual origins of psychic activity, and particularly with the ego-instinctual dialectic as a function of man's evolutionary process, physical and social. What implications does a heightened awareness of the environmental factor—horizontal and vertical—have for our understanding of original sin, which is by definition of historical derivation, and which is more and more being considered in connection with the sin of the world? And finally, in the third chapter, the central role which the sexual instincts and their evolution play in psychic formation, particularly in the capacity to love, was discussed. Special consideration was given to narcissism as an early phase in psychosexual development and as part of a constant polarity in psychic life. These considerations suggest

103

perspectives on man as developmental, on his capacity for truth, and on love as a healing or salvific force.

Psychic Dualism and Concupiscence

The heart of Freud's contribution to a reconsideration of the reality of original sin is his exposition of the unconscious mind. More than any man before him, he insisted that the unconscious be taken seriously and therefore explored with curiosity and a high degree of scientific integrity. The opposition which his works still provoke—in such subtle forms as brief textbook caricatures of his theories or exclusive attention to his hypothetical sociological works—derives for the most part from his insistence on the psychic dualism of man.[1] The proximity of the unconscious to man's instinctual life is surely the major factor in that resistance.

The fact that a systematic investigation into the unconscious had to wait until the end of the 19th century and that it remains to this day an intensely emotional issue is surely of striking significance. I submit that this phenomenon is intimately linked with another in the area of theology. That is the comparative obscurity with which the subject of original sin has been surrounded. Traditional theological efforts to explain it have diverted attention onto tenets such as the existence of limbo and of a state of original privilege, which have been a source of malaise to thinking Christians. Thus the essentials have suffered: the material aspect of original sin as concupiscence has been deprived of resourceful and inquisitive attention from theologians. Concupiscence is a term at once "loaded" and indefinite. While Christian moral theology over the centuries has been impressive in its use of philosophical insight into conscious moral decision, no comparable resourcefulness has been brought to bear on the subject of concupiscence. In the West, from the time of St. Augustine (who first used the term "original sin"), that issue has been peculiarly susceptible to isolation from the mainstream of the Christian message, to heterodox influences, and to obscurantist and almost pseudo-mystical attitudes.[2]

"Concupiscence", it seems to me, describes a situation which derives from the conscious/unconscious dualism in man. The same resistance to elucidation attends the one and the other, and for the same profound reasons. There is, of course, an all-important distinction insofar as concupiscence is seen as the material aspect of *peccatum originale originatum,* namely, that in the one case certain phenomena are considered in man as related to God, and in the other are not so considered. In the absence of that formality, a recognition of pathology is possible, but not of sin.

The meanings of the term concupiscence are clearly set forth in a recent article by J. P. Kenny. Concupiscence in its broadest sense, he writes, "comprises the whole sweep and range of appetite or desire (stressing its activity as against the relative passivity of knowledge), both sensory and spiritual, both faculty as well as its acts—and these latter whether deliberate or spontaneous. It includes not only the seeking of a good but also the rejecting of what is judged to be harmful". In the narrower sense, concupiscence can still be either sensory or spiritual, but is restricted in a twofold manner: "first insofar as it is limited to the *act* of desire; second, insofar as this is *in*deliberate. The indeliberate act of desire, springing from the very dynamism of man's nature, gives to the will the object about which it deliberates and decides. Every human being (therefore Christ in His human nature, Our Lady, Adam prior to his fall) must have concupiscence in this sense; absence of it would spell paralysis of the will." Finally, concupiscence is used in a technical, theological sense:

> Concupiscence again is involved in the indeliberate act of desire but only and precisely insofar as this is pitted against the free decision, hindering and hampering it, wrestling with and diverting it. In this technical sense, then, concupiscence acts in three ways. (1) It forestalls the free decision; already before any choice is finally made, concupiscence is present threatening liberty of action. (2) In the very process of one's choosing, concupiscence is at work as a countertension. (3) Even when vanquished, it still asserts itself and is not totally submissive.[3]

It is in this last sense—as the failure of *integritas*—that concupiscence is held to be the material aspect of original sin. ("Self-alienation" sometimes describes the same dilemma). The formal aspect of original sin is the privation of a right relationship with God. In the disturbance of this rectitude is the source of the disturbance of *integritas* or harmony within the self, in relation to other men and to the whole created order.[4] Concupiscence and *peccatum originale originatum* are not therefore identical: the formality of man's relationship to God can and has been changed; this is the Good News.[5] But concupiscence is healed only gradually and never entirely, for men realize their justification in the context of a still sinful world.

N.B.

This formality is clearly absent in Freud's treatment of the divided self. But the materiality, concupiscence, is unmistakably in question in his descriptions of unconscious activity. The foundational elements of that description, the *raisons d'être* of psychic dualism, as they were somewhat lengthily discussed, particularly in Chapter One, expose more clearly the terms of the dialectic referred to by the word concupiscence. Thus the psyche is described as evolving out of the life of the instincts. The archaic psyche is the id, the nucleus of all psychic development. The instincts lie on the threshold between the mental and the somatic, but can be subjectively experienced only through mental representations more or less remote from the primary impulses. The id comprises the psychic forces most adjacent to those of the instincts and is virtually co-extensive with the psyche at the beginning of life. But the human being is radically and formatively related to the world outside himself. Out of the gradual reckoning with that polarity by the primitive psyche, there evolves an ego, the psyche as subjective, as self-directing. It so evolves to a greater or lesser degree in each human being, but the extent of that development defines the extent of maturity. Stated in different terms, the primary mode of mental functioning—impersonal, diffuse, reflexive, mentality in the service of instinctual satisfactions—must be overtaken by a secondary mode which organizes and synthesizes instinctual demands in the context of external reality. The process inevitably involves struggle; the secondary nature of the one and the primitive strength of the other make for an uneasy peace, for both tyranny and lesions of integration. The various forms of self-alienation discussed earlier, especially under the rubrics of the dynamic unconscious and the defence mechanisms, derive from this tension between different modes of mental functioning. The domination by the secondary mode involves a certain division of the mind against itself.

The struggle between primary and secondary is epitomized in the evolution of the sexual instincts. They constitute the most powerful challenge to integration. Auto-erotic, narcissistic and extremely diffuse at the beginning of life, they must undergo a complex development, yet are particularly immunized against the exigencies of reality. The narcissistic-altruistic or love-hate ambivalence stands behind all the stages of growth. The sexual instincts are the sources of desire in the sensual-spiritual being. And what is more radical than desire? Ultimately, growth, regression or stagnation happens according to its conditions.

There are innumerable passages in which Freud depicts the struggle which is at issue in the traditional descriptions of concupiscence. If reread at this point, the passages on the ego and the id quoted at the end of Chapter One are particularly striking. More succinctly: "These two discoveries—that the life of our sexual instincts cannot be wholly tamed, and that mental processes are in themselves unconscious and only reach the ego and come under its control through incomplete and untrustworthy perceptions—these two discoveries amount to a statement that *the ego is not master in its own house.*" [6] Concupiscence is self-alienation—self-alienation which has its roots in appetitive autonomy.

Chapter Seven of St. Paul's Epistle to the Romans, and especially the section on man "sold to sin" (vv. 14-25), is the classic source for the doctrine on *peccatum originale originatum.*[7] Not that St. Paul is writing of this with scholastic precision, but he is examining the condition of man left to himself without grace.[8] The parallels there to Freud's descriptions of unconscious activity as schematized above are striking. St. Paul's lamentation is initiated by a clear statement of his self-alienation, that is to say, by the awareness of an unconscious dimension to his activity: "I cannot understand my own behaviour. I fail to carry out the things I want to do, and I find myself doing the very things I hate" (v. 15). He speaks of his "true self" (v. 20) or his "inmost self" (v. 22). This is the "I" of the lament, the possessed, directive, truly personalized self. Its frustration and grief is directed against the impersonal area which all too consequentially remains. So keenly is this impersonality experienced that St. Paul speaks of it as if it were an alien entity: "The thing behaving in that way is not my self but sin living in me" (v. 17). This metaphorical tendency is common in the Christian tradition and finds ultimate expression in ascription to demonic possession.[9] Nevertheless, as St. Paul acknowledges in the last sentences of the passage, all of these impulses are his own: "In short, it is I who with my reason serve the Law of God, and no less I who serve in my unspiritual self the law of sin" (v. 25).

One could almost imagine that Freud had this Pauline passage in mind in his own analysis of self-alienation:

> Obviously one must hold oneself responsible for the evil impulses of one's dreams. What else is one to do with them? Unless the content of the dream (rightly understood) is inspired by alien spirits, it is a part of my own being. . . . What I am disavowing not only "is" in me, but sometimes "acts" from out of me as well.
>
> It is true that in the metapsychological sense this bad repressed content does not belong to my "ego"—that is, assuming that I am a morally blameless individual—but to an "id" upon which my ego is seated. But this ego developed out of the id; it forms with it a single biological unit, it is only a specially modified peripheral portion of it, and it is subject to the influences and obeys the suggestions that arise from the id. For any vital purpose, a separation of the ego from the id would be a hopeless undertaking.

He remarked a few lines further: "The ethical narcissism of humanity should rest content with the knowledge that the fact of distortion in dreams as well as the existence of anxiety-dreams and punishment-dreams, afford just as clear evidence of his *moral* nature as dream interpretation gives of the existence and strength of his *evil* nature." [10]

The inclinations of his better self are identified by St. Paul with the inclinations of his will (see vv. 16, 18, 20). And will is the appetite of reason (see vv. 23, 25). In reason-will are focussed man's dignity and rectitude.[11] Yet the effectiveness of both is dependent on the extent of self-comprehension. St. Paul elegizes the paralysis of his faculties by his self-ignorance, and Freud reiterates that dilemma: "In the ordinary way, I will admit, the intelligence which reaches your consciousness is enough for your needs, and you may cherish the illusion that you learn of all the more important things. But in some cases, as in that of an instinctual conflict such as I have described, your intelligence service breaks down and your will then extends no further than your knowledge." [12]

It is only by the expression of himself as reason-will, the expansion of his consciousness, that man transcends fatal enclosure in a merely biological self. This is the real meaning of man's spirituality. It has two directions: one, the ever-expanding appreciation of the cosmos of which he finds himself at once a humble part and a master through understanding; the other, a passionate and painful work of understanding his own inner self as at once a manifestation of God's image and as constituted by the earth, his mother and father, and the society which makes him human.[13] Paul's anguish about the quasi-autonomous impulses of the "unspiritual self" (v. 18) is rooted in his awareness of their power to subvert and destroy this spiritual flowering of man.

Though St. Paul does little more than name these impulses and decry their treachery, their blind and narrow self-interest is conveyed. Freud spoke of the impulses alien to the ego as under the domination of the primary process, indifferent to everything save diffuse and simplistic satisfaction, and when alienated from and by the ego, as tending towards the construction of a closed system along the model of primitive (unspiritual) forms of life. Or to speak in terms of the sexual instincts, which are integrally involved in that view as they are in the experience of concupiscence, these impulses would revert to a narcissistic, auto-erotic regime that is appropriate only to the infant. Significantly, St. Paul repeats in his brief designation of these unspiritual impulses that their provenance is the body: "In my inmost self I dearly love God's Law, but I can see that my body follows a different law that battles against the law which my reason dictates. This is what makes me a prisoner of that law of sin which lives inside my body" (vv. 22f.). Unconscious activity was, for Freud, unconscious or alienated precisely because it follows another law of functioning than does conscious activity. It is mentality at the service of instincts, whose sources are sub-psychic or bodily.

The nature of the instinctual and somatic role in our psychic life, this is clearly essential to a phenomenological understanding of concupiscence. It was signalled by Freud as "at once the most important and the most obscure element of psychological research".[14] He himself cast a great deal of light on the relationship, but it also happens to be one of the most exciting areas of contemporary science.[15] The impact of these discoveries has yet to be felt in a theological appreciation of concupiscence. What they promise is a formidable blow at certain heretical assumptions which have always haunted the theology of original sin, and which have not been successfully warded off by even the most careful expositions. They are promising inasmuch as they are gradually sketching in the lines of a new anthropology—it must be that radical.

Throughout the Christian tradition, there has been a powerful tendency to blur the distinction between alienated elements of psychic life and morally degenerate ones. In short, concupiscence has too readily and implicitly been identified with sin and its fruits.[16] This implicit association has not been checked by the clear distinction drawn between concupiscence and sin in dogmatic statements by the Church.[17] Nor has it been successfully undermined by sound theological exposition. It cannot be so long as concupiscence remains a term at once so indefinite and so provocative, so long, that is, as investigation proceeds virtually no further than delineation, however eloquent. The problematic appears in a singular and striking manner to have forbidden investigation—for it must lead into the unconscious and instinctual reaches of human experience.

The confusion between natural and sinful dualism implicitly

assumes that self-alienation is not properly human. It evidences a deep-seated reluctance to include the fact of the unconscious— which constantly testifies to man's prehuman and infantile origins —at the radical level of theological foundations.

Perhaps the clearest expression of this tendency is to be found in the tradition of a state of original privilege. Although the details of its description were never elevated to the level of dogmatic teaching,[18] they occupied an important and unquestioned place in treatises on original sin and in catechesis until very recently. In the classical presentation of original sin,[19] man before the fall was free from concupiscence in the technical sense or from desires not integrated within the will (the condition of integrity). He was gifted with special knowledge regarding himself and his life-giving relationship to God. He was not to experience the deterioration of death or even physical pain. Though this state was carefully designated as preternatural and not therefore pertaining to the human condition, what is significant is that speculation proceeded in this direction at all. The first man, because he was (gratuitously)[20] regarded as deciding for all his progeny, could not be entrusted with such awesome responsibility unless he was also endowed with superhuman or preternatural gifts. To choose with human capacities infused with God's grace was apparently unequal to the moment. There is a profound malaise at work in this speculative development. What is excluded in the preternatural state is self-alienation in all its forms. It represents a failure to appreciate man's relationship to God as *man,* as naturally self-alienated. Ultimately, it is a failure to accept God's love for man.

Another instance of the identification of concupiscence with sin and its fruits is afforded by the statements of Martin Luther. What he railed against and feared as sin seems in very significant part to have been unconscious influences which, as he justly emphasized, pervade all the actions of pagan and Christian alike. "Doué d'un sens extrêmement aigu du péché, il aimait répéter que celui-ci ne consiste pas uniquement dans la transgression extérieure de la loi, mais surtout dans la mauvaise disposition intérieure, dans cet egoisme radicale et fondamentale qui caracterise toutes nos actions, même quand elles sont apparemment conformes aux prescriptions légales." [21] Because this is the sinner's condition throughout life, it is of prime importance that he remain always conscious of his sin; in fact, that constant awareness is a *sine qua non* of justification. Positively speaking, Luther had a keen and just sense of man's ambivalence and of the necessity for continual awareness of that dimension. According to Aarne Siirala, Luther's position on concupiscence forced an implicit recognition of the pervasive and indestructible influences of the unconscious. The forcing of that issue was a factor in the vehement and contentious atmosphere that surrounded the Reformation controversies.[22] However, what was lacking in Luther and his contemporaries was a kind of moral neutrality regarding concupiscence, a recognition that the ambivalence was definitely not sin and not even necessarily the fruit of sin.

If Freud's discoveries were accurate, the study of concupiscence must be revolutionized. It must be approached from a fresh anthropological starting point. Louis Beirnaert makes this point in a wider context:

> Il n'est pas possible, en effet, de situer correctement la psychothérapie sans accepter que celle-ci introduit dans l'anthropologie une dimension nouvelle qui la modifie elle-même. A vouloir, à tout prix, faire entrer la nouvelle discipline dans des catégories toutes faites, à chercher des concordismes, nous ne pouvons qu'échauer. Les oppositions âme-corps, clerc-laïc, sacré-profane, haut-bas, effort-laisser-aller, sont elles absolues? N'y a-t-il pas lieu de se demander à quoi elles répondent, de découvrir l'unité dynamique qui les suscite et les surmonte à la fais? Travail considérable qui est à peine ébauché, et dont nous pressentons la partie. Il s'agit d'un renouvellement de l'anthropologie chrétienne.[23]

So long as one's paradigm is man as conscious, concupiscence becomes a scandal, not only because it stands for unharnessed perversity, but also because it continually disconcerts the illusion that mentality and consciousness are synonymous. It is not always easy to tell which condition is being decried in discussions on concupiscence. But insofar as it is this latter, it constitutes a rebellion against the human condition as human.

However, if one radicalizes discussion by proceeding from a

more comprehensive anthropology, the implications are far-reaching. The mental processes of the human being "are in themselves unconscious" and are only in part consciously possessed. Moreover, psychic economics are such that certain mental acts are designedly kept from conscious purview. This latter is not always pathological ruse, but a function of the psyche insofar as it passes through a long period of development and is faced with a gargantuan task, insofar as it must preserve at all times its own competence, however limited. From such a vantage point, concupiscence is no longer viewed as frustrating and disheartening evidence of the fall from Adam. It emerges for what before all else it is: a natural quality of man.

N.B.

What are some of the implications of this shifted perspective? For one thing, it is a promising complement to new directions in the theology of original sin, particularly to the incorporation of an evolutionary perspective. This latter has brought into fresh relief the necessity for discerning in the self-alienated human condition what is natural to man as *homo viator* and what is the fruit of sin.

1.

Secondly, concupiscence emerges not only as a mystery of faith but as a frontier for human investigation and change. The statement that concupiscence—like the poor—will be always with us eclipses the resourcefulness still demanded of man within that condition. Now one has empirical referents for theological statements such as Rahner's denial that

2.

> the Christian is condemned to passive resignation, individual or collective. For on the one hand the eschatological power of grace to overcome suffering and death is already operative everywhere. And on the other hand the Christian, by his active planning and shaping of the future in justice and love, must produce a concrete historical manifestation of this presence of grace. The doctrine of original sin is a warning that this task is a duty but cannot be completed in this world.[24]

Thirdly, and this is no small advantage, the dimensions of the moral struggle become immensely richer and more interesting. Though psychic dualism is not an aberration of an ideal, but a datum, that condition is nevertheless peculiarly susceptible to

3.

pathological intensification. Theologically speaking, human nature as we experience it historically is markedly susceptible to
sin. But how much of the properly human has been sacrificed to
the shadows of a fallen condition? To what extent has that revealed truth been used to ease fear and confusion, to minimize the
grandeur, complexity and challenge of being *homo viator?* The
message of psychoanalysis is that self-alienation or concupiscence
can be diminished, not simply by fighting the good fight at the
level of conscious moral choice, but by entering the inner world
and understanding its impulses. The difference lies between
amplifying our consciousness (an invitation which in many forms
and from many provenances has taken hold of the contemporary
imagination) and narrowing it to provide against the emergence
of what is too quickly deemed the "fruits of sin". In a remark that
savors at once of tight moral categories and experiential courage,
Luther said, "I did not learn my theology all at once, but I had to
search deeper for it, where my temptations took me".[25] It is
true that Freud as an atheist could have no sense of sin properly
speaking. But he was unusually gifted with a disconcerting
honesty and a curiosity untrammeled by antecedent moral judgement. He was particularly shrewd about the questionable re-
course to morality: "Our suspicion that 'morality' is put forward as the repressing force merely as an excuse is confirmed by
the experience that resistance during the therapeutic work makes
use of every possible motive for defence".[26] The suspension of
moral anxiety is a condition for understanding the inner life.
Ultimately, it is a concomitant of that conviction the Church has
always protected in its pronouncements on original sin: *"Bonum
naturae nec tollitur nec diminuitur per peccatum"*.[27]

The spectre of Manichaeism has always loomed over attempts
to understand original sin. St. Thomas' efforts to purify the
doctrine and to move the emphasis to the privation of justice so
that man's natural constitution is seen as originally sinful only
in that context was a major effort against the Manichaean tendency to treat the material conditions of man as intrinsically sinful. As the interrelation between psyche and soma is being detailed in modern psychology, the inveterate hold of an old foe

weakens. Those discoveries ground in a quite unique way the
Church's insistence on not only the goodness but also the integrity
of man's materiality.

The Environmental Factor:
Original Sin and the Sin of the World

The doctrine of original sin dis-
tills two profound truths of human experience: that man is
divided within himself and that he is formed by his environment
at a level anterior to choice. The first and second chapters of this
work present themes from Freud that respectively elaborate on
these convictions. The relationship between psychic dualism and
original sin was touched upon in the preceding pages. Dubarle
refers to the relationship existing between original sin and environmental influences when he says

> la liberté de chacun s'exercise initialement dans des conditions pertur-
> bées par le péché d'autrui et ne peut échapper complètement au désordre
> de la conduite, au moins objectivement. La doctrine du péché originel
> est la formulation abstraite de ce fait, qui a trouvé une expression con-
> crète et symbolique dans le récit de l'Eden, sans parler d'innombrable
> attestations bibliques de l'interdépendances des hommes dans une his-
> toire de péché et de grâce.[28]

Nevertheless, in classical treatises on original sin, from which
catechesis has until the present derived, the consideration of environmental influences has been virtually non-existent. In fact,
they were limited to the sin of a remote ancestor. That event was
definitive, its results unmodified and unmodifiable by any successive events until the saving actions of Christ. Such an interpretation is at odds with the sense of a cumulative, collective
hardening in sin which is conveyed in the chapters of Genesis
immediately following the paradisiac narrative and which is
thematic in the Old Testament.[29] Nor can it claim parentage in
St. Paul.[30] The exclusion of environmental influence from the
exposition of original sin must, in part, explain why a subject

which is so profoundly significant has for so long remained an obscure, at worst, far-fetched and peripheral issue in theology. In the words of Karl Rahner, it is "atrophied and largely a catechism truth, mentioned at its place in the system and then forgotten in daily life and average preaching. Unfortunately it no longer has any really formative influence in contemporary man's vital conception of human reality".[31]

Fortunately, environmental influence on indeliberate or semi-deliberate alienation is being brought to the fore in recent discussions on the sin of the world and in the tendency to associate the latter with original sin. This development promises to bring into relief the centrality and contemporaneity of the latter doctrine.

A brief delineation of the realities referred to by the term the sin of the world would be profitable here. In the words of Piet Schoonenberg: "We use this Johannine expression (Jn. 1.29) to sum up the social nature of sin or solidarity in sin. . . . Sin remains a power in the world, and the 'world' remains a fellowship in sin. This fits in with our experience of the 'contamination' of evil and in general, the 'infectiousness' of moral action. One may speak of the sins, or perhaps also the virtues, of a given people or epoch of culture." Because guilt derives from the personal free act of each individual, one cannot speak here of "collective guilt". "Nonetheless, the influence of one free agent on another is unmistakable. This can be formally described with the help of the term 'situation'. As a free person, I cannot be deprived of my freedom by the free decision of others, but they may well place me in a situation which may determine me inwardly even in my freedom." The most insidious aspect of the sin of the world is its stunting effect on impulses that are good and vital. This is the "scandal" against which Jesus inveighed so severely:

The persistent absence of positive testimony to a value and the persistent display of evil example can weaken and quench the appeal of the value. The grasp of the value can become so obscure that a real blindness to the value can occur. Such pernicious influence can be seen at work even in adults, who still need the guarantee of others in moral action. They are still more effective on children, inasmuch as they are still dependent on moral education. Children or even a whole generation can be "born blind" to certain values, when they are born in a milieu where the values in question have been obscured or eliminated. This is how it is possible to speak of the "sins" of a people or a culture, though the sins are to a great extent merely the material sins of individuals born blind to a given value.[32]

Authors such as A.-M. Dubarle, Piet Schoonenberg and A. Hulsbosch are tending towards a virtual identification of original sin and the sin of the world.[33] Original sin would then seem to imply only the additional note of the *introduction* of sin into the world, of a disorientation which was hardened and extended, of a quasi-dispensation into which all are born. Thus Schoonenberg writes that the sin which enters into the world and will rule over it, the sin of the world, is concentrated (in the Genesis narrative) in the sin of one figure. He stands in Genesis at the beginning of a whole history of worry and sin.[34] The point of initiation is important and deserving of particular consideration because it expresses a conviction of faith: that the presence of sin in the world is not of God, but is man's own doing.

There are difficulties, perhaps only superficial ones, in the way of such an identification. The sin of the world implies a personal collusion in the sin of one's milieu, an eventually personal ratification of a sinfulness that precedes conscious choice. The classical presentation of original sin pointedly excludes personal sinfulness, but this seems to be in the interests of emphasizing the real existence of a state of sinfulness that is not voluntary, and which is the condition of all men before the capacity for moral choice develops. It is a concept in which that factor is formally and justifiably isolated. In the existential situation of the adult, however, it never exists in isolation. St. Paul, whose teachings represent the clearest, most direct and definitive exposition of original sin in Revelation, wrote of it in this latter, existential sense. The subject of his expositions was the adult—every adult—who had already submitted to the pernicious influences of sin. The case of the unbaptized infant, who would instantiate this factor in isolation, never entered into his perspective. Nor is it to be found in any biblical passage.[35]

A second difficulty is perhaps more serious. Original sin is transmitted to every human being "by propagation and not by imitation".[36] Can environmental influence satisfy this doctrinal definition? It can, surely, if environmental influences are understood, not in the superficial Pelagian sense of examples that are freely chosen for imitation, but in the profound sense brought into fresh prominence by the investigation of Freud and the social sciences. In this sense, the child is born into a situation which is sinful (as well as wholesome), and one which forms him before he can choose with respect to it. It is operative from the moment of birth.[37]

Some theologians are hesitant to identify original sin and the sin of the world for another reason: the latter so evidently affects individuals in different degrees, whereas original sin is the same in all.[38] If this constitutes a serious objection, it is strange, for St. Thomas obviated the posing of the issue in these terms in the 13th century. Then the problem was posed more individualistically in that the objection he countered argued from the varying degrees of bondage to concupiscence in each individual. But the same method of solution—clarification of formal and material elements—can be applied to the modern problem. St. Thomas argues that the essence of original sin lies in two things: the privation of original justice and the relation of this defect to its cause in the past. These two, total deprivation and relation, do not admit of degree. Stated in other terms, all participate equally in original sin inasmuch as it is a universal sharing in a privation which is related causally to the past. However, St. Thomas has to face the objection that some men seem to experience a more powerful disharmony than others in the area of concupiscence, which is an effect of original sin. He replies that the consequence of the privation is to leave men to their own powers, "each of which tends to its own proper action". The variety in the force of concupiscence he relates to the bodily differences among men equally deprived of justice: "It happens that some powers of the soul are stronger in one than in another on account of the different bodily constitutions (*corporis complexiones*)".[39] The extension of the distinction between formal and material to man in his social existence—that is, to considerations on the sin of the world—is a natural one. Once the formality of original sin is clearly recognized, there is room for all manner of material diversity.

It is in order to amplify this awareness of solidarity in good and evil that a special discussion of environmental influences is included in the second chapter of this work. The susceptibility of each to each, most importantly at a preverbal level, the extent of what is perceived and communicated unconsciously, explains the singular virulence of the sin of the world. Freud's insistence on the crucial importance of the long period of childhood peculiar to the human species is also relevant here. Childhood implies a heightened and uncritical susceptibility to environmental influence. At the same time, however, it is the period in which the deepest inner formation is effected, where dispositions are assumed so intimately that they can only rarely be distanced from in adulthood. The moments in which we can do so are experienced as moments of grace (and derive from fresh environmental models). The expedient of repression, which is especially favored in times of fear and inadequacy, explains the inaccessibility of these interior dispositions. Dubarle explicates the bearing of these considerations on the theology of original sin:

> It is worth while calling to mind what modern research in psychoanalysis has made us understand more deeply. There can be no comparison between the influences brought to bear on a child at an early age, when it is still lacking internal structure, and those brought to bear on an adult, who is already in possession of his autonomy, his reflex consciousness and his moral principles. . . . During this period of childhood the human being is extremely open to injuries that may be inflicted on it by defective behaviour on the part of those about it. But it does not necessarily react by strict imitation; for example it may respond to harshness but by weakness and fear.

And more pointedly a few lines later:

> Between generation in the strict sense of the word and the bad example received from an adult there is an incalculable mass of social and psychological influences brought to bear on a subject in the process of formation, providing him of necessity with the instruments of his psychic life (language for example). It is fair to say of the interior result of all this physical heredity and spiritual heritage that it exists in each person

'propagatione non imitatione', to repeat the formula of the Council of Trent on the subject of original sin.[40]

The solidarity of human beings for good or ill is a profoundly biblical truth; this condition is not a matter of choice for any man. Pelagius apparently claimed that it was. His heresy derived from the species of megalomania that claims immunity from historical and environmental determination.

The sense of vertical environment is also present in Freud's exposition of the psyche. From the outset of his investigations, he quite naturally turned to the evolutionary process to seek explanation for the constitution of the psyche and particularly the nature of the psychic struggle as we experience it now. The evolutionary process included both the physical and cultural evolution of man. It was only against that backdrop that the power of repressive forces and the depth of fear of the instincts —individually and collectively—could find adequate explanation. The consequences of evolutionary options are, after all, survival or extinction. Man's development, attended by the profound fear both of what is ahead and what lies behind, has always vacillated between the extremes of surrender to instinct and heavy-handed repression of instinct. All this is reflected on the psychic level in the troubled integration of primary and secondary processes. Unless the reality of psychic dualism is considered in an evolutionary context, the seriousness of the tensions involved therein cannot be appreciated. The man facing psychotic breakdown experiences something of the depths of that seriousness. The terror that overwhelms him on the threshold of that disintegration is equalled only by the ordinary man's fear of the insane. Further, the ignorance and brutality with which the insane have consistently been treated by society exposes the profound and fearful nature of the instinctual problematic. Civil anarchy or its threat touches on the same depths.

Original sin and/or the sin of the world are involved at the heart of this struggle. Unless this is recognized, the deadly seriousness of sin, which is reiterated throughout the Scriptures, particularly in the Johannine writings, cannot be appreciated. Sin is a misdirection of the most consequential kind. The human psyche is a delicate and complex balance of counter-tensions, and that condition is, in part, the result of an intricate and troubled evolutionary process. There is a fierce insecurity involved in the human condition. Its complexity renders it peculiarly vulnerable to pathological developments. The sin of the world, the cumulative and hardened pathology in the environment, preys upon that vulnerability. Stated in other terms, concupiscence, which is a natural quality of evolving man, is the point of susceptibility to the sin of the world.

Freud's sense of the psyche as a function of evolutionary process speaks directly to contemporary discussions on original sin. A. Hulsbosch, for example, describes the state of man as one of not-yet-possessing, of unfinished creaturehood. The act of creation is still in progress, and man, whose capacity for completion derives from his natural desire for God, plays a cooperative role in it. The incompletedness is sinful only insofar as it is the result of human choice, or better, refusal. "Then what was at the start purely a not-yet-possessing, becomes a sinful absence, because the incompletedness, in conflict with God's will, is affirmed as a positive condition." [41] It is into such a world, debilitated by the refusal to evolve, that each person is born. Thus, "original sin is the powerlessness, arising from nature, of man in his incompletedness as creature to reach his freedom and to realize the desire to see God, *insofar as* this impotence is put into the context of a sinful world".[42]

One can imagine four distinct existential cases of pathological resistance. The first is the case of a person who, without any personal fault, is so ill-founded emotionally that the pathological resistance includes no element of personal responsibility. Then the resistance must be completely described as coming from original sin or its historical reinforcement anterior to the individual's life. Secondly, a pathological resistance may be so much part of the constitution of the social life that an individual cannot resist it without endangering survival. Then his participation in that pathology is to be attributed to original sin and its historical reinforcement. An example of this would be our necessary use of money which involves us inevitably in all that is paranoid and exploitative in this human institution. Thirdly, a person whose life is, through personal fault, basically oriented against life and love will in his resistance conflate, as it were, both personal fault and active reaffirmation of original sin and its historical reinforcement. And finally, a person whose life is basically oriented for life and love (the state of grace) and who in personal freedom in some way acts minimally against this orientation, revives in some way his participation and reinforcement of original sin and its historical confirmation.

Authors such as Hulsbosch, Schoonenberg and Tresmontant point out the distortions introduced into the understanding of original sin by the static image of history, by the vision of a Golden Age in the past from which man has fallen. They urge a rediscovery of the eschatological and prophetic nature of Revelation: "God's world is *in the making* . . . the paradise-state depicts how we stand *essentially* before God, though this essential condition has to be slowly, hence historically realized in and through God's saving action".[43] Man's Golden Age is in the future: it is the fullness of Christ towards which we all labor. As long as the static image of a fall from privilege in the past prevails, the understanding of concupiscence is threatened. In the first place, the tendency to regard it too narrowly as the fruits of sin is encouraged. Secondly, its challenge and seriousness as urged above is emasculated by nostalgia.

The last pages of the second chapter go more deeply into environmental influences as interiorized. The question of whether this interiorization extends so radically as to constitute heredity remains open. Perhaps in the last analysis, one may question whether it matters, since those influences are so intimate and determinate. What is important is the fact that increasing insight into the unconscious mind reinforced in Freud an impression of the conservative nature of the psyche, of its archaic roots, and of the timeless, reiterative quality of the spiritual-instinctual struggle. Despite his dislike for anything smacking of the mystical,[44] that theme runs throughout his writings from first to last. He spoke of mental disturbance and of dreams—externalizations of unconscious psychic life—as reservoirs of "the antiquities of human development",[45] individual and collective. He frequently stated that the psychic life of the individual recapitulates the life of the race. He was convinced that the more profoundly the inner life is probed, the more profoundly will the sense of the human struggle throughout the ages be grasped. If his instinct is correct, then insight into the unconscious will have much to teach regarding the nature of sin.

The Primacy of Love:
The Importance of the Formality

Contemporary theologians have pointed out that one of the disastrous attendants to isolating the doctrine of original sin has been a dimmed vision of the deepest truth of Revelation: God's love for man. In Rahner's words:

> From Augustine onwards this doctrine was in fact linked with pessimistic feelings (a tragic conception of man) and with a view of salvation as restricted in extent, which was not identical with the doctrine of original sin itself. Original sin was not taken as designating a feature in the constitution of human reality which is always and from the start comprised within God's salvific will for all and the powerful grace of Christ, but as the situation of all, out of which a subsequent grace saves only some; the universality of original sin was clearer than the universality of man's redeemed condition, chiefly because it was not clearly seen how the universality of God's saving will and the fact that Christ died for all men could be translated into a structural feature intrinsically characterizing the personal life of every man even prior to his justification. Consequently the universal redemption by Christ was regarded as affecting the individual only when the process of justification itself or baptism took place.[46]

St. Paul's context for discussing original sin was his larger faith in the conquering love of Christ Jesus.[47] "Adam prefigured the One to come, but the gift itself considerably outweighed the fall. If it is certain that through one man's fall so many died, it is even more certain that divine grace, coming through the one man, Jesus Christ, came to so many as an abundant free gift." [48] St. Paul ends his interpretation of salvation history with a hymn to the inscrutable grandeur of God's salvific plan. "How rich are the depths of God—how deep his wisdom and knowledge—and how impossible to penetrate his motives or understand his methods! 'Who could ever know the mind of the Lord? Who could ever be his counsellor? Who could ever give him anything or lend him anything? All that exists comes from him; all is by him and for him. To him be glory for ever! Amen' ".[49] The Council of Trent reiterated the primacy of the formality when it declared its faith in the power of love, a radical healing power, over the wounds of alienation.

Through investigation of the unconscious the centrality of love (a truth much abused by unconvincing rhetoric) is empirically re-emphasized. This statement is the burden of these last pages: its exposition will focus on the sexual instincts, or rather, on the sexual instincts as evolutive, with a view to theological implications.

The contemporary freshness of insight into an ancient doctrine, that of original sin, has resulted in part from viewing that doctrine in an evolutionary perspective. Thus original sin is being described as the condition of evolving man insofar as his evolution is pathologically resisted or misdirected. If this position has merit, then the appreciation of what is sinful demands deeper insight into the developmental process as it is evidenced at an individual level (assuming that individual in some sense recapitulates collective evolution). For if that process is not first understood, how can the pathology within it be discerned?

There is a certain disposition that is called for with regard to phenomena that unfold gradually. It is one of curiosity, respect, encouragement. Maternal love serves as perhaps the best paradigm of man's response to himself as developmental. The essence of maternal love is its profound respect for the dynamics of growth. It grasps what the loved one is capable of, where he must be challenged and where protected, where allowed to pursue his impulses and where curbed. It is never condemning or punitive of inadequacy, nor does it fear its open manifestation. It springs from the unshakable conviction that the loved one and all his impulses are fundamentally good. It can therefore provide the environment in which they can unfold. Without maternal love, the development of a human being from its infantile state of help-lessness and self-centered need would be impossible. It is part of the human plan insofar as the human being is evolutive. In Scripture, God tells Israel, whom He has nurtured through several centuries of development, that He loves her as one loves a child.[50] Maternal love is the quintessential response of human beings to their own condition.

The basic disposition with which Freud approached psychic life instantiates the attitude in another way. The stance of Freud the investigator was first and foremost one of curiosity.[51] It was the kind of curiosity that has impelled the great human innovators: a consuming force that is served without regard for one's own comforts and smaller hopes, and without respect for established viewpoints. It was his curiosity that made him an effective therapist, for he early realized that moral blandishments were ineffective in most cases and only superficially effective in all. He had to *see* into the nature of things more deeply in order to reach the patient's desire and ability to change. Whatever the investigator may protest to the contrary, he wants to see reality because he already loves it as the good. How else can the compelling force of this drive, to which so much is willingly sacrificed, be explained? Unremitting curiosity is the creature's response to God's creation, which He declared to be good. It is founded on love: the stunting of curiosity is impossible with regard to an object as loved; it can only result from hatred and fear. To the degree that moral theology is not inspired by that curiosity, it is in fact immoral.[52]

The indispensability of a loving, curious disposition and the dangers which its opposites pose are brought out especially clearly in the context of the developing sexual instincts. Freud revealed the complex evolution which they must undergo and the relationship between their development and that of the most spiritual psychic capacities. What stands out is the dependence of their wholesome development on love from others. In the first place, the human being is born narcissistic, his pleasures and interests focused on himself. Only maternal love can warmly accept and give to such a being—until, from within, he is capable of giving in turn. "The libido attaches itself to the satisfaction of the great vital needs, and chooses as its first objects the people who have a share in that process. And in the development of mankind as a whole, just as in individuals, love alone acts as the civilizing factor in the sense that it brings a change from egoism to altruism".[53] To the extent that narcissism meets with love, it gradually changes to love. If it is despised or left to itself, it becomes a prison. The narcissistic adult has been deprived of loving communication in his earliest stages of growth—there is for him no vital invitation to a wider reality. What is first a basic stage of growth can be reverted to, hardened into. Secondary narcissism —the illusion of self-sufficiency—is a biblical prototype of sin.[54] Psychoanalytically speaking, it is the most pathological of psychic disturbances. The absence of love at the outset of life inflicts the deepest wound.

Secondly, love is the only disposition that can reckon wholesomely with the place of sensuality in human life. The human being is sensual from birth. Sensuality is an integral force within the major vital drives: the taking of nourishment, excretion and reproduction. At first auto-erotic, it is the basis for the love of one's body, one's natural functions, and those who serve them. Yet because of the auto-erotic possibility, sensuality can also provide a narrow haven from the real demands of life. In fact, when the life situation is brutal, overwhelming, or unloving, the imprisonment in auto-erotism is almost inevitable (which fact negatively testifies to its foundational importance). Human sexuality, moreover, is extremely diffuse; virtually any emotional state can be made to yield sensualized satisfaction. Especially, therefore, in its natural transitions through progressive organization (oral, anal, oedipal, genital) is sexual evolution peculiarly vulnerable to an environment or parents that give no loving encouragement to these transitions, but rather work to fixate sexuality at earlier stages.

The capacity to love has humble origins. It constitutes no denial of the transcendent in man to say that that capacity has sensual, instinctual sources, for man is bodily. The fear and hatred of concupiscence is deadly because it refuses to honor the sensual sources of love. But if these are not accepted, then neither is the nature of love. The hatred of instinctual impulses throws the individual back onto the unenlightened tyranny of those same forces or the severe inner reaction (the super-ego) to them. Love that is unafraid to see human nature deeply is the strongest preventative of and corrective to concupiscence in its pathological sense.

What is more, the very capacity to see without distortion is a function of that love. The defence mechanisms discussed in Chapter One are intensifications of self-deception; the defensive individual literally cannot see himself and his surroundings truly. For when these mechanisms—repression, paranoia, obsessions, reaction-formation, obtuseness to areas of reality—are successful, they cannot be recognized as such by their subject. He succeeds in building a false self on the foundations of mistrust of his deeper impulses. The self-preservative instinct has been overworked and has drowned out the more delicate operation of developing gradually in terms of a reality more and more clearly seen. That instinct is not so provoked in a loving environment. Defences in the adult will crumble only when he can entrust another with his own survival interests, that is, only when they are disarmed by love.

The same dependence of perceptive capacity upon loving and enlightened acceptance of the instinctual life was brought out in Chapter Three in two other contexts. The curiosity drive in children is integrally related to the efflorescence of their sexuality, so that abusive (which includes "moralistic") handling of the latter can damage the natural desire to know. Secondly, mature moral conscience is formed from, yet threatened by, the super-ego, which is the infantile stance towards instinctual life.

Vices and virtues, particularly those so deep-seated as to constitute part of the character formation and therefore antecedent in large part to conscious choice, cannot be understood in abstract treatises that lack any sense of the developmental process. Narcissism, megalomania, irascibility, rebelliousness, jealousy, sexual perversity are first and foremost concomitants of certain stages of growth. When these negative qualities continue to dominate the disposition of the adult, they point to areas of irresolution in his development. They can only be changed when that is first grasped. Both their subject and those who love him must understand and trust the growth process.

Lofty and premature moral censure mistrusts the underlying rectitude of the growth process; in fact, it only covers despair of the possibility of real inner change. This allegation is borne out by the complete ineffectualness of moralism in work with the mentally disturbed. Only enlightened honesty and genuine love are effective, and they are tested by fire! The disturbed cannot pretend superficial resolution in the interests of adjustment. Change occurs only when they know themselves to be understood accurately and without blame, and when their desire to change has been roused by the love they see in others.

A developmental sense of the human condition arms us with the instruments for healing it. It also frees us from the disease of judgement and blame. If human beings are evolutive, then a sense of time must be part of moral confrontation. For if they are evolutive, then negativity and inadequacy will inevitably attend their evolution, and may not for some time be morally reprehensible.[55]

Dubarle brings considerations such as these to bear on the doctrine of original sin and the sin of the world. He cites the parable of the weeds, in which the master of the vineyard tells his servants to let grain and weeds grow alike, for to uproot the evil might involve uprooting the good as well. The separation must wait until the harvest.[56]

Here again the lesson of Genesis appears, in a new guise. The fault committed by the first couple has its repercussions in every generation, just as the destiny of each ancestor continues in that of the particular race which takes its origin from him. The Gospel parable underlines the fact that they can no longer be separated. This is also the lesson to be drawn from the sentences pronounced by Yahweh on the guilty. The blessing of fecundity is not withdrawn, but childbirth is henceforth to be painful. The union of the two sexes is not suppressed, but the wife is to be subject to the husband. The earth will continue to give food, but it will be at the price of hard labour. So at the heart of everyone's life good and bad are inextricably mixed.

His following remarks speak even more directly to the issue here, namely, that a kind of discernment that is part of a developmental sense is necessary to a theology of original sin:

> The parable of the weeds unites the two ideas of a perversion of the initial work and of a development. And this calls to mind once more the description of a simultaneous growth of mankind and of sin in the stories of primitive history. St. Paul will reap the fruits of this legacy, for in his eyes the religious destiny of mankind consists not only in the spread of sin from one person, but in the growth of a son to the time of his majority.[57]

A good resolution in sexual development is crucial to the whole project of humanization, for sexual desire, in the broad developmental perspective here in question, is the appetitive force behind all human stagnation and change. At the apex of sexual development is the capacity for heterosexual love, the outcome of the successful resolution of the Oedipus complex. One is reminded here of the artful contrast drawn in Genesis between the relationship of the man and woman before sin and that after sin when a troubling divisiveness has entered.[58]

When the evolving human being meets with dispositions alien to that of maternal love, his incompleteness is highly susceptible to fixation. Others may secretly or openly connive with his short-sighted negativity because they have not outgrown it either. Or perhaps they may protest against their inner irresolution by moralism that encourages repression and self-division. In such ways, the neutral meets with the pathological and is vitiated. The sin of the world is compounded and fosters its own continuance. A deep sense of the developmental heightens sensitivity to the sin of the world in its manifold and subtle forms.

The Church is the community of men entrusted with Revelation—that is, with the deepest understanding of man's process—and with the overflowing Spirit of Love. It is there that the direction of evolution is therefore most surely discerned, criticized and fostered. The Church is the community of men freeing themselves from the sin of the world; it is the body of the consummate Man. Baptism is initiation into that community, into its formative influence and the gradual work of salvation.[59] These remarks are at once a statement and a challenge.

These remarks on the importance of a developmental sense and of love in those terms are resumed and sharpened when one examines the Tridentine position on original sin and justification. The Council of Trent declared that when a man is in a loving relationship with God, the very nature of his concupiscence changes. It is impossible to say that the acceptance of God's love makes no interior difference. It gives a man direction and the resources to see what is pernicious to his directedness. It gives him the desire to grow.[60] According to the classical teaching embodied in the Tridentine decree, the relationship is the very formality of the condition, sinful or justified. If it is rejected, man is left to his non-integration. If it is accepted, then integration (of identical components) begins around that focal point.

This truth is vindicated with singular force in Freud's exposure of the transference dynamic. Since the latter was only more or less obliquely referred to in Part One, some explanation will be necessary to see its implications.

Each person "has acquired a specific method of his own in his conduct of his erotic life—that is, in the preconditions to falling in love which he lays down, in the instincts he satisfies and the aims he sets himself in the course of it".[61] It is repeated constantly in the course of his life. But only a portion of his instinctual expectations is conscious; another has not kept up with his overall development and either exists in phantasy or is unconscious. In the relationship with the therapist, these regressive elements are provoked because the therapist, by definition, is intent upon bringing everything significant to light. A struggle ensues:

> The unconscious impulses do not want to be remembered in the way the treatment desires them to be, but endeavour to reproduce themselves in accordance with the timelessness of the unconscious and its capacity for hallucination. Just as happens in dreams, the patient regards products

of the awakening of his unconscious impulses as contemporaneous and real; he seeks to put his passions into action without taking any account of the real situation.[62]

The attraction of such elements to the unconscious mode of possession must be overcome. "This is responsible for by far the largest part of the resistance, which so often causes the illness to persist even after the turning away from reality has lost its temporary justification." [63]

At this point, the transference dynamic is reverted to: the patient transfers the elements of the repressed material onto the therapist, so that he assumes the features of an important person or persons in the past. He will become the object of forbidden impulses—negative and sexual. The therapist then

> tries to compel him [the patient] to fit these emotional impulses into the nexus of the treatment and of his life history, to submit them to intellectual consideration and to understand them in the light of their psychical value. This struggle between the doctor and the patient, between intellect and instinctual life, between understanding and seeking to act, is played out almost exclusively in the phenomena of transference. It is on that field that the victory must be won—the victory whose expression is the permanent cure of the neurosis.[64]

The successful outcome of this struggle depends, however, on the existence of a "positive" transference of feelings onto the therapist: of feelings that are friendly, affectionate and conscious as well as negative, forbidden, and unconscious. It is on the strength of that response that the patient will ultimately accept objective confrontation. The positive transference, then, is the vehicle of success. It will "induce the patient to perform a piece of psychical work—the overcoming of his transference resistances— *which involves a permanent alteration in his mental economy*".[65] The relationship, in other words, is the agent of real inner transformation.

The transference dynamic is by no means limited to the psychoanalytic session. On the contrary, "it is a universal phenomenon of the human mind . . . and in fact dominates the whole of each person's relations to his human environment".[66] It is called into play in all meaningful relationships and accounts both for their strength and their troubled elements. To the degree that one or both of the partners can engage the love and trust of the other, and to the degree that he is or they are integrated, they call out the refractory, primary components in the other into the light of mature judgement.

In other words, truthful love heals concupiscence.[67]

Freud was a complex man. Successors have accused him of reductionism in his treatment of love and can marshall texts to support their criticism. On the other hand, there are texts which soberly set forth the role of love as a *sine qua non*. And more significantly, though less tangibly, there is his therapeutic stance—the patience, respect and integrity with which he approached individuals in their least attractive moments—an appreciation of which can be gained only through reading his case histories. Whatever the reefs and shoals that have threatened the Freudian succession (rigidity, adjustment, the encouragement of infantile self-involvement), it is impossible to overlook the mighty instrument for humanization it has been in the hands of fine therapists, and, more diffusely, the change it has brought about generally in our attitude towards human disturbance.

There are many ways to get a measure of a contribution such as Freud's. One is the sheer pleasure of meeting an intelligence so penetrating and relentless. Another takes the passing of years: when the foundations he laid prove so deep and true that they are claimed by others as the basis for criticizing his own conclusions and for proposing fresh directions. I have referred to Reich and to Suttie. There is also Laing with his stress upon mutuality as a neglected dimension in Freud's metapsychology.[68] And there is Ricoeur who indicates other psychoanalytic approaches to the Judaeo-Christian tradition:

> Freud seems to me to exclude without reason, I mean without any psychoanalytic reason, the possibility that faith is a participation in the source of Eros and thus concerns, not the consolation of the child in us, but the power of loving; he excludes the possibility that faith aims at making this power adult in the face of the hatred within us and outside

of us—in the face of death. The only thing that can escape Freud's critique is faith as the kerygma of love: "God so loved the world. . . ." But in return his critique can help me discern what this kerygma of love excludes—a penal Christology and a moral God—and what it implies—a certain coincidence of the tragic God of Job and the lyric God of John.[69]

In the confrontation of the believer with the psychoanalysis of religion, Ricoeur concludes, neither emerges intact. Idols are separated from symbols for the believer, while resignation to Ananke is separated from the love of creation in that psychoanalysis.[70]

NOTES

Introduction

1. The nature of the historicity of the Genesis narrative on the fall has had an important place in exegetical and theological discussion recently. These brief sentences seem to express the emerging consensus. See, for example, A. -M. Dubarle's discussions in *The Biblical Doctrine of Original Sin,* tr. E. M. Stewart (New York: Herder & Herder, 1964), pp. 52-65. Karl Rahner, *Hominisation: The Evolutionary Origin of Man as a Theological Problem,* tr. W. J. O'Hara (New York: Herder, 1965); Henricus Renckens, *Israel's Concept of the Beginning. The Theology of Genesis 1-3,* tr. Charles Napier (New York: Herder & Herder, 1964); Luis Alonso-Schökel, "Sapiential and Covenant Themes in Genesis 2-3", *Theology Digest;* XIII, 1 (1965), 3-10; Norbert Lohfink, "Genesis 2-3 as Historical Etiology", *Theological Digest;* XIII, 1 (1965), 11-17.

2. It is in terms of the universality of sin and the unity of mankind that the question of monogenism has theological significance and has inspired so much debate. See the survey in Karl Rahner's "Monogenism", in *Sacramentum Mundi: An Encyclopedia of Theology,* ed. Karl Rahner and Others (New York: Herder & Herder; London: Burns & Oates, 1969), IV, 105-107.

3. C. J. Peter, "Original Sin", in the *New Catholic Encyclopedia* (New York: McGraw-Hill, 1967), X, 777.

4. St. Thomas Aquinas, *Summa Theologiae;* I-IIae, Q. 82, a. 3.

5. The literature referred to in this survey is listed in the bibliography.

6. "Prospective Theology", *The Ecumenist;* VIII, 5 (1970), p. 73.

7. *Ibid.,* pp. 73f.

Chapter 1

1. Speaking of the years since 1923 when his life was threatened by cancer, Freud said that older and original interests had once more become prominent, in a kind of "phase of regressive development". "My interest, after making a lifelong *détour* through the natural sciences, medicine and psychotherapy, returned to the cultural problems which had fascinated me long before, when I was a youth scarcely old enough for thinking." He specifies his hypothesis of two classes of instinct *("Eros"* and the death instinct) and the division of the mental personality into an ego, a super-ego, and an id (1923) as his "last decisive contributions to psycho-analysis" *(An Autobiographical Study:* Postscript (1935); XX, 71f.). Volume reference is to the Standard Edition of Freud's Collected Works (see Bibliography), and so throughout.

2. See, for examples, "On Psycho-Analysis"; XII, 210; "A Short Account of Psycho-Analysis"; XIX, 197f.; *An Autobiographical Study;* XX, 31, 40.

3. Lecture XXXI, "The Dissection of the Psychical Personality", of the *New Introductory Lectures on Psycho-Analysis;* XXII, 57.

4. See J. Breuer, Part III. "Theoretical", in *Studies on Hysteria;* II, 250; Freud, Letters 56 (17.1.97) and 57 (24.1.97) in *The Origins of Psycho-Analysis*. Letters to Wilhelm Fliess, Drafts and Notes: 1887-1902 by Sigmund Freud, ed. Marie Bonaparte, Anna Freud, Ernst Kris, tr. Eric Mosbacher and James Strachey (New York: Basic Books, 1954), pp. 187-191 (Vol. I, 242-4 in the Standard Edition. Only portions of the Fliess correspondence have been printed in the Standard Edition, so that the first or only reference will henceforth be to *The Origins of Psycho-Analysis); A Seventeeth Century Demonological Neurosis;* XIX, 72.

5. *Five Lectures on Psycho-Analysis;* XI, 10. The case of Anna O. is described by Breuer in *Studies on Hysteria;* II, 21-47, and by Freud in *Five Lectures on Psycho-Analysis;* XI, 9-20; *An Autobiographical Study;* XX, 19-23.

6. *Five Lectures on Psycho-Analysis;* XL, 13f. See also Breuer and Freud, "On the Psychical Mechanism of Hysterical Phenomena: Preliminary Communication" (to the *Studies on Hysteria;* II, 6. Though the process appears simple, it required laborious and repeated effort (Freud, *Studies on Hysteria;* II, 271, 278, 287-298).

7. *Ibid.,* pp. 38f.

8. *Ibid.,* pp. 44, 46.

9. *An Autobiographical Study;* XX, 19.

10. *Ibid.,* pp. 19f.

11. See the Editor's Introduction; II, xvi.

12. The first published occurrence of the term in what was to be its psycho-analytic sense is in Breuer's case history of Anna O. (II, 45). Freud's first use of the word in print appears on p. 76, n. 1.

13. *Ibid.,* p. 45.

14. *Ibid.,* p. 76.

15. The existence of unconscious mental processes was recognized by J. F. Herbart, who not only greatly influenced Freud's medical teachers but was studied at his secondary school. Nevertheless, Freud did not immediately adopt this position. It was Breuer who was the first to make a reasoned defence of the existence of unconscious ideas *(Studies on Hysteria;* II, 222-239). See the Editor's Note to "The Unconscious"; XIV, 161-165; Ernest Jones, *Sigmund Freud: Life and Work* (London: Hogarth, 1953), Vol. I, pp. 397f.

16. Lecture XXXI, "The Dissection of the Psychical Personality", of the *New Introductory Lectures on Psycho-Analysis;* XXII, 70.

17. *Ibid.* In this particular passage, Freud turned immediately to the phenomenon

of parapraxes: slips of the tongue, of the pen, idle but extremely revealing gestures, acts of forgetting. The subject precipitated a long study on his part, *The Psycho-pathology of Everyday Life*, which he published six years after the *Studies on Hysteria*. He found parapraxes to result from a conflict between two or more intentions, one of which the subject was unwilling to so betray, but which was nevertheless active enough to interfere with his dominant, conscious intention. It was not merely latent, therefore, but also psychical. "From this experience we retrospectively obtain the right also to pronounce as something unconscious what had been described as latent" (p. 71).

18. Freud stated the issue most succinctly in one of his last writings. See "Some Elementary Lessons in Psycho-Analysis"; XXIII, 285f.

19. The *Project for a Scientific Psychology* was published only posthumously. Freud himself refused to have it published, though at the time of its germination he had written to his friend Fliess, "I am so deep in the 'Psychology for Neurologists' that it quite consumes me, until I have to break off out of sheer exhaustion. I have never been so intensely preoccupied by anything" (Letter 23 (27.4.95), in *The Origins of Psycho-Analysis*, p. 118). Nevertheless, aspects of the *Project* were to be paradigmatic for his later expositions, particularly for the seventh chapter of *The Interpretation of Dreams*. The *Project* is reproduced in Volume I of the Standard Edition, pp. 295-387, and in *The Origins of Psycho-Analysis*, pp. 347-445. See the respective editors' introductions and Jones, *Sigmund Freud: Life and Work*, I, 316-318 for a more complete discussion of the *Project*.

20. *Studies on Hysteria;* II, 268. For Freud's assessment of the cathartic method (which involved hypnosis), see pp. 267f., 283-285; "On Psychotherapy"; VII, 260f.; *Five Lectures on Psycho-Analysis;* XI, 21-28; *An Autobiographical Study;* XX, 19-31.

21. *Studies on Hysteria;* II, 269. The last sentence describes the mechanism of repression. Cf. "Repression"; XIV, 147. At this early period, Freud used the terms repression and defence almost equivalently. (See the Editor's Note to "Repression"; XIV, 143f., for Freud's alternation between usages and his eventual precision on their distinction). Resistance is a more general term than repression. In *Inhibitions, Symptoms and Anxiety* (XX, 157), Freud describes it as "the action undertaken to protect repression".

22. "On the History of the Psycho-Analytic Movement"; XIV, 16; cf. the Editor's Note to *Project for a Scientific Psychology;* I, 351, n. 2; *Studies on Hysteria;* II, 157; *An Autobiographical Study;* XX, 29f.

23. *Beyond the Pleasure Principle;* XVIII, 9; cf. "Instincts and Their Vicissitudes"; XIV, 120f. For early formulations of the principle, see Draft D (5.94) and *Project for a Scientific Psychology,* I, 1; *Origins of Psycho-Analysis,* pp. 87f., 357f. (Standard Edition; I, 187, 197). For a discussion of the occurrences and significance of this principle in Freud's writings see the Editor's Appendix to "The Neuro-Psychoses of Defence"; III, 65f.

24. Breuer, Part III. "Theoretical", in *Studies On Hysteria;* II, 200.

25. Letter 137 (12.9.1900); *The Origins of Psycho-Analysis,* pp. 321f.; cf. *The Interpretation of Dreams;* IV, 116-120, 122-133. References to the theme are frequent in the Fliess correspondence: e.g., Letters 28 (23.9.95), 60 (28.4.97), Draft L (2.5.97); *The Origins of Psycho-Analysis,* pp. 125, 193-196, 199f. (Standard Edition; I, 245-247, 250).

26. *The Interpretation of Dreams;* IV, 267. On children's dreams, see *On Dreams;* V, 643-645.

27. *The Interpretation of Dreams;* V, 567f.

28. *Ibid.;* IV, 191.

29. *Ibid.;* V, 567-570.

30. *Ibid.;* V. 608.

31. See n. 29 above, and Letters 82 (16.1.98) and 105 (19.2.99) for Freud's early

formulation of this insight (*The Origins of Psycho-Analysis,* pp. 243f., 277-279, or Standard Edition; I, 287f.).

32. Preface to the Third (Revised) English Edition of *The Interpretation of Dreams* (1931); VI, xxxii.

33. *Ibid.;* V, 608f.; "Preface to Reik's *Ritual: Psycho-Analytic Studies";* XVII, 259.

34. *An Outline of Psycho-Analysis;* XXII, 169.

35. *The Interpretation of Dreams;* IV, 283.

36. *Ibid.;* IV, 122-133, 277-508.

37. Interview filmed for the presentation of the Academy Awards, April 15, 1971.

38. See, for example, Draft N (31.5.97); *The Origins of Psycho-Analysis,* p. 208 (Standard Edition; I, 256); "Creative Writers and Daydreaming"; IX, 143-153; "Formulations on the Two Principles of Mental Functioning"; XII, 224; Lecture XXIII, "The Paths to the Formation of Symptoms", of the *Introductory Lectures on Psycho-Analysis;* XVI, 375-377; *Delusions and Dreams in Jensen's* Gradiva; IX, 7-95; "Dreams in Folklore"; XII, 180-203; "The Occurrence in Dreams of Material From Fairy Tales"; XII, 281-287; "The Theme of the Three Caskets"; XII, 291-301; "The Moses of Michelangelo"; XII, 211-236; *Leonardo da Vinci and A Memory of His Childhood;* XI, 63-137. See also Ernest Jones, *Sigmund Freud: Life and Work,* Vol. I, p. 253.

39. *The Interpretation of Dreams;* IV, 134-162.

40. Lecture XXXI, "The Dissection of the Psychical Personality", of the *New Introductory Lectures on Psycho-Analysis;* XXII, 70.

41. *Ibid.,* pp. 70f.; Lecture XIX, "Resistance and Repression", of the *Introductory Lectures on Psycho-Analysis;* XVI, 295f.; "Some Elementary Lessons in Psycho-Analysis"; XXIII, 283f.

42. *An Outline of Psycho-Analysis;* XXIII, 159.

43. *Ibid.,* 157-164; *The Ego and the Id;* XIX, 13-15.

44. Lecture XXXI, "The Dissection of the Psychical Personality", of the *New Introductory Lectures on Psycho-Analysis;* XXI, 71. See *Moses and Monotheism* on the unsatisfactory elements involved in a topographical approach (notably its non-dynamic nature); XXIII, 97. Freud's topographical conception implied no connection with the anatomy of the brain. See *An Autobiographical Study;* XX, 32; *The Interpretation of Dreams;* V, 536-542.

45. That Freud saw psycho-analysis as a science is clear from the following passages: *Beyond the Pleasure Principle;* XVIII, 60; *An Autobiographical Study;* XX, 32f., 58f.; "Some Elementary Lessons in Psycho-Analysis"; XXIII, 282-286. Contemporary philosophers have been more stringent in their analysis of the nature of depth-psychology. Ricoeur discusses their viewpoints at length, and concludes that it is neither an observational science nor phenomenology. It "is a unique and irreducible form of praxis" (p. 418). What is important for our purposes is in the first place, that Freud's expositions grew directly from his analytic experience and throughout the course of his life were confirmed or modified by fresh developments. He disciplined his own speculative penchant through laborious observation and application. Secondly, he was aware of the diverse nature of his statements, aware that some were directly descriptive of his therapeutic experience (e.g., the qualities conscious, preconscious and unconscious); others were postulates (e.g., the topographical approach, the classifications of the instincts), and so on. He was also explicit about the figurative nature of his terminology, a characteristic which they shared with the natural sciences, such as physics.

46. "The Unconscious"; XIV, 171.

47. *An Autobiographical Study;* XX, 31. See also *Moses and Monotheism;* XXIII, 97; *The Interpretation of Dreams;* V, 615-617; Lecture XIX, "Resistance and Repression", of the *Introductory Lectures on Psycho-Analysis;* XVI, 295, n. 1.

48. Lecture XVIII, "Fixation to Traumas—The Unconscious", of the *Introductory Lectures on Psycho-Analysis;* XVI, 284f. "Two discoveries amount to a statement that *the ego is not master in its own house*". They are: "that the life of our sexual instincts cannot be wholly tamed, and that mental processes are in themselves unconscious and only reach the ego and come under its control through incomplete and untrustworthy perceptions" ("A Difficulty in the Path of Psycho-Analysis; XVII, 143).

49. Lecture XXXI, "The Dissection of the Psychical Personality", of the *New Introductory Lectures to Psycho-Analysis;* XXII, 70.

50. *The Ego and The Id;* XIX, 18. See also "The Unconscious"; XIV, 172; "Some Elementary Lessons in Psycho-Analysis"; XXIII, 286f.

51. Freud considered this theory to embody one of his most fundamental insights. See the *Project for a Scientific Psychology;* I, 15; I, 324-327; "The Unconscious"; XIV, 188; *Beyond the Pleasure Principle;* XVIII, 34; *An Outline of Psycho-Analysis;* XXIII, 164. The fullest treatment is to be found in *The Interpretation of Dreams;* V, 588-609.

52. *The Interpretation of Dreams;* V, 665.

53. *Beyond the Pleasure Principle;* XVIII, 7. In the beginning Freud seems to have assumed the identity of the pleasure principle and the law of constancy (or Nirvana principle), so that the drive towards pleasure and that towards discharging excitation were the same. (See *Project for a Scientific Psychology*, I, 8; I, 312; *The Interpretation of Dreams;* V, 598). But his later observations on the nature of pleasure: the pleasure involved in states of increasing tension (e.g., sexual excitement). the connection between pleasure and rhythmic patterns of excitation and the apparent exceptions to the pleasure principle—these led him to conclude to a distinction between the two basic trends. See *Beyond the Pleasure Principle;* XVIII, 8, 63; "The Economic Problem of Masochism"; XIX, 159-161. See also the Editor's Note, "Instincts and Their Vicissitudes"; XIV, 121.

54. *The Interpretation of Dreams;* V, 565-567; *Project for a Scientific Psychology*, I, 1, 2, 11; I, 295-298, 317-319.

55. *Leonardo da Vinci and a Memory of His Childhood;* XI, 75f. See Ricoeur's remarks in *Freud and Philosophy*, p. 550.

56. See, for example, Erik Erikson, *Young Man Luther* (New York: W. W. Norton and Co., 1962), pp. 116-119, 141. Ian Suttie is explicitly critical of Freud for his failure to give this reality its due (*The Origins of Love and Hate*) (Harmondsworth: Penguin Books, 1963), pp. 31f, etc.

57. *The Interpretation of Dreams;* V, 598-603.

58. *The Question of Lay Analysis;* XX, 194f.

59. Letter 105 (19.2.99); *The Origins of Psycho-Analysis*, p. 277. See also *Beyond the Pleasure Principle;* XVII, 63. The question of "reality-testing", i.e., the mental ability to distinguish reality from phantasy, was one that interested Freud all his life. One can trace the development of his thinking in the passages cited above from the *Project for a Scientific Psychology* and *The Interpretation of Dreams* through the following works: "Formulations on the Two Principles of Mental Functioning"; XII, 218-226; "A Metapsychological Supplement to the Theory of Dreams"; XIV, 222-235 (see also the important Editor's Note, pp. 219-221); *The Ego and the Id;* XIX, 28, n. 2; "Negation"; XIX, 235-239; "Neurosis and Psychosis"; XIX, 149-153; "Fetishism"; XXI, 152-157; Lecture XXX, "Dreams and Occultism" of the *New Introductory Lectures on Psycho-Analysis;* XXII, 33; *An Outline of Psycho-Analysis;* XXIII, 195-204.

60. *The Interpretation of Dreams;* V, 567. See the entire section, pp. 533-549, and IV, 189-219.

61. "Formulations on Two Principles of Mental Functioning"; XII, 225; "The

Unconscious"; XIV, 186-189. Detailed attention is given to these characteristics of the unconscious as revealed in dreams in *The Interpretation of Dreams;* IV, 279-338.

62. "The way in which dreams treat the category of contraries and contradictories is highly remarkable. It is simply disregarded. 'No' seems not to exist so far as dreams are concerned. They show a peculiar preference for combining contraries into a unity or for representing them as one and the same thing. Dreams feel themselves at liberty, moreover, to represent any element by its wishful contrary; so that there is no way of deciding at a first glance whether any element that admits of a contrary is present in the dream-thoughts as a positive or as a negative. The dream-interpreters of antiquity seem to have made the most extensive use of the notion that a thing in a dream can mean its opposite" (*The Interpretation of Dreams;* IV, 318).

Evidences of the same combination of contradictions in linguistic usage fascinated Freud. In Latin, for example, *"altus"* means both "high" and "deep"; *"sacer"* both "sacred" and "accursed". "Boden" in German means both "garret" and "ground". The Old Saxon *"bat"* ("good") corresponds to the English "bad". See "The Antithetical Meaning of Primal Words"; XI, 155-161.

63. "The Unconscious"; XIV, 187. In this quotation, there is mention of a term that frequently occurs in Freud's writings, namely, "cathexis". It is a translation of the German *"Besetzung"* which can mean "occupation" or "filling". The fact that it was a term in ordinary usage endeared it to Freud. He disliked unnecessary technical terms and was not happy with James Strachey's introduction of "cathexis" for the English translation. Strachey invented the term after the Greek verb, χατέχειν, "to occupy". Freud did, however, use it himself in an English article he wrote for the *Encyclopaedia Britannica* ("Psycho-Analysis"; XX, 266). The word cathexis embodies a theory which Strachey points to as the most fundamental of all Freud's hypotheses, and which he calls for convenience "the theory of cathexis": "that in mental functions something is to be distinguished—a quota of affect or sum of excitation—which possesses all the characteristics of a quantity (though we have no means of measuring it), which is capable of increase, diminution, displacement and discharge, and which is spread over the memory-traces of ideas somewhat as an electric charge is spread over the surface of a body" ("The Neuro-Psychoses of Defence (I)"; III, 60). It very early became standard usage, but was preceded in Freud's early writings by phrases such as "loaded with a sum of excitation", "provided with a quota of affect", and "supplied with energy". His concept of cathexis underlay the theoretical understanding of the cathartic method and the law of constancy. The word has an entirely non-physical meaning in all his writings from the time of *The Interpretation of Dreams.* See the Editor's Appendix, "The Emergence of Freud's Fundamental Hypotheses", to "The Neuro-Psychoses of Defence (I)"; III, 62-68.

64. *Freud and Philosophy,* pp. 159f. The dream seems to be an indispensable form of psychic discharge. Part of the reason why prolonged lack of sleep can lead to insanity is because this discharge is denied. In fact the victim of this state will eventually hallucinate. See *An Outline of Psycho-Analysis;* XXIII, 165f.

65. Lecture XXII, "The Paths to the Formation of Symptoms", of the *Introductory Lectures on Psycho-Analysis;* XVI, 372; cf. "Remarks on the Theory and Practice of Dream-Interpretation"; XIX, 127.

66. See "Analysis of a Phobia in a Five-Year Old Boy" (the Case of "Little Hans"); X, 5-149; *Three Essays on the Theory of Sexuality;* VII, 194-197. The child analyst, Melanie Klein, had an exceptional understanding of the child's world of phantasy and conjecture. Her works are still foremost in the field. See *The Psychoanalysis of Children* (London: Hogarth, 1959).

67. Letter 69 (21.9.97), *The Origins of Psycho-Analysis,* pp. 215-217. Cf. "The Neuro-Psychoses of Defence (II)", III, 168, n. 1.

68. *An Outline of Psycho-Analysis;* XXIII, 168; *Moses and Monotheism;* XXIII, 96, 98.

69. Freud spoke in several contexts of the relationship between words and the preconscious, the province of the secondary mode. The essence of his therapeutic method was to bring hitherto unconscious memories, wishes and ideas to verbal expression, thereby definitively freeing them from their relegation to the unconscious and to infantilism. Speech and full consciousness are thus synomymous. See "The Unconscious"; XIV, 186-188, 202f.; *The Ego and the Id;* XIX, 20. In *Moses and Monotheism* (XXIII, 95), Freud wrote that "the repressed retains its upward surge, its effort to force its way to consciousness". It achieves its aim under the following conditions: (1) a weakening of the ego, such as happens in sleep or psychotic breakdown; (2) when related instincts are reinforced, such as at the time of puberty; (3) when an experience occurs which is like the repressed, so that the latter is reawakened.

70. "It cannot be a matter of indifference psychologically that the period of infantile amnesia coincides with this early period of sexuality. It may be that this state of things provides the true determinant for the possibility of neurosis, which is in a sense a human prerogative and from this point of view appears as a vestige— a 'survival'—of primaeval times like certain portions of our bodily anatomy" *(Moses and Monotheism;* XXIII, 75). For further discussions of infantile amnesia, the diphasic nature of sexual development and hominization, see *An Outline of Psycho-Analysis;* XXIII, 153; *Three Essays on the Theory of Sexuality;* VII, 174-176.

71. See n. 17 above.

72. *Inhibitions, Symptoms and Anxiety;* XX, 163; cf. "Analysis Terminable and Interminable"; XXIII, 234-240, and n. 21 above.

73. "Analysis Terminable and Interminable"; XXIII, 235.

74. *Ibid.* See also *Inhibitions, Symptoms and Anxiety;* XX, 155f.

75. Freud concluded that "repression is not a defensive mechanism which is present from the very beginning, and that it cannot arise until a sharp cleavage has occurred between conscious and unconscious mental activity—that *the essence of repression lies simply in turning something away, and keeping it at a distance, from the conscious"* ("Repression"; XIV, 147).

Freud discovered the same mechanisms of condensation and displacement which are operative in dreams to be responsible for the falsification of memory which is characteristic of individual history (Lecture XIII, "The Archaic Features and Infantilism of Dreams" of the *Introductory Lectures on Psycho-Analysis;* XV, 200f.). Hence the apparent forgetting of significant events of early childhood but the remembering of (associated) indifferent events, persons and things. Freud therefore called the latter "screen memories" *(The Psychopathology of Everyday Life;* VI, 43, 47f.).

76. See "The Neuro-Psychoses of Defence (I)"; III, 59f.; "Neurosis and Psychosis"; XIX, 149-153; "The Loss of Reality in Neurosis and Psychosis"; XIX, 183-187; "Fetishism"; XXI, 152-157; "Splitting of the Ego in the Process of Defence"; XXIII, 275-278.

77. Draft H (24.2.95), Draft K (1.1.96), in *The Origins of Psycho-Analysis,* pp. 110-115, 152-155 (Standard Edition; I, 206-212, 200-229); "The Neuro-Psychoses of Defence (II)"; III, 174-185.

78. "Psycho-Analytic Notes on an Autobiographical Account of a Case of Paranoia *(Dementia Paranoides)"* (The Case of Schreber); XII, 59-68; "A Case of Paranoia Running Counter to the Psycho-Analytic Theory of the Disease"; XIV, 263-272; "Some Neurotic Mechanisms in Jealousy, Paranoia and Homosexuality"; XVIII, 223-232.

79. Lecture XIX, "Resistance and Repression", of the *Introductory Lectures on Psycho-Analysis;* XVI, 293.

80. "The Neuro-Psychoses of Defence (I), (II)"; III, 52f., 168-174; "Obsessive Actions and Religious Practices"; IX, 117-127; "From the History of an Infantile Neurosis" (The Case of the "Wolf-Man"); XVII, 61-71, etc.

81. *Inhibitions, Symptoms and Anxiety;* XX, 101-110; "Obsessions and Phobias: Their Psychical Mechanism and Their Aetiology"; III, 74-82, and the Editor's Appendix, pp. 83f.; "Analysis of a Phobia in a Five-Year Old Boy" (The Case of "Little Hans"); X, 5-149; *Totem and Taboo;* XIII. 127-132, etc.

82. On "reaction-formation", see *Three Essays on The Theory of Sexuality;* VII, 238f.; *Inhibitions, Symptoms and Anxiety;* XX, 102f., 116, 157-159. It should be noted here that reaction-formation (like repression) plays a positive role as well in the developmental process. Both are characteristic features of the latency period. Freud called reaction-formation "a sub-species of sublimation" (*Three Essays on the Theory of Sexuality;* VII, 238).

83. *Inhibitions, Symptoms and Anxiety;* XX, 153.

84. *Ibid.* Cf. p. 93 for a discussion of the repetition of earlier fears underlying irrational responses.

85. *Ibid.,* p. 99; cf. pp. 153, 160.

86. See Part Two, Chapter Four, n. 26.

87. Lecture XXXI, "The Dissection of the Psychical Personality", of the *New Introductory Lectures on Psycho-Analysis;* XXII, 71.

88. *Ibid.,* p. 74.

89. *An Outline of Psycho-Analysis;* XXIII, 163.

90. "The ego is that portion of the id which was modified by the proximity and influence of the external world, which is adapted for the reception of stimuli and as a protective shield against stimuli, comparable to the cortical layer by which a small piece of living substance is surrounded" (Lecture XXXI, "The Dissection of the Psychical Personality", of the *New Introductory Lectures on Psycho-Analysis;* XXII, 75).

91. The secondary mode of mental functioning is the mode peculiar to and formative of the ego. It is the mode which dominates conscious and preconscious mental activity. Thus, the true ambit of ego functioning is the conscious and preconscious, despite the fact that much of its activity may also be in the nature of unconscious checks and balances. See *Beyond the Pleasure Principle;* XVIII, 34; *An Outline of Psycho-Analysis;* XXIII, 162, 164; *Moses and Monotheism;* XXIII, 96.

92. Lecture XXXI, "The Dissection of the Psychical Personality", of the *New Introductory Lectures on Psycho-Analysis;* XXII, 75f.

93. *Ibid.,* p. 76.

94. "Inhibitions, Symptoms and Anxiety"; XX, 97.

95. *Ibid.* "The ego is an organization. It is based on the maintenance of free intercourse and of the possibility of reciprocal influence between all its parts . . . this necessity to synthesize grows stronger in proportion as the strength of the ego increases" (p. 98).

96. *Ibid.,* p. 92. Freud emphasized (p. 95) that the recognition of the strength of the ego must attend the considerations which follow, namely of the ego's weakness with respect to the id, if a balanced comprehension is to be had.

97. *Ibid.,* pp. 76f. "The repressed is now, as it were, an outlaw; it is excluded from the great organization of the ego and is subject only to the laws which govern the realm of the unconscious" ("The Instincts and Their Vicissitudes"; XIV, 153; cf. also p. 97).

98. *Ibid.,* pp. 77f. See corresponding passages in *The Ego and the Id;* XIX, 55-57. "In its position midway between the id and reality, it too often yields to the temptation to become sycophantic, opportunist and lying, like a politician who sees the truth but wants to keep his place in popular favour" (p. 55).

99. *Beyond the Pleasure Principle;* XVIII, 34. See also "The Unconscious"; XIV, 186.

100. See *An Outline of Psycho-Analysis;* XXIII, 157-164.

101. Lecture XXXI, "The Dissection of the Psychical Personality", of the *New Introductory Lectures on Psycho-Analysis;* XXII, 73f.

102. *Ibid.,* pp. 74f. See also *An Outline of Psycho-Analysis;* XXII, 163.

Chapter 2

1. Lecture XXXI, "The Dissection of the Psychical Personality", of the *New Introductory Lectures on Psycho-Analysis;* XXII, 73, 74.

2. *Beyond the Pleasure Principle;* XVIII, 34.

3. "On Narcissism: An Introduction"; XIV, 78.

4. Lecture XXXII, "Anxiety and Instinctual Life", of the *New Introductory Lectures on Psycho-Analysis;* XXII, 95.

5. "Instincts and Their Vicissitudes"; XIV, 121f. See the Editor's Introduction on the history of Freud's understanding of the instincts.

6. "The Unconscious"; XIV, 177.

7. Freud commonly spoke of the psychic representative as the instinct (see n. 1 above). As time went on, however, he tended to limit the term to the non-psychical process, but both usages will be found to the end of his writings. It is an ambiguity that derives from the threshold nature of the instincts. By reason of that same threshold nature, biological advances in the study of the instincts are of primary interest to psychoanalysis. Freud frequently expressed the hope for this sort of re-search (see, for example, *Beyond the Pleasure Principle;* XVIII, 60). Nevertheless, the study of the somatic sources of the instincts lies outside the scope of psycho-analysis ("Instincts and Their Vicissitudes"; XIV, 123). See Ricoeur, *Freud and Philosophy*, p. 137.

8. "Instincts and Their Vicissitudes"; XIV, 122.

9. *Ibid.*

10. *Ibid.*, pp. 122f.; cf. *Beyond the Pleasure Principle;* XVIII, 34.

11. "Instincts and Their Vicissitudes"; XIV, 127. On the content of this para-graph, see the entire section, pp. 126-140; "Repression"; XIV, 147, 151.

12. *Three Essays on the Theory of Sexuality;* VII, 238.

13. "Repression"; XIV, 148.

14. Draft K (1.1.96), Letters 58 (8.2.97) and 75 (14.11.97), in *The Origins of Psycho-Analysis*, pp. 147-149, 192, 232-234 (Standard Edition; I, 221-223, 268-271); *Three Essays on the Theory of Sexuality;* VII, 162, 191, 231, etc. This point was frequently repeated by Freud; it was part of his broader sense of the opposition between in-stinctual life and civilization that was to be thematic in his last writings.

15. Such derivatives are phantasies, both of normal and disturbed people, and the various substitutive formations studied earlier with regard to defence. Freud compared these derivatives of unconscious instinctual impulses to "individuals of mixed race, who, taken all round, resemble white men, but who betray their coloured descent by some striking feature or other, and on that account are ex-cluded from society and enjoy none of the privileges of white people" ("The Un-conscious"; XIV, 191). The derivatives mark the point at which unconscious thoughts and desires betray their existence to the conscious mind. They are not so disconcerting to consciousness as the primitive and unruly impulses that character-ize unconscious activity because "they are highly organized, free from self-contra-diction, have made use of every acquisition of the system *Cs.* and would hardly be distinguished from the formations of that system" (*ibid.*, p. 190). Nevertheless, they are not allowed to enter into the full stream of conscious life, because their origins in repressed impulses are too thinly concealed. Thus an individual will experience an unmistakable aversion to attention—on his own part and from others—to certain of his fragmentary phantasies or defense mechanisms. On the other hand, certain of the latter, particularly if they constitute an "over-protest" will become conscious, and, in fact, obsessively so.

16. "Repression proper, therefore, is actually an after-pressure" ("Repression"; XIV, 148). See also "The Unconscious"; XIV, 180f. For an early statement of the view and for its elaboration in concrete instances, see "Psycho-Analytic Notes on An Autobiographical Account of a Case of Paranoia *(Dementia Paranoides)*" (The Case of Schreber); XII, 58-67. In this study, Freud examines extreme paranoidal positions taken to solidify the core repression of infantile homosexual tendencies.

17. See "Analysis of a Phobia in a Five Year Old Boy" (The Case of "Little Hans"); X, 5-149. See Ch. 1, n. 66, p. 215 above.

18. "Repression"; XIV, 149.

19. "Psycho-Analytic Notes on an Autobiographical Account of a Case of Paranoia" (The Case of Schreber); XII, 71. See also "Instincts and Their Vicissitudes"; XIV, 125; *Moses and Monotheism;* XXIII, 124-127.

20. "Instincts and Their Vicissitudes"; XIV, 124; *Civilization and Its Discontents;* XXI, 117. Freud's earliest writings scarcely mention the word instinct, but expressions such as "excitations", "affective ideas", "wishful impulses" and "endogenous stimuli" refer to the same reality. See, for example, *Project for a Scientific Psychology,* I, 1; I, 297, 316, and the Editor's Introduction to "Instincts and Their Vicissitudes"; XIV, 114.

21. "It may be asked whether and how far I am myself convinced of the truth of the hypotheses that have been set out in these pages. My answer would be that I am not convinced myself and that I do not seek to persuade other people to believe in them. . . . I do not dispute the fact that the third step in the theory of the instincts, which I have taken here, cannot lay claim to the same degree of certainty as the two earlier ones—the extension of the concept of sexuality and the hypothesis of narcissism. These two innovations were a direct translation of observation into theory and were no more open to sources of error than is inevitable in all such cases. It is true that my assertion of the regressive character of instincts also rests upon observed material—namely on the facts of the compulsion to repeat. It may be, however, that I have overestimated their significance. And in any case it is impossible to pursue an idea of this kind except by repeatedly combining factual material with what is purely speculative and thus diverging widely from empirical observation". He adds that where the great problems of life and science are concerned, each of us is governed "by deep-rooted internal prejudices, into whose hands our speculation unwittingly plays. Since we have such good grounds for being distrustful, our attitude towards the results of our own deliberations cannot well be other than one of cool benevolence". He describes his position in proposing this line of speculation "as an *advocatus diaboli,* who is not on that account himself sold to the devil" *(Beyond the Pleasure Principle;* XVIII, 59; cf. p. 64).

22. "Instincts and Their Vicissitudes"; XIV, 120. This sentence contains the germs of the later theory of a death instinct.

23. *The Interpretation of Dreams;* V, 602f.

24. *Civilization and Its Discontents;* XXI, 106, 99f., n. 1. See also *The Origins of Psycho-Analysis,* pp. 186f. and 231f.; "Notes Upon a Case of Obsessional Neurosis" (The Case of the "Rat Man"); X, 247f.; "On the Universal Tendency to Debasement in the Sphere of Love (Contributions to the Psychology of Love II)"; XI, 189; and the Editor's Introduction to *Civilization and Its Discontents;* XXI, 60f.

25. A. T. W. Simeons, M.D., *Man's Presumptuous Brain.* An Evolutionary Interpretation of Psychosomatic Disease (London: Longman's, Green and Co., Ltd., 1960). See Chapter Two, "The Evolution of the Human Psyche", pp. 31-59.

26. *Ibid.,* p. 32. The reptile scuttles away to shelter when it perceives a large shadow in the sky above it. The small tree-living mammal waits, its body prepared physiologically for instant flight, but its cortex sifting all evidence in order to ascertain how imminent is the danger. That activity of "judging" is one of the indices of higher development (pp. 32-34).

27. *Ibid.*, pp. 44f.

28. *Ibid.*, pp. 46-48.

29. The passage is quoted in n. 90, p. 220 above. See also *Moses and Monotheism;* XXIII, 97; *Beyond the Pleasure Principle; XVIII, 24; The Ego and the Id; XIX, 19.

30. Simeons, *Man's Presumptuous Brain,* pp. 45-54.

31. "'Saintliness' is something based on the fact that, for the sake of the larger community, human beings have sacrificed some of their freedom to indulge in sexual perversions. The horror of incest (as something impious) is based on the fact that, as a result of a common sexual life (even in childhood), the members of a family hold together permanently and become incapable of contact with strangers. Thus incest is anti-social and civilization consists in a progressive renunciation of it. Contrariwise the 'superman'" (Draft N (31.5.97); *The Origins of Psycho-Analysis.* pp. 209f. (Standard Edition; I, 257). See also *Totem and Taboo;* XIII, 1-17; *Civilization and Its Discontents;* XXI, 104; *Moses and Monotheism;* XXIII, 120-122).

32. "Fragment of An Analysis of a Case of Hysteria" (The Case of Dora); VII, 50. The same theme is elaborated in Letters 52 (6.12.96), 55 (11.1.97) and 57 (24.1.97); *The Origins of Psycho-Analysis,* pp. 180, 185-187, 189 (Standard Edition; I, 239, 241, 244); *Three Essays on the Theory of Sexuality;* VII, 165-167, etc.

33. See Freud's very interesting analysis of this quality in "The 'Uncanny'"; XVII, 219-256.

34. This point is thematic in *Totem and Taboo* (XIII, 1-161).

35. Lecture XXIII, "The Paths to the Formation of Symptoms", of the *Introductory Lectures on Psycho-Analysis;* XVI, 371.

36. *The Interpretation of Dreams;* 548f. To this statement he added: "so that psycho-analysis may claim a high place among the sciences which are concerned with the earliest and more obscure periods of the human race".

37. The proposal began to appear around 1912. See the important editorial note in *Moses and Monotheism;* XXIII, 102.

38. Freud specifies as archaic heritage what is excluded from the individual's personal experience or acquisition: what "was innately present in him at his birth, elements with a phylogenetic origin" (*Moses and Monotheism;* XXIII, 98). In this heritage are included the disposition to react and to develop in a certain manner, a characteristic of all living organisms within their species, but also the disposition to react in a way distinctive from that of other individuals. This latter is the "constitutional factor" in the individual. The conjectural element enters with Freud's inclusion of rudimentary memory traces.

39. Lecture X, "Symbolism in Dreams", of the *Introductory Lectures on Psycho-Analysis;* XV, 165.

40. *Ibid.*, p. 160.

41. *Ibid.*, p. 166.

42. *Ibid.*, p. 168.

43. *Ibid.*, p. 166. See also *Moses and Monotheism;* XXIII, 99.

44. Lecture XIII, "The Archaic Features and Infantilism of Dreams", of the *Introductory Lectures on Psycho-Analysis;* XV, 199. See also *Moses and Monotheism;* XVIII, 98f.; *The Interpretation of Dreams;* V, 350-404.

45. Lecture XXIII, "The Paths to the Formation of Symptoms", of the *Introductory Lectures on Psycho-Analysis;* XVI, 371.

46. Letter 69 (21.9.97); cf. Letter 54 (24.1.97); *The Origins of Psycho-Analysis,* pp. 216, 188-190 (Standard Edition; I, 260); "Further Remarks on the Neuro-Psychoses of Defence"; III, 161, n. 1.

47. Lecture XXIII, "The Paths to the Formation of Symptoms", of the *Introductory Lectures on Psycho-Analysis;* XVI, 370f. This seems to be Freud's first definite reference to the inheritance of primal phantasies. Though the text of this thesis speaks only of archaic memory traces in the individual, one would naturally

and rightly infer that Freud alleged their presence in the group as well: "In my opinion there is an almost complete conformity in this respect between the individual and the group: in the group too an impression of the past is retained in unconscious memory traces" (*Moses and Monotheism;* XXIII, 94).

48. Passages on the Oedipus complex abound in the Freudian corpus. It was described for the first time in print in *The Interpretation of Dreams;* IV, 260-266; and was given its name in "A Special Type of Choice of Object Made by Men (Contributions to a Psychology of Love I)"; XI, 171. Other important facets of the complex are described in *Totem and Taboo;* XIII, 141-146, 149, 160f., etc.; *The Ego and the Id;* XIX, 31-39; "The Dissolution of the Oedipus Complex"; XIX, 173-179.

49. At first, Freud declared the complex in small girls to be "precisely analogous" to that in small boys (*The Ego and the Id;* XIX, 32). But from 1925 on, he introduced important distinctions and fresh insight into his exposition. See "Some Psychical Consequences of the Anatomical Distinction Between the Sexes"; XIX, 248-258, and the Editor's Note, pp. 243-247; "Female Sexuality"; XXI, 225-243; Lecture XXXIII, "Femininity", in the *New Introductory Lectures on Psycho-Analysis;* XXII, 112-135. To the end of his life, Freud admitted to the obscurities with which the more complex sexual development of women was still surrounded.

50. See the discussion of *Oedipus Rex* and *Hamlet* in Letter 71 (15.10.97); *The Origins of Psycho-Analysis,* pp. 223f. (Standard Edition; I, 265f.); *The Interpretation of Dreams;* IV, 261-266.

51. *Totem and Taboo;* XIII, 141-146, 149, 160f., cf. pp. 125f. Freud discusses anthropological works of the time which arrived at the same conclusions. Ultimately, all of them trace their parentage to the theories of Charles Darwin (p. 142, n. 1).

52. It was explicitly so called in "Thoughts for the Times on War and Death", XIV, 292f.; *An Autobiographical Study; XX,* 68; *Moses and Monotheism;* XXIII, 135.

53. *Totem and Taboo;* XIII, pp. 142f., n. 1.

54. On Freud's fascination with antiquity and social anthropology, see the Editor's Note to *Totem and Taboo;* XIII, xf.; Ernest Jones, *Sigmund Freud: Life and Work;* II, 381f., 200-205; and III, 307 for his views on the inheritance of acquired characteristics.

55. "The Unconscious"; XIV, 195; see n. 38 above.

56. "Analysis Terminable and Interminable"; XXIII, 240.

57. *The Ego and the Id;* XIX, 38.

58. See, for example, Draft F (18.8.94), Letter 55 (11.1.97); *The Origins of Psycho-Analysis,* pp. 96f., 184-187 (Standard Edition; 195-198, 240f.).

59. Works such as *The Future of An Illusion, Civilization and Its Discontents, Moses and Monotheism* (1927-1938), as well as the earlier *Totem and Taboo* (1913) fall into this category. See n. 1, p. 205 above.

60. *Totem and Taboo;* XIII, 159.

61. The factor of what might be called organic communication of emotional states is relatively undeveloped by Freud. Along with the concept of "character armouring", it has been brilliantly pursued by Wilhelm Reich and his students (notably, Alexander Lowen). See the bibliography.

62. Lecture XXI, "The Dissection of the Psychical Personality", of the *New Introductory Lectures on Psycho-Analysis;* XXII, 74.

63. *An Outline of Psycho-Analysis;* XXIII, 147; *Moses and Monotheism;* XXIII, 117; *The Ego and The Id;* XIX, 34-39. Edmund Bergler was particularly aware of the child's part in later disturbances. See, for example, *Parents Not Guilty of Their Children's Neuroses* (New York: Liveright, 1964).

64. *An Outline of Psycho-Analysis;* XXIII, 146f.

Chapter 3

1. "Sketches for the 'Preliminary Communication' of 1893"; I, 150; cf. *Project for a Scientific Psychology;* II, 3; I, 352. The sexual instinct is "the most unruly of all the instincts" (*Three Essays on the Theory of Sexuality;* VII, 161).

In my estimation, the statements regarding the sexual instinct in the text hold true even when one considers the aggressive instinct, which the average man at least episodically experiences in its powerful and primitive forms. It must be remembered that aggression very commonly has sexual components. Freud's early attention to it was only in the context of the evolution of the sexual instincts. The aggressive instinct is mentioned in this thesis only within the context of other considerations, though it is obviously of major importance in psychic life. There are two reasons for this. First, except for its inverted expression in masochism, it did not strike me as being one of the major Freudian themes which would correspond to traditional preoccupations in the theology of original sin. The second reason is closely related: Freud's treatment of aggression is problematic. In his early works, (e.g., *Three Essays on the Theory of Sexuality*), he discussed it only as a dimension of the sexual instinct (eg., VII, 157-160; 192f.). It was not until 1930, when he wrote *Civilization and Its Discontents,* that he gave special consideration to the aggressive and destructive instincts; and there he explained them (along with masochism) as derivatives of the controversial death instinct (see XXI, 117-122). See the remarks on masochism in the introduction to the thesis, p. 13. One might read further in this matter in Anthony Storr's *Human Aggression* (Harmondsworth: Penguin Books, 1968).

2. "The Aetiology of Hysteria"; III, 199.

3. Freud mentions three such eminent colleagues in "On the History of the Psycho-Analytic Movement"; XIV, 13-15; cf. "An Autobiographical Study"; XX, 24, 26.

4. See Ernest Jones' remarks on Jung, in *Sigmund Freud: Life and Work,* II, p. 137-151. See also *Reich Speaks of Freud,* tr. Therese Pol (New York: Noonday Press, 1967).

5. Editor's Introduction to *Three Essays on the Theory of Sexuality;* VII, 126.

6. Ernest Jones, *Sigmund Freud: Life and Work;* I, p. 350.

7. Draft D (5.94), in *The Origins of Psycho-Analysis,* pp. 86-88 (Standard Edition; I, 186f.); "On the Grounds for Detaching a Particular Syndrome from Neurasthenia under the Description 'Anxiety Neuroses' "; I, 106-111; "Sexuality in the Aetiology of the Neuroses"; III, 263-285. The unhealthy sexual conditions referred to were excessive masturbation, *coitus interruptus* and impotence or frigidity in a marriage partner.

8. See the brief discussion in the Editor's Note, *Project for a Scientific Psychology;* I, 12; I, 321; *Three Essays on the Theory of Sexuality;* VII, 168, 215f., 243.

9. Letter 52 (6.12.96), Draft K (1.1.96), in *The Origins of Psycho-Analysis,* pp. 173-181, 146-155 (Standard Edition; I, 233-239, 220-228). See p. 93 above.

10. "The Aetiology of Hysteria"; III, 191-221.

11. Ernest Jones, *Sigmund Freud: Life and Work;* I, pp. 319-324.

12. Draft M (1.1.96), in *The Origins of Psycho-Analysis,* p. 146; cf. n. 10 above.

13. Letter 69 (21.9.97), in *The Origins of Psycho-Analysis,* pp. 215f.

14. Letter 71 (15.10.97), in *The Origins of Psycho-Analysis,* pp. 233f.

15. "Sexuality in the Aetiology of the Neuroses"; III, 268-280.

16. *Ibid.,* pp. 280f.; "The Aetiology of Hysteria"; III, 191-221; "Heredity and the Aetiology of the Neuroses"; III, 143-156, etc.

17. *Three Essays on the Theory of Sexuality;* VII, 115.

18. *Group Psychology and the Analysis of the Ego;* XVIII, 90f. See also Preface to the Fourth Edition (May, 1920) of *Three Essays on the Theory of Sexuality;* VII, 134 (for reference to Plato's *"Eros"*); "Introduction to *Psycho-Analysis and the War Neuroses";* XVII, 208; " 'Wild' Psycho-Analysis"; XI, 222f.; "The Resistances to Psycho-Analysis"; XIX, 215.

19. *Three Essays on the Theory of Sexuality;* VII, 217.

20. *Five Lectures on Psycho-Analysis;* XI, 45; cf. *Three Essays on the Theory of Sexuality;* VII, 235.

21. *Three Essays on the Theory of Sexuality;* VII, 232; cf. "The Sexual Aetiology of the Neuroses"; III, 280f.

22. *Three Essays on the Theory of Sexuality;* VII, p. 180.

23. *Ibid.,* p. 169.

24. See *Three Essays on the Theory of Sexuality;* VII, 161; "Formulations on the Two Principles of Mental Functioning"; XII, 222f.

25. *Three Essays on the Theory of Sexuality;* VII, 198.

26. *Ibid.,* pp. 185-187, 203; "Character and Anal Erotism"; IX, 169-175; "On Transformations of Instinct as Exemplified in Anal Erotism"; XVII, 127-133.

27. *An Autobiographical Study;* XX, 35.

28. "A Difficulty in the Path of Psycho-Analysis"; XVII, 137.

29. *Three Essays on the Theory of Sexuality;* VII, 191.

30. *An Autobiographical Study;* XX, 35.

31. See " 'Civilized' Sexual Morality and Modern Nervous Illness"; IX, 189; "Two Encyclopaedia Articles, (B) The Libido Theory"; XVIII, 256; "On Narcissism"; XIV, 95; *The Ego and the Id;* XIX, 30.

32. Mark 4:25; cf. Matt. 13:12; Luke 8:18, 19:26.

33. *Civilization and Its Discontents;* XXI, 121, n. 1.

34. Letter 125 (9.12.99), in *The Origins of Psycho-Analysis,* pp. 303f. "The lowest of the sexual strata is auto-erotism, which renounces any psychosexual aim and seeks only local gratification. This is superseded by allo-erotism (homo- and hetero-), but undoubtedly survives as an independent tendency" (Standard Edition; I, 280).

35. *Three Essays on the Theory of Sexuality;* VII, 187.

36. *The Question of Lay Analysis;* XX, 215. See "On the Sexual Theories of Children"; IX, 209-226.

37. *The Future of An Illusion;* XXI, 47.

38. *Leonardo da Vinci and A Memory of His Childhood;* XI, 75-80; *Three Essays on the Theory of Sexuality;* VII, 238f.; "The Resistances to Psycho-Analysis": XIX, 218.

39. *Three Essays on the Theory of Sexuality;* VII, 200; *The Question of Lay Analysis;* XX, 210f.; *Group Psychology and the Analysis of the Ego;* XVIII, 143. See Ch. 1, n. 70 above.

40. *Three Essays on the Theory of Sexuality;* VII, 226, n. 1; cf. " 'A Child is Being Beaten': A Contribution to the Study of the Origin of Sexual Perversion"; XVII, 193.

41. *Three Essays on the Theory of Sexuality;* VII, 210f.

42. "The Taboo on Virginity" ("Contributions to the Psychology of Love III"); XI, 203. See also "On the Universal Tendency to Debasement in the Sphere of Love" ("Contributions to the Psychology of Love II"); XI, 184-190.

43. This sentence states in a more comprehensive fashion the Freudian dictum that sexuality is the key to the neuroses. In the words of Ricoeur: "the concepts of analytic theory are the notions that must be elaborated so that one may order and systematize analytic experience; I will call them the conditions *of possibility of a semantics of desire" (Freud and Philosophy,* p. 375).

44. "Some Psychical Consequences of the Anatomical Distinction Between the

Sexes"; XIX, 252-258; "Female Sexuality"; XXI, 225-243; Lecture XXXIII, "Femininity", in the *New Introductory Lectures on Psycho-Analysis;* XXII, 112-135; *Three Essays on the Theory of Sexuality;* VII, 144f., 195, etc.

45. "The Dissolution of the Oedipus Complex"; XIX, 173-179; *The Ego and the Id;* XIX, 31-39. Bergler has a good exposition of the pre-Oedipal phase of the formation of the super-ego, in *Parents Not Guilty,* pp. 19-51.

46. See n. 36 above; *Three Essays on the Theory of Sexuality;* VII, 177 179, *An Autobiographical Study;* XX, 37; *The Question of Lay Analysis;* XX, 223.

47. *The Ego and the Id;* XIX, 28-39.

48. See n. 64, p. 232.

49. *Three Essays on the Theory of Sexuality;* VII, 144f., n. 1 (added 1910); *Leonardo da Vinci and a Memory of His Childhood;* XI, 100; "Psycho-Analytic Notes on an Autobiographical Account of a Case of Paranoia *(Dementia Paranoides)"* (The Case of Schreber); XII, 60-62. Freud first introduced this theme in 1909 at a meeting of the Vienna Psycho-Analytic Society. See the Editor's Introduction to "Narcissism"; XIV, 69.

50. "Psycho-Analytic Notes on an Autobiographical Account of a Case of Paranoia *(Dementia Paranoides)";* XII, 61; *Three Essays on the Theory of Sexuality;* VII, 144; *Leonardo da Vinci and a Memory of His Childhood;* XI, 96. Freud was emphatic on the universality of a predisposition to homosexuality (see p. 99, n. 2 of the latter work). In the second work cited he stated: "psycho-analysis considers that a choice of an object independently of its sex—freedom to range equally over male and female objects—as it is found in early childhood, in primitive states of society and early periods of history, is the original basis from which, as a result of restriction in one direction or the other, both the normal and the inverted types develop." See his comments on "the narcissism of minor differences" in "The Taboo of Virginity" ("Contributions to the Psychology of Love III"); XI, 199.

51. "Psycho-Analytic Notes on an Autobiographical Account of a Case of Paranoia *(Dementia Paranoides)";* XII, 318; Lecture XXVI, "The Libido Theory and Narcissism", of the *Introductory Lectures on Psycho-Analysis;* XVI, 415f.; "On Narcissism"; XIV, 74f.

52. "On the Universal Tendency to Debasement in the Sphere of Love" ("Contributions to the Psychology of Love II"); XI, 181.

53. "Psycho-Analytic Notes on an Autobiographical Account of a Case of Paranoia" (The Case of Schreber); XII, 61.

54. "On Narcissism"; XIV, 73f.; cf. *Totem and Taboo;* XIII, 88-90.

55. Lecture XXVI, "The Libido Theory and Narcissism" of the *Introductory Lectures on Psycho-Analysis;* XVI, 417.

56. *Totem and Taboo;* XIII, 88-90.

57. "On Narcissism"; XIV, 76. In and after the study "On Narcissism" (1914), Freud frequently spoke of the ego as the "reservoir" of the libido: "Narcissistic or ego-libido seems to be the great reservoir from which the object-cathexes are sent out and into which they withdraw once more; the narcissistic libidinal cathexis of the ego is the original state of things, realized in earliest childhood, and is merely covered by the later extrusions of libido, but in essentials persists behind them" (*Three Essays on the Theory of Sexuality;* VII, 218; added in 1915). See also "On Narcissism"; XIV, 75; "A Difficulty in the Path of Psycho-Analysis"; XVII, 139; Lecture XXVI, "The Libido Theory and Narcissism", of the *Introductory Lectures on Psycho-Analysis;* XVI, 416; *Beyond the Pleasure Principle;* XVIII, 51; "Two Encyclopaedia Articles (B) The Libido Theory"; XVIII, 257. However, in *The Ego and the Id* (XIX, 30, n. 1), he said, "Now that we have distinguished between the ego and the id, we must recognize the id as the great reservoir of libido indicated in my paper on narcissism". (It will be recalled that only with the publication of this work in 1923 did Freud distinguish the id from the unconscious. See pp. 66f.

above.) On p. 46, he stated: "This would seem to imply an important amplification of the theory of narcissism. At the very beginning, all the libido is accumulated in the id, while the ego is still in process of formation or is still feeble. The id sends part of this libido out onto erotic object-cathexes, whereupon the ego, now grown stronger, tries to get hold of this object-libido and to force itself on the id as a love object. The narcissism of the ego is thus a secondary one, which has been withdrawn from objects".

In spite of this modification, Freud continued to speak of the ego as the reservoir of libido. See *Beyond the Pleasure Principle;* XVIII, 51f.; *An Autobiographical Study;* XX, 56 and *An Outline of Psycho-Analysis;* XXIII, 150. From other remarks, one gathers that the modification seems to have been preserved but regarded less antithetically. The ego referred to in the state of primary narcissism is the undifferentiated ego-id: "We picture some such initial state as one in which the total available energy of Eros, which henceforward we shall speak of as 'libido' is present in the still undifferentiated ego-id" (*An Outline of Psycho-Analysis;* XXIII, 149). The comprehensive nature of his use of "ego" is clear also in his remark, "The ego—but what we have in mind here is rather the id, the whole person—originally includes all the instinctual impulses" (Lecture XXXII, "Anxiety and Instinctual Life", of the *New Introductory Lectures on Psycho-Analysis;* XXII, 105).

Freud seems to have envisaged two movements out of primary narcissism towards object-choice, but nowhere did he compare or reconcile his descriptions. On the one hand, he spoke of the ego trying to claim the love invested on objects and so constitute itself as the object of libidinal movements from the id. On the other hand, he suggested that the first love was invested in the inchoate ego and through it onto other objects (thus in *An Outline of Psycho-Analysis;* XXIII, 150, he said that the state of primary narcissism in which all libido is stored up in the ego "lasts until the ego begins to cathect the ideas of objects with libido, to transform narcissistic libido into object-libido"). See the discussion in the Editor's Appendix (B "The Great Reservoir of Libido") to *The Ego and the Id;* XIX, 63-66.

58. "On Narcissism"; XIV, 85.

59. *Ibid.,* p. 75. The withdrawal constituted by secondary narcissism will clearly also involve an attempt to repress former attachments. See *The Ego and the Id;* XIX, 46; *An Autobiographical Study;* XX, 56f.

60. Lecture XXVI, "The Libido Theory and Narcissism", of the *Introductory Lectures on Psycho-Analysis;* XIV, 417.

61. "On Narcissism"; XIV, 82.

62. *Ibid.,* p. 76; "Psycho-Analytic Notes on an Autobiographical Account of a Case of Paranoia" (The Case of Schreber); XII, 68-70.

63. "Psycho-Analytic Notes on an Autobiographical Account of a Case of Paranoia" (The Case of Schreber); XII, 61. See also Lecture XXVI, "The Libido Theory and Narcissism" of the *Introductory Lectures on Psycho-Analysis;* XVI, 421f.

64. Lecture XXVI, "The Libido Theory and Narcissism", of the *Introductory Lectures on Psycho-Analysis;* XVI, 416; "On Narcissism"; XIV, 75.

65. "On Narcissism"; XIV, 100.

66. *Totem and Taboo;* XIII, 90, n. 2.

67. "On Narcissism"; XIV, 93-102.

68. *Ibid.* Cf. *Group Psychology and the Analysis of the Ego;* XVIII, 109f.

69. "On Narcissism"; XIV, 88.

70. *Ibid.,* p. 90; cf. pp. 87-90; Lecture XXVI, "The Libido Theory and Narcissism", of the *Introductory Lectures on Psycho-Analysis;* XVI, 418f.

71. "On Narcissism"; XIV, 88.

72. *Ibid.,* p. 91.

73. See *Group Psychology and the Analysis of the Ego;* XVIII, 100-128.

74. "Instincts and Their Vicissitudes"; XIV, 135.

75. *Ibid.*, p. 137.

76. *Ibid.*

77. "Instincts and Their Vicissitudes"; XIV, 138f.

78. *Group Psychology and the Analysis of the Ego;* XVIII, 115. Affection grows from sexual impulsions which have been modified in their aims.

79. "On the Universal Tendency to Debasement in Love" ("Contributions to the Psychology of Love II"). XI, 180f.

80. "On Narcissism"; XIV, 100.

81. See Rom. 8:39; Song of Songs 7:6f.

82. See, for example, "On Narcissism"; XIV, 88-91.

83. *Freud and Philosophy*, p. 154.

84. See, for example, "Femininity", of the *New Introductory Lectures on Psycho-Analysis;* XXII, 135.

Chapter 4

1. An arch dismissal of Freud is impossible for the honest and intelligent investigator. The violence done to his contribution is reminiscent in its forms of the violence done to St. Thomas' contribution: the formation of rigid and stagnant groups of followers, compromise and dilution of points of impact, acquaintance through secondary sources only.

An example of "exclusive attention to his hypothetical sociological works" can be seen in an article by P. Grelot, entitled "Péché originel et rédemption dans l'épître aux Romains. Freud devant la théologie paulinienne", *Nouvelle Revue Théologique*, XC, 4 (1968), 449-478. The critique centers almost entirely on *Moses and Monotheism*, in which Freud gave his own explicit doctrine of original sin and a blatantly reductionist view of the Judaeo-Christian tradition. As the author rightly (and easily) points out, Freud's inadequate understanding of the latter leaned heavily on liberal studies in the history of religion that now seem so overweening and dated. Attention is paid to some rather obviously relevant insights, but in the last analysis, a redoubtable spokesman is disposed of in much the same way he, Freud, disposed of the Judaeo-Christian reality.

2. See A. Vanneste, "La préhistoire du décret du concile de Trente sur le péché originel", *Nouvelle Revue Théologique*, LXXXVI, 4 (1964), p. 359. He notes that only good sense and adhesion to Catholic dogma prevented certain Augustinian authors from slipping into Manichaeism.

3. J. P. Kenny, "Concupiscence", in the *New Catholic Encyclopedia*, IV, p. 122.

4. St. Thomas Aquinas, *Summa Theologiae*, I-IIae, Q. 82, a. 3: "Peccatum originale materialiter quidem est concupiscentia; formaliter vero, defectus originalis iusititias". On integritas, see Karl Rahner, "The Theological Concept of Concupiscentia", in *Theological Investigations*, tr. Cornelius Ernst (Baltimore: Helicon Press, 1961), I, pp. 347-382.

5. "If anyone denies that the guilt of original sin is forgiven by the grace of our Lord Jesus Crist which is given in baptism, or even asserts that not everything that is truly and properly sin is removed, but says it is only smoothed away (*radi*) or not imputed: let him be anathema. For in the reborn God hates nothing, because 'there is nothing to be condemned in those who have been truly buried with Christ through baptism into his death' [Rom. 6, 4], those who 'walk not according to the flesh' [Rom. 8, 1], but putting off the old man and 'putting on the new, created' according to God [cf. Eph. 4, 22ff.; Col. 3, 9f.], have been made beloved sons of God, innocent, immaculate, pure and sinless, 'heirs indeed of God, co-heirs with Christ' [Rom. 8, 17], so that entrance to heaven is completely open to them.

"This holy Synod however confesses and believes that there remains in the baptized concupiscence or tinder (*fomes*), which, since it is left for the sake of struggle, cannot hurt those who do not consent to it, but manfully fight it off by the grace of Jesus Christ. Rather, 'he will be crowned who has lawfully struggled' [2 Tim. 2, 5]. The holy Synod declares that the Catholic Church has never understood this concupiscence remaining in the reborn to be sin in the true and proper sense even though the Apostle sometimes calls it sin because it is from sin and inclines to sin. If anyone holds the contrary, let him be anathema" (Canon 5 of Decree on Original Sin, the Council of Trent. DS 1515. Translation mine).

6. "A Difficulty in the Path of Psycho-Analysis"; XVII, 143.

7. "Le passage où saint Paul s'explique sur ce point [le problème du *peccatum originale originatum*] avec le plus de clarté est le chapitre 7 de l'épître aux Romains"

(P. Grelot, "Péché originel dans l'épître aux Romains", p. 338). In an (appreciative) review of Grelot's exegesis, A.-M. Dubarle says: "Dans l'Ecriture le péché originel originé tient plus de place que le péché originant. Il est l'objet d'une considération directe dans Rom 7 et non pas simplement d'une allusion latérale comme dans Rom 5" ("Le péché originel: recherches récentes et orientations nouvelles", *Recherches scientifiques, philosophiques et théologiques*, LII, 1 (1969), 86f.) Marc Oraison notes that there is no passage in Scripture more complete and explicit on the Christian notion and psychology of sin than Romans 7 and 8 ("Psychologie et sens du péché", in *Le Péché*, M. Oraison and Others, [Bruges: Desclée de Brouwer, 1959], p. 48).

8. See the magisterial study by S. Lyonnet in *Les étapes de l'histoire du salut selon l'épître aux romains* (Paris: Editions du Cerf, 1969). He indicates the growing consensus in exegesis of Romans 7 by quoting from the note to v. 15 in the *Traduction Oecuménique de la Bible:* La pensée de Paul se transcrirait assez exactement en termes d'aliénation (au sens profond de ce mot, conforme à son étymologie: appartenir à un autre). Le péché aliene l'homme, en ce sens qu'il l'engage dans un destinée qui contredit ses aspirations profondes et la vocation à laquelle Dieu l'appelle" (pp. 159f).

9. "In our eyes, the demons are bad and reprehensible wishes, derivatives of sexual impulses that have been repudiated and repressed. We merely eliminate the projection of these mental entities into the external world which the middle ages carried out; instead we regard them as having arisen in the patient's internal life, where they have their abode" ("A Seventeenth Century Demonological Neurosis"; XIX, 72). See n. 4, p. 205 above.

10. "Some Additional Notes on Dream Interpretation as a Whole"; XIX, 133f.

11. Reason, in Western culture, has always heavily implied an orientation "outwards" despite Socrates' attempt to direct philosophy towards self-knowledge and to assert the primacy of a moral problematic. It has been seen as the capacity to understand the self in terms of external reality (which is epitomized in the knowledge of God's law). This has left us with a definition of human spirituality as unrooted reason-will coping with intransigent reality. Thus the Western view of man's spirituality issues in a technological explosion of control over environment, and we find Descartes the supreme philosophical consequence and symbol of this view of reason, regretting passionately the years of man wasted in childhood, when reason is unable to stand as critical observer to all reality (including the body). Cf. the discussion by Aarne Siirala, *Divine Humanness*, tr. T. A. Kantonen (Philadelphia: Fortress Press, 1970), pp. 115-117.

12. "A Difficulty in the Path of Psycho-Analysis"; XVII, 142.

13. St. Thomas, whose initial framework manifests some of the dichotomizing tendency described in the note on reason, gives many evidences of breaking out of it to the more whole and interiorized concept of reason-will. Nowhere is this more finely evident than in the treatise on law. Law is first seen as God's external instruction to man (I-IIae, Q. 90, prologue), but he pursues a path of interiorizing law at the two crucial poles of natural law and the New Law. Natural law becomes man's self-determination on the basis of inner drives; one could aptly call it the operation of spiritual instinct (I-IIae, Q. 91, a. 2). The New Law is seen only secondarily as a written law and primarily and essentially as "the grace of the Holy Spirit, which is given to believers in Christ" (I-IIae, Q. 106, a. 1). I am indebted for the remarks in nn. 11 and 13 to discussions with T. P. McKenna and (n. 13) to the unpublished lectures of the late Rev. I. Eschmann.

14. *Beyond the Pleasure Principle;* XVIII, 34.

15. Some results of this research are accessible to the lay reader in recent works by Simeons, Luce, Janov and Weil. See the bibliography.

16. "With such emphasis laid on concupiscence as a force hostile to God, the

thought of its 'naturalness' and of its possibly positive function in the attainment
of human salvation was bound to be lost sight of. But the recognition that concupiscence is present even in the redeemed (Rom. 7:5, 8:8; 13:14; Gal. 5:24), and
its link with the sin of Adam in the history of salvation, would eventually raise
the question of the relationship of concupiscence to human nature as such and
of its concrete manifestations" (Leo Scheffczyk, "Concupiscence", in *Sacramentum
Mundi. An Encyclopedia of Theology*, I, p. 404). Karl Rahner cites the general
tendency to identify concupiscence and (personal) sin as a reason for the obscurity
so characteristic of the doctrine of original sin: "Original sin is sometimes regarded
in an univocal way even by Christians, misinterpreting the Church's teaching, as
the same as personal sin, if not in its cause at least in its nature (as 'habitual' sin).
The problems thus created (a collective guilt produced by someone else) then
cause original sin to be either accepted as a 'mystery' or rejected as an intrinsic
contradiction" ("Original Sin", in *Sacramentum Mundi*, IV, p. 328). Dubarle says
of St. Paul's thought—which is the most definitive word of Revelation on original
sin—that while he "does not consider the present state of mankind, in which sin
comes from the flesh by a sort of necessity, entirely normal", nor does he "consider that every difficulty or need for struggle is the result of sin". Our troubles
may, at least to some extent, be part of the divine pedagogy (*The Biblical Doctrine
of Original Sin*, pp. 190f.).

   17. Namely, in Canon 5 of the Tridentine Decree on Original Sin (see n. 5
above). In this text, the Church declared that concupiscence which remains in the
baptized is not "sin in the true and proper sense". On the other hand, it defines
concupiscence as from sin and inclining to sin, so that the text cannot be used
to vindicate the distinction between natural self-alienation and the alienation
which is the fruit of sin that is being urged in this discussion. Leo Scheffczyk remarks: "When the Council of Trent, in apparent contradiction to this 'natural'
interpretation, declares that concupiscence 'comes from sin and inclines to sin'
(D792), the assertion is made in the perspective of the history of salvation and
sees the concrete form and the actual intensity of concupiscence in strict dependence on sin. But because even here, in its clearest expression as a factor in the
economy of redemption, concupiscence presupposes a natural condition, it remains possible to maintain its natural structure and at the same time to attribute
to it a sort of ethical ambivalence. This leaves room for a positive evaluation of
the spontaneous movements of passion and a general rehabilitation of human 'sensuality' " ("Concupiscence" in *Sacramentum Mundi*, I, p. 404). See also J. P. Kenny,
"Concupiscence", in the *New Catholic Encyclopedia*, IV, p. 122.

   18. The Tridentine description of primaeval innocence is very restrained. The
Council anathematized denial that man was constituted in justice and holiness,
and that, in losing it, he incurred the anger of God, death, subjection to the
devil, and a vitiated state of body and soul. (Cf. DS 1511). Though the statements
of the Councils of Carthage (416 A.D.) and Orange (529 A.D.) were taken over
almost literally in the Tridentine pronouncements, the Carthaginian profession
that man would not have died if he had not sinned (DS 222) was omitted. See the
discussion by Piet Schoonenberg, *Man and Sin*, tr. Joseph Donceel (University of
Notre Dame Press, 1965), pp. 157-177. It might be noted that "le décret promulgée
par le Concile de Trent (1546) est le seul enseignement solennel de l'Eglise catho-
lique sur le péché originel. Les canons de conciles provinciaux antérieurs, important
pour leur influence sur les théologiens, n'ont pas été repris tels quels à Trente et leur
approbation totale et sans restriction par les papes est fort douteuse" (Dubarle, "Le
péché originel: recherches récentes et orientations nouvelles", p. 112).

   19. See the discussion by Peter de Rosa in *Christ and Original Sin* (Milwaukee:
Bruce, 1967), pp. 81f. He notes that the gifts of Adam's special knowledge and his
freedom from pain were less widely held. See also Michael J. Cantley, "The

Biblical Doctrine of Original Sin", in *Proceedings of the Catholic Biblical Society of America,* XXII (1967), pp. 147-150.

20. The reference here is to the weight St. Augustine placed on a variant reading of Rom. 5:12, a reading reinforced in the Latin rendering by Ambrosiaster and adopted in the Vulgate. In this interpretation, one only rarely accepted by modern exegetes, all men are sinners because "in Adam" all have sinned. A second and more probable reading, which prevailed among the Greek Fathers and is adopted in the Revised Standard Version and the Bible of Jerusalem says that sin entered the world through one man and has spread throughout the world "because" all men have ratified it by their personal sins. Still another interpretation of the Greek is possible: by reason of the sin and death introduced into the world, all men have sinned. See the note to this verse in the English edition of the Bible of Jerusalem. In short, one interpretation of a verse so ambiguous and one which departed from that of most of the earlier Greek Fathers cannot support the weight of the very specific doctrine St. Augustine erected upon it. (He was also strongly influenced by the practice of infant baptism). See the discussions in Schoonenberg, *Man and Sin,* pp. 131-140 ("The Apostle takes original sin into account insofar as it expresses itself in personal sins; the situation of mere original sin has not yet come to life for him", p. 139); Dubarle, *The Biblical Doctrine of Original Sin,* pp. 144-171, 190-200; de Rosa, *Christ and Original Sin,* pp. 99f. Karl Rahner distinguishes a state of original integrity from its preternatural supports, and argues that it is conceivable not only as a human quality, but also as a quality of primitive man. See *Hominisation. The Evolutionary Origin of Man as a Theological Problem,* pp. 102-109.

21. Vanneste, "La préhistoire du décret du concile du Trente sur le péché originel", p. 359.

22. This view was communicated in a conversation with Professor Siirala. It prevails more implicitly in his book *Divine Humanness.* See, for example, pp. 54, 86, nn. 127, 132, pp. 165f.

23. "L'integration de la psychotherapie dans l'anthropologie chretienne", *Supplement de la Vie Spirituelle* No. 68 (1964), p. 5.

24. "Original Sin", in *Sacramentum Mundi,* IV, p. 333. Paul Lee remarks on the similarity between Freud's confrontation of religion and that of Bonhoeffer, in *Freud and the Problem of Guilt* (Harvard University Press, 1964), p. 112, n. 16.

25. As quoted in Erikson, *Young Man Luther,* p. 251. The existential and intellectual struggles of Augustine and Luther to understand man's confrontation with sin come closest perhaps to the kind of searching anthropology here insisted on as necessary. However, neither were able ultimately to give themselves distance from the tight moral categories of consciousness. This fatal flaw shows its fruits in the life-hating way subsequent ages used the work of these two giants.

26. Draft K (1.1.96), in *The Origins of Psycho-Analysis,* p. 152, or Standard Edition; I, 226. "Resistance, which is in the last resort the thing that stands in the way of the work, is nothing but the child's character, its degenerate character, which has, or would have, developed as a consequence of those experiences which one finds in conscious form in so-called degenerate cases; in these cases, however, the degenerate character is overlaid by the development of repression. In my work I dig it out, it rebels, and the patient, who started by being so civilized and well-mannered, becomes vulgar, untruthful or defiant, a malingerer, until I tell him so, and this makes him able to overcome this degenerate character" (Letter 72 (27.10.97), in *The Origins of Psycho-Analysis,* p. 226, or Standard Edition; I, 266f.).

27. St. Thomas Aquinas, *Summa Theologiae,* I-IIae, Q. 85, a. 1. St. Thomas specifies a few lines earlier in what way he is speaking of *bonum naturae:* it is as "ipsa

principia naturae, ex quibus natura constituitur, et proprietates ex his causatae sicut potentiae animae et alia huiusmodi".

28. "Le péché originel: recherches récentes et orientations nouvelles", pp. 98f.

29. "Therefore it would be contrary to the thought of the biblical author to think of the original fault as an isolated fact whose consequences do not follow the same general law as the other sins committed in the course of time. This faculty for involving the fate of a whole race is something it has in common with many other events described by the book as it continues. Only, there is a unique gravity in the first disorder of the series, for it causes the loss of a perfect harmony, which cannot be entirely restored, even though divine mercy intervenes to remedy the evil. But it does not lead to the loss of all possibility of a religious life or human development. After it, the heads of a line will be able either to better or to worsen its common fate" (Dubarle, *The Biblical Doctrine of Original Sin*, pp. 82f.). See also Louis Ligier, *Péché d'Adam et péché du monde. L'Ancien Testament* (Paris: Aubier, 1960). Michael Cantley's discussion of Adam as a corporate personality and the related Hebrew concept of history and time (wherein the present moment recapitulates the entire past and contains the entire future) is also relevant here. See "The Biblical Doctrine of Original Sin", *Proceedings of the Catholic Theological Society of America*, XXII (1967), pp. 138-141.

30. "But any attempt to claim that evil desires, to the extent that they are an affliction that preys on men, come exclusively from Adam's sin and not also from the corrupting influence of the world surrounding a child from birth, prior to any possibility of personal reaction on his part, would be going beyond the letter of the very sketchy teachings of Paul, who did not pause to describe the psychological and moral state of the first man before the Fall" (Dubarle, *The Biblical Doctrine of Original Sin*, p. 190). See also the discussion by de Rosa in *Christ and Original Sin*, pp. 98-100, and n. 20 above.

31. "Concupiscence", in *Sacramentum Mundi*, IV, p. 329.

32. Schoonenberg, "Sin", in *Sacramentum Mundi*, VI, pp. 90f.

33. Dubarle writes: "The question may be left open. But what should not create any difficulties is the recognition that in the perspective of Scripture original sin is continued, relayed and conveyed to us by the sin of the world. It is well, then, to complete and balance an oversimplified view of things by the inexhaustible riches of biblical ideas" (*The Biblical Doctrine of Original Sin*, p. 229). The identification is more clearly urged by P. Schoonenberg (*Man and Sin*, pp. 177-191). He finds that this position, which he calls a hypothetical beginning, is not in opposition to the essentials of the doctrine of original sin (as distinct from speculative developments) as they are revealed in Scripture and defined by the Council of Trent. Hulsbosch seems to identify the two (*God's Creation. Creation, Sin and Redemption in an Evolving World*, tr. Martin Versfeld (London, etc.: Sheed and Ward, 1965), pp. 50-56). Rahner's position seems very similar to Dubarle's when the latter is speaking most carefully and directly to the question. Rahner says that the history of original sin is to be read in the history of the sin of the world. "And today it is perhaps easier to see how the 'sin of the world' directly affects human existence, while original sin is less easily noted in this role. Hence the 'sin of the world' could well be the starting-point for a treatise on the sin of man, which could then be a vantage-point for an examination of original sin, since this is the 'beginning' of the sin of the world. But it is a beginning which is not merely the first temporal moment . . . and one which is unique in its kind" ("Original Sin", in *Sacramentum Mundi*, IV, p. 333). The theme common to Dubarle and Rahner that the history of original sin lies in the history of the sin of the world seems to imply an identification at least of *peccatum originale originatum* and the sin of the world. See also the discussions in Ligier, *Péché d'Adam et péché du monde. L'Ancien Testament*, pp. 165-231; Louis Monden, *Sin,*

Liberty and Law, tr. Joseph Doncell (New York: Sheed and Ward, 1965), pp. 71f.

34. *Man and Sin,* p. 139; cf. pp. 177-199.

35. *Ibid.,* pp. 132-139; Dubarle, *The Biblical Doctrine of Original Sin,* 156f.

36. Canon 3 of the Decree on Original Sin, the Council of Trent (DS 1513): "Si quis hoc Adae peccatum, quod origine unum est et propagatione, non imitatione transfusum omnibus inest unicuique proprium".

37. See Dubarle, *The Biblical Doctrine of Original Sin,* pp. 238-245; Schoonenberg, *Man and Sin,* pp. 180f., 185-187.

38. De Rosa, *Christ and Original Sin,* p. 132. (N.B. This position is only surveyed, not claimed, by de Rosa).

39. *Summa Theologiae,* I-IIae, Q. 82, a. 4. Freud said of the archaic heritage that it has to be worked over: it is unacceptable as such in our civilized social life ("Preface to Reik's *Ritual: Psycho-Analytic Studies"; XVII, 261-263). There are more or less acceptable ways of so doing, and in certain milieux, the resolution is at a more developed stage, so that one can speak meaningfully of common dispositions (See "Analysis Terminable and Interminable"; XXIII, 240; cf. p. 102 above). The unwise rearing of an individual can leave him victim to the instinctual, archaic forces within himself.

40. *The Biblical Doctrine of Original Sin,* pp. 240-242. So also Hulsbosch (*God's Creation,* pp. 54f): "If the world as a whole lies in the power of the Evil One, this power extends to the child when it is born, not in the form of personal guilt, but as a datum which is codeterminative for his relationship with God . . . The traditional conception of original sin accompanies a way of thinking in which the significance of the relationship [to the world] is underestimated, and attention directed almost exclusively to what can be referred to the individual subject . . . Actual personal relations with our fellows are therefore much more constitutive of what a man is, than common descent from one progenitor".

41. *God's Creation,* p. 50.

42. *Ibid.,* pp. 55f. Dubarle seems to agree with Hulsbosch's position, though he would formulate it more clearly (cf. "Le péché originel: recherches récentes et orientations nouvelles", pp. 96f.).

43. De Rosa, *Christ and Original Sin,* p. 111. De Rosa surveys statements to this effect by the authors cited in this paragraph (pp. 87f., p. 111).

44. An acquaintance of both Freud and Jung, Viktor von Weizsaecher, describes their differences in this respect ("Reminiscences of Freud and Jung", *Freud and the 20th Century,* ed. Benjamin Nelson (Cleveland and New York: Meridian Books, 1967).

Freud himself wrote (*From the History of an Infantile Neurosis; XVII,* p. 97): "All that we find in the prehistory of neuroses is that a child catches hold of this phylogenetic experience where his own experience fails him. He fills in the gaps in individual truth with prehistoric truth; he replaces occurrences in his own life by occurrences in the life of his ancestors. I fully agree with Jung in recognizing the existence of this phylogenetic heritage; but I regard it as a methodological error to seize on a phylogenetic explanation before the ontogenetic possibilities have been exhausted. I cannot see any reason for obstinately disputing the importance of infantile prehistory while at the same time freely acknowledging the importance of ancestral prehistory. Nor can I overlook the fact that phylogenetic motives and productions themselves stand in need of elucidation, and that in quite a number of instances this is afforded by factors in the childhood of the individual. And, finally, I cannot feel surprised that what was originally produced by certain circumstances in prehistoric times and was then transmitted in the shape of a predisposition to its re-acquirement should, since the same circumstances persist, emerge once more as a concrete event in the experience of the individual".

45. Lecture XXIII, "The Paths to the Formation of Symptoms", of the *Introductory Lectures on Psycho-Analysis;* XVI, 371.

46. "Original Sin", in *Sacramentum Mundi,* IV, p. 329.

47. "Paul's object is to extol God's way of ensuring salvation and he takes this opportunity [the reference here is to Rom. 5:12-21] to give a new insight into the origin of sin and the need of salvation for all" (Dubarle, *The Biblical Doctrine of Original Sin,* p. 144). See also Schoonenberg, *Man and Sin,* pp. 129-131.

48. Rom. 5:15.

49. Rom. 11:33-36.

50. See Is. 49:15; Hos. 11:1-4.

51. Freud once wrote the following self-description in a letter to his betrothed: "There is some courage and boldness locked up in me that is not easily driven away or extinguished. When I examine myself strictly, more strictly than my loved one would, I perceive that Nature has denied me many talents and has granted me not much, indeed very little, of the kind of talent that compels recognition. But she endowed me with a dauntless love of truth, the keen eye of an investigator, a rightful sense of the values of life, and the gift of working hard and finding pleasure in doing so" (Jones, *Sigmund Freud: Life and Work,* I, 118). In *An Autobiographical Study* (XX, 8). Freud again referred to the powerful curiosity about the riddles of Nature that had dictated his choice of life work.

52. It is of interest here to consider the development of the Wisdom tradition in the Scriptures. What began as aphoristic, practical advice to courtiers and the learned gradually expanded until Wisdom is personified as God himself and the pursuit of man's relation to God (wisdom in lower case) is seen to include a serene understanding and love of God's creation (man in particular) in all its elements and developing history. (Cf. Jerusalem Bible, Introduction to the Wisdom Books, pp. 723-725).

53. *Group Psychology and the Analysis of the Ego;* XVIII, 103. A few lines earlier he wrote: "Love for oneself knows only one barrier—love for objects" (p. 102).

54. See G. Kittel's discussion in *Bible Key Words,* tr. and ed. J. R. Coates (New York: Harper and Brothers, 1951), pp. 26-28, 38, 78.

55. See Piet Fransen's discussion of what he calls the fundamental option ("Towards a Psychology of Divine Grace", in *Cross Currents of Psychiatry and Catholic Morality,* ed. W. Birmingham and J. E. Cunneen (New York: Pantheon, 1964), pp. 31-61; Andre Snoeck, "Moral Reflections on Psychiatric Abreaction", *Theological Studies* XIII, 2 (1952), pp. 173-189; Gregory Zilboorg, *Psychoanalysis and Religion,* ed. M. S. Zilboorg (New York: Farrar, Straus & Cudahy, 1962), pp. 117-139.

56. Matt. 13:24-30, 36-43.

57. *The Biblical Doctrine of Original Sin,* pp. 140-141.

58. See Gen. 2:20-25 and 3:7, 12, 16. See the discussions in de Rosa, *Christ and Original Sin,* p. 79; Gerhard Von Rad, *Genesis: A Commentary,* tr. J. H. Marks (London: SCM Press, 1961), pp. 89, 97.

59. New perspectives on original sin, notably the tendency to associate it with the sin of the world, have led to a re-emphasis on the ancient concept of baptism as the initiation to a saving community, a dying out of the sin of the world. Hulsbosch writes: "The existence of the child cannot be abstracted from his surroundings. Just as for physical well-being he is dependent on adults, so for spiritual development he is bound up with the community in which he is born and reborn. Thus baptism is not merely a transaction between God and the child, but also puts the child into the sacred space of the Church, which is necessary to the living out of his supernatural orientation to God which is given in baptism. Baptism withdraws the child from the world as the domain of the enemy. It frees the child from the compulsive power of sin" (*God's Creation,* pp. 252f.).

60. See Canon 5 of the Decree on Original Sin (DS 1515); it is quoted in n. 5, pp. 249f. above.

61. "The Dynamics of Transference"; XII, 99.

62. *Ibid.*, p. 108.

63. *Ibid.*, p. 103.

64. *Ibid.*, p. 108.

65. *An Autobiographical Study;* XX, 43 (italics mine).

66. Ibid., p. 42. For other texts on transference see "On Beginning the Treatment"; "Remembering, Repeating and Working Through"; "Observations on Transference-Love" ("Further Recommendations on the Technique of Psycho-Analysis", I, II, III respectively); XII, 121-171.

67. Schoonenberg states the same relationship, though without much elaboration. He is arguing for a concept of original innocence more in line with modern scientific discovery and theory. It is possible "to explain the freedom from concupiscence *(immunitas a concupiscentia, integritas)* before the fall and the presence of concupiscence since the fall by admitting a modification not in the relation between body and soul, but in the relation of man's freedom to the world. Hence, there would be a situation of integration in love, or its possibility, before the fall versus a nonintegrated striving of all man's tendencies, on account of a lack of love, after the fall. If one understands the doctrine of original sin in this way, there is no difference in this respect from what we have said above about the implications of 'being situated' through the sin of the world" *(Man and Sin,* p. 182).

68. See for example pp. 41f. of *The Politics of Experience and the Bird of Paradise* (Harmondsworth: Penguin Books, 1967).

69. *Freud and Philosophy,* p. 536. Ricoeur points to Freud's exposition of Eros—the sexual and self-preservative instincts—and its relationship to the God of Deuteronomy and Hosea, the God of John Who is Light and Love.

70. *Ibid.*, p. 551.

BIBLIOGRAPHY

Books and Pamphlets

Aquinas, St. Thomas. *Summa Theologiae*. Prima Pars (I), Prima Secundae (I-II). Rome: Marietti, 1950.

Beinaert, Louis. *Expérience chrétienne et psychologie*. Paris: Editions de l'Epi, 1964.

Bergler, Edmund. *Parents Not Guilty of Their Children's Neuroses*. New York: Liveright, 1964.

Birmingham, William and Joseph E. Cunneen, eds. *Cross Currents of Psychiatry and Catholic Morality*. New York: Pantheon, 1964.

Braceland, Francis J., ed. *Faith, Reason and Modern Psychiatry*. New York: P. J. Kenedy and Sons, 1955.

Dalbiez, Roland. *Psychoanalytic Method and the Doctrine of Freud*. Translated by T. F. Lindsay. London and New York: Longmans, Green, and Co., 1941.

Delhaye, P., A. Gélin et al. *Théologie du Péché*. Tournai: Desclée, 1960.

Denziger, Henricus and Adolphus Schonmetzer. *Enchiridion Symbolorum. Definitionem et Declarationum de rebus fidei et morum*. 32nd ed. Barcelona, Fribourg: Herder, 1963.

✓ De Rosa, Peter. *Christ and Original Sin*. Milwaukee: Bruce Publishing Company, 1967.

Dominian, J. *Psychiatry and the Christian*. Vol. 93 of the *Twentieth Century Encyclopedia of Catholicism*. New. York: Hawthorn, 1962.

✓ Dubarle, A.-M. *The Biblical Doctrine of Original Sin*. Translated by E. M. Stewart. New York: Herder and Herder, 1964.

Erikson, Erik. *Young Man Luther*. New York: W. W. Norton and Co. Inc., 1962.

Freud, Sigmund. *Letters of Sigmund Freud*. Edited by Ernest L. Freud. Translated by Tania and James Stern. New York, Toronto, London: McGraw-Hill, 1964.

————. *The Standard Edition of the Complete Psychological Works of Sigmund Freud*. Translated from the German under the General Editorship of James Strachey, in collaboration with Anna Freud; assisted by Alix Strachey and Alan Tyson. 24 vols. London: Hogarth Press and the Institute of Psycho-Analysis, 1955-. (Index and bibliography volume still in preparation.)

————. *The Origins of Psychoanalysis: Letters to Wilhelm Fleiss, Drafts and Notes, 1887-1902*. Edited by Maria Bonaparte, Anna Freud, and Ernst Kris. Translated by Eric Mosbacher and James Strachey. New York: Basic Books, 1954.

Freud, Sigmund and Oskar Pfister. *Psychoanalysis and Faith: The Letters of Sigmund Freud and Oskar Pfister*. Edited by Heinrich Meng and Ernst T. Freud. New York: Basic Books, 1963.

Goldbrunner, Josef. *Holiness Is Wholeness and Other Essays*. Translated by Stanley Godman. University of Notre Dame Press, 1964.

Hesnard, A. *Morale sans péché*. Paris: Presses Universitaires de France, 1954.

✓ Hulsbosch, A. *God's Creation. Creation, Sin and Redemption in An Evolving World*. Translated by Martin Versfeld. London: Sheed & Ward, 1965.

Janov, Arthur. *The Anatomy of Mental Illness: The Scientific Basis of Primal Therapy*. New York: G. P. Putnam's Sons, 1971.

Jones, Ernest. *Sigmund Freud: Life and Work*. 3 vols. London: Hogarth, 1953-57.

Keenan, Alan. *Neurosis and Sacraments*. New York: Sheed & Ward, 1950.

Kittel, G. *Bible Key Words*. Translated and edited by J. R. Coates. New York: Harper and Brothers, 1951.

Klein, Melanie. *The Psychoanalysis of Children.* Translated by Alix Strachey. London: Hogarth, 1959.

Laing, R. D., *The Politics of Experience and The Bird of Paradise.* Harmondsworth: Penguin Books, 1967.

Lee, Paul Albert. *Freud and the Problem of Guilt.* Harvard University Press, 1964.

Ligier, Louis. *Péché d'Adam et péché du monde: L'Ancien Testament.* Paris: Aubier, 1960.

Lowen, Alexander. *The Language of the Body.* (Originally published as *Physical Dynamics of Character Structure*). New York: Collier Books and London: Collier-Macmillan Ltd., 1971.

Luce, Gay Gaer. *Body Time. Physiological Rhythms and Social Stress.* New York: Pantheon Books, 1971.

Luce, Gay Gaer and Segal, Julius. *Sleep.* New York: Lancer Books, 1966.

Lyonnet, S. *Les étapes de l'histoire du salut selon l'épître aux romains.* Paris: Editions du Cerf, 1969.

Margolis, Joseph. *Psychotherapy and Morality. A Study of Two Concepts.* New York: Random House, 1966.

Monden, Louis. *Sin, Liberty and Law.* Translated by Joseph Donceel. New York: Sheed and Ward, 1965.

Nelson, Benjamin, ed. *Freud and the 20th Century.* 11th printing. Cleveland and New York: Meridian Books, 1967.

Odier, Charles. *Les deux sources, consciente et inconsciente de la vie morale.* Neuchâtel: Ed. de la Baconnière, 1943.

Oraison, Marc, et al., eds. *Le Péché.* Bruges: Desclée de Brouwer, 1959.

Oraison, Marc. *Une Morale pour notre temps.* Paris: Fayard, 1967.

Rahner, Karl. *Hominisation. The Evolutionary Origin of Man as a Theological Problem.* Translated by W. T. O'Hara. Freiburg: Herder, 1965.

————. *Theological Investigations.* Vol. I. Translated by Cornelius Ernst. Baltimore: Helicon Press, 1961.

Reich, Wilhelm. *Character Analysis.* Translated by Theodore P. Wolfe. Third and enlarged edition. New York: Noonday Press, 1961.

————. *The Emotional Plague of Mankind: Vol. I. The Murder of Christ.* Translated by Theodore P. Wolfe. New York: Noonday Press, 1966.

————. *The Function of the Orgasm.* Translated by Theodore P. Wolfe. New York: Noonday Press, 1961.

————. *Listen, Little Man!* Translated by Theodore P. Wolfe. New York: Noonday Press, 1968.

————. *The Mass Psychology of Fascism.* Translated by Mary Boyd Higgins. New York: Noonday Press, 1970.

————. *Reich Speaks on Freud.* Edited by Mary Boyd Higgins and Chester M. Raphael. Translated by Therese Pol. New York: Noonday Press, 1967.

————. *Selected Writings.* New York: Farrar, Straus & Cudahy, 1960.

————. *The Sexual Revolution.* Translated by Theodore P. Wolfe. New York: Noonday Press, 1962.

Renckens, Henricus. *Israel's Concept of the Beginning. The Theology of Genesis 1-3.* Translated by Charles Napier. New York: Herder & Herder, 1964.

Ricoeur, Paul. *Freud and Philosophy.* Translated by Denis Savage. New Haven and London: Yale University Press, 1970.

————. *The Symbolism of Evil.* Translated by Emerson Buchanan. New York: Harper and Row, 1967.

Rondet, Henri. *Notes sur la théologie du péché.* Paris: P. Lethielleux, 1957.

Schoonenberg, Piet. *Man and Sin. A Theological View.* Translated by Joseph Donceel. University of Notre Dame Press, 1965.

Siirala, Aarne. *Divine Humanness*. Translated by T. A. Kantonen. Philadelphia: Fortress Press, 1970.

Simeons, A. T. W. *Man's Presumptuous Brain. An Evolutionary Interpretation of Psychosomatic Disease*. London: Longmans, Green and Co., Ltd., 1960.

Stern, Karl. *The Pillar of Fire*. New York: Harcourt, Brace & Company, 1951.

Storr, Anthony. *Human Aggression*. Harmondsworth: Penguin Books, 1968.

Suttie, Ian D. *The Origins of Love and Hate*. Harmondsworth: Penguin, 1963.

Szasz, Thomas S. *Law, Liberty and Psychiatry*. New York: Macmillan, 1963.

Vanderveldt, James H. and P. Odenwald. *Psychiatry and Catholicism*. New York, Toronto, and London: McGraw-Hill, 1957.

Vergote, A. *Psychologie religieuse*. Bruxelles: Dessart, 1966.

Von Rad, Gerhard. *Genesis: A Commentary*. Translated by John H. Marks. London: SCM Press, 1961.

Weil, Andrew. *The Natural Mind*. Boston: Houghton-Mifflin Co., 1972.

White, Victor. *Soul and Psyche*. London: Harvill, and New York: Harper, 1960.

Zilboorg, Gregory. *Freud and Religion*. Woodstock Papers, No. 3. Westminster, Maryland: The Newman Press, 1964.

————. *Mind, Medicine and Man*. New York: Harcourt, Brace and Co., 1943.

————. *Psychoanalysis and Religion*. Edited by Margaret Stone Zilboorg. New York: Farrar, Straus & Cudahy, 1962.

————. *Sigmund Freud*. His Exploration of the Mind of Man. New York: Charles Scribner's Sons, 1951.

Articles and Parts of Books

Alonso-Schökel, Luis. "Sapiential and Covenant Themes in Gensis 2-3", *Theology Digest*, XIII, 1 (1965), 3-10.

Bartemeier, Léo H. "Psychanalyse et Religion", *Supplément de la Vie Spirituelle*, 80, XX (1967), 176-184.

Baum, Gregory. "Prospective Theology", *The Ecumenist*, VIII, 5 (1970), 72-75.

Beirnaert, L. "Does Sanctification Depend on Psychic Structure?" *Cross Currents*, I, 2 (1951), 39-43.

————. "L'intégration de la psychothérapie dans l'anthropologie chrétienne", *Supplément de la Vie spirituelle*, 68, XVII (1964), 3-7.

Buber, Martin. "Guilt and Guilt Feelings", *Cross Currents*, VIII, 2 (1958).

Cantley, Michael J. "The Biblical Doctrine of Original Sin", *Proceedings of the Catholic Theological Society of America*, XXII (1967), 133-171.

Casey, R. P. "Oedipus Motivation in Religious Thought and Fantasy", *Psychiatry*, V (1942), 212-228.

Choisy, Maryse. "Psychoanalysis and Catholicism", in *Cross Currents of Psychiatry and Catholic Morality*. Edited by William Birmingham and Joseph E. Cunneen. New York: Pantheon, 1964, pp. 62-83.

Dalmais, I. "Original Justice", in *God and His Creation*. Vol. II of *Theology Library*. Edited by A. M. Henry. Translated by Charles Miltner. Chicago: Fides, 1955.

Dominian, J. "Psychanalyse et vie spirituelle", *Supplément de la Vie Spirituelle*, 88, XXII (1969), 29-44.

Dubarle, A.-M. "Le Péché originel: recherches récentes et orientations nouvelles", in *Recherches des Sciences Philosophiques et Theologiques*. LII, 1 (1969), 81-113.

Feiner, Joannes. "Man's Origin and Contemporary Anthropology", in *Renewal in Dogma*, Vol. I of *Theology Today*. Edited by Johannes Feiner and others.

Translated by Peter White and Raymond H. Kelly. Milwaukee: Bruce Publishing Company, 1965.

Fransen, Piet. "Towards a Psychology of Divine Grace", in *Cross Currents of Psychiatry and Catholic Morality*. Edited by William Birmingham and Joseph E. Cunneen. New York: Pantheon, 1964, pp. 31-61.

Graef, H. C. "Eros et Agapè", *Supplément de La Vie Spirituelle*, 12, III (1950), 99-105.

✓ Grelot, P. "Péché originel et redemption dans l'épître aux Romains. Freud devant la théologie paulinienne", *Nouvelle Revue Théologique*, XC, 4 (1968), 337-362.

Hunt, I., and C. J. Peter. "Original Sin", in the *New Catholic Encyclopedia*. New York: McGraw-Hill, 1967. Vol. X, 776-781.

Kenny, J. P. "Concupiscence", in the *New Catholic Encyclopedia*. New York: McGraw-Hill, 1967. Vol. IV, 121-125.

Lohfink, Norbert. "Genesis 2-3 as Historical Etiology", *Theology Digest*, XIII, 1 (1965), 11-17.

Mailloux, N. "Déterminisme psychique, liberté et développement de la personnalité", *Supplément de la Vie Spirituelle*, 22, V (1952), 257-276.

Maritain, Jacques. "Freudianism and Psychoanalysis", in *Cross Currents*, VI, 4 (1956), 307-324.

Oraison, Marc. "A propos de l'action thérapeutique du sacrement de pénitence", *Supplément de la Vie Spirituelle*, 31, VII (1954), 412-430.

Peter, C. J. "Original Justice", in the *New Catholic Encyclopedia*. New York: McGraw-Hill, 1967. Vol. X, 774-776.

――――. "Original Sin", in the *New Catholic Encyclopedia*. New York: McGraw-Hill, 1967. Vol. X, 776-781.

Plé, Albert. "L'Acte morale et la 'pseudo-morale' de l'inconscient", *Supplément de la Vie Spirituelle*, 40, X (1957), 24-68.

――――. "Saint Thomas d'Aquin et la psychologie des profondeurs", *Supplément de la Vie Spirituelle*, 19, IV (1951), 402-434.

――――. "Sexualité et culpabilité", *Supplément de la Vie Spirituelle*, 72, XVIII (1965), 143-151.

✓ Rahner, Karl. "Evolution and Original Sin", *Concilium*. Edited by Johannes Metz et al. New York and Glen Rock: Paulist Press, 1967. Vol. XXVI, 61-73.

✓ ――――. "Monogenism", *Sacramentum Mundi. An Encyclopedia of Theology*. Edited by Karl Rahner and others. New York: Herder and Herder; London: Burns and Oates, 1969. Vol. IV, 105-107.

✓ ――――. "Original Sin", *Sacramentum Mundi. An Encyclopedia of Theology*. Edited by Karl Rahner and others. New York: Herder and Herder; London: Burns and Oates, 1968. Vol. IV, 328-334.

Rimaud, Jean. "Psychologists versus Morality", *Cross Currents*, I, 2 (1951), 26-38.

✓ Scheffczyk, Leo. "Concupiscence", *Sacramentum Mundi. An Encyclopedia of Theology*. Edited by Karl Rahner and others. New York: Herder and Herder; London: Burns and Oates, 1968. Vol. I, 403-405.

✓ Schoonenberg, P. "Sin", *Sacramentum Mundi. An Encyclopedia of Theology*. Edited by Karl Rahner and others. New York: Herder and Herder; London: Burns and Oates, 1968. Vol. VI, 87-94.

Smulders, Piet. "Evolution and Original Sin", *Theology Digest*, XIII, 3 (1965), 172-176.

Snoeck, Andre. "Moral Reflections on Psychiatric Abreaction", *Theological Studies*, XIII, 2 (1952), 173-189.

Vanneste, A. "La Préhistoire du decret du Concile de Trente sur le péché originel", *Nouvelle Revue Théologique*, LXXXVI (1964), 355-368, 494-510; LXXXVII (1965), 688-726; LXXXVIII (1966), 581-602.

THE SURVIVOR

THE
SURVIVOR

AN ANATOMY OF LIFE IN THE DEATH CAMPS

TERRENCE DES PRES

OXFORD UNIVERSITY PRESS
Oxford   New York   Toronto   Melbourne

Oxford University Press
Oxford   London   Glasgow
New York   Toronto   Melbourne   Wellington
Nairobi   Dar es Salaam   Cape Town
Kuala Lumpur   Singapore   Jakarta   Hong Kong   Tokyo
Delhi   Bombay   Calcutta   Madras   Karachi

Portions of this book have been previously published elsewhere: Chapter 1 in
Encounter (September 1971); Chapter 2 in *Social Research* (Winter 1973);
part of Chapter 5 in *Dissent* (Winter 1976); *Moment* (February 1976); and *Harper's* (February 1976).

Library of Congress Cataloging in Publication Data

Des Pres, Terrence.
The survivor.

Bibliography: p.
1. Holocaust, Jewish (1939-1945)—Psychological
aspects. 2. Concentration camps—Psychological aspects.
I. Title.
D810.J4D474   1980   940.54'72   79-21479
ISBN 0-19-502703-5 pbk.

printing, last digit: 20 19 18 17 16 15 14 13

PREFACE

My subject is survival, the capacity of men and women to live beneath the pressure of protracted crisis, to sustain terrible damage in mind and body and yet be there, sane, alive, still human. I am not directly concerned with the concentration camps, but with the people who suffered those places, who endured that evil and returned to bear witness. Even so, an experience such as theirs cannot be understood apart from its context, and in the following pages there is much description, amounting almost to a comprehensive view, of camp conditions. Unavoidably, a spectacle of death and mutilation opens upon us, an endless silent scream rising to a sky forever heedless of men's anguish. But what mattered most for survivors—and what matters now for us—is a different aspect of the camp ordeal. Their testimony reveals a world ruled by death, but also a world of actual living conditions, of *ways of life* which are the basis and achievement of life in extremity. It turns out that survival is an experience with a definite structure, neither random nor regressive nor amoral. The aim of this book has been to make that structure visible.

And how does one handle this subject? One doesn't; not well, not finally. No degree of scope or care can equal the enormity of such events or suffice for the sorrow they encompass. Not to betray it is as much as I can hope for. The work itself took nearly four years, years of reading through vast amounts of eyewitness testimony, of cutting through accepted notions of the camp experience, of informal talk with survivors, and finally, before getting firmly underway, a time of search for a way to set myself in relation to them.

I could not take a stance of detachment, could not be "clinical" or "objective" in the way now thought proper. A curious fact about language, which Tolstoy and then Hemingway used to advantage, is that to write about terrible things in a neutral tone or with descriptions barren of subjective response tends to generate an irony so virulent as to end in either cynicism or despair. On the other hand, to allow feeling much play when speaking of atrocity is to border on hysteria and reduce the agony of millions to a moment of self-indulgence. There seemed one language left —a kind of archaic, quasi-religious vocabulary, which I have used not as a reflection of religious sentiment, but in the sense that only a language of ultimate concern can be adequate to facts such as these.

As for point of view, I gradually came to see that I would have to stay within the survivor's own perspective. This will perhaps bother the historian, with his distrust of personal evidence; but radical suffering transcends relativity, and when one survivor's account of an event or circumstance is repeated in exactly the same way by dozens of other survivors, men and women in different camps, from different nations and cultures, then one comes to trust the validity of such reports and even to question rare departures from the general view. I had little choice, therefore, but to proceed by a dense use of quotation, by constant reference to examples and stories bearing the survivor's immediate authority. The book thus becomes a compilation of actual testimony—the voices of many men and women gathered to a critical mass of rage and sorrow and truth. My job has been to provide a medium through which these scattered voices might issue in one statement.

The survivor is the figure who emerges from all those who fought for life in the concentration camps, and the most significant fact about their struggle is that it depended on fixed activities: on forms of social bonding and interchange, on collective resistance, on keeping dignity and moral sense active. That such thoroughly *human* kinds of behavior were typical in places like Buchenwald and Auschwitz amounts to a revelation reaching to the foundation of what man is. Facts such as these discredit the claims of nihilism and suggest, further, that when men and women must face months and years of death-threat they endure less through cultural than through biological imperatives. The biological sciences have begun to point in the same direction, and toward the end of the book I have incorporated some of their broader insights to clarify what survivors mean when they speak of *a talent for life,* or of life as a *power,* or of their reliance on *life in itself.* But here the reader should not be misled: speculation about the relation between survival behavior and basic life-processes is speculation only. The experience itself is what counts. An agony so massive should not be, indeed cannot be, reduced to a bit of datum in a theory.

In the concentration camps, as everyone knows, vastly more people died than came through. Statisticians may therefore wish to quarrel with my concern for the survivors. Fernand Braudel, a historian I greatly admire, argues that human destiny is shaped by sheer weight of numbers. Perhaps so, but that is not the issue here. We must not, in any case, confuse history with the constituent activities of selfhood. The image of the survivor includes any man or woman striving to keep life and spirit intact—not only those who returned, but the hundreds of thousands who stayed alive sometimes for years, only to die at the last minute. Nor do I think that numbers are as significant as the fact that survival behavior reveals typical forms of response to extremity.

I have tried to keep a wide range of reference, and to draw on descriptions from as much of the camp world as possible. For reasons which will be apparent, documentation of the Nazi experience is more extensive than that of its Soviet counterpart. And although the survivor is anyone from any corner of Europe or the Soviet Union (and often far beyond), this book is very much about the fate of the Jews, who fared worst in both German and Russian camps. But finally it is with ordinary people that I am concerned; with how they felt and what they did. At moments, the possibility that in some of the camps not one man or woman survived has caused a sense of futility strong enough to make going on seem pointless. Did anyone come back from Chelmno? Yet if no more than a dozen men and women stayed human and came through, if only the barest trace of humanness was *there* in the whole of that world, the survivor's experience would still be invaluable. And as Albert Camus put it, "human evidence must be preserved."

Hamilton, New York   T.D.P.
May 1975

ACKNOWLEDGMENTS

I began this book while a Junior Fellow at Harvard, and to the Society of Fellows, especially to Wassily Leontief and Reuben Brower, I owe an endless debt. I also owe special thanks to Alan Heimert, Master of Eliot House, who saw to it that I had a place to live and work unbothered. The book was completed while teaching at Colgate University, and for the kind support of my colleagues, Robert Blackmore in particular, I am most grateful. I received aid and encouragement from many people—friends, scholars, and not least the survivors I have come to know personally. At critical moments, assistance came from Lionel and Diana Trilling, E. O. Wilson, Patricia Blake, Liz Kornblee, Frederick Busch and James Raimes. Most of all I thank Stephanie Golden and Anthea Waleson.

CONTENTS

THE SURVIVOR

THE SURVIVOR IN FICTION

The writer's role is not free of difficult duties. By definition he cannot put himself today in the service of those who make history; he is at the service of those who suffer it.

ALBERT CAMUS

EACH THING, said Spinoza in the "Ethics," *insofar as it is in itself, endeavors to persevere in its being.* That may not be true for rocks and stars, but for societies and men it is undeniable. Survival of the body and its well-being take priority over everything else, although this imperative is transcended and lost sight of when the machinery of civilization is working as it should. The remarkable fact, however, is that while the business of living goes forward from day to day we reserve our reverence and highest praise for action which culminates in death. I am referring to images of the hero in Western religion and literature, and here there is no doubt: our serious models draw their sanction and compelling force from death. Those who for centuries have commanded love and imitation—Christ, Socrates, the martyrs; the tragic hero always; the warrior from Achilles to the Unknown Soldier—all are sacrificial victims, all resolve conflict by dying and through death ensure that the spirit they spoke or fought for shall not perish. The pattern is so honored and familiar that a connection between heroism and death seems natural.

The struggle to survive, on the other hand, is felt to be suspect. We speak of "merely" surviving, as if in itself life were not worth much; as if we felt that life is justified only by things which negate it. The contradiction is real; it goes to the root of how we envision death in relation to life, and I shall try to account for it. We may find, in the end, that the hero's death is appointed—that one of the functions of culture is to provide symbolic systems which displace awareness of what is terrible, and that through death the hero takes upon himself the condition of victimhood and thereby grants the rest of us an illusion of grace. Dying gods and sacrificial victims have regularly attended the rise of civilizations; and often, as in the case of Greek tragedy, societal well-being and ritual death seem inseparable. The problem now is that symbolic manipulations of consciousness no longer work. Death and terror are too much with us.

Men have always been ready to die for beliefs, sacrificing life for higher goals. That made sense once, perhaps; but no cause moves without live men to move it, and our predicament today—as governments know—is that ideas and ideologies are stopped by killing those who hold them. The "final solution" has become a usual solution, and the world is not what it was. Within a landscape of disaster, places like Auschwitz, Hiroshima or the obliterated earth of Indo-China, where people die in thousands, where machines reduce courage to stupidity and dying to complicity with aggression, it makes no sense to speak of death's dignity or of its communal blessing. We require a heroism commensurate with the sweep of ruin in our time: action equal to situations in which it becomes less self-indulgent and more useful to live, to be there. History moves, times change, men find themselves caught up in unexpected circumstance. The grandeur of death is lost in a world of mass murder, and except for special cases the martyr and his tragic counterpart are types of the hero unfit for the darkness ahead. When men and women must live against terrible odds, when mere existence becomes miraculous, to die is in no way a triumph.

If by heroism we mean the dramatic defiance of superior individuals, then the age of heroes is gone. If we have in mind glory and grand gesture, the survivor is not a hero. He or she is anyone who manages to stay alive in body *and* in spirit, enduring dread and hopelessness without the loss of will to carry on in human ways. That is all. What this kind of struggle entails, and in what the survivor's "humanness" consists, are the joint themes of this book. They are also themes in important recent novels, and although in a strict sense I am concerned only with the experience of actual survivors, fiction serves here as it has always served: it provides images whose formal purity brings some part, at least, of the world's confusion to focus. Existence in extremity is not an easy subject. It is hard to approach and harder still to understand. Through fiction, however, some start can be made, some framework fixed which mediates the difference between that world and ours.

In novels by Camus and Malamud, accordingly, survival is represented as an action with a political outcome. Here the survivor is a protagonist in the classic sense, for by staying alive he becomes an effective agent in the fight against evil and injustice. The survivors in Solzhenitsyn's novels, on the other hand, change nothing. To keep life and decency intact is the limit of their achievement. But by choosing not only to live, but to live humanly, they take upon themselves the burden of an action requiring much will and courage, much clearsightedness and faith in life.

One more distinction: because the traditional hero chooses to find consummation in death, he controls the condition for his fulfillment. The survivor's choice is not absolute in the same way. To stay alive is of course the whole point, but unlike those who die deliberately, the survivor can never be sure of success. Any day sickness or the whim of a vicious guard can cut short the struggle. That is one more circumstance the survivor must face. If he or she should die, it is the fight to live and not the manner of dying which matters. And finally there is this: in extremity, the bare possibility of survival is not enough. There must also be a move beyond despair and self-pity to that fierce determination which survivors call up in themselves. To come through; to keep a living soul in a living body. ∎

The first condition of extremity is that there is no escape, no place to go except the grave. It is like a city under siege, Paris in 1870, Leningrad of the 900 days, or like the town of Oran in *The Plague:* "But once the town gates were shut, every one of us realized that all . . . were . . . in the same boat, and each would have to adapt himself to the new conditions of life" (61). So begins Camus' allegory of the extreme situation. New conditions become "normal conditions—in other words, the plague" (166); and this, in its immense power, is like "the slow, deliberate progress of some monstrous thing crushing out all upon its path" (163). The city becomes a "victim world," and the old order is transformed. Schools turn into hospitals, the stadium becomes a quarantine camp, streetcars are used as death wagons. This is a world in which living and dying are no longer held separate; in which the forms of life are determined by death.

The plague is ubiquitous and no place is safe. Death waits at home, in the street, on the stage; and slowly the condition of anti-life, because it cannot be veiled in myth or held in the balance of combat, becomes anti-human as well. Subject to this pressure and unable to draw inspiration from traditional forms of courage-in-adversity, the people of the town suffer general collapse. They despair, become selfish and mean; they will not face facts, and behave as if asleep. Confronted with a terror that has no foretellable end, they are reduced to helplessness. If they had been attacked by something on the human scale, an invasion of hostile neighbors for example, the citizens of Oran would have rallied to the cause and given their lives as the martyr and the patriot have always done. But the extreme situation is not an event, not a period of crisis with its proper beginning, middle and end. It is a state of existence which persists beyond the ability of men to alter or end it. And because there is no opportunity for one all-out effort, no single battle to be fought come what may, the honored forms of heroism fail as models for action and spiritual support. A sense of impotence prevails and dehumanization sets in. Against *this* enemy the people of the town see no way left to act.

Extremity requires an attitude which allows men and women to act, and thereby to keep faith in themselves as something more than victims. First of all, then, the survivor is not a victim merely. He refuses to see his victimization as total, fights it as best he can, and will not consent to death in any form. He will not, that is, accept the logic of the situation imposed upon him. So there are two kinds of people in *The Plague,* the "townspeople" and the "volunteers." Both react to the plague, the former on its terms, the latter on terms partially their own. The "townspeople" remain subject to necessity, at one with the situation destroying them. The "volunteers" respond to the same necessity, but by opposing it. They turn reaction into action self-directed, and in this way move far enough beyond death's rule to keep themselves intact as human beings. Rieux, Tarrou and their co-workers pit themselves against the plague, with no conviction of success, but only determined not to stand idle while others suffer. Together, therefore, they organize hygienic programs, they tend the stricken, they dispose of the dead. They work twenty hours a day amid the stench and agony of the dying, spending themselves in that endless, empty time of day upon day, without the encouragement of visible progress, without the hope of a positive end in sight, and always with the knowledge that death may win. They carry on all the same, because "they knew it was the only thing to do" (121).

It is plainly the human thing to do. In ordinary times, to protect the living, aid the sick and bury the dead are taken for granted as elementary forms of human activity. In extremity, however, simply continuing to do one's job as part of the human community becomes difficult to the point of heroism. Yet Camus insists that his protagonists are not heroic in a traditional sense. As Rieux puts it: "there's no question of heroism in all this. It's a matter of common decency. . . . Heroism and sanctity don't really appeal to me. . . . What interests me is being a man" (150, 231). Rieux's characteristic understatement serves to point up the humility, the hardminded realism and rejection of drama which are essential to the survivor's outlook. His is a matter-of-factness rooted in the knowledge that survival *depends* on staying human. That, in fact, is the great theme of *The Plague*, and although to be human under pressure takes extraordinary effort, there is really no alternative: "The only means of fighting a plague is—common decency" (150). Hard as it is, therefore, the survivor's struggle is without glamor or special destiny. Camus' "volunteers" are doing what anyone should do, and doing it simply to live. As Rieux concludes: "there was nothing admirable about this attitude; it was merely logical" (122).

The tragic hero finds in death a victory. Thereby he places

himself beyond compromise, beyond the erosion of time, and the truth for which he stood is solemnized, pressed deep in the hearts of his audience through the drama of his sacrifice. He is proof of spirit's contempt for the flesh, and death itself becomes the confirmation of greatness. There is much to be admired in such a stance, but not in time of plague. For the survivor all things— himself, his works, the race of man—are painfully mortal, and when all are endangered there may be no audience to count on. Hemingway has said of the tragic hero that he is "destroyed but not defeated," implying a capacity to stand firm to the end. The survivor too stands firm; but for those who choose life, to die is to lose. ■

The Plague can be read as an account of France under Nazi occupation, and *The Fixer,* to which I now turn, is based on a notorious case of anti-Semitism (the Beiliss trial in Kiev in 1913). Camus and Malamud, each in a way peculiar to his art and personal experience, are responding directly to the climate of atrocity which like a leveling wind has touched and unsettled every aspect of existence in our century. Their vision is informed by genocide and the concentration camps, and it becomes particular through individuals caught up in events which threaten to destroy not only populations but the human spirit itself. "We're dealing nowadays," says Malamud's small hero, "with the slaughter of large numbers and it's getting worse" (258). Against an evil so vast, individual actions seem slight indeed, in no way victorious or spectacular, but not, for all that, without intense significance. Individual men and women, either alone or in concert with their fellows, must still be *there,* in that place at that time, and by the fact of their existence be proof that no matter how bold and massive the machinery of power becomes it does not prevail.

Yakov Bok leaves the pale, goes to Kiev, and finds himself in the hands of his enemies, "unjustly accused, helpless, unable to offer proof or be believed" (104). His fate is like the larger fate of the Jews: "Overnight a madman is born who thinks Jewish blood is water. Overnight life becomes worthless. . . . So what can Yakov Bok do about it?" (274). If he dies, nothing, and that he will die is probable: "It was a natural thing for prisoners to die in prison. They died like flies all over Russia" (273). Accused of killing a Christian child, the fixer is held for two years in prison where every pressure against life and mind, short of outright murder, is inflicted upon him. With only a rabid anti-Semitism to support its case, the government is afraid to bring him to public trial. The alternative is to break his spirit and obtain a confession, while at the same time arranging conditions which will increase the probability of sickness and accident—in the hope that, once more, death will resolve an otherwise unresolvable situation.

The fixer is held in isolation and has no sense of the political situation, but he knows that if the government should "prove" its case, the Black Hundreds will be vindicated and pogroms will wring yet more blood from his people. Against this possibility he will do what he can. To die in prison would be to accept his role as victim and confirm his appointed guilt. Therefore he must stay alive, and by refusing to disappear in death, force the government to bring him to trial. His mission, he comes to see, is simply to survive: "Therefore he must endure to the trial and let them confirm his innocence by their lies. He has no future but to hold on, wait it out" (274).

To hold on and wait are imperatives which define the survivor's struggle, but against what? Against conditions opposed to life as we know it, conditions which civilization works to transcend and keep us, the lucky ones, from falling back into—random death and spiritual vacuum, physical anguish and empty time. The fixer lives in an unrelieved state of physical pain, enduring unmet needs for food, air, sanitation and light, as well as intenser moments of sickness and beating. His existence is a closed circuit of physical-spiritual erosion which the tragic hero, his moment of agony surpassed in the glory of death, knows little of. This is the undramatic, unglorified sorrow of the body, a permanent part of the human condition which most of us prefer to ignore in favor of "inner" suffering—as if mind and body were separate worlds. But pain which goes on and on seeps through body *and* mind, and in this as in other respects, survival inverts the values of civilization. Physical existence can no longer be dismissed as unworthy of concern. The body's will and the will of the spirit must join in common cause.

The survivor must personally oppose conditions which the edifice of civilization was built to transcend. Structured time, the blessing of a foundation for measure and purposive action, is one of civilization's great gifts. But in extremity the forms of time dissolve, the rhythms of change and motion are lost. Days pass, seasons, years pass and the fixer has no idea how long his ordeal will go on: "Time blew like a steppe wind into an empty future. There was no end, no event, indictment, trial" (238). His predicament is not a crisis, not a determinate span in a curve of significant time. It is an emptiness complete in itself, a suspension in the sameness of identical days which could last a year or a lifetime. Russian prisons have been notorious for lives spent this way, and the fixer could remain in his cell, a young man becoming an old man, without so much as a sentence to measure the the waste of his life. The death of time destroys the sense of growth and purpose, and thereby undermines faith in the possibility that any good can come from merely staying alive. This too the survivor must face and withstand.

Holding on, the fixer is repeatedly forced to recognize that "whenever he had been through the worst, there was always worse" (295). The spirit's element is space, and among other things civilization is the creation of a steady space in which our humanity can freely hatch and thrive. It is a space of sustaining plenitude, a network of meaning and interchange, the matrix of human communion. Certainly it is not an empty space, for nothing, we are sure, can live in a vacuum. But for the fixer, the emptiness of time is compounded by the emptiness of total isolation. The one man with whom he communicates is murdered, the only other men he sees are his jailors. He has no contact with the world outside, no sense of his plight as part of a larger whole. His life, his suffering, seem severed from human community, and he is forced to endure with the thought that "he suffers for no one except himself" (240).

But as a man unjustly condemned, he *is* connected to others, to the Jews first of all and then to men and women everywhere who like himself are the victims and scapegoats of power. At first he insists that he is not a "political person." But gradually his suffering brings home to him the pain of all men in extremity, and he comes finally to realize that when the exercise of power includes the death of innocent people, "there's no such thing as an unpolitical man" (335). The "political person," in the pure sense Malamud intends, is the man or woman conscious of the individual's implicit relation to the community of others, and therefore the person who takes intelligent action to make explicit and effective this vital connection of one to all. For the fixer, intelligent action means to survive and by his irreducible presence, by refusing to go away or be simply a victim, to force the government to expose itself by bringing him to trial. ∎

Survivors do not choose their fate and would escape it if they could. They are trapped in a world of total domination, a world hostile to life and any sign of dignity or resistance—a world, finally, in which an anti-human order is maintained by the bureaucratic application of death. Here, to remain alive and human demands not only a certain kind of action, as we have seen, but also a radical shift in the sense of selfhood. Survivors are uncommonly conscious of limits and foundations, of the strength to be found in innocence, and especially of the sustaining power which life itself provides when all else has been stripped away. Precisely because it does not die or give up, the self comes upon itself and the ground of itself as it could never do while enjoying the delicate, efflorescing extensions of selfhood which civilization creates and fosters. From this experience comes a special integrity, a clearness of vision indispensable to those for whom, outwardly, helplessness and victimization are major facts of existence.

No novelist has described this kind of consciousness better than Solzhenitsyn. His survivor is the man in love with his people and their cause, the man who stood against the Nazi onslaught only to find himself thrown into a slave camp; this same man, helpless but unreconciled to his fate, determined to remain innocent and unbroken under conditions specifically devised to crush out life and spirit. His energies burn with the pointed fury of an extreme tension between the will to live and the will to remain pure—between an almost mystical thirst for life and an unwavering refusal to capitulate, sell out, or in any way become accessory to a system which reduces men to puppets and meat. He rejects the benefits of abdication and, powerless, chooses not to compromise. Thereby he becomes a sliver in the throat of power, and is proof, to himself and others who would join him, that men and women can sustain enormous damage and still go on as human beings.

Shukhov, the hero of *One Day in the Life of Ivan Denisovich*, is this kind of man. He has been unjustly imprisoned, and has lived through years of sub-zero weather without decent clothing or a warm place to sleep, rising each day before the sun to twelve hours of heavy labor on a starvation diet. He steers his life through sickness and exhaustion, through the random cruelty of camp procedure and the betrayal of fellow prisoners, and yet he is not broken: "even eight years as a convict hadn't turned him into a jackal—and the longer he spent at the camp the stronger he made himself" (142). Shukhov is willing to give way to other prisoners, to perform services for men he respects, but he will not make a deal with those in power, never inform, never do a favor for the cooks or ask one of them. He has developed the *zek*'s special ability to cheat the officials and camp regulations, by which he saves his strength and now and then gets an extra bowl of soup (these are major victories), but he will not cheat others in the same situation as himself. And through it all he maintains an elementary sense of self-respect: "Every nerve in his body was taut, all his longing was concentrated in that cigarette butt—which meant more to him now, it seemed, than freedom itself—but he would never lower himself . . . he would never look at a man's mouth" (40).

Due to his situation as much as to his character, Shukhov has come a long way in the wisdom of simplicity. He has learned to extract sharp satisfaction—a sense of animal well-being which saves him from self-pity and despair—from slight and infrequent moments of pleasure. Working with his squad to build a wall (the temperature is $-17°$), Shukhov is inspired to delight by the rhythm of the work and the interplay of skills. He enjoys the warmth which spreads through his body, and later, the firmer joy of a job well done. He has come to appreciate, deeply and to the full, every inch of life that transcends pain and hopelessness. By far the most important event in his life is food, and like all of Solzhenitsyn's characters, Shukhov has developed an extraordinary attitude toward the watered soup and black bread which sustain him. Eating becomes a small ritual, an experience which provides a physical ground for faith in the value of life. Souptime is for Shukhov a "sacred moment," a revelation deep in the body's pleasure that, at bottom and in spite of everything, life is strong and worth its pain:

> Shukhov took off his hat and laid it on his knees. He tasted one bowl, he tasted the other. Not bad—there was some fish in it. . . .
> He dug in. First he only drank the broth, drank and drank. As it went down, filling his whole body with warmth, all his guts began to flutter inside him at their meeting with that stew. Goo-ood! . . .
> And now Shukhov complained about nothing: neither about the length of his stretch, nor about the

> length of the day, nor about their swiping another Sun-
> day. This was all he thought about now: we'll survive.
> We'll stick it out, God willing, till it's over (136).

He eats his soup and bliss wells up like a benediction, like an extravagant blessing, as though this second bowl, tricked from the cooks, were life's finest gift. Shukhov attains that rarest of moments, when a person is simply, and against all evidence, happy to be alive. The importance of food to people starving is perhaps not easy for us to imagine. It is even more difficult for us to understand that this man's affirmation is made in the middle of a concentration camp.

But the whole point of *One Day* is that such a man exists in such a place. Surrounded by the inhumanity of man and nature, Shukhov has made a life for himself, with its gross imbalance of pain and pleasure, privation and fulfillment. And to a slight but crucial degree it is *his* life, affirmed anew in each violation of camp regulations, in each moment of pleasure. He knows, of course, that *this* day was uncommon for luck, and that pain is the substantial element in which he must live. But he has come to terms with it, transcended his victimization by refusing self-pity or the temptation to hope for anything but life itself, and then gone on to find what goodness he can in the life he has. Like all survivors, he has squarely faced the basic problems of existence in extremity. The first is how not to despair. The second, how to keep moral sense and dignity intact. ∎

Like thousands of actual P.O.W.'s, Shukhov was sent to the camps because during the war he had been captured by the Germans. According to his interrogator, "he'd surrendered to the Germans with the intention of betraying his country" (71). Millions of men and women under Soviet rule were imprisoned for similar—and similarly insane—reasons. In *The First Circle*, Gerasimovich becomes a *zek* for "intent to commit treason," Kagan for "failure to inform." These strictly imaginary crimes were defined and made real by *Article 58* of the penal code. Anyone who stood out, either by accident or decision, sooner or later could expect to be arrested—anyone incompatible with the system in which he or she was trapped. The Soviet camps were full of people arrested *because* they were innocent, because they would not cooperate with evil, because they possessed the integrity to think and judge for themselves. In *Cancer Ward* Kostoglotov and his fellow students get seven years plus exile: "We used to come together, court the girls, dance; but the boys also talked about politics. And about HIM. . . . In May, just before the examinations, we were all arrested, the girls too" (193).

When a government rules by force and falsehood, when people are murdered in great numbers and the prisons are jammed with men and women who even the interrogators know are innocent, then to escape involvement becomes impossible. Some work with the system, become murderers. Others—millions—become victims. Still others watch and pretend they do not see. Many men and women were swept into the Soviet camps by pure accident. They happened to be in the wrong place at the right time, they became part of a quota. But there was always an outside chance that if one stayed far enough in the background and was very quiet, one might be overlooked. In a totalitarian state which uses the threat of imprisonment to maintain its power, an element of choice thus arises. In *Cancer Ward* Shulubin, bitter because he saw and remained silent, quotes Pushkin:

> **In this our age of infamy**
> **Man's choice is but to be**
> **A tyrant, traitor, prisoner;**
> **No other choice has he.**

People still free must decide how much their "freedom" is worth: how many lies they will live by, how far they will acquiesce while their neighbors are destroyed. The choice is always there. Those arrested for "failure to inform" might have decided to go along with the police that far at least. Kostoglotov and his friends did not have to discuss politics, did not have to criticize HIM. "If one is forever cautious, can one remain a human being?" (3). So thinks Innokenty Volodin, the young diplomat in *The First Circle* whose simple act of humanity will send him into the camps. In extremity that question is everyman's. Each must decide how he or she will reconcile the desire for life and comfort with the desire for purity and self-respect. In relation to this choice, each character in Solzhenitsyn's world takes his or her position on a scale of moral being which reaches from monstrosity to sainthood.

The low end is occupied by men in positions of authority: petty bureaucrats, state officials, Stalin first of all. Minister of State Security Abakumov, for example, is the model of official success: "it turned out that Abakumov conducted interrogations effectively; his long arms were an asset when it came to smashing people in the face" (72). His talent has brought him close to Stalin, increasing the chance of a bullet in the neck, and his dread filters down through the hierarchy, each man beneath the heel of the man above him. All the ministers, bureaucrats, jailors, etc. who serve the system comprise the "they" to which the *zeks* refer, men without character or depth, the product of the machine they service. And although their safety is never assured, they are one kind of survivor, a kind to be found in the camps as well. Siromankha, king of the camp informers in *The First Circle,* is a kind of survivor whose behavior is legendary. He is one of "those who, as camp guards, could club their countrymen in the face; those who, as bread cutters and cooks, could eat the bread of others who were starving" (466). Plainly, there is more than one way to survive, and a point after which the heroism of survival turns into its opposite. The distinction is between those who live at any price, and those who suffer whatever they must in order to live humanly. As Solzhenitsyn sums it up, "The wolfhound is right and the cannibal is wrong" (401).

There are, then, prisoners who have come into the camps not because they gave up, but because they refused to give up. They are there because they persist in the desire to preserve their innocence and to keep themselves intact as human beings. This desire, and the possibility of this choice, is the axis of concern in *The First Circle*. Foremost among Solzhenitsyn's band of survivors, and the center of moral intelligence in the novel, is Gleb Nerzhin, "a prisoner in his fifth year in harness who never hurries because he expects only worse from what lies ahead" (37). Like Solzhenitsyn himself, Nerzhin was arrested at the front for private criticism of Stalin, and given a ten-year term. He is a mathematician, brought to the special prison at Mavrino after four years of labor in the northernmost camps. Mavrino, by comparison, is a godsend: "Hands not flayed with work. Fingers not frozen" (42). Here the *zeks* are scientists and technicians, but they are forced to work on the refinement of a special technology—devices which will serve the growth of totalitarian control. Most of them only pretend to work, but anyone who directly refuses to cooperate is certain to be in the next transport back to the camps, which means—

> Perhaps he will not arrive at his destination. In a cattle car he may die either of dysentery or of hunger, because the zeks will be hauled along for six days without bread. Or the guard may beat him with a hammer because someone has tried to escape. Or, at the end of the journey in an unheated car, they may toss out the frozen corpses of the zeks like logs (558).

At Mavrino Nerzhin is forced to work, but he does not give himself to the purpose imposed upon him. His desk is piled with books and folders, but "in fact, it was all a false front" (19). His real work is a collection of notes in which he analyzes the failure of the Revolution—how, that is, history purifying itself came to result in concentration camps. But then he is called before the officials and asked to volunteer for a special project, and this he will not do. If he were to agree, he might earn his release. His refusal, on the other hand, "was certain to result, perhaps very soon, in a long and arduous journey to Siberia or the Arctic, to death or to a hard victory over death" (65). Other prisoners, like Rubin and Sologdin, decide to work for their freedom (and Solzhenitsyn allows them a sympathetic understanding). But Nerzhin is uncompromising; he will keep himself pure and take his chances. As soon as the decision is made his spirit begins to shore its strength, drawing on the survivor's special wisdom:

> Nerzhin . . . was now thinking that only the first year of camp could finish him, that he had achieved a completely different tempo, that he would not try to scramble into the ranks of the goldbrickers, that he would not be afraid of camp labor, but would slowly, with an understanding of life's depths, go out for morning line-up in his padded jacket smeared with plaster or fuel oil and tenaciously drag through the twelve-hour day—and so on, for the whole five years remaining until the end of his term. Five years is not ten. One can last five (136).

That is the survivor's predicament: like the "volunteers" in *The Plague,* he must be prepared to run risks which keep him alive by bringing him closer to death. The odd thing is that Nerzhin expects to gain in strength and in knowledge by an existence so radically pared down—as if *there,* at the absolute limit of body and soul, truths might be found on which a human being may firmly build. "Camp life," Solzhenitsyn tells us, "exceeds in its ruthlessness anything known of the lives of cannibals and rats" (208). But at the same time he speaks of "the harsh apprenticeship of camp" (388). To what can that refer, if not to the apprenticeship of one's own soul, to the crystallization of that essence all men and women share but seldom realize or even acknowledge? As Nerzhin puts it, "one must try to temper, to cut, to polish one's soul so as to become *a human being*" (389). That recalls Shukhov: "the longer he spent at the camp the stronger he made himself." It seems clear that the ordeal of survival becomes, at least for some, an experience of growth and purification.

By virtue of the extraordinary demands made upon men and

women in extremity, their struggle to live humanly involves a process of becoming more—essentially, firmly—human. Not the humanness of refinement and proliferation, of course, but of the fundamental knowledge of good and evil, and of the will to stand by this knowledge, on which all else depends. Nerzhin says: "I had no idea what good and evil were, and whatever was allowed seemed fine to me. But the lower I sink into this inhumanly cruel world, the more I respond to those who, even in such a world, speak to my conscience" (515). For this kind of survivor, the way down is the way up.

Like other types of the hero, survivors take their stand directly on the line, but they are unique in that they *stay* there. And it is there, in the balance of being and non-being, that their peculiar freedom becomes real and effective. Their vision is not clouded by sheltering illusions; they do not suddenly, in the ambush of crisis, discover their mortality, for in order to remain alive they must at every moment acknowledge the centrality of death. This familiarity has not failed to breed a proper contempt: survivors may be killed, but as long as they live they will not be afraid. And closer to death, survivors are rooted more urgently in life than most of us. Their will to survive is one with the thrust of life itself, a strength beyond hope, as stubborn as the upsurge of spring. In this state a strange exultation fills the soul, a sense of being equal to the worst. And as long as they live, survivors *are* equal to the worst. This, finally, is the attitude of those *zeks*—Nerzhin, Gerasimovich and their friends—who at the end of *The First Circle* are shoved into a meat truck and shipped off to the camps:

> Concentrating on the turns the van was making, the zeks fell silent.
> Yes, the taiga and the tundra awaited them, the record cold of Oymyakon and the copper excavations of Dzhezkazgan; pick and barrow; starvation rations of soggy bread; the hospital; death. The very worst.
> But there was peace in their hearts.
> They were filled with the fearlessness of those who

have lost *everything,* the fearlessness which is not easy
to come by but which endures (579). ■

Having fought against the Nazi invasion, Solzhenitsyn's survivors are also soldiers, and that is how they think of themselves
as day by day they withstand extremity with the modest tactics
which keep them alive. "A soldier gets along best on the defensive" (89), says Kostoglotov in *The Cancer Ward;* and in
fact the survivor's struggle is very much like guerrilla warfare—
"tactical offensives within the strategic defense," as Mao Tse-
tung defined it (157). But the survivor's enemy is death, and in
the end he is a soldier who can never hope for more than small
and temporary victories. The cancer ward is death's home field,
and those who find themselves there have no thought but to survive, to employ any medical tactic which may strengthen their defense. They fight as best they can, but since death will not retreat,
they must come to terms with their situation so as to live beyond
fear and despair: "In the face of death, in the face of the striped
panther of death who had already lain down beside him, in the
same bed, Vadim, as a man of intellect, had to find a formula for
living" (293). Kostoglotov's answer is to live as the soldier lives:
aware of danger and ready to die, yet putting up the longest fight
possible, and regarding all men kindly but without pity as brothers in a losing war.

This hardness of the living heart is something a man like Kostoglotov cannot do without. After the war he entered the university, but before his life could begin to take shape he was arrested
and sent to the camps. After that came exile, and then cancer, so
we cannot avoid the impression that Kostoglotov, still in his thir-
ties, is an old man. The pathos of his situation is that, on the
verge of death, he is a man who never had a life—"A river that
doesn't go anywhere, that haphazardly gives away all its best water
and power along the way" (345). He has survived years of incredible hardship, missed death by a hair's breadth, only to find,

not the tree of life flaming with promise and budding fruits, but an implacable cancer which will soon shut life from him. Kostoglotov thirsts for fulfillment with a fierceness equaled only by his despair of attaining it. And having acquired in the camps "the ability to shake off all but the main thing" (170), he comes at last to the humblest kind of hope: "I want to live for a bit without guards and without pain, and that's the limit of my dreams" (345).

This is as much as he can hope for from treatment in the cancer ward:

> not for a complete new life, but for an extra portion, like the make-weight end of a loaf fastened onto the main part of the ration, a twig stuck through the two to hold them together—part of the same ration, but a separate piece (565).

The image here comes from the camp experience, and what it tells us is that the survivor only lasts. He does not reach victory or a new existence but only some "small, additional, added-on life" (566). And even that has its price, for in extremity every moment of life is purchased at exorbitant cost, forcing the survivor repeatedly to consider the balance of values. As Kostoglotov says, "I have often wondered before, and now particularly I wonder: What, after all, is the highest price one should pay for life? How much should one pay, how much is too much?" (346). The question is always there, and each turn of events requires a new answer. So it is when Kostoglotov enters the cancer ward. His chance for a bit more life depends on a hormone treatment which will deprive him of his virility, and this is the decision he must face: "To become a walking husk of a man—isn't that an exorbitant price? It would be a mockery. Should I pay it?" (346). And if he pays, what then?

> Whom shall I seek, with whom share
> The heavy-hearted joy of my survival?

In this small verse the whole of his fate is expressed. We can suppose that this lusty man would once have led a simple fruitful life, shared with the woman he has come to love. But now he must continue to live against encroaching cancer with the knowledge that he has lost everything; that love and work, children, life ripening within, will not be his to try. But he does choose to live, once more giving up a part of himself in order to preserve what he calls "the main thing." He will not stop now, because after the camps he cannot, in this last extremity, negate the only meaning his life has had; and because to continue to live, even for a few months, is worth it absolutely.

Survivors *choose* life, and the basis of their choice is apparent in the happiness of Kostoglotov's final walk through the city—his rapport with the teeming life and motion around him, the intense relish with which he eats some roasted meat, the tender gratitude he feels toward Vega for her love. It is a wonderful day, and the wisdom of his deep delight is evident: "Even if next spring never came, even if this was the last, it was one *extra* spring! And thanks be for that!" (571). Like Shukhov and like Nerzhin, he is able to respond to life's least gift with a fullness of joy which is, finally, greater and more powerful than hope. That is the survivor's small but invaluable return. In this state of mind Kostoglotov leaves the cancer ward in search of a flowering apricot tree. Not to possess it, but only for a moment's time to behold it, and allow the beauty of its delicate blossoming to confirm the enduring *Yes* he has so often and at such cost said to life.

Then back into exile. He boards the train, finds a place in the baggage rack, and settles for the journey thinking: "Others had not survived. He had survived" (615). That is all. Kostoglotov is a man without hope, but even so, he has lived as long as he could, without damage to his innocence, without harm to others. And in this effort—to carry on when ordinary avenues of life are closed and death lies visible ahead—the survivor reaches his limit. In the end he has nothing, nothing at all but this short reprieve, this extra life free and his own. The loss of particular hope opens on the power of life in itself, something unexpectedly uncovered when the spirit is driven down to its roots and through its pain is brought to a stillness and finality which—as men once said—surpasses understanding. For survivors that is enough. ∎

THE WILL TO BEAR WITNESS

Rejected by mankind, the condemned do not go so far as to reject it in turn. Their faith in history remains unshaken, and one may well wonder why. They do not despair. The proof: they persist in surviving—not only to survive, but to testify.

The victims elect to become witnesses.

ELIE WIESEL
One Generation After

During the terrible years of Yezhovshchina I spent seventeen months in the prison queues in Leningrad. One day someone recognized me. Then a woman with lips blue with cold who was standing behind me, and of course had never heard of my name, came out of the numbness which affected us all and whispered in my ear —(we all spoke in whispers there):

"Can you describe this?"

I said, "I can!"

Then something resembling a smile slipped over what had once been her face.

ANNA AKHMATOVA
Requiem

To COME from fiction to documents is to move from an ideal lucidity to the dense anguish of men and women telling as straightforwardly as they know how the story of what they saw and endured in their passage through the concentration camps. Their testimony is given in memory, told in pain and often clumsily, with little thought for style or rhetorical device. The experience they describe, furthermore, resists the tendency to fictionalize which informs most remembering. We have accepted the idea that when the past is described the narrator selects and arranges, points up and slides over, maneuvering the facts to produce an acceptable image. And no doubt that is true for men and women in civilized circumstances, where there is always more than one level of meaning to choose from, more than one way to view the facts. But the world survivors speak of has been so rigidly shaped by necessity, and so completely shared—almost all survivors say "we" rather than "I"—that from one report to the next the degree of consistency is unusually high. The facts lie embedded in a fixed configuration; fixed, we may come to believe, by the nature of existence when life is circumscribed by death.

Men and women are happy in a multitude of ways, but in sorrow's deepest moments all are one. The experience of extremity issues always in the same need and pain, always in what Barrington Moore, Jr., has called "the unity of misery" (11). We may prefer to ignore the world's anguish, and those who must bear it have seldom been articulate. But radical suffering, as Moore observes, "has been the lot of a very large portion of humanity for nearly all of recorded history. The inarticulateness of the victims, very few of whom have left any records, has to a great extent masked its extent" (11-12). By "suffering" he does not mean embattled love or yearning for God, but the gross pain of flesh and of physically uprooted lives. The First World War was the first mass disaster experienced by large numbers of people who were literate and therefore able to leave records. And what they reveal of human struggle is not high cause and glorious downfall, but defilement and dazing fear, dumb hurt and bodies rotting in mud.

In the concentration camps there was an even wider margin of literacy, and many men and women returned who if not sophisticated were certainly articulate enough to give clear accounts. Through survivors a vast body of literature has thus come into being—diaries, novels, documentary reports, simple lists and fragments, books in many languages, which all tell one story. This kind of writing is unusual for the experience it describes, but also for the desire it reveals to remember and record. The testimony of survivors is rooted in a strong need to make the truth known, and the fact that this literature exists, that survivors produced these documents—there are many thousands of them—is evidence of a profoundly human process. Survival is a specific kind of experience, and "to survive as a witness" is one of its forms. ∎

What happened in the Warsaw Ghetto is known in detail because many people made it their job to write down what they saw and experienced. The *Warsaw Diary* of Chaim A. Kaplan is one example. From September 1, 1939, when Hitler invaded Poland, until the afternoon of August 4, 1942, when Kaplan was sent to the extermination camp at Treblinka, he set down each day's disasters in a child's copybooks. At different moments he refers to his job as a "duty," as a "mission," and as a "sacred task." "My utmost concern," he tells us, "is for hiding my diary so that it will be preserved for future generations" (395). This thrust of urgent purpose never left him. He describes it, at one point, as "a flame imprisoned in my bones, burning within me, screaming: Record!" (144). Kaplan's sense of this command was absolute, and neither periods of desperation nor the coming of death could weaken the almost mystical compulsion which governs his work: "But this despair does not last forever. The spirit of dedication which had left me in my moments of spiritual agony returns, as though some hidden force were ordering me: Record!" (233).

Why this feeling was so strong, or what he expected to achieve, are issues Kaplan does not discuss. What is clear, however, is his passionate will to preserve the memory of the horror he has witnessed. And this desire was not his alone. When men and women are forced to endure terrible things at the hands of others—whenever, that is, extremity involves moral issues—the need to remember becomes a general response. Spontaneously they make it their business to record the evil forced upon them. "The drive to write down one's memoirs is powerful," observes Emmanuel Ringelblum in his *Notes from the Warsaw Ghetto;* "even young people in labour camps do it" (133). "In spite of hunger, illness and privation, there was a compulsion to record this period in all its details" (83), says David Wdowinski in *And We Are Not Saved.* Those caught were shot, but that did not keep Ringelblum and his friends from organizing a clandestine group whose job was to gather information for deposit in a secret archive (much of which survived). Here, and in similar situations, survival and bearing witness become reciprocal acts.

For most survivors the chance to speak comes later. To bear witness is the goal of their struggle. This was true, certainly, for many in the concentration camps—as Alexander Donat, for example, makes clear in *The Holocaust Kingdom.* Donat fought in the Warsaw Ghetto uprising, then went through Maidanek, Auschwitz and Dachau. From the start he had one intention: "I felt I was a witness to disaster and charged with the sacred mission of carrying the Ghetto's history through the flames and barbed wire until such time as I could hurl it into the face of the world. It seemed to me that this sense of mission would give me the strength to endure everything" (183). Donat's desire to be a witness was so strong that this task became, finally, the essence of his identity as a survivor:

> I was now an old-timer, resistant to pain and cold;
> inured to beating, opprobrium and heavy labor; insen-
> sitive to pain and unhappiness. All I retained was the
> newspaperman's greedy curiosity, the desire to see and
> find out everything, to engrave in my memory this Dan-
> tesque world (253).

Donat had been a journalist before the war, but the impulse
he describes is not limited to men and women of that profession.
"While still in the camp," says Halina Birenbaum in *Hope Is the
Last To Die,* "I decided that if I lived to see liberation, I would
write down everything I saw, heard and experienced" (244). In
Survival in Auschwitz Primo Levi recalls his drift toward fatal
indifference, and the moment when a simple expression of care
pulled him back together: "Steinlauf, a man of good will, told
me . . . that even in this place one can survive, and therefore
one must want to survive, to tell the story, to bear witness" (36).

The survivor's aim, as Margarete Buber says in *Under Two
Dictators,* is "to let the world know" (xii). Each piece of testimony by a survivor answers this need. Behind the individual witness, furthermore, lies the collective effort of many others. Here,
too, there is plenty of evidence. Most dramatic, perhaps, is what
happened at Treblinka. At the peak of operations, 15,000 men,
women and children died there each day. Death on that scale
took enormous labor, and toward the end, when the SS began to
fear discovery, the mass graves were opened and the rotting
bodies burned. All the actual work was done by several hundred
prisoners called the *Sonderkommando.* Forced to wade through
corpses, with SS bullets thinning their ranks, the work squads at
Treblinka contained a core of men who managed to survive. And
not just to save their skins. Against impossible odds they organized a resistance, they revolted, and on August 2, 1943, they
burned down the camp.

It took months and months of preparation, cutting down the
suicides, insisting that survival even in such a place is not without
value. Their purpose—strong enough to lift the spirit from truly

inhuman depths—was to destroy the camp and allow at least one man or woman to escape and bear the tale. "I found it most difficult to stay alive," says a survivor of Treblinka, "but I had to live, to give the world the story of this depravity, this bestial depravity" (Glatstein, 180). Meanwhile, the dead were being unearthed and burned, and soon the work squads too would go up in smoke. If that had come to pass, Treblinka would never have existed. The aim of the revolt was to ensure the memory of that place, and we know the story of Treblinka because forty survived.

In *Where Are My Brothers?* Sarah Berkowitz records a small incident: "One night a girl in our barrack started to scream terribly in her sleep. Within minutes all of us found ourselves screaming without knowing why" (82). Why? The place was Auschwitz; surely that was reason enough. The Holocaust produced an endless scream which, given time, has transmuted itself into the voice of many witnesses. This would seem, in fact, to be one of the primary aspects of the survival experience: the will to bear witness issues as a typical and in some sense necessary response to extremity. Confronting radical evil, men and women instinctively feel the desire to call, to warn, to communicate their shock. Terror dissolves the self into silence, but its aftermath, the spectacle of human mutilation, gives birth to a different reaction. Horror arises and in its presence men and women are seized by an involuntary outburst of feeling which is very much like a scream—sometimes, as we have seen, literally a scream. And in this crude cry the will to bear witness is born:

> This pitiful sound, which sometimes, goodness knows how, reaches into the remotest prison cell, is a concentrated expression of the last vestige of human dignity. It is a man's way of leaving a trace, of telling people how he lived and died. By his screams he asserts his right to live, sends a message to the outside world demanding help and calling for resistance. If nothing else is left, one must scream. Silence is the real crime against humanity (42-43).

These are the words of Nadezhda Mandelstam, whose *Hope Against Hope* stands second only to Solzhenitsyn's massive *GULAG* as an account of survival in Russia during the years of Stalin's terror. Her husband was Osip Mandelstam, one of Russia's finest poets. He made the mistake of writing a poem against Stalin, someone informed, and from then on their life was doomed and they knew it. After Mandelstam's disappearance into the camps, his wife lived on the move, leaving places sometimes hours before the police arrived to arrest her. She lied to get jobs, she lied to keep them. She watched those around her withdraw and grow silent, and she too said nothing. But all the time she was observing and remembering. And all the time the scream was growing. Nadezhda Mandelstam survived to testify, and in that purpose found strength to continue. The moral nature of this act, furthermore, shielded her from the debilitating fear which mere self-interest generates. To "survive as a witness," she came to believe, is *the* imperative of men in murderous times:

> Most accounts of life in the camps appeared on first hearing to be a disconnected series of stories about the critical moments when the narrator nearly died but then miraculously managed to save himself. The whole of camp life was reduced to these highlights, which were intended to show that although it was almost impossible to survive, man's will to live was such that he came through nevertheless. Listening to these accounts, I was horrified at the thought that there might be nobody who could ever properly bear witness to the past. Whether inside or outside the camps, we had all lost our memories. But it later turned out that there were people who had made it their aim from the beginning not only to save themselves, but to survive as witnesses. These relentless keepers of the truth, merging with all the other prisoners, had bided their time—there were probably more such people in the camps than outside, where it was all too common to succumb to the temptation to make terms with reality and live out one's life in peace. Of course those witnesses who have kept a clear memory of the past are few in number, but their very

survival is the best proof that good, not evil, will prevail in the end (379).

Death is compounded by oblivion, and the foundation of humanness—faith in human continuity—is endangered. The final horror is that no one will be left. A survivor of Dachau told me this:

> The SS guards took pleasure in telling us that we had no chance of coming out alive, a point they emphasized with particular relish by insisting that after the war the rest of the world would not believe what happened; there would be rumors, speculations, but no clear evidence, and people would conclude that evil on such a scale was just not possible.

Without the past we have nothing to stand on, no context from which to organize the energies of moral vision. Against such possibilities survivors do what they can. Facing man-made horror, their need becomes strong to remember and record—to ensure, through their own survival or the survival of their word, that out of horror's very midst (from where else can it come?) the truth shall emerge. ∎

"There was," says Elie Wiesel in *One Generation After*, "a veritable passion to testify for the future, against death and oblivion, a passion conveyed by every possible means of expression"; he goes on to cite "accounts told with childlike artlessness" and "precisely kept ledgers of horrors," all of which "waver between scream and silent anger" (53). In *Night*, his first book, Wiesel describes the agony of his boyhood in Auschwitz, and it is that experience which becomes central to the spiritual position of the protagonists in later books, novels like *The Accident* and *The Gates of the Forest*, in which Wiesel attempts to interpret, not the experience itself, but the survivor's relation to it in retrospect. Before all else, Wiesel has been concerned with the problems of the survivor *as a witness*. In *One Generation Afer* he says: "All questions pertaining to Auschwitz lead to anguish. Whether or not the death of one million children has meaning, either way man is negated and condemned" (56). But if faith in humanity is no longer possible, what then is the point of bearing witness? "Was it not a mistake to testify, and by that very act, affirm . . . faith in man and word?" (15).

Silence is the only adequate response, but the pressure of the scream persists. This is the obsessive center of Wiesel's writing: his protagonists desire a silence they cannot keep. In *The Oath* the members of a Jewish community, awaiting the pogrom that will destroy them, make a solemn promise never to reveal their fate; but the sole survivor finds that such a silence is more than he can bear. In *Beggar in Jerusalem* the hero crawls out of a mass grave and makes his way to Israel where, as witness, he becomes the necessary connection between past and future. Through him the silence speaks and the new spirit of resistance stays loyal to the suffering which was its birth. The conflict between silence and the scream, so prominent in Wiesel's novels, is in fact a battle between death and life, between allegiance to the dead and care for the living, which rages in the survivor and resolves itself in the act of bearing witness.

Silence, in its primal aspect, is a consequence of terror, of a dissolution of self and world that, once known, can never be fully dispelled. But in retrospect it becomes something else. Silence constitutes the realm of the dead. It is the palpable substance of those millions murdered, the world no longer present, that intimate absence—of God, of man, of love—by which the survivor is haunted. In the survivor's voice the dead's own scream is active. A man named Alexander Donat accidentally took the place of a man named Michael Berg in a death brigade; and Berg, in his capacity as witness, writes *The Holocaust Kingdom* in Donat's name. This is a primary source of the will to bear witness: the survivor allows the dead their voice; he makes the silence heard.

There is evidence of this impulse in most books by survivors. In *Eleven Years in Soviet Prison Camps,* Elinor Lipper speaks of

> the silence of the Siberian graveyards, the deathly silence of those who have frozen, starved, or been beaten to death. This book is an attempt to make that silence speak (viii).

To speak in memory of the dead becomes a kind of "mandate," as in Olga Lengyel's *Five Chimneys:*

> In setting down this personal record I have tried to carry out the mandate given to me by the many fellow internees at Auschwitz who perished so horribly. This is my memorial to them (208).

Eugene Heimler wrote *Night of the Mist* to fulfill a similar need:

> There were things I had to do, words I had to speak, moments which I had to dissect in order to show the world what I had seen and lived through, on behalf of the millions who had seen it also—but could no longer speak. Of their dead, burnt, bodies I would be the voice (191).

Statements like these suggest many things. Most evident is the survivor's compassion, and after that, his loyalty. He survived, others did not, but all were there together. He knows he did not come through alone. Nobody survived without help. Life in the camps was savage, and yet there was *also* a web of mutual aid and encouragement, to which all books by survivors testify. As we shall see, some minimal fabric of care, some margin of giving and receiving, is essential to life in extremity. In a literal sense, therefore, the survivor owes his life to his comrades.

This debt to the dead, furthermore, is reinforced by the special kind of identity which survivors share. In the camps men and women were reduced to a single human mass. They all looked alike—the same filthy rags, shaved heads, stick-thin festering bodies—and the same hurt and need was each one's lot. Survivors are not individuals in the bourgeois sense. They are living remnants of the general struggle, and certainly they know it. First-hand accounts of life in the concentration camps almost never focus on the trials of the writer apart from his or her comrades, apart from the thousands of identical others whose names were never known. Books by survivors are invariably group portraits, in which the writer's personal experience is representative and used to provide a perspective on the common plight. Survival is a collective act, and so is bearing witness. Both are rooted in compassion and care, and both expose the illusion of separateness. It is not an exaggeration, nor merely a metaphor, to say that the survivor's identity includes the dead.

And there is also this: in extremity men and women make a special promise among themselves, always implicit and often openly declared. Scrawled on the latrine wall in a Soviet camp was this inscription: "May he be damned who, after regaining freedom, remains silent" (Ekart, 12). Whoever comes through will take with him the burden of speaking for the others. Someone will survive and death will not be absolute. This small pledge, this gigantic demand, is intensely important to people facing extinction. In the survivor's own case, furthermore, it becomes a way to transcend the helplessness which withers hope and self-respect in the presence of so much affliction. Surrounded by suffering he cannot comfort or prevent, this much at least he *can* do: the deaths, the sorrow, the infinite dragging pain shall not be lost completely. In this way the survivor's relation to the dead is compounded and made final:

> His [fate] had fallen on the side of life, and yet he felt that he would henceforth carry with him the fate of all these thousands. No, he had not gone through it "like a stone." The blood of all these sufferers had fused with his and made it dark and heavy with all their pain. . . .
> "Do not forget us!" was their silent cry.
> "Think of us! Help us! Do not forget us!"
> No, he would never forget them (Wiechert, 125, 129). ▪

Nevertheless, this concern for the dead has been taken as evidence of something irrational and therefore suspect in the survivor's behavior. Observers call it "survival guilt," a term much used and almost wholly negative in emphasis. The concept of guilt, in this respect, is most clearly developed in the work of Robert Lifton. In *Death in Life: Survivors of Hiroshima*, Lifton argues that guilt is the key to the survivor's mentality. The survivor has a "need to justify his own survival in the face of others' deaths" (35). This need arises from a "process of identification which creates guilt over what one has done to, or not done for, the dying while oneself surviving" (496). Lifton reduces the problem to the "inseparability of death and guilt" (499), and as might be expected, he focuses on "the survivor's tendency to incorporate within himself an image of the dead, and then to think, feel and act as he imagines they did or would" (496). I have tried to suggest some of the ways in which this "tendency to incorporate" comes about. In Lifton's view, however, the fact that living men and women insist upon remembering the dead is clear proof of neurosis. The aim of psychiatric treatment is adjustment, acceptance, forgetting—goals which constitute a condition the survivor rejects. The urgency of his need to bear witness puts him in open conflict with the system being imposed to explain away his behavior, and such opposition, from the psychiatric point of view, is further evidence of neurotic reaction.

Lifton's good will is evident, but as a psychiatrist he can only assume that behavior as intense and singleminded as the survivor's is abnormal. Lifton's original focus on atomic-bomb survivors, furthermore, obscures an essential aspect of bearing witness which becomes clear in instances of protracted crisis. The will to bear witness arises early, not after guilt has had time to accrue, but during the *initial* stage of adjustment to extremity. This is an important point, and it is confirmed repeatedly in the descriptions survivors give of their experience. The following passage is from a survivor's letter to me, and plainly, the idea of a "task" precedes any notion of guilt:

> I feel no guilt in being a survivor, but I feel that I have
> a task to fulfill. We may call it the survivor task, and it
> is part of my ego ideal, not of my superego. This task
> crowded into my thinking when I participated for the
> first time at the roll call of the captives in the concen-
> tration camp Buchenwald thirty-four years ago when I
> had no guarantee whatsoever that I would be a survivor.

Another survivor, Leon Thorne, began *Out of the Ashes* in hiding, before he was captured and sent to the camps: "I dare not
hope that I shall live through this period, but I must work as
though my words *will* come through. I shall act and write as
though there were hope for me" (13).

The survivor's behavior looks different when seen in terms of
a "task," and Lifton too has noticed this. In *History and Human
Survival* he refers to "the survivor's intense concern with historical record" (197); and although the "sense of special mission
characteristic of survivors" is still explained by "the need to
render significant the deaths they have seen" (204), Lifton's emphasis is now on a positive outcome. He wishes to retain the concept of guilt, but—as in the following remarks from an article in
Partisan Review—finally he wants to suggest a new way of thinking about it: "although as a psychiatrist I was brought up to look
upon guilt as a profound problem within neurosis, as indeed it
can be, one comes in certain situations to value it as a process"
(518). This, in turn, leads to the formulation of an "energizing
or animating guilt" (517), and ultimately to a redefinition of
survival guilt as "the anxiety of responsibility" (519). At which
point—and this is the conclusion I draw from Lifton's work—the
idea of guilt transcends itself. As the capacity for response to
deeds and events; as care for the future; as awareness of the inter-
dependency of human life, it becomes simply conscience.

Ernest A. Rappaport has reached a similar conclusion. Drawing
on personal experience (he was in Buchenwald) and on years of
psychiatric work with survivors of the Nazi camps, Rappaport
argues that their experience was so radically unique that the the-

ory of neurosis is inadequate to deal with it. Much of their psychological difficulty is an outcome of the social resistance they encounter when they do not go along with "the preferred attitude of forgetting." Which is to say that apart from the idea of survival guilt, there is still the problem of its usage, of how we deploy it as a defense.

The "world" to which survivors speak is very much a part of their condition as witnesses. They speak *for* someone, but also *to* someone, and the response they evoke is integral to the act they perform. And here an unexpected ambiguity arises. As a witness the survivor is both sought and shunned; the desire to hear his truth is countered by the need to ignore him. Insofar as we feel compelled to defend a comforting view of life, we tend to deny the survivor's voice. We join in a "conspiracy of silence," and undermine the survivor's authority by pointing to his guilt. If he is guilty, then perhaps it is true that the victims of atrocity collaborate in their own destruction; in which case blame can be imputed to the victims themselves. And if he is guilty, then the survivor's suffering, all the sorrow he describes, is deserved; in which case a balance between *that* pain and our own is restored.

Strategies like these are commonly employed against survivors. Most simply, of course, the imputation of guilt is a transfer from spectator to victim. People living safe and at ease are understandably disturbed; they are not, as civilized beings, prepared for what the survivor has to say. But the operation of denial runs deeper. Refusal to acknowledge extremity is built into the structure of existence as we, the lucky ones, know it. More perhaps than we care to admit, spiritual well-being has depended on systems of mediation which transcend or otherwise deflect the sources of dread. In the beginning, Genesis tells us, the earth was "without form and void." Out of nothing the human world was made, out of nothingness and terror. Man's ascent to dominion depended on mechanisms which deny, symbolically if not in fact, those primal negations of human value which we would rather ignore. Too close a knowledge of vulnerability, of evil, of human insufficiency, is felt to be ruinous. And therefore we assert that death is *not* the end, the body is *not* the self. The world is *not* a film upon the void, and virtue is *not* without Godhead on its side. So too with the survivor. The ostracism of outsiders, of bearers of bad news, is a very old practice. In order to gain momentum the human enterprise bought time and assurance by taking refuge in myth, in numbers, in any makeshift strategy of distance or denial. But what was wisdom once is not so now. The gates of pearl have turned to horn, and the appearance of the survivor suggests—indeed this is his message—that we embrace illusion at our peril.

The survivor is ignored for at least one other reason. Since the middle of the nineteenth century, suffering has come to be equated with moral stature, with spiritual depth, with refinement of perception and sensibility. I can only guess at the sources of this idea: the Christian belief in salvation through pain; Kierkegaard's emphasis on despair and Nietzsche's on the abyss; and not least, the Marxist celebration of the oppressed and downtrodden. The roots are manifold, but the net result is simple: the more poignant one's own suffering (or so the argument goes), the more one rises superior to others, the more authentic one becomes. Then too, if dross turns to gold, one's own private hurt is easier to bear. A prominent scholar (his speciality is Dickens) told me that the trouble with characters in Solzhenitsyn's novels is that they do not seem to suffer—as if open pain were possible in *their* shoes. Odd as this sounds, there is among us an envy of suffering. It increases with education, and it reveals the bitterness felt when history renders our own pain trivial. But of course, to put a value on suffering is something only the happy few can afford. One of the strongest themes in the literature of survival is that pain is senseless; that a suffering so vast is completely without value *as suffering*.

The survivor, then, is a disturber of the peace. He is a runner of the blockade men erect against knowledge of "unspeakable" things. About these he aims to speak, and in so doing he undermines, without intending to, the validity of existing norms. He is a genuine transgressor, and here he is made to feel real guilt. The world to which he appeals does not admit him, and since he has looked to this world as the source of moral order, he begins to doubt himself. And that is not the end, for now his guilt is doubled by betrayal—of himself, of his task, of his vow to the dead. The final guilt is not to bear witness. The survivor's worst torment is not to be able to speak.

Life lives upon life. That is a truth which civilized people may choose to ignore, but which the survivor must face at every turn. We live, all of us, in a realm of mutual sacrifice, and it seems possible that those of us in the civilized state—where victimization is selective—accrue greater guilt than men and women trapped in open horror, where life's cost is general and not borne by any one person or class apart from the rest. Here in particular the survivor's experience qualifies what is called "collective" or "metaphysical" guilt. In *The Question of German Guilt*, Karl Jaspers put it this way:

> **Metaphysical guilt is the lack of absolute solidarity with the human being as such—an indelible claim beyond morally meaningful duty. This solidarity is violated by my presence at a wrong or a crime. It is not enough that I cautiously risk my life to prevent it; if it happens, and if I was there, and if I survive where the other is killed, I know from a voice within myself: I am guilty of being still alive (71).**

In *The Reawakening*, Primo Levi refers to this same feeling as

> **the shame . . . the just man experiences at another man's crime; the feeling of guilt that such a crime should exist, that it should have been introduced irrevocably into the world of things that exist, and that his will for good should have proved too weak or null, and should not have availed in defense (12).**

There is nothing metaphysical about this kind of perception. It stems, rather, from awareness of the empirical fact that any person's existence depends on the work, the sacrifice, and often the oppression and death of many other men and women. Each one of us is bound both near and far to others in what becomes, finally, the totality of human life on earth. The age-old belief in "the oneness of man" has become, in our time, a visible actuality —the result of war and mass murder, of world politics and the economic interdependence of classes and nations. The sense of responsibility arising from this kind of awareness is not peculiar to survivors, and ought not to be imputed to them as if theirs were a special case.

With very few exceptions, the testimony of survivors does not concern itself with guilt of any sort. Their books neither admonish nor condemn nor beg forgiveness; not because survivors are drained of their humanity, but because their attention lies wholly elsewhere—in scenes which they can never forget and which, sometimes in hatred, sometimes with amazing tenderness, they feel compelled to record. To assume that the need to bear witness is rooted in neurosis is to ignore entirely the nature of extreme experience, and I quote the following passage to illustrate a central point: we cannot know, we have no *way* of knowing, what provokes the survivor's behavior unless we accept at face value the content of his or her story. The time is winter, 1944. The place is Neumark, a minor concentration camp for women. The name "Stuthofers," mentioned here, is derived from a typical kind of SS joke. Those about to be shot—there is no logic to this— are told that they will be "transported to Stuthof":

> No one was allowed into the Stuthofers' tent. If any-one was caught visiting a mother or a sister, she was never allowed to leave the tent again. The Stuthofers were seldom given food, and on the rare occasions when it was supplied, it was placed on the ground in the dark in front of the tent. Then the strongest of them fetched it and distributed it.
> Entering the tent from the blinding snow-whiteness, I could hardly distinguish anything in the semi-darkness, least of all the women lying on the ground. The stench was over-powering despite the airy tent. After awhile

my eyes became accustomed to the light, and I was completely overcome by what I saw.

I screamed in horror and shut my eyes to the sight. My knees trembled, my head began to swim, and I grasped the central tent-prop for support. It was hard to believe the women on the ground were still human beings. Their rigid bodies were skeletons, their eyes were glazed from long starvation. . . .

For two months the Stuthofers had lain on the ground, stark naked. The meagre bundles of straw on which they lay were putrid from their urine and excreta. Their frozen limbs were fetid and covered with wounds and bites to the point of bleeding, and countless lice nested in the pus. Their hair was very short indeed, but the armies of lice found a home in it. No stretch of the imagination, no power of the written word, can convey the horror of that tent. And yet . . . they were *alive* . . . they were hungry and they tore at their skeletal bodies with their emaciated hands covered in pus and dirt. They were beyond help. The SS guards denied them the mercy of shooting them all at once. Only three or four were called out daily to be shot. . . .

For days I couldn't swallow even a crumb of bread. The horror I lived through watching this agony will remain with me to the end of my days. Later I saw thousands of my fellow prisoners die from rifle shots, but even that could not compare with the terrible and unspeakable ordeal of the Stuthofers (Weiss, 188-89).

We will not understand the survivor's behavior apart from its context. That is the context. ■

The survivor preserves his life, but also his humanness, against a situation in which, at every turn, decency seems stupid or impossible. He anchors himself in the moral purpose of bearing witness, and thereby he maintains, in himself and in the action he performs, an integrity which contradicts the savagery surrounding him. His task is like one of those small rocks to which vast seaplants hold upon the ocean floor—a point of stability and rooted strength against the brunt of each day's peril. In the introduction to his book of camp sketches, Alfred Kantor remarks not only upon his "overwhelming desire to put down every detail," but also on the saving grace of an activity like this:

> my commitment to drawing came out of a deep instinct of self-preservation and undoubtedly helped me to deny the unimaginable horrors of life at that time. By taking on the role of an "observer" I could at least for a few moments detach myself from what was going on in Auschwitz and was therefore better able to hold together the threads of sanity (unpaged).

A purpose of this kind, moreover, remains undiminished through time—years in some cases—because it is integral to the survivor's situation. Its source is in the moral emotion which horror provokes, a response intensified rather than weakened by the accumulation of detail.

Horror arises from the visible wreckage of moral and physical being. We instinctively feel that a mangled body reveals a mangled soul, and that is an accurate perception when we are dealing, as now, with the spiritual consequences of torture and extermination. In the presence of things which negate all claim to life and value—the bomb-scapes, the death-stench, the ditches of gunned-down children—mind and flesh recoil in a single expression of shock. The whole body screams, and this "last vestige of human dignity," as Nadezhda Mandelstam suggested, is life's own cry of dread and care, of recognition and refusal and appeal to resistance. On the surface men go numb, but deeper down the scream is there, "like a flame imprisoned in my bones," as Chaim Kaplan put it. We tend to forget, or perhaps never knew, how vigorous and strongminded the reaction to horror can be.

This response, this *response-ability,* is what I wish to call "conscience"—conscience in its social form; not the internalized voice of authority, not the introspective self-loathing of the famed "Puritan" or "New England" conscience. And not remorse. If bearing witness were an isolated private act, a purely subjective event,

[46]

then perhaps the theory of guilt would serve. But as we have seen, the survivor's behavior is typical, and more, it is integral to conditions which reach beyond personal involvement. Horrible events take place, that is the (objective) beginning. The survivor feels compelled to bear witness, that is the (subjective) middle. His testimony enters public consciousness, thereby modifying the moral order to which it appeals, and that is the (objective) end. Conscience, in other words, is a social achievement. At least on its historical level, it is the collective effort to come to terms with evil, to distill a moral knowledge equal to the problems at hand. Only after the ethical content of an experience has been made available to all members of the community does conscience become the individual "voice" we usually take it for.

And like any witness, the survivor gives testimony in situations where moral judgment depends on knowledge of what took place. Through him the events in question are verified and their reality made binding in the eyes of others. The survivor-as-witness, therefore, embodies a socio-historical process founded not upon the desire for justice (what can justice mean when genocide is the issue?), but upon the involvement of all human beings in common care for life and the future. "I want the world to read and to resolve that this must never, never be permitted to happen again"—so concludes one survivor of Auschwitz (Lengyel, 208). "I believe it is my duty," says another, "to let the world know on the basis of first-hand experience what can happen, what does happen, what must happen when human dignity is treated with cynical contempt" (Buber, xii). This is an attitude expressed often indeed by survivors. The assumption is that good and evil are only clear in retrospect; that moral vision depends on assimilation of the past; that man as man cannot dispense with memory. Wisdom depends on knowledge and it comes at a terrible price. It comes from consciousness of, and then response to, the deeds and events through which men have already passed. Conscience, as Schopenhauer put it, is "man's knowledge concerning what he has done" (104).

By now it should be evident that survival is an act whose value

[47]

extends beyond the individual who survives. One way to make this clear is formulated by Hannah Arendt in the last pages of *Eichmann in Jerusalem:*

> It is true that totalitarian domination tried to establish these holes of oblivion into which all deeds, good and evil, would disappear, but just as the Nazis' feverish attempts, from June, 1942, on, to erase all traces of the massacres—through cremation, through burning in open pits, through the use of explosives and flame-throwers and bone-crushing machinery—were doomed to failure, so all efforts to let their opponents "disappear in silent anonymity" were in vain. The holes of oblivion do not exist. Nothing human is that perfect, and there are simply too many people in the world to make oblivion possible. One man will always be left alive to tell the story (211-12).

That one man or woman is enormously important. In Turkey in 1915, for example, a million people were massacred as part of a deliberate policy to rid the country of its Armenian population. There were pogroms in the cities; villages were burned; men, women and children were driven into the desert to starve and be cut down. Against this event very few voices were raised, so few, in fact, that when Hitler proposed the idea of genocide to his General Staff, he could dismiss world conscience by saying: "Who, after all, speaks today of the annihilation of the Armenians?" (Housepian, 61). Those who possess enormous means of destruction actually believe—and this is the logic of power in our time—that death is stronger than life. They believe that over bone and flesh a withering silence *can* be imposed.

We live in an age of genocide, a time of willingness to remove humanity in chunks from the path of this or that policy. Hitler set out to eliminate, among others, the Jews, the Poles, the Communists. Stalin began by crushing the Old Bolsheviks, the intellectuals, the recalcitrant peasantry, and then went on to spread a web of random death through the very fabric of social interdependence. In Hiroshima it was the population at large, and in

Indochina all life—plant, human, animal—in the countryside. Genocide is a "crime against humanity" because it negates human value as such. Its victims are the innocent occupants of a certain amount of human space which henceforth will be empty. Mass murder is nothing new, of course. Incredibly enough, that argument is still used to dampen response to present atrocities. But when the administration of death becomes a bureaucratic procedure, when killing is computerized and efficiency is the only value left, then clearly we behold something more than the age-old disregard for life. In our time the outcome of power is hostility to life itself.

Modern history has created the survivor as a moral type. His or her special task, moreover, has become indispensable. When terrorism and mass murder prevail, there will be no sources of concrete information unless men and women survive. Conscience is not awakened by hearsay or surmise. Care for life beyond ourselves is born of personal knowledge, of the compassion which comes from knowing the fate of actual lives. In an age of total propaganda, furthermore, there is no way past falsehood and confusion, save in the testimony of eyewitnesses. Distrust of official information has produced a paralyzing hesitation toward facts not verified in direct experience. The stories survivors tell are limited, of course, but they possess the kind of certainty, wholly human and involved, that moral resistance needs. And in these ways survivors do have influence. The Left gradually withdrew support from Stalinist politics in many countries, in part because of books like Alexander Weissberg's *The Accused;* and the beginning of a libertarian movement in Russia is directly related to the survival and outspokenness of Solzhenitsyn.

Survivors do not bear witness to guilt, neither theirs nor ours, but to objective conditions of evil. In the literature of survival we find an image of things so grim, so heartbreaking, so starkly unbearable, that inevitably the survivor's scream begins to be our own. When this happens the role of spectator is no longer enough. But the testimony of survivors is valuable for something else as well. By the very fact that they came to be written, these documents are evidence that the moral self can resurrect itself from the inhuman depths through which it must pass. These books are proof that human heroism is possible. At the end of *Journey Through Hell,* Reska Weiss says: "I rejoice that I am alive and can bear witness to the miracle of survival" (253). The miracle is that she can make such a statement. Ordinary people, in no way different from ourselves, go through infernal agony; they keep moral sense and memory intact; and afterwards, they take upon themselves the pain of living through it again, in order to fix its detail and make it known. ∎

EXCREMENTAL ASSAULT

As the column returns from work after a whole day spent in the open, the stench of the camp is overwhelmingly offensive. Sometimes when you are still miles away the poisoned air blows over you.

SEWERYNA SZMAGLEWSKA
Smoke over Birkenau

He had stopped washing a long time before . . . and now the last remnants of his human dignity were burning out within him.

GUSTAV HERLING
A World Apart

IT BEGAN in the trains, in the locked boxcars—eighty to a hundred people per car—crossing Europe to the camps in Poland:

> The temperature started to rise, as the freight car was enclosed and body heat had no outlet. . . . The only place to urinate was through a slot in the skylight, though whoever tried this usually missed, spilling urine on the floor. . . . When dawn finally rose . . . we were all quite ill and shattered, crushed not only by the weight of fatigue but by the stifling, moist atmosphere and the foul odor of excrement. . . . There was no latrine, no provision. . . . On top of everything else, a lot of people had vomited on the floor. We were to live for days on end breathing these foul smells, and soon we lived in the foulness itself (Kessel, 50-51).

Transport by boat, in the case of many Soviet prisoners, was even worse: "most people were seasick and they just had to vomit on those down below. That was the only way to perform their natural functions too" (Knapp, 59). From the beginning, that is, subjection to filth was an aspect of the survivor's ordeal. In Nazi camps especially, dirt and excrement were permanent conditions of existence. In the barracks at night, for example, "buckets of excrement stood in a little passage by the exit. There were not enough. By dawn, the whole floor was awash with urine and feces. We carried the filth about the hut on our feet, the stench made people faint" (Birenbaum, 226). Sickness made things worse:

> Everybody in the block had typhus . . . it came to Belsen Bergen in its most violent, most painful, deadliest form. The diarrhea caused by it became uncontrollable. It flooded the bottom of the cages, dripping through the cracks into the faces of the women lying in the cages below, and mixed with blood, pus and urine, formed a slimy, fetid mud on the floor of the barracks (Perl, 171).

[53]

The latrines were a spectacle unto themselves:

> There was one latrine for thirty to thirty-two thousand
> women and we were permitted to use it only at certain
> hours of the day. We stood in line to get into this tiny
> building, knee-deep in human excrement. As we all suf-
> fered from dysentery, we could rarely wait until our
> turn came, and soiled our ragged clothes, which never
> came off our bodies, thus adding to the horror of our
> existence by the terrible smell which surrounded us like
> a cloud. The latrine consisted of a deep ditch with planks
> thrown across it at certain intervals. We squatted on
> these planks like birds perched on a telegraph wire, so
> close together that we could not help soiling one an-
> other (Perl, 33).

Prisoners lucky enough to work in one of the camp hospitals, and
therefore able to enjoy some measure of privacy, were not thereby
exempt from the latrine's special horror: "I had to step into human excreta, into urine soaked with blood, into stools of patients
suffering from highly contagious diseases. Only then could one
reach the hole, surrounded by the most inexpressible dirt" (Weiss,
69). The new prisoner's initiation into camp life was complete
when he "realized that there was no toilet paper"—

> that there was no paper in the whole of Auschwitz, and
> that I would have to "find another way out." I tore off
> a piece of my scarf and washed it after use. I retained
> this little piece throughout my days in Auschwitz;
> others did likewise (Unsdorfer, 102).

Problems of this kind were intensified by the fact that, at one
time or another, *everyone* suffered from diarrhea or dysentery.
And for prisoners already starved and exhausted, it was fatal
more often than not: "Those with dysentery melted down like
candles, relieving themselves in their clothes, and swiftly turned
into stinking repulsive skeletons who died in their own excrement" (Donat, 269). Sometimes whole camp populations sick-
ened in this way, and then the horror was overwhelming. Men
and women soiled themselves and each other. Those too weak to

move relieved themselves where they lay. Those who did not recover were slowly enveloped in their own decomposition: "Some
of the patients died before they ever reached the gas chambers.
Many of them were covered all over with excrement, for there
were no sanitary facilities, and they could not keep themselves
clean" (Newman, 39).

Diarrhea was a deadly disease and a source of constant befoulment, but it was also dangerous for another reason—it forced prisoners to break rules:

> Many women with diarrhea relieved themselves in soup
> bowls or the pans for "coffee"; then they hid the utensils
> under the mattress to avoid the punishment threatening
> them for doing so: twenty-five strokes on the bare but-
> tocks, or kneeling all night long on sharp gravel, hold-
> ing up bricks. These punishments often ended in the
> death of the "guilty" (Birenbaum, 134).

In another case a group of men were locked day after day in a
room without ventilation or toilet facilities of any kind. Next to
a window by which guards passed they discovered a hole in the
floor. But to use it a man had to risk his life, since those caught
were beaten to death. "The spectacle of these unfortunates, shak-
ing with fear as they crawled on hands and knees to the hole and
relieved themselves lying down, is one of my most terrible memories of Sachsenhausen" (Szalet, 51).

The anguish of existence in the camps was thus intensified by
the mineral movement of life itself. Death was planted in a need
which could not, like other needs, be repressed or delayed or pas-
sively endured. The demands of the bowels are absolute, and under such circumstances men and women had to oppose, yet somehow accommodate, their own most intimate necessities:

> Imagine what it would be like to be forbidden to go to
> the toilet; imagine also that you were suffering from in-
> creasingly severe dysentery, caused and aggravated by a
> diet of cabbage soup as well as by the constant cold.
> Naturally, you would try to go anyway. Sometimes you
> might succeed. But your absences would be noticed and

you would be beaten, knocked down and trampled on.
By now, you would know what the risks were, but urgency would oblige you to repeat the attempt, cost
what it might. . . . I soon learned to deal with the dysentery by tying strings around the lower end of my
drawers (Maurel, 38-39). ∎

With only one exception, so far as I know, psychoanalytic studies
of the camp experience maintain that it was characterized by regression to "childlike" or "infantile" levels of behavior. This conclusion is based primarily on the fact that men and women in the
concentration camps were "abnormally" preoccupied with food
and excretory functions. Infants show similar preoccupations,
and the comparison suggests that men and women react to
extremity by "regression to, and fixation on, pre-oedipal stages"
(Hoppe, 77). Here, as in general from the psychoanalytic point
of view, context is not considered. The fact that the survivor's
situation was itself abnormal is simply ignored. That the preoccupation with food was caused by literal starvation does not count;
and the fact that camp inmates were *forced* to live in filth is likewise overlooked.

The case for "infantilism" has been put most forcefully by
Bruno Bettelheim. A major thesis of his book *The Informed
Heart* is that in extreme situations men are reduced to children;
and in a section entitled "Childlike Behavior" he simply equates
the prisoners' objective predicament with behavior inherently regressive. Bettelheim observes, for example—and of course this
was true—that camp regulations were designed to transform excretory functions into moments of crisis. Prisoners had to ask permission in order to relieve themselves, thereby becoming exposed
to the murderous whim of the SS guard to whom they spoke. During the twelve-hour workday, furthermore, prisoners were often
not allowed to answer natural needs, or they were forced to do so
while they worked and on the actual spot *where* they worked. As
one survivor says: "If anyone of us, tormented by her stomach,

would try to go to a nearby ditch, the guards would release their dogs. Humiliated, goaded, the women did not leave their places—they waded in their own excrement" (Zywulska, 67). Worst of all were the days of the death marches, when prisoners who stopped for any reason were instantly shot. To live they simply had to keep going:

> Urine and excreta poured down the prisoners' legs, and by nightfall the excrement, which had frozen to our limbs, gave off its stench. We were really no longer human beings in the accepted sense. Not even animals, but putrefying corpses moving on two legs (Weiss, 211).

Under such conditions, excretion does indeed become, as Bettelheim says, "an important daily event"; but the conclusion does not follow, as he goes on to say, that prisoners were therefore reduced "to the level they were at before toilet training was achieved" (132). Outwardly, yes; men and women were very much concerned with excretory functions, just as infants are, and prisoners were "forced to wet and soil themselves" just as infants do—except that infants are not forced. Bettelheim concludes that for camp inmates the ordeal of excremental crisis "made it impossible to see themselves as fully adult persons any more" (134). He does not distinguish between behavior in extremity and civilized behavior; for of course, if in civilized circumstances an adult worries about the state of his bowels, or sees the trip to the toilet as some sort of ordeal, then neurosis is evident. But in the concentration camps behavior was governed by immediate death-threat; action was not the index of infantile wishes but of response to hideous necessity.

The fact is that prisoners were *systematically* subjected to filth. They were the deliberate target of excremental assault. Defilement was a constant threat, a condition of life from day to day, and at any moment it was liable to take abruptly vicious and sometimes fatal forms. The favorite pastime of one *Kapo* was to stop prisoners just before they reached the latrine. He would force an inmate to stand at attention for questioning; then make him "squat in deep knee-bends until the poor man could no longer control his sphincter and 'exploded' "; then beat him; and only then, "covered with his own excrement, the victim would be allowed to drag himself to the latrine" (Donat, 178). In another instance prisoners were forced to lie in rows on the ground, and each man, when he was finally allowed to get up, "had to urinate across the heads of the others"; and there was "one night when they refined their treatment by making each man urinate into another's mouth" (Wells, 91). In Birkenau, soup bowls were periodically taken from the prisoners and thrown into the latrine, from which they had to be retrieved: "When you put it to your lips for the first time, you smell nothing suspicious. Other pairs of hands trembling with impatience wait for it, they seize it the moment you have finished drinking. Only later, much later, does a repelling odor hit your nostrils" (Szmaglewska, 154). And as we have seen, prisoners with dysentery commonly got around camp rules and kept from befouling themselves by using their own eating utensils:

> The first days our stomachs rose up at the thought of using what were actually chamber pots at night. But hunger drives, and we were so starved that we were ready to eat any food. That it had to be handled in such bowls could not be helped. During the night, many of us availed ourselves of the bowls secretly. We were allowed to go to the latrines only twice each day. How could we help it? No matter how great our need, if we went out in the middle of the night we risked being caught by the S.S., who had orders to shoot first and ask questions later (Lengyel, 26).

There was no end to this kind of degradation. The stench of excrement mingled with the smoke of the crematoria and the rancid decay of flesh. Prisoners in the Nazi camps were virtually drowning in their own waste, and in fact death by excrement was common. In Buchenwald, for instance, latrines consisted of open pits twenty-five feet long, twelve feet deep and twelve feet wide.

There were railings along the edge to squat on, and "one of the favorite games of the SS, engaged in for many years," was to catch men in the act of relieving themselves and throw them into the pit: "In Buchenwald ten prisoners suffocated in excrement in this fashion in October 1937 alone" (Kogon, 56). These same pits, which were always overflowing, were emptied at night by prisoners working with nothing but small pails:

> The location was slippery and unlighted. Of the thirty men on this assignment, an average of ten fell into the pit in the course of each night's work. The others were not allowed to pull the victims out. When work was done and the pit empty, then and then only were they permitted to remove the corpses (Weinstock, 157-58). ■

Again, conditions like these were not accidental; they were determined by a deliberate policy which aimed at complete humiliation and debasement of prisoners. Why this was necessary is not at first apparent, since none of the goals of the camp system—to spread terror, to provide slaves, to exterminate populations—required the kind of thoroughness with which conditions of defilement were enforced. But here too, for all its madness, there was method and reason. This special kind of evil is a natural outcome of power when it becomes absolute, and in the totalitarian world of the camps it very nearly was. The SS could kill anyone they happened to run into. Criminal *Kapos* would walk about in groups of two and three, making bets among themselves on who could kill a prisoner with a single blow. The pathological rage of such men, their uncontrollable fury when rules were broken, is evidence of a boundless desire to annihilate, to destroy, to smash everything not mobilized within the movement of their own authority. And inevitably, the mere act of killing is not enough; for if a man dies without surrender, if something within him remains unbroken to the end, then the power which destroyed him has not, after all, crushed everything. Something has escaped its

[59]

reach, and it is precisely this something—let us call it "dignity"—that must die if those in power are to reach the orgasmic peak of their potential domination.

As power grows, it grows more and more hostile to everything outside itself. Its logic is inherently negative, which is why it ends by destroying itself (a consolation which no longer means much, since the perimeter of atomic destruction is infinite). The exercise of totalitarian power, in any case, does not stop with the demand for outward compliance. It seeks, further, to crush the spirit, to obliterate that active inward principle whose strength depends on its freedom from entire determination by external forces. And thus the compulsion, felt by men with great power, to seek out and destroy all resistance, all spiritual autonomy, all sign of dignity in those held captive. It was not enough just to shoot the Old Bolsheviks; Stalin had to have the show trials. He had to demonstrate publicly that these men of enormous energy and spirit were so utterly broken as to openly repudiate themselves and all they had fought for. And so it was in the camps. Spiritual destruction became an end in itself, quite apart from the requirements of mass murder. The death of the soul was aimed at. It was to be accomplished by terror and privation, but first of all by a relentless assault on the survivor's sense of purity and worth. Excremental attack, the physical inducement of disgust and self-loathing, was a principal weapon.

But defilement had its lesser logic as well. "In Buchenwald," says one survivor, "it was a principle to depress the morale of prisoners to the lowest possible level, thereby preventing the development of fellow-feeling or co-operation among the victims" (Weinstock, 92). How much self-esteem can one maintain, how readily can one respond with respect to the needs of another, if both stink, if both are caked with mud and feces? We tend to forget how camp prisoners looked and smelled, especially those who had given up the will to live, and in consequence the enormous revulsion and disgust which naturally arose among prisoners. Here was an effective mechanism for intensifying the already

[60]

heightened irritability of prisoners towards each other, and thus for stifling in common loathing the impulse toward solidarity. Within the camp world all visible signs of human beauty, of bodily pride and spiritual radiance, were thereby to be eliminated from the ranks of the inmates. The prisoner was made to feel subhuman, to see his self-image only in the dirt and stink of his neighbor. The SS, on the contrary, appeared superior not only by virtue of their guns and assurance, but by their elegant apartness from the filth of the prisoner's world. In Auschwitz prisoners were forced to march in the mud, whereas the clean roadway was reserved for the SS.

And here is a final, vastly significant reason why in the camps the prisoners were so degraded. This made it easier for the SS to do their job. It made mass murder less terrible to the murderers, because the victims appeared less than human. They *looked* inferior. In Gitta Sereny's series of interviews with Franz Stangl, commandant of Treblinka, there are moments of fearful insight. Here is one of the most telling:

> *"Why,"* I asked Stangl, *"if they were going to kill them anyway, what was the point of all the humiliation, why the cruelty?"*
>
> "To condition those who actually had to carry out the policies," he said. "To make it possible for them to do what they did" (101).

In a lecture at the New School (New York, 1974), Hannah Arendt remarked that it is easier to kill a dog than a man, easier yet to kill a rat or frog, and no problem at all to kill insects—"It is in the glance, in the eyes." She means that the perception of subjective being in the victim sparks some degree of identification in the assailant, and makes his act difficult in proportion to the capacity for suffering and resistance he perceives. Inhibited by pity and guilt, the act of murder becomes harder to perform and results in greater psychic damage to the killer himself. If, on the other hand, the victim exhibits self-disgust; if he cannot lift his eyes for humiliation, or if lifted they show only emptiness—then

[61]

his death may be administered with ease or even with the conviction that so much rotten tissue has been removed from life's body. And it is a fact that in camp the procedure of "selection"—to the left, life; to the right, death—was based on physical appearance and on a certain sense of inward collapse or resilience in the prospective victim. As a survivor of Auschwitz puts it:

> Yes, here one rotted alive, there was no doubt about it, just like the SS in Bitterfield had predicted. Yet it was vitally important to keep the body clear. . . . Everyone {at a "selection"} had to strip and one by one, parade before them naked. Mengele in his immaculate white gloves stood pointing his thumb sometimes to the right, sometimes to the left. Anyone with spots on the body, or a thin *Muselmann,* was directed to the right. That side spelt death, the other meant one was allowed to rot a little longer (Hart, 65). ∎

With water in permanent shortage; with latrines submerged in their own filth; with diarrhea rife and mud everywhere, strict cleanliness was just not possible. Simply to *try* to stay clean took extraordinary effort. As one survivor says: "To pick oneself up, to wash and clean oneself—all that is the simplest thing in the world, isn't it? And yet it was not so. Everything in Auschwitz was so organized as to make these things impossible. There was nothing to lean on; there was no place for washing oneself. Nor was there time" (Lewinska, 43). That conditions *were* "so organized" was a dreadful discovery:

> At the outset the living places, the ditches, the mud, the piles of excrement behind the blocks, had appalled me with their horrible filth. . . . And then I saw the light! I saw that it was not a question of disorder or lack of organization but that, on the contrary, a very thoroughly considered conscious idea was in the back of the camp's existence. They had condemned us to die in our own filth, to drown in mud, in our own excrement. They wished to abase us, to destroy our human

dignity, to efface every vestige of humanity, to return us to the level of wild animals, to fill us with horror and contempt toward ourselves and our fellows (Lewinska, 41-42).

With this recognition the prisoner either gave up or decided to resist. For many survivors this moment marked the birth of their will to fight back:

But from the instant when I grasped the motivating principle . . . it was as if I had been awakened from a dream. . . . I felt under orders to live. . . . And if I did die in Auschwitz, it would be as a human being, I would hold on to my dignity. I was not going to become the contemptible, disgusting brute my enemy wished me to be. . . . And a terrible struggle began which went on day and night (Lewinska, 50).

Or as another survivor says:

There and then I determined that if I did not become the target of a bullet, or if I were not hanged, I would make every effort to endure. No longer would I succumb to apathy. My first impulse was to concentrate on making myself more presentable. Under the circumstances this may sound ludicrous; what real relation was there between my new-found spiritual resistance and the unsightly rags on my body? But in a subtle sense there *was* a relationship, and from that moment onwards, throughout my life in the camps, I knew this for a fact. I began to look around me and saw the beginning of the end for any woman who might have had the opportunity to wash and had not done so, or any woman who felt that the tying of a shoe-lace was wasted energy (Weiss, 84).

Washing, if only in a ritual sense—and quite apart from reasons of health—was something prisoners needed to do. They found it necessary to survival, odd as that may seem, and those who stopped soon died:

At 4:30, "coffee"—a light mint infusion without nourishment and with a repulsive taste—was distributed. We

[63]

often took a few swallows and used the rest for washing, but not all of us were able to do without this poor substitute for coffee and consequently many inmates ceased to wash. This was the first step to the grave. It was an almost iron law: those who failed to wash every day soon died. Whether this was the cause or the effect of inner breakdown, I don't know; but it was an infallible symptom (Donat, 173).

Another survivor describes the initial disappearance of concern for his appearance, and the gradual realization that without such care he would not survive:

Why should I wash? Would I be better off than I am? Would I please someone more? Would I live a day, an hour longer? I would probably live a shorter time, because to wash is an effort, a waste of energy and warmth. . . . But later I understood. . . . In this place it is practically pointless to wash every day in the turbid water of the filthy wash-basins for purposes of cleanliness and health; but it is most important as a symptom of remaining vitality, and necessary as an instrument of moral survival (Levi, 35).

By passing through the degradation of the camps, survivors discovered that in extremity a sense of dignity is something which men and women cannot afford to lose. Great damage has to be borne, much humiliation suffered. But at some point a steady resistance to their obliteration as human beings must be made. They learned, furthermore, that when conditions of filth are enforced, befoulment of the body is experienced as befoulment of the soul. And they came to recognize, finally, that when this particular feeling—of something inwardly untouchable—is ruined beyond repair, the will to live dies. To care for one's appearance thus becomes an act of resistance and a necessary moment in the larger structure of survival. Life itself depends on keeping dignity intact, and this, in turn, depends on the daily, never finished battle to remain *visibly* human:

[64]

So we must certainly wash our faces without soap in dirty water and dry ourselves on our jackets. We must polish our shoes, not because the regulation states it, but for dignity and propriety. We must walk erect, without dragging our feet, not in homage to Prussian discipline but to remain alive, not to begin to die (Levi, 36). ∎

The basic structure of Western civilization or perhaps of any civilization, insofar as the processes of culture and sublimation are one, is the division between body and the spirit, between concrete existence and symbolic modes of being. In extremity, however, divisions like these collapse. The principle of compartmentalization no longer holds, and organic being becomes the immediate locus of selfhood. When this happens, body and spirit become the ground of each other, each bearing the other's need, the other's sorrow, and each responds directly to the other's total condition. If spiritual resilience declines, so does physical endurance. If the body sickens, the spirit too begins to lose its grip. There is a strange circularity about existence in extremity: survivors preserve their dignity in order "not to begin to die"; they care for the body as a matter of "moral survival."

For many among us, the word "dignity" no longer means much; along with terms like "conscience" and "spirit" it has grown suspect and is seldom used in analytic discourse. And certainly, if by "dignity" we mean the projection of pretense and vainglory, or the ways power cloaks itself in pomp and ritual pride; if, that is, we are referring to the parodic forms of this principle, as men exploit it for justification or gain—just as honor and conscience are exploited and likewise parodied, although real in themselves—then of course the claim to dignity is false. But if we mean an inward resistance to determination by external forces; if we are referring to a sense of innocence and worth, something felt to be inviolate, autonomous and untouchable, and which is most vigorous when most threatened; then, as in the survivor's case, we come upon one of the constituents of humanness, one of the irreducible elements of selfhood. Dignity, in this case, appears as a self-conscious, self-determining faculty whose function is to insist upon the recognition of itself *as such.*

Certainly the SS recognized it, and their attempt to destroy it, while not successful in the survivor's case, was one of the worst aspects of the camp ordeal. When cleanliness becomes impossible and human beings are forced to live in their own excretions, their pain becomes intense to the point of agony. The shock of physical defilement causes spiritual concussion, and, simply to judge from the reports of those who have suffered it, subjection to filth seems often to cause greater anguish than hunger or fear of death. "This aspect of our camp life," says one survivor, "was the most dreadful and the most horrible ordeal to which we were subjected" (Weiss, 69). Another survivor describes the plight of men forced to lie in their own excreta: they "moaned and wept with discomfort and disgust. Their moral wretchedness was crushing" (Szalet, 78). In the most bizarre cases, defilement caused a desperation bordering on madness, as when a group of prisoners were forced "to drink out of the toilet bowls":

> The men could not bring themselves to obey this devilish order; they only pretended to drink. But the block-fuehrers had reckoned with that; they forced the men's heads deep into the bowls until their faces were covered with excrement. At this the victims almost went out of their minds—that was why their screams had sounded so demented (Szalet, 42).

But why is contact with excrement unbearable? If actual discomfort is minor, why is the reaction so violent? And why does the sense of dignity feel most threatened in this particular case? The incident of the toilet bowls, cited above, has been examined from a psychoanalytic point of view, the conclusion being this:

> infantile satisfactions . . . could be acquired only by means against which culture has erected strong prohibitions. . . . Enforced breakdown of these barriers

was capable of bringing the prisoner near to mental disintegration (Bluhm, 15).

The extreme suffering of those men thus resulted from a breach in cultural taboo. Their demented screams issued from the rending of subliminal structures, in response to violation of those "cleanliness habits" which are "enforced by any culture at an early stage of training" (17). The survivor's struggle against an excremental fate, to speak more plainly, is a function of "toilet training"—although that term is not used in the article from which I am quoting, since the degree of reduction it implies, even from a psychoanalytic perspective, seems altogether disproportionate to the violence of the prisoners' experience. The article goes on, however, to suggest that the depth at which the scream originates may reveal, beyond the relative and flexible demands of culture, the violation of a limit or boundary not relative in the same sense:

> however, the normal adult of our civilization shares the disgust toward the contact with his excrements with members of tribes who live on the lowest levels of culture. This disgust seems to be a demarkation line, the transgression of which can produce effects much more devastating than the appearance of more or less isolated regressive symptoms (17).

From the psychoanalytic point of view, moral anguish is a product of conflict between cultural demands and the regressive desire to subvert them. But if we keep in mind that all regression is in the service of pleasure, or release from pain (which was Freud's definition of pleasure), then the whole theory of infantile regression, in the survivor's case, becomes absurd. The scream of those desperate men was indeed a defense against dissolution, but to reduce their extraordinary pain to the violation of a taboo, or any restriction merely imposed, seems entirely to miss the point. In any case, the inhibiting authority of toilet training is not so central to selfhood that infraction causes the personality to disintegrate. Only once in Western culture has this been viewed in terms of psychic crisis—among the bourgeois classes in the nineteenth century, with their radical reliance on physical rigidity and, as a consequence, their prurient forms of sexual satisfaction; and I would suggest, finally, that such training is the ritual organization of an inherent biological process. Plenty of taboos went by the board in the concentration camps, but not this one—not, that is, transgression of a "demarkation line" which runs deeper than cultural imposition. What human beings will or will not tolerate depends, up to a point, on training of all kinds. Beyond that, however, there are things absolutely unacceptable because something—let us keep the word "dignity"—in our deepest nature revolts. And on such revolt, life in extremity depends. ■

In *The Symbolism of Evil,* Paul Ricœur defines "dread of the impure" as the special kind of fear we feel in reaction to "a threat which, beyond the threat of suffering and death, aims at a diminution of existence, a loss of the personal core of one's being" (41). That, I think, is a good description of what survivors feel when threatened by excremental attack. Ricœur goes on to argue that the feeling of defilement underlies concepts like "sin" and "guilt," and finally that as "the oldest of the symbols of evil," defilement "can signify analogically all the degrees of the experience of evil" (336). And indeed, why does imagery of washing and physical purgation underlie our ideas of sanctity and spiritual purification? Why do we use images associated with excrement—imagery of corruption and decay, of dirt and contagion, of things contaminated, rotting or spoiled—to embody our perceptions of evil? Ricœur concludes that all such imagery is symbolic only, that it represents inner states of being—and for us no doubt he is right. But in the concentration camps, defilement was a condition known by actual sight and touch and smell, and hence this question: when survivors react so violently to contact with excrement, are they responding to what it symbolizes, or is their ordeal the concrete instance from which our symbolism of evil derives?

The implication of Ricœur's analysis is that "the consciousness of self seems to constitute itself at its lowest level by means of symbolism and to work out an abstract language only subsequently" (9). As far as it goes that is true, yet where does the symbolism originate? How did defilement come to symbolize evil? Ricœur can only answer that in the beginning was the symbol— that human selfhood became aware of itself through symbolic objectification of its own structure and condition. This kind of starting point, however, is also a culmination; it is nothing less than the goal of civilization, the outcome of a process of sublimation or transcendence or etherealization (call it what you wish) by which actual events and objects become the images, myths and metaphors that constitute man's spiritual universe. Transformation of the world into symbol is perpetual; thereby we internalize actuality and stay in spiritual, if not in concrete, connection with those primal experiences from which, as civilized beings, we have detached ourselves.

But this activity can be reversed. When civilization breaks down, as it did in the concentration camps, the "symbolic stain" becomes a condition of literal defilement; and evil becomes that which causes real "loss of the personal core of one's being." In extremity man is stripped of his expanded spiritual identity. Only concrete forms of existence remain, actual life and actual death, actual pain and actual defilement; and these now constitute the medium of moral and spiritual being. Spirit does not simply vanish when sublimation fails. At the cost of much of its freedom it falls back to the ground and origin of meaning—back, that is, to the physical experience of the body. Which is another way of saying that, in extremity, symbols tend to actualize.

We might say, then, that in extremity symbolism *as symbolism* loses its autonomy. Or, what amounts to the same thing, that in this special case everything is felt to be inherently symbolic, intrinsically significant. Either way, meaning no longer exists above and beyond the world; it re-enters concrete experience, becomes immanent and invests each act and moment with urgent depth.

And hence the oddly "literary" character of experience in extremity, to which I shall return in Chapter Six. It is as if amid the smoke of burning bodies the great metaphors of world literature were being "acted out" in terrible fact—death and resurrection, damnation and salvation, the whole of spiritual pain and exultation in passage through the soul's dark night.

The following event, for example, seems literary to the point of embarrassment. It is the kind of incident we might expect at the climax of a novel, valid less in itself than as a fiction bearing meaning, and therefore acceptable through the symbolic statement it makes, the psychic drama it embodies. This event, however, happens to be real. It occurred during the last days of the Warsaw Ghetto uprising, it was the fate of many men and women. Armed with handguns and bottles of gasoline, the ghetto fighters held out for fifty-two days against tanks, field artillery and air strikes. So stubbornly did they resist that the Germans finally resorted to burning down the ghetto building by building, street by street, until everything—all life, all sign of man—was gone. The last chance for escape was through the sewers, and down into that foul dark went the remnant of the ghetto:

> On the next day, Sunday, April 25, I went down . . .
> into the underground sewer which led to the "Aryan"
> side. I will never forget the picture which presented it-
> self to my eyes in the first moment when I descended
> into the channel. Dozens of refugees . . . sought shel-
> ter in these dark and narrow channels awash with filthy
> water from the municipal latrines and foul refuse
> flushed down from the private apartments. In these low,
> narrow channels, only wide enough for one person to
> crawl forward in a bent position, dozens of people lay
> jammed and huddled together in the mud and filth
> (Friedman, 284).

They stayed below, sometimes for days, making their way toward the "free" side, coming up occasionally to see where they were, and then simply waiting. Many died, but through the combined effort of Jewish and Polish partisans, some were rescued and survived:

> On May 10, 1943, at nine o'clock in the morning, the lid of the sewer over our heads suddenly opened, and a flood of sunlight streamed into the sewer. At the opening of the sewer Krzaczek [a member of the Polish resistance] was standing and calling all of us to come out, after we had been in the sewer for more than thirty hours. We started to climb out one after another and at once got on a truck. It was a beautiful spring day and the sun warmed us. Our eyes were blinded by the bright light, as we had not seen daylight for many weeks and had spent the time in complete darkness. The streets were crowded with people, and everybody . . . stood still and watched, while strange beings, hardly recognizable as humans, crawled out of the sewers (Friedman, 290).

If that were from a novel, how easily we might speak of rites of passage; of descent into hell; of journey through death's underworld. We would respond to the symbolism of darkness and light, of rebirth and new life, as, blessed by spring and the sun, these slime-covered creatures arise from the bowels of the earth. And we would not be misreading. For despite the horror, it all seems familiar, very much recalling archetypes we know from art and dreams. For the survivor, in any case, the immersion in excrement marks the nadir of his passage through extremity. No worse assault on moral being seems possible. Yet even here there was life and will, as if these shit-smeared bodies were the accurate image of how much mutilation the human spirit can bear, despite shame, loathing, the trauma of violent recoil, and still keep the sense of something inwardly inviolate. "Only our feverish eyes," said one survivor of the sewers, "still showed that we were living human beings" (Friedman, 289). ∎

IV

NIGHTMARE AND WAKING

Whenever I recall the first days at the camp, I still grow hot and cold with nameless terror. . . . Three weeks after I arrived at Auschwitz, I still could not believe it. I lived as in a dream, waiting for someone to awaken me.

OLGA LENGYEL
Five Chimneys

It seemed almost a luxury to die, to go to sleep and never wake up again.

GERDA KLEIN
All But My Life

ONE SURVIVOR remarks that in camp he did not wake fellow prisoners when one of them was having a nightmare; he knew that no matter how bad the dream might be, reality was worse. And what, really, could be worse than to wake up in a concentration camp? "The most ghastly moment of the twenty-four hours of camp life," says a survivor of Auschwitz, "was the awakening, when, at a still nocturnal hour, the three shrill blows of a whistle tore us pitilessly from our exhausted sleep and from the longings of our dreams" (Frankl, 31). "The moment of awakening," says another, "was the most horrible" (Zywulska, 33). Or finally:

> Awakening is the hardest moment—no matter whether these are your first days in the camp, days full of despair, where every morning you relive the painful shock, or whether you have been here long, very long, where each morning reminds you that you lack strength to begin a new day, a day identical with all previous days (Szmaglewska, 4).

The wonder is they got up at all. Camp prisoners were permanently exhausted, they were often sick, and a night's sleep was four or five hours at most. Under such stress we might expect a retreat into unconsciousness, into coma, as when a person faints from shock or excess of pain. Where did the strength to get up come from? And why return to a reality so terrible? Prisoners were driven awake by fear, by anxiety, and often by the blows of a whip or club. But mainly they got up for the same reason any of us do: essential activities have to be performed; organisms must interact with, and find protection from, their environment. Prisoners either got up or died; they either faced an unbearable world knowing they would have to bear it, or gave up.

The whole of the survivor's fate is in that moment. It was always a battle in itself, but it was also part of a larger fight, not just against weakness and despair, but finally against sleep itself because sleep was dangerous. There was never time for sufficient rest, and this elementary need thus became a constant temptation, enforced by extreme exhaustion but even more by the yearning to quit, to sink into the blank peace of oblivion and stay there. Many prisoners were shot or beaten to death for crawling off to some corner and falling asleep. Many others froze to death while sleeping in the snow. At any moment of relaxed striving, sleep could become a part of the slide toward death, a surrender of the will to shove on. "There was absolutely no relaxation possible at Auschwitz" (Kessel, 106). Or again, "The only escape is in sleep, but sleep means death" (Ekart, 46).

The fact that prisoners remained sane with so little rest and under such pressure argues a radical revision of the body's basic rhythms and therefore an agency beyond will alone. Sleep and waking are phases in a process biologically determined, and we may speculate that in extremity men and women find a foundation for struggle in the organic activities of daily life, as if these were indeed *acts of life*. Every morning the survivor's will had to be renewed, and it was: not through some secret fortitude of the heart, but through the physical act of getting up. The pain might be enormous, despair complete, but the commitment—to that day, to that much more of existence—was made. A survivor of Auschwitz describes it this way: "I climb down on to the floor and put on my shoes. The sores on my feet reopen at once, and a new day begins" (Levi, 57). ∎

When the camp experience is viewed as a whole, a remarkable parallel appears between each morning's waking and a larger aspect of the survivor's ordeal. The first encounter with extremity immersed prisoners in a world of pure terror, a world in which nothing made sense or promised hope. The impact was so sudden and overwhelming that the self floundered and began to disintegrate. In shock and disbelief, prisoners went about as if asleep, as if locked in horrid dream, not responding intelligently, not looking out for themselves. The first phase of survival experience may thus be described as a period of *initial collapse.* Given time, however, breakdown was followed by a second stage, characterized by reintegration and recovery of stable selfhood. Very much as if they were waking up, survivors went from withdrawal to engagement, from passivity to resistance. They emerged from their dream-state to face what had to be faced.

Coming from our world, with no prior knowledge of extremity, new prisoners were in no way prepared for the frenzy of their first days in camp. Here is what it was like—after days in a cattlecar without water or room for rest, standing in excrement and vomit—to arrive:

> the wagon doors were torn ajar. The shouts were deafening. S.S. men with whips and half-wild Alsatian dogs swarmed all over the place. Uncontrolled fear brought panic as families were ruthlessly torn apart. Parents screamed for lost children and mothers shrieked their names over the voices of the bawling guards. Everyone without exception lost both nerves and senses (Unsdorfer, 72).

It was an onslaught not to be withstood. When the train doors opened, prisoners were faced with an incomprehensible world: beating and shooting; families dispersed; and those not "selected" for immediate extermination driven into crowded buildings where everything—possessions, clothes, hair, name—was stripped from them. The magnitude and speed of these events made sane response impossible. What kind of sense, after all, was the incoming prisoner to make of his or her first march through Auschwitz:

> Corpses were strewn all over the road; bodies were hanging from the barbed-wire fence; the sound of shots rang in the air continuously. Blazing flames shot into the sky; a giant smoke cloud ascended above them. Starving, emaciated human skeletons stumbled toward

us, uttering incoherent sounds. They fell down right in front of our eyes, and lay there gasping out their last breath (Newman, 18).

The otherness of the camps, their horror and apparent chaos, was not real by past standards; unable to root itself in familiar ground, the old self fell apart. A similar disintegration was suffered by Soviet prisoners who, as soon as they were arrested, were subjected to a process which would not end until the prisoner broke down and signed a false confession:

> Interrogations by night and special cells ensure that the prisoner is not allowed to sleep for one moment. After five to eight days without sleep he is subject to increasingly severe hallucinations and these can be further intensified by blows. The prisoner loses his self-control. His personality begins to split, to dissolve and to be transformed. . . . He loses the power to distinguish between reality and possibility. He loses touch with himself. All that remains of him is a twitching point of reference between vague terror without an object, the pervasive feeling of imposed guilt and confusing hallucinations (Roeder, 11).

There are heroic accounts of resistance to that kind of treatment, especially Artur London's *The Confession* and Alexander Weissberg's *The Accused*. London broke down in the end, and even Weissberg, whose endurance seems superhuman, went through brief periods of collapse:

> it had now been made clear that the examiner was not interested in the truth and wanted fictitious self-accusations. If that were the case then I was really lost. . . . This feeling of being hopelessly trapped paralysed me. . . . So far I had confessed nothing, but I felt now that my reason was about to break down (Weissberg, 219).

Or as an American survivor of the Soviet camps told me: "Oh yes, after enough beating at the base of the spine, after enough kicks in the genitals, you would sign anything." To sign was to say to them and to yourself that you were not who you had been.

Temporarily, the old self dissolved. And for Soviet and Nazi prisoners alike, this first stage was decisive:

> every new-comer immediately had to traverse a course of profound personal degradation and humiliation. Naked he was driven through the unbridgeable abyss that separated the two worlds, "outside" and "inside." It was the immediate effects of this terrifying act of compulsion that determined the ultimate destiny of a prisoner. There were two possibilities and within three months it became apparent which one would apply. By that time a man would have gone into an almost irresistible mental decline—if, indeed, he had not already perished in a physical sense; or he would have begun to adapt himself to the concentration camp (Kogon, 274).

In *The Informed Heart* Bruno Bettelheim observes that the "vast majority of the thousands of prisoners who died at Buchenwald each year died soon" (146). That was true everywhere in the world of the camps: newcomers had the highest death rate. We might therefore ask, as Bettelheim does, "why, in the concentration camp, although some prisoners survived and others got killed, such a sizable number simply died" (145). His answer is that they "died of exhaustion, both physical and psychological, due to a loss of desire to live" (146). Loss of desire to live is one of the primary symptoms of the period of initial collapse, and large numbers of men and women died because during this crucial stage of imprisonment they failed to strive for life with every fiber of their being. But still, loss of the will to live is a symptom, not a cause. The fact is that prisoners "died soon" from a complex of conditions and forces which nothing in the whole of their lives had prepared them to face or even imagine: from prolonged terror and shock; from radical loss, both of identity and of faith in the capacity of goodness to prevail against the evil surrounding them. They died simply for lack of information, because they did not know what to do or how to act. Very often, too, they died of mourning, of grief for the deaths of their family and friends. As one survivor remembers of the time when her friends were killed: "That day I no longer wanted to fight for my life" (Hart, 81). And when the death of one's children or parents or spouse or all of these at once was involved, the state of mourning —of the desire to rejoin those whose death is experienced as a death in the self—could last months, a time during which the mourner was especially vulnerable.

Here, in fact, is the deepest cause of early death: the horror and irreparable hurt felt by the prisoner when he or she first encounters the spectacle of atrocity. Moral disgust, if it arises too abruptly or becomes too intense, expresses itself in the desire to die, to have done with such a world. Perhaps to some small degree we feel this ourselves, a little more each evening as news of the day's evil—the massacres, the mass starvations, the betrayals of leadership—batters away at our faith in human virtue. How much more compelling for those actually *there,* suddenly a part of the worst world possible. For them there comes a point after which no feeling remains except absolute refusal to go on existing when existence itself seems vile beyond redemption. One survivor, having experienced this feeling herself, includes in her testimony a letter from a friend who died. I quote it at length, asking the reader to ignore the pathos in order to understand without special sentiment how "loss of desire to live" comes about:

> Do you know what happened? No, you don't know. Yesterday, yes, it was yesterday, early in the morning we heard a lot of noise—screams and crying and begging for mercy. . . . Quickly my father and I ran down the back stairs to hide in the basement, while Mother went to get the baby. . . . We heard distant screams for hours and hours. Only when night fell was it quiet. We hoped and prayed that Mama and the child had found refuge somewhere. After it had been dark for hours we crawled out of the cellar. . . . We went to the street. We went to all the homes. We met a few ghostlike people who were swaying as if coming from another world. . . . Finally, we met a young man who told us the tragic tale. Old people, young people, and children all had been taken to the market place. There

they had undressed and lain naked on the stones, face
down, and the murderers on horses and brandishing
guns trampled on that screaming human pavement.
. . . those who remained alive had to march naked outside the town. They had to dig their own grave and
stand on the rim until a hail of bullets killed them.
. . . We went there. . . . We saw a great square
grave, half-open yet, a mountain of naked bodies in it.
Many we recognized. We found my mother. She was all
bloody. We did not find my little brother. I found
Henek, the one I loved more than life, who was to be
my husband. . . . Not one tear did I shed in that
grave. Only my heart died. Do you know what? If they
would come tomorrow and kill my father I would not
care. I would not cry. I would be glad for him. I wish
they would kill me. From now on I will walk wherever
it is not permitted. I want them to catch me. I want
them to kill me because I don't care (Klein, 69-70).

For that girl one question was left: "Why does the world go
on when things like this happen?" Every survivor must face this
question. It bothers us too, now and then, except that for us despair is not fatal. Life goes on, if only through routine and habit.
For all those who "died soon," however, the initial immersion in
horror was like a well of sorrow to which there is no bottom. Survivors are proof that the desire to live returns. It returns, but
slowly, through an inner process of regeneration which takes
time. Vast numbers of men and women died because they did not
have time, the blessing of sheer time, to recover. Something—typhus, starvation, an SS bullet—killed them before they regained
their will to live. As a survivor of Buchenwald says: "It took a
long time for a mind, torn from the anchorages of the outside
world and thrust into life-and-death turmoil, to find a new inward
center of gravity" (Kogon, 276). ■

Speaking of his own camp experience, Bettelheim observes that
"right from the beginning I became convinced that these dreadful and degrading experiences were somehow not happening to

'me' as a subject, but only to 'me' as object" (127). Elie Cohen, another psychiatrist who survived the camps, calls this the "stage of initial reaction"; he too emphasizes the "subject-object split," and identifies it by describing his own response to atrocity: "My reaction to this, I observed, was an apparent splitting of my personality. I felt as if I did not belong, as if the business did not concern me" (116). Viktor Frankl, a third psychiatrist to pass through the camps, divides the period of initial collapse into two stages: first shock, then apathy. The new prisoner undergoes "a kind of emotional death" (18), which Frankl sees as a "necessary mechanism of self-defense" (27). Cohen, however, points out that although apathy keeps madness and despair at a distance, it produces a dangerous disregard for the environment:

> In my opinion the after-effect of the fright reaction in most prisoners was followed by the phase of apathy, which for many was a period fraught with extreme danger. As they took no interest in their surroundings and did not strive after self-preservation, reacting tardily and behaving as if they had been "sandbagged," their behavior was not such as is best suited to a concentration camp. The duration of this fright apathy is limited; I would estimate it at no more than one or two weeks. But after this the prisoner was not yet in a condition to make an attempt at adaptation, for with the dwindling of his apathy, mourning made itself felt to its fullest extent, and the mournfully depressive phase set in. . . . For very many prisoners [this] period proved too long, so that they never had an opportunity to engage in the struggle for adaptation (169).

That is the experience of initial collapse in clinical terms. The majority of survivors, however, do not use technical language. For them, entry into the camp world was characterized by an overriding sense of *nightmare* and *unreality*—two words which appear constantly when survivors refer to their first days and weeks:

> All around us were screams, death, smoking chimneys making the air black and heavy with soot and the smell

> of burning bodies. . . . It was just like a nightmare
> and it took weeks and weeks before I could really be-
> lieve this was happening (Hart, 92-93)

But unlike our use of such words (to inject a little drama into ordinary life), survivors speak this way because by any standard of communicable perception or past experience, the first weeks in camp were literally unreal and embedded in nightmare. "Not only during the transport," says Bettelheim, "but for a long time to come, prisoners had to convince themselves that this was real and not just a nightmare" (127).

To the extent that "reality" is a cultural construct, then of course the camps were unreal. At least in Western Europe there had been two centuries of steady advance in political and economic well-being, with much praise of "Progress" and "Humanity," on the assumption that these providential agencies were fully capable of taking a lost God's place. The homeland of Kant and Goethe was renowned for its *Kultur,* for its *Geistesbildung,* and in Russia the new age of justice had arrived. Man was emerging from the dark past of his childhood. Imbued with such preponderant "faith in humanity," how indeed were the victims to believe, let alone make sense of, the inhumanity massing to destroy them? Evil on such a scale was not believable. As one survivor says, "We fell victim to our faith in mankind, our belief that humanity had set limits to the degradation and persecution of one's fellow man" (Donat, 103). Or as another survivor puts it, this time in direct answer to our questions:

> Why? Why did we walk like meek sheep to the
> slaughter-house? Why did we not fight back? . . . I
> know why. Because we had faith in humanity. Because
> we did not really think that human beings were capable
> of committing such crimes (Klein, 89).

The concentration camps were *in* this world and yet *not* in this world, places where behavior was grossly exaggerated, without apparent logic, yet fiercely hostile and encompassing. These are the components of nightmare, and if they join with the prisoner's psychic state—the confusion and stunned emotion, the dread and impotence, the split between a self that is victim and a self which, as through the wrong end of a telescope, merely watches —then the sense of nightmare is bound to prevail. During this time the prisoner suffers a terrible sleep, as when the young Wiesel saw what in shape and feeling could only be a nightmare:

> Not far from us, flames were leaping up from a ditch, gigantic flames. They were burning something. A lorry drew up at the pit and delivered its load—little children. Babies! Yes, I saw it—saw it with my own eyes. . . . Was I awake? I could not believe it. . . . No, none of this could be true. It was a nightmare (*Night,* 42).

Wiesel is not being literary, he is not using metaphor to enforce his perceptions. He is making the only reference remotely adequate to what he saw and felt. The dream of Hell, which for millennia had haunted Western consciousness, was now actual. Prisoners found themselves *in* it, just as we might find ourselves in a bad dream, without sense or perspective or relation. And as with nightmare, one tries to escape: either by saying that it is "only a dream," or by striving to "wake up."

But it was deadly to remain within the dream. Prisoners unable to shake off their sense of unreality could only drift as one drifts in dream, defenseless and stupid. Viktor Frankl observes that to regard camp existence as "unreal was in itself an important factor in causing the prisoners to lose their hold on life" (71). The alternative was to wake up, to replace apathy with struggle and transcend the derangement of nightmare by recovering moral perspective:

> Many times I felt I must be dreaming, and I would call to myself: "Wake up! Wake up! You are having a nightmare!" I would look around me, trying to wake up, but alas, my eyes kept on seeing the same dismal picture. Finally, I would start to shake all over, and I would say to myself: "You are in a concentration camp, in an annihilation camp. Don't let them get you down."

> **I didn't want to end up in the furnace; I wanted to live
> to tell of this** (Newman, 20).

This survivor of Auschwitz would "call" to herself as if split
into distant selves, the one passive, the other helpless but aware
of the need to act. The dream is not a dream, there is no way out,
and once she begins to admit the truth of her predicament the
sense of unreality fades. By coming to face the evil of the world
she is in she gains a perspective which sets her apart. Selfhood,
realism, and the desire to live emerge together ("I didn't want
to end up in the furnace") and culminate in the will to bear witness ("I wanted to live to tell of this"). ■

The survivor turns back to life because a process of healing, of
inner repair, has had the time to complete itself. The mind grows
able to respond once more, and here a final factor is evident, for
very often the moment of waking occurred in response to a specifically human act or circumstance. In the following instance a
survivor of Maidanek and Auschwitz describes her breakdown
and the care of a friend which gave her the time and encouragement to recover:

> **The shock that followed the unexpected loss of my
> mother, my frantic terror at the sight of the watchtow-
> ers, the machine-guns . . . drove me almost to the
> point of insanity. . . . and at a time when I should
> have forced myself to be as resistant as possible, I broke
> down completely. . . . Meanwhile Hela fought with
> redoubled strength—for herself and for me. She shared
> every bite she acquired with me. . . . Had it not been
> for Hela's efforts, I would not have roused myself from
> my apathy and despair** (Birenbaum, 94-96).

Suicide, or rather its failure, was also effective. It shocked the
prisoner back to life as if—and this may actually apply to all survivors who come through the period of collapse—the will to
survive were born by subjectively passing through death. I have

[85]

talked about this with survivors, and their stories are repeated in the case of a Soviet prisoner who attempted to hang himself. With the return to consciousness came a feeling of intense decision:

> During the following 17 years I was to go through unbelievable trials, trials in which death would have come as a real balm, but I never thought for a second to try it again. From that one wretched moment I was determined to survive (Solomon, 16).

Sometimes the catalyst was shock, sometimes the slow penetration of care. Often it was a new-found purpose—as when a survivor of Maidanek began "card-filing" the incoming prisoners:

> I thought of my arrival and my first impressions of the camp. I knew that a person coming to a camp was afraid of everything and everybody, that she was distracted and terrified. The first word was so important. I decided to be patient, to answer all questions, to calm them and give them courage. My life began to hold meaning (Zywulska, 113).

Typically also, the moment of waking coincided with the resolution to bear witness or with the decision to resist defilement. And often, too, survivors were jarred back to life by the same horror that, earlier, had paralyzed them. During one survivor's first days "there were moments when I could scarcely resist the temptation to end my life"; but one morning when he saw how the guards "piled up the dead bodies like steps of stairs, how the blockfuehrers played football with them, I put from me all thought of suicide" (Szalet, 52). Another survivor, a doctor, accidentally witnessed the end of a group of pregnant women and came to see that against such evil the alternative to death is revolt:

> They were beaten with clubs and whips, torn by dogs, dragged around by the hair and kicked in the stomach.
> . . . Then, when they collapsed, they were thrown into the crematory—alive. I stood, rooted to the ground,

unable to move, to scream, to run away. But gradually
the horror turned into revolt and this revolt shook me
out of my lethargy and gave me a new incentive to live.
I had to remain alive. . . . It was up to me to save the
life of the mothers, if there was no other way, then by
destroying the life of their unborn children   (Perl,
80-81).

That kind of decision—to save life through death—was forced
upon survivors repeatedly, and I shall return to it in Chapter
Five. The point now is that like each morning's waking, these
moments of return to the world are psychic acts of *turning,* from
passivity to action, from horror to the daily business of staying
alive—as if one turned one's actual gaze from left to right, from
darkness to possible light. As one survivor says, "I simply did not
dwell on the horrors I was living through" (Donat, 304). There
was no other way, and to become a survivor, every inmate had to
make this turn. Once it was made the possibility of coming
through was greatly increased, for now some part, at least, of
their fate was up to them. They now paid sharp attention, not to
the horror or to their own pain, but to the development of objective conditions which had to be judged constantly in terms of
their potential for life or for death. Survivors thus acquire a
capacity for realism, impersonal and without the least illusion, a
realism which one survivor has called "the inhuman frankness of
Auschwitz," and with it the ability to learn, to know, to fight
back in small ways:

> The longer we stayed in the camp, the more we gained
> in experience, our instincts sharpened, our vigilance de-
> veloped and our reactions quickened. We acquired a
> greater capacity for adapting ourselves to conditions
> (Birenbaum, 103).

They turned to face the worst straight-on, without sentiment or
special hope, simply to keep watch over life. And when the moment of turning came, finally, it was attended by a strong sensa-
tion of choice, a feeling of new determination, as if the decision

to survive were an inner fate expressing itself through a conscious assent of the will. As one survivor says, "It was then, faced with this spectacle of physical decay, with death rising like a tide on all sides, that I decided in my mind that I must live" (Bernard, 87). That is the moment of waking, of return; and this book, as I write, enacts the same resolution, the same kind of turn—away from the monstrous inhumanity of the concentration camps, away from the despair and nihilism they authorize, back to the small strands of life and decency which constitute, however faint and scattered, a fabric of discernible goodness amid that evil. ∎

But for many the turn never came. For them there was neither luck nor time. These people, thousands of them, were called the *Muselmänner,* the "moslems" or "walking dead," for whom time ran out before they were able to shake the sense of nightmare and wake to their predicament. They starved, they fell sick, they stumbled into situations which got them killed. For them the collapse was too much, too many psychic and physical blows too fast, until the momentum of decline increased beyond reversal. They died inwardly, and as their spirit withered their outward aspect was terrible to see:

> they behaved as if they were not thinking, not feeling, unable to act or respond. . . . Typically, this stopping of action began when they no longer lifted their legs as they walked, but only shuffled them. When finally even the looking about on their own stopped, they soon died (Bettelheim, 152-53).

This is the empirical instance of death-in-life. No more awful thing can be said of the concentration camps than that countless men and women were murdered in spirit as the means of killing them in body. Primo Levi has suggested that if we were to pull all the evil of our age into one image, it would be this face with dead eyes. In Levi's description we get some idea of the logical fate, the fate most feared, most nearly suffered, by everyone who passed through the camps:

> On their entry into the camp, through basic incapacity, or by misfortune, or through some banal incident, they are overcome before they can adapt themselves; they are beaten by time, they do not begin to learn German, to disentangle the infernal knot of laws and prohibitions until their body is already in decay, and nothing can save them from selections or from death by exhaustion. Their life is short, but their number is endless; they, the *Muselmänner,* the drowned, form the backbone of the camp, an anonymous mass, continually renewed and always identical, of non-men who march and labour in silence, the divine spark dead within them, already too empty to really suffer. One hesitates to call them living; one hesitates to call their death death (82).

To say "they went to their death like sheep" is easy enough, and we say it often indeed. Thereby our own fear finds expression, our own terror and doubt to be concealed even as we imply that we know better than they what it must be like to wake up in a concentration camp, to carry on through nightmare, to turn back somehow to that world. Whatever our reasons, we can make such assumptions only by disregarding a cardinal fact about the survivor's experience: *all things human take time,* time which the damned never have, time for life to repair at least the worst of its wounds. It took time to wake, time for horror to incite revolt, time for the recovery of lucidity and will. Imagine the time necessary to carry through a major resistance action in a concentration camp—the infinitely slow work of regenerating will and self-respect, of building trust, of making contacts, getting arms, sustaining deaths and betrayals, establishing accurate plans and then, together, moving as they did in Buchenwald, in Auschwitz, Sobibor, Treblinka. Everything depended on time, and in the interim chance ruled supreme. Any accumulation of too much bad luck at once —to be exhausted and starving and *then* get sick and *then* be savagely beaten—and the frail spirit broke. This happened most often to new prisoners; but it could happen to anyone, and the survivor's greatest fear was that through a run of bad luck he or she would sink irreversibly into the masses of the doomed.

In almost all accounts by survivors the spectacle of these truly "dead souls" is mentioned, and always with the same mixture of pity and revulsion. In the Soviet camps they were called *dokhodyaga,* the "goners," and the fear they inspire arises from the *visible* process of spirit in decay:

> **There was a man squatting on a rubbish heap. He must have broken down—mentally, I mean, and that was the end, physically too, in every case—and if he found a fish head, he tried to suck the eyes and did things like that** (Knapp, 77).

That, for survivors, was worse than being killed outright. And it was always possible, for once the will to live had been regained it was constantly undermined by chance and despair. Prisoners survived by chance, they died by chance, and they *knew* it. In one instance a group of women were rounded up at random and locked in the gas chamber. All night they stood jammed against each other waiting; at dawn they were released because the SS had run out of gas, and by the time the next supply arrived it was someone else's turn. And always, around that corner, around this one, there might be an SS man drunk and killing for the fun of it: "Their hands were never far from their revolvers and even without provocation they would draw them and shoot a prisoner in the face at close range" (Vrba, 209). It was indeed hopeless, and yet the alternative was either to quit and join the *Muselmänner,* or to strive anyway, *as if* chance were to some extent on one's side. A survivor of Birkenau put it this way: "She knows that a number of circumstances evoked by orders or accidents may cause her annihilation, but she knows too that there is a chance to escape death and that it is up to her to win the game" (Szmaglewska, 117).

But still it was hopeless. The striking fact is that from a logical point of view, resistance and survival were just not possible.

The following dialogue, between two women in Auschwitz, expresses the general outlook among survivors:

> "There's no hope for us."
> And her hand makes a gesture and the gesture evokes rising smoke.
> "We must fight with all our strength."
> "Why? . . . Why fight since all of us have to . . ."
> The hand completes the gesture. Rising smoke.
> "No. We must fight."
> "How can we hope to get out of here. How could anyone ever get out of here. It would be better to throw ourselves on the barbed wire right now."
> What is there to say to her. She is small, sickly. And I am unable to persuade myself. All arguments are senseless. I am at odds with my reason. One is at odds with all reason (Delbo, 18).

The survivor's will to go on is illogical, irrational, stupid with another wisdom. Just to *read* descriptions of camp conditions leads to loss of faith in the prospect of survival. Life seems so clearly impossible against such odds. Yet in extremity the function of intelligence is not to judge one's chances, which are nearly zero, but to make the most of each day's opportunity for getting through *that* day: "I realized, after what I had seen, that my attitude to Auschwitz would have to change. No longer was it simply a question of surviving. It was a question of surviving today without thinking too much about tomorrow" (Vrba, 108). At any moment the survivor might be killed, might be hurt badly enough in mind and body to make *another* return impossible. But until then, he or she hangs on despite evidence on all sides that death is inevitable. As long as the spirit does not break, the survivor keeps mute faith in life. Against the knowledge of chance and hopelessness there is another, more intimate knowledge—an awareness of "that puzzling potential of inner strength," as one survivor says,

> which permits your body to keep warm though the penetrating chill freezes the soil and clots the damp

sand, which permits you to keep the cheerfulness of spirit though death and extermination are all about you, which permits you to have faith that the Germans will lose though you are surrounded—take that railroad track, for instance, with its purposeful shipments—by evidences of their power (Szmaglewska, 125). ▪

Life in extremity reveals in its movement a definite rhythm of decline and renewal. The state of wakefulness is essential, but in actual experience it is less an unwavering hardness of spirit than a tenuous achievement with periods of weakness and strength. Survivors not only wake, but reawake, fall low and begin to die, and then turn back to life. This happened to individual inmates all the time. Sometimes just the shock of realizing that one was becoming a *Muselman* was enough to inspire new will. But often, too, the experience of renewal was shared, sometimes in moments of intense solidarity:

> Pain and . . . fear . . . kept us awake. A cloudless sky, thickly set with glittering stars, looked in upon our grief-filled prison. The moon shone through the window. Its light was dazzling that night and gave the pale, wasted faces of the prisoners a ghostly appearance. It was as if all the life had ebbed out of them. I shuddered with dread, for it suddenly occurred to me that I was the only living man among corpses.
>
> All at once the oppressive silence was broken by a mournful tune. It was the plaintive tones of the ancient "Kol Nidre" prayer. I raised myself up to see whence it came. There, close to the wall, the moonlight caught the uplifted face of an old man, who, in self-forgetful, pious absorption, was singing softly to himself. . . . His prayer brought the ghostly group of seemingly insensible human beings back to life. Little by little, they all roused themselves and all eyes were fixed on the moonlight-flooded face.
>
> We sat up very quietly, so as not to disturb the old man, and he did not notice that we were listening. . . . When at last he was silent, there was exaltation among

us, an exaltation which men can experience only when they have fallen as low as we had fallen and then, through the mystic power of a deathless prayer, have awakened once more to the world of the spirit (Szalet, 70-71).

On its collective level, this movement away from, and then back toward, life and humanness was more apparent in the Soviet camps, where the impact of some rumor or special event would cause the mood of the entire camp to rise or fall. In the following instance a kind of general resurrection occurred when everyone in camp was allowed a "free" day, with no work and maybe a bit of extra food:

At every step, in every corner of the barrack, the approaching holiday could be sensed. I could never understand how so much politeness suddenly appeared from under the shell of indifference and mutual hatred. As they talked, the men showed each other so much courtesy and friendliness that, looking at them, I could almost forget that I was in prison. There was a stench of bad breath and sweat in the barrack, clouds of steam seeped in from the door and the faces seemed to blur in the murky light, but despite all this there was so much life and happy excitement there, so much hope and feeling. . . . Good-night, good-night, excited voices whispered all around, sleep well, tomorrow is our holiday, tomorrow is a day of rest (Herling, 116).

And sometimes, finally, this kind of rebirth came with all the pain and mystery of actual birth, as if the two were but different instances of an identical process. To go into a camp "hospital" was not to expect improvement, since the main function of such places was to gather up the dead and dying. There was little treatment, often none at all, and here the diseases of the camp were assembled without precaution. In the Nazi camps, the worst cases were regularly "selected" for extermination, and terrible "experiments" were performed. A prisoner went into the camp hospital fairly sure that life was finished. The temptation to quit was very

[93]

strong, and yet in these places too, many men and women regained the desire to live. And as experienced, it felt as if the power of life itself were pulling them back to the world:

> **The first thing the dying woman feels upon return to consciousness is pain. She is not yet fully awake after her exhausting delirium and she already feels a pain deep within her, near the heart, just as if a kind hand lovingly hugged the heart, forgetting that this may hurt. . . . When the body lies shrunken to a childish form, when arms and legs have become like thin twigs, when the mouth is parched and puckered, when every bite of food causes the return of dysentery, when the very smell of the camp soup brings on nausea, when there is no help, no care, no medicine—whence comes this magic will to live? Where is it born, in which recess of the human body does it bud and blossom so strongly that it can conquer Death in his many shapes? Whence comes that imperishable will power to find the means of defense? (Szmaglewska, 49).**

These are the questions, addressed not to the fact that so many died, but to the fact that some survived. And the answers can only lie in life itself. There is a power at the center of our being, at the heart of all things living. But only in man does it assume a spiritual character. And only through spirit does life continue by decision. "Human beings are like weeds," said a Soviet prisoner to his cellmates. "They take some killing. Now if you treated horses like this they'd be dead in a couple of days" (Weissberg, 389). But this answer only points to a deeper question. Perhaps we shall not fathom the wonder of life at its roots, or discern how strength can rest on such frail foundations. Only within the last hundred years have the biological sciences begun to formulate objectively what might be meant by "life in itself." I shall return to this in Chapter Seven, but already we can grasp some part, at least, of what the survivor's experience reveals: that whether felt as a power, or observed as a system of activities, life is existence laboring to sustain itself, repairing, defending, healing. ∎

LIFE IN DEATH

In my happier days I used to remark on the aptitude of the saying, "When in life we are in the midst of death." I have since learnt that it's more apt to say, "When in death we are in the midst of life."

A BELSEN SURVIVOR

In our group we shared everything; and the moment one of the group ate something without sharing it, we knew it was the beginning of the end for him.

A TREBLINKA SURVIVOR

IN *NIGHT,* Elie Wiesel records two moments of advice, two prescriptions for survival in the concentration camps. The first came from an "old" prisoner speaking to the new arrivals:

> We are all brothers, and we are all suffering the same fate. The same smoke floats over all our heads. Help one another. It is the only way to survive (52).

The second was an anonymous inmate's comment:

> Listen to me, boy. Don't forget that you're in a concentration camp. Here, every man has to fight for himself and not think of anyone else. Even of his father. Here, there are no fathers, no brothers, no friends. Everyone lives and dies for himself alone (122).

Help one another. Every man for himself. The conflict is classic, and nowhere more starkly stressed than in the concentration-camp ordeal. For as soon as survivors wake to the reality of their predicament they must choose. They must decide which view will govern their behavior and their perception of camp life as a whole. In extremity the claims of self-interest seem sounder, more logical; and the second prescription—help only thyself—dominates the description of events in Wiesel's books: men fight among themselves, fathers contend with sons to the death. The rule of war was total, or so he implies. Yet Wiesel did not abandon his father, and the prisoner who gave kind advice was, after all, a man living in Auschwitz.

There is a contradiction in Wiesel's view of the camps, a contradiction which occurs so often in reports by survivors that it amounts to a double vision at the heart of their testimony. In *The Holocaust Kingdom,* Alexander Donat describes Maidanek as a world in which "the doomed devoured each other," but he includes another kind of evidence as well, for instance his near death from a beating he received for refusing to beat others, and the help he was given, when he was desperately in need of time to recover, by someone who found him a clerking job. Likewise, in his account of survival in Auschwitz Sim Kessel says: "Intelligence, courage, knowledge, vitality, the desire to live—all counted for nothing. . . . common misery reduced everyone to the same level, erasing all values, breaking down all wills" (10). He sticks to this assessment, despite examples of courage and quick-wittedness, despite his own slow coming to terms with the knowledge of how to survive. He says all concern for others vanished; yet one morning when, like countless others, Kessel collapsed in the snow and could not get up, "two neighbors leaned over me, saying that I was feverish and they would help me. And so they did; they supported me, almost carrying me at times" (161). They never knew his name, nor he theirs.

Acts of care and decency seem so out of place in the camps that survivors themselves are perplexed. In his description of the Soviet camps, Jerzy Gliksman states that "the conditions in which we had to live aroused the worst instincts in all of us. All trace of human solidarity vanished" (217). But here again the principle of jungle rule is belied by events which Gliksman describes in the course of his story. Most striking, perhaps, is the moment when night-blindness (a frequent illness among vitamin-starved prisoners in the northern camps) made his predicament "most desperate":

> One evening as I was walking . . . with my arms stretched out in front of me, like a real blind man, an unknown individual took me by the arm and conducted me to a spot that had more light. . . . "Don't you recognize me? . . . I am Berg . . . don't you remember me from Kotlas?" (301).

Kotlas was the transit camp where they had met and briefly talked. Berg knew his way around better and was able to get a job for Gliksman in one of the innumerable GULAG file rooms, with an improvement in shelter and light which saved his life. Gliksman concludes the episode by saying: "To the present day I do not know why this man, almost a total stranger, did me such a good turn" (304).

Incidents like these seem exceptional, as indeed they were, and yet they happened all the time—a fact which does not negate the savagery of existence in the camps, but which qualifies the view of "all against all" and needs accounting for. Reports by survivors regularly include small deeds of courage and resistance, of help and mutual care; but in the larger picture, the image of viciousness and death grows to such enormous intensity that all else— any sign of elementary humanness—pales to insignificance. And surely this is understandable. The element of chance was so pervasive, the moments of salvation so unexpected, that the power of human encounters seemed slight and difficult to make sense of. Shock was another factor; what impressed survivors most indelibly was death, suffering, terror, all on a scale of magnitude and monstrosity not to be faced without lasting trauma. Primarily, however, survivors stress the negative side of camp existence because their accounts are governed by an obsessive need to "tell the world" of the terrible things they have seen. This determines not only the kind of material they select to record, but also the emphasis they give it. As a witness, the survivor aims above all to convey the otherness of the camps, their specific inhumanity. ∎

But the contradiction goes deeper than that. The essential paradox of extremity is that life persists in a world ruled by death. Life-in-death characterizes every aspect of the survivor's experience, for in order to live and stay human, the survivor must be in the world but not of it. That, of course, is an old distinction. For the Stoic or the Christian it was mainly a matter of spiritual detachment. For the survivor the problem is more difficult. He too must maintain detachment; he too must preserve an identity apart from the one imposed by his environment. But since for him death is the immediate determinant of behavior, he must find a realm of separateness not in mind only but also in action. The survivor must act on two levels, be "with and against," as Eugen Kogon says. And what this means in practice is that to stay alive survivors often worked for, or even in, camp administration. As a Soviet survivor said, "you can only survive on a function" (Ekart, 53). To one degree or another, many survivors were spokes in the wheel of mass murder, the ultimate instance being those members of the *Sonderkommandos* who ran the Nazi gas chambers—but who also burned down Treblinka and Sobibor, and blew up the crematorium at Auschwitz.

Under normal circumstances, assistance in crime is condemned, if only because (and this amounts to a definition of the civilized state) there is always a margin of choice, always another way to live. But in extremity there may be no other way to live. In the concentration camps, to choose life means to come to terms with, but also to resist, the forces of destruction. And although this imperative opens the door to every manner of hypocrisy and lie, and therefore becomes a permanent occasion for corruption, it cannot be avoided. The luxury of sacrifice—by which I mean the strategic choice of death to resolve irreconcilable moral conflicts —is meaningless in a world where any person's death only contributes to the success of evil.

Overtly the survivor defers to death, covertly he or she defies it. This duality of behavior, of concrete action on separate levels, is one of the principal characteristics of existence in extremity— or in any institution, slavery for example, which through threat and force attempts to reduce its members to nothing but functions in the system. The structure of behavior in "total institutions" has been analyzed by Erving Goffman in *Asylums,* and he arrives at the following distinction:

> When an individual co-operatively contributes required activity to an organization and under required conditions . . . he is transformed into a co-operator; he becomes the "normal," "programmed," or built-in member. He gives and gets in an appropriate spirit what has been systematically planned for, whether this

entails much or little of himself. . . . I shall speak in these circumstances of the individual having a *primary adjustment* to the organization. . . .

I have constructed this clumsy term in order to get to a second one, namely, *secondary adjustments,* defining these as any habitual arrangement by which a member of an organization employs unauthorized means, or obtains unauthorized ends, or both, thus getting around the organization's assumptions as to what he should do and get and hence what he should be. Secondary adjustments represent ways in which the individual stands apart from the role and the self that were taken for granted for him by the institution (188-89).

Goffman concludes by suggesting that "these [secondary adjustments] together comprise what can be called the *underlife* of the institution, being to a social establishment what an underworld is to a city" (199). In extremity this "underlife" becomes the literal basis of life.

During the ordeal of the Warsaw Ghetto, for example, and precisely in Goffman's sense, Chaim Kaplan made the following remark in his *Diary*:

In these days of our misfortune we live the life of Marranos. Everything is forbidden to us, and yet we do everything. Every Jewish occupation is under a ban, yet nevertheless we somehow support ourselves; true, we do it with grief, but we do survive" (174).

Trade was illegal, procuring medicines was illegal, schooling the children was illegal. So were things like meetings, movement outside the ghetto, and traveling the streets after curfew. The punishment was death, and yet all these activities were necessary to life and had to be carried on covertly, at constant risk.

One of the most persistent forms of "secondary adjustment," in both the camps and the ghettos, was smuggling. In the Warsaw Ghetto this kind of "illegal" activity involved everyone; it proceeded daily on both individual and organized levels, and as death by starvation increased, it grew to heroic proportions. There were periodic crackdowns, when dozens of smugglers were shot, and other, looser times when bizarre methods of every sort were used:

> Specially constructed mobile ramps were set against the walls on both sides to smuggle over live cows and oxen. . . . From the window of a building . . . which overlooked the ghetto . . . a sheet metal pipe was lowered and milk poured across the racial boundary (Goldstein, 78).

Operations on this scale depended on collaboration with the oppressor—in other words, on "one simple and powerful mechanism, bribery, which reached to the police of all varieties and the gendarmes of all ranks" (Goldstein, 75). The complexity of such deals was amazing, as in this example from Ringelblum's *Notes*:

> A ladder is thrown over the Wall and smuggling goes on all night. But this night the smugglers quarrel among themselves, and one of them informs where it will do the most good. The police come at once and catch a whole crowd in the middle of operations. Machine guns begin shooting, one smuggler is shot dead on the spot, one or two others wounded. Then they search every apartment in the building, take away a great deal of goods, and arrest forty smugglers. For 40,000 zlotys, they return the goods and set the smugglers free. That is the sum that the police claim to have lost because the smugglers used the Wall to bring goods in, rather than taking them through the watch at the Ghetto gate, where the police get a cut (264-65).

Organized smuggling brought profits, and no doubt that was a powerful incentive. But Ringelblum observed a devil-may-care attitude among smugglers, a kind of stark bravado which kept them going and gave their deeds a desperate glamor: "One of the smugglers told a friend that he would keep on smuggling, because if he didn't, he would starve to death. Rather die fast from a bullet than slow from hunger" (293). For the children, however, glamor faded to pathos, a pathos infinite and never to be answered, as in this example from Mary Berg's *Diary*:

> Whole gangs of little children are organized, boys and girls from five to ten years of age. The smallest and most emaciated of them wrap burlap bags around their bony little bodies. Then they slink across to the "Aryan" side. . . . Often peasants give them potatoes for nothing. Their terrible appearance arouses pity. . . . On this side of the barbed wire their older partners wait for them. Very often they stay there for hours waiting until the Nazi guard is busy checking the passport of some foreign citizen or Polish Gentile visiting the ghetto. This gives them an opportunity to smuggle their foodstuffs. Sometimes the German sentry does not notice them, sometimes he does, but pretends that he does not. . . . But most of the German guards fire in cold blood at the running children, and the Jewish policemen must then pick up the bleeding victims, fallen like wounded birds, and throw them on passing rikshas (72-73).

Here we should also remember—especially when we talk about people dying "like sheep"—that any kind of armed uprising within the ghettos or the camps depended on smuggling; and that arms were a great deal harder to obtain, and certainly harder to hide, than food. When Bruno Bettelheim criticizes everyone in Auschwitz who did not act as did the *Sonderkommando* which blew up the crematorium and shot it out with the SS (Nyiszli, "Foreword"), he does not allow for the fact that the arms and explosives which made that particular revolt possible took years to accumulate. An organization had to be forged and made trustworthy amid constant depletion of members who were killed. Contacts with partisan groups outside the camp had to be made and, more difficult yet, maintained through time against informers. Finally, arms had to be found, paid for (which involved another network of smuggling), and successfully carried through an intricate system of surveillance. Only then was revolt possible.

And all this had to be done while, ostensibly, the prisoners were cringing like dogs before their Nazi masters.

They cringed and hurried to perform their ugly jobs, but they did not justify themselves by saying, "I *do* one thing but I *think* another." The survivor is not a type of the "beautiful soul," as Hegel called those who embrace pristine principles but dare not tarnish them through action. Inward resistance is indispensable, but for survivors something more is needed. Their lives and humanness directly depend on active *works*. And since on the "primary" level they are meshed in destruction, they must find another, "secondary" level of action—ways which will keep themselves and each other alive in spirit as well as in body. Survivors often remark that if a prisoner were to obey all camp rules he or she would be dead in a month. As a woman who survived Auschwitz says, "According to even the Camp Commandant . . . the obedient *Häftlinge* could only survive for three months at the very most. Those who lived longer did so only by cheating the authorities" (Hart, 66). Or as a survivor of Buchenwald says, they "gradually realized that obedience meant death. The only hope of survival lay in resistance" (Weinstock, 34). ∎

Ghetto and camp regulations were designed to make life impossible. Survival therefore depended on an "underworld" of activities, all of them illegal, all of them risky, but all essential to life. There was a special word for this, current in all the camps: to carry out any kind of illegal action was "to organize." As one survivor says, "I was later to know that 'organize' was *the* most important word in the Auschwitz language. It meant: to steal, buy, exchange, get hold of" (Hart, 54). Another survivor, also from Auschwitz, gives a fuller description:

> In the language of a political prisoner the word "organize" means to acquire a thing you need without wrong-

ing another prisoner. For instance: to take a shirt from a warehouse full of underwear left to rot and be gnawed by rats because a German Kapo would rather see it destroyed than give it to prisoners is to organize. But to take someone else's shirt which she washed and put on the grass to dry is not to organize—that is stealing. When a prisoner gives other prisoners a few loaves of bread filched from the supply room—this is organization. But when the block supervisor takes loaves from the rations of other prisoners and hands them out to privileged prisoners, for some underhand additional services—that is theft. On the area of the camp there are many storerooms filled with all kinds of goods. From time to time their contents are sent to the interior of Germany. To manage to get at those shipments and distribute some articles of daily need over the camp uncaught, and thus make life easier for fellow prisoners means to know how to organize (Szmaglewska, 66-67).

Food had to be organized, because no one could subsist on camp rations. Things like shoes, blankets and warm clothing had to be organized, as did jobs. Spoons and bowls—without which one could not even get soup—had to be organized, because in many cases these essential items were not provided. And although on occasion the individual prisoner had a chance to grab something for himself, most of the time the items of daily need could only be acquired through collective action; hence the social significance of the word *organize,* used to cover all forms of illegal, life-sustaining activity. This was one of the primal facts about Auschwitz, or any of the camps, and it was something the new prisoner had to learn fast if he or she expected to live:

And all the time there was this awful fight for one's bare existence. The essential thing of course, was not to lose the will to live, for this definitely meant death. I soon realized that alone one could not possibly survive. It was necessary therefore to form little families of two or three. In this way we looked after one another (Hart, 63).

The most important kind of organizing (apart from that of the political underground) was smuggling food, shoes and clothing out of warehouses into the rest of the camp. The Nazi extermination plant included gigantic systems of storage and transport, places where the belongings of millions of victims—money and foodstuffs, blankets, cooking utensils and all kinds of clothing— were gathered and packed for shipment back to the Reich. The largest of these was at Auschwitz. It was called "Canada," which in camp slang meant "an abundance of everything." There was so much sheer bulk to be processed that "the Germans became generous with manpower and put nearly twelve hundred men and two thousand women into the work" (Lengyel, 77). And although the least punishment a prisoner could expect for "stealing" was the customary and often fatal twenty-five lashes, each evening members of the Canada squads returned with vital loot:

> One had six tins of sardines, another, two pounds of figs. Shirts and fruit and soap, salami, sausages and ham appeared until the barracks began to look like a well-stocked grocery. . . . The block senior strolled in to collect his percentage. . . . The camp doctors, themselves prisoners, were there, too, looking for drugs, for medicines, for anything which might help them in their hopeless task (Vrba, 132).

The crucial moment was the search, and all kinds of tricks were devised to get through:

> Every evening, before returning to camp, we were put through three spot-checks. These were carried out by dead-drunk Storm Troopers. . . . Anyone on whom was found the smallest trifle was beaten terribly. . . . Even so, everyone smuggled things back into camp. . . . Every day I put on a new pair of shoes at work, came back wearing them and gave them to comrades in the camp. . . . We smuggled gloves, blouses, underwear on our stomachs, under the coarse striped camp chemise. I hid pieces of bread, cake, bacon under my clothing as I held it during the searches (Birenbaum, 169-70).

Each Canada worker had his or her own special methods, on which the lives of others depended: "I usually wore at least three of everything. . . . I pinned towels along the inside back of the dresses. . . . I carried rings and even gold watches inside my mouth" (Hart, 95).

Such places as Canada were like infernal funnels through which the wealth of the victims was sucked in—tons of gold, millions of dollars in jewelry—supposedly to be sent to Berlin, but much going into SS pockets. Some of it, however, went for purposes far different from those prescribed:

> **We used the bank notes as toilet paper. We buried boxes full of gold and valuables in the ground. We handed much to the men, if and whenever possible, for it was generally believed that the men had contact with an underground movement and that any valuables might come in useful in obtaining ammunition for an uprising** (Hart, 88).

Smuggling is only one example of "organizing." Prisoners working in factories performed daily acts of sabotage and theft. Those who worked in the notorious medical blocks stole medicines, jockeyed names, lied about symptoms, and in Buchenwald they used the typhus wards, which the SS would not go near, to hide men whose names had come up on the death lists. Others kept up contact with partisan groups and helped arrange escapes. Still others circulated news of the progress of the war—news on which camp morale depended. In Soviet camps there was mass theft of camp supplies, especially coal and construction materials, both essential to survival in an arctic climate. Camp facilities were used for "illegal" activities: "Buildings designed for the manufacture of heavy equipment also housed independent workshops for producing goods out of pilfered materials, waste, and remnants" (Gilboa, 197). And since, in the Soviet camps, the worker's daily food allotment, as well as the privileges of those in administration, depended on fulfillment of "work norms," everyone, from the common worker to the Camp Commandant, falsified work reports. Prisoners fulfilled their timber-cutting norm by stealing from yesterday's output. If a work brigade produced fourteen cars of coal in a day, the brigade leader put down fifteen in his report, in order to meet the norm and insure a decent food allotment for his men. In GULAG, cheating was universal.

The distinction between "primary" and "secondary" levels of behavior was central to the concentration-camp experience. Men and women conformed because otherwise they died. But they also resisted, and for the same reason: otherwise they died. Only by resisting could they sustain themselves and each other through despair and hardship. As a survivor of Auschwitz puts it:

> Oppression as violent as that under which we lived automatically provoked resistance. Our entire existence in the camp was marked by it. When the employees of "Canada" detoured items destined for Germany to the benefit of their fellow internees, it was resistance. When labourers at the spinning mills dared to slacken their working pace, it was resistance. When at Christmas we organized a little "festival" under the noses of our masters, it was resistance. When, clandestinely, we passed letters from one camp to another, it was resistance. When we endeavoured, and sometimes with success, to reunite two members of the same family—for example, by substituting one internee for another in a gang of stretcher bearers—it was resistance (Lengyel, 154).

On the surface, cooperation with camp administration appeared total. But underneath, moral sanity reasserted itself, response to necessity was characterized by resistance, and the worst effects of extremity were thereby transcended. In a literal sense, these countless, concrete acts of subterfuge constituted the "underlife" of the death camps. By doing what had to be done (disobey) in the only way it could be done (collectively) survivors kept their social being, and therefore their essential humanity, intact. ■

The effectiveness of "organizing" depended on teamwork, and stable social units were thereby created in which relations were personal and friendly. These small groups sprang up everywhere, but in addition there was another, much broader network of interaction. This was the black market, an impersonal system of acquisition and barter which ran full tilt in all the concentration camps. Like any black market, this one took advantage of privation and thrived on scarcity. It was exceptional only in the scope and daring of its operations, and perhaps also for the improbable items—bottles of Clos Vougeot, caviar, packs of Lucky Strike—which appeared as if by magic. Goods were acquired in all sorts of ways, from "organizing" and manufacture to theft and deals with guards and camp officials. Elaborate methods of trading evolved, many of them dangerous and all of them open to betrayal. Yet here was a vigorous underworld of interchange. Prisoners met as buyers and sellers, sometimes in friendship, more often in suspicion and cunning, but nevertheless as participants in a steady stream of activity which, in the end and despite grave abuse, supported the general struggle for life. A survivor of Auschwitz describes it this way:

> Prices were determined by the scarcity of commodities, the inadequacy of rations, and, of course, by the risks in securing the article. . . . The barter was a natural result of local conditions. It was difficult not to take part in it. I paid eight days' ration of bread for a piece of cloth to make a nurse's blouse. I also had to pay three soups to have it sewn (Lengyel, 78-79).

This was the underside of the underside, a dimension of "secondary" action which exploited vital needs but at the same time helped to fulfill them. And it was important for another reason. By playing on SS greed, the black market contributed to the spread of corruption in high places; and this in turn, weakened the discipline of the SS, not only among themselves, but more importantly in their control of camp affairs and therefore the lives of the prisoners. "Large-scale theft was possible," says a survivor of Auschwitz, "only because the S.S. men and women, who were supposed to supervise the prisoners at their work in the stores, stole themselves, in competition and accord with the prisoners" (Lingens-Reiner, 48). Power declined as guards and officers came more and more to depend on their victims:

> For instance, the camp doctor, Dr. Rohde, before going on leave which he was spending with his wife, went to a Polish prisoner and asked the man to find him a nice present for her. What he got was a large pigskin dressing-case. When he returned from leave he told the prisoner that his wife had liked it very much and sent many thanks (Lingens-Reiner, 48).

The by-ways of trade and theft were often quite complicated, and sometimes even humorous:

> I remember the round trip of a pair of battle-dress trousers. An S.S. man stole them from a comrade and sold them for stolen sugar to a prisoner working in the kitchen. The prisoner gave them to his girl friend in the woman's camp, from whom they were stolen by another prisoner, a prostitute. Another S.S. man "confiscated" them as "illicit property," and gave them to a second prostitute with whom he had an affair. She sold them for spirits to a wardress, who bartered them for margarine, after which they returned to the first prisoner working in the men's kitchen. . . . So it happened with small things and with far more important things. And perhaps it was not altogether an evil, because even a black market is better than none at all (Lingens-Reiner, 46).

Relatively few prisoners had the energy and time for intrigue of that sort. Traffic in "illicit property" touched the rest of the camp population mainly on the level of small thefts, and these were so constant and widespread as to constitute a perpetual mode of exchange:

> the uniformed SS Doctor Koenig rushes among the standing women. . . . Bowls and spoons fly with a

clash, bread, rations of margarine and sausage end in the ditch. . . . From behind the brick barracks gypsies cautiously creep out. . . . In one second the ditch is empty, and the property has changed hands (Szmaglewska, 71).

In the Soviet camps, stealing was nothing less than *the* way of life. As one survivor says:

> Stealing was prevalent . . . in every camp in Russia. For eight years I never heard any denial of this. It could not be called dishonesty: it was simply a fight for life at any price (Ekart, 204).

The point is not so much the prevalence of stealing as the fact that amid this scramble of trickery and theft a semblance of order emerged—conditions of interchange which were tolerated in much the same way as we, when we play games, agree to abide by the "rules." Through practices that could be justified only by extreme need, a system of barter became possible, a partial recovery of human community through inhuman means. The wonder is not that a black market thrived or that stealing was rampant, but that these activities did not thrive more, did not become absolute. There was in all the camps a significant drive toward decency, a persistent tendency to transcend the amorality of initial conditions and to establish modes of interchange which were life-supporting and a basis for relations truly social:

> Small cooperatives were formed. One member contributed his kettle, another some water, a third a slice of bread and another a pinch of salt. The biggest capitalist of all was Joachim . . . who had hidden away in his underwear a small packet of saccharine tablets. Breaking each tablet in half, and sometimes into quarters, he would give a piece to the cooperatives in exchange for a good share of the brew. But I did all right too. I had a little bar of concentrated pea soup, so everyone was willing to do business with me (Fittkau, 121).

This kind of "business" was universal and was governed by "one of the basic laws of prison-camp life":

Any small possessions that others might use became a man's capital and he was entitled to make profit from them. A knife earned you a sliver of any food it was used to cut. A needle could be rented for anything the man who wanted to use it could pay (Fittkau, 84).

Pushed by necessity, prisoners became masters of invention; they acquired items useful for camp "business" by an endless proliferation of cunning and ingenious techniques:

> To begin with first things: you want a needle in prison, if you are to keep your clothes and socks—don't forget you have no change of clothing—in any sort of repair. But you have no tools; everything has been taken away from you. What you do then is to smash the light bulb . . . and from the fragments select a sharp, pointed piece of glass. With that you can bore a hole through a fishbone and there is your needle (Knapp, 29).

Or consider the use of the latrine in a Soviet prison:

> there were a few loose bricks in the wall, which were excellent for sharpening bits of metal. In this way we were able to make the tools necessary for our continued existence. . . . As knives and needles were needed by all, . . . the majority had to borrow them, and the service was repaid by some makhorka [tobacco], a piece of bread or some sugar (Ekart, 26).

And as in any system of manufacture and services, methods of distribution were also invented:

> The next step was the division of the bread into the required number of portions, which was done by a man specially elected for that function. . . . The sugar was also divided out with the aid of scales made from matchboxes, wood and pieces of string. But as even with all these precautions there was no guarantee that the shares would be equal, lots were drawn in the following manner. The rations of bread and sugar were divided into batches for five people and then placed on the table. Then five people messing together would appoint a delegate, who was given a number for his

group. One delegate would stand with his back to the table, and another would point at a group of rations and say, "For whom?" The one with his back to the table might say, "Number twelve," which meant that the delegate from number twelve group would collect the particular lot of rations and divide it with his four messmates (Ekart, 28-29).

Next to food, the most prized commodity for trade, especially in the Soviet camps, was tobacco—not tobacco such as we know, but "the well-known Russian *makhorka* (a special plant-stem cut into small pieces), which tastes right only when it is wrapped up in Russian newspaper, as this does not burn while smoking, but only glows" (Nork, 32). Almost all prisoners came to use this stuff, not only because "it was an excellent remedy against hunger" (Nork, 32), but also because in extreme deprivation some slight pleasure is imperative, some physical stimulation indispensable—not to mention the psychic lift that such a drug can produce when the body is starving. To say that tobacco served a steady social function is not to exaggerate:

> There was no such thing as matches or flint, but the prisoners had an ingenious system of their own for lighting the cigarettes. A fellow named Vasha was a past master at the technique. He was also jealous of his talent, because he exacted two puffs from every cigarette he lit. He'd take a piece of cotton, or stuffing from a pillow, or the lining of a quilted jacket, fluff it up and stretch it out very thin, then roll it up tight. Next he would put the cotton between two boards and rub them vigorously, faster and faster, sometimes for as long as fifteen minutes. . . . As soon as he smelled smoke, Vasha pulled out the rolled-up cotton, broke it at the point where it was smoldering, and very gently began to blow on it until it was completely aglow. Then, while he carefully shielded it in his hand, everyone who had a cigarette crowded eagerly around for a light. Vasha would take the first two puffs from every cigarette, drawing the smoke deep down into his lungs on each puff until it looked as if he were about to burst,

hold the smoke as long as he could, then exhale it—into
someone else's mouth (Ciszek, 91).

Strange practices, but organized with ritual correctness, with
division of labor and reward. In the camps any kind of talent,
any sort of item or possession, was put to enterprising use. Prisoners became expert scavengers, forever on the lookout for anything at all—"a piece of tinplate, a nail, a stick or a cigarette end"
(Ekart, 32)—with which to transact "business." In *One Day in
the Life of Ivan Denisovich,* Solzhenitsyn's hero risks severe punishment to smuggle a piece of broken saw-blade past the guards.
He knows that sooner or later another prisoner will be "in the
market" and ready to trade. On such modes of exchange survivors
depended for a life that was primitive and barren, but not without
dignity, and not completely savage. Always on the verge of social dissolution, men and women managed to achieve sustaining
order through forms of interchange which life itself—in all
things the mother of invention—demanded of them. ∎

Between conditions in Soviet and in Nazi camps there were obvious differences; and some of the latter, furthermore, were "official" killing centers while others were "merely" labor camps.
Yet I have not hesitated to call all these places "death camps."
More than three million people died in Auschwitz, but if the incoming prisoner was not killed immediately, his or her chance
for life was much better than that of the prisoner sent to one of
the smaller camps where there was less food and more random
killing. And what, really, is the difference if Buchenwald was not
classified as an extermination camp and had no gas chamber, but
had special rooms for mass shooting and a level of privation so
severe that prisoners died in hundreds every day? Starvation
claimed victims by the thousand everywhere. Apart from that,
Nazi victims were usually gassed or shot, whereas Soviet prisoners died mainly of exhaustion and sickness. There was likewise a

difference in atmosphere: horror and dread were overwhelming in the Nazi camps, while in Soviet camps the predominant mood was a blend of rage and hopelessness. But again, these are secondary distinctions so far as survivors are concerned. For them any camp was a closed world in which one's chance of coming through was nearly zero.

To describe existence in the camps as a condition of life-in-death is neither to exaggerate nor to fall back on metaphor. To preserve life survivors had to use the means at their disposal; they had to manipulate facilities within the camp itself, and chief among these were functionary jobs which, if strategically used, became a principal weapon of defense. Occupying such a position made the prisoner less vulnerable to chance and "selection"; it also meant better food and shelter; and finally it allowed a vital margin of influence in situations where camp policy was carried out by the prisoners themselves. "You must get yourself a 'function,'" said one Soviet inmate to a newcomer, "it is your only chance" (Ekart, 61). And as Eugen Kogon observes, "there were few long-time concentration-camp inmates who did not in the course of time rise to more favourable, if not comfortable, working conditions. Those who failed in this endeavour simply perished" (85).

And how did one "rise"? By chance and intrigue; by being around after others had died off or, once the political underground gained control, by being chosen as a man or woman likely to be of use in resistance operations. If the incoming prisoner had a craft, his or her chances were immeasurably better than average, since all kinds of skilled workers, from electrician to glassblower to cabinetmaker, were in constant demand. The one thing needful was a job which kept the prisoner away from "general work assignment" where inmates were inevitably shot or beaten to death. One might therefore work as a tailor, be a room orderly or a file clerk, a mechanic or a shoemaker. Many new prisoners were advised by seasoned inmates to lie: to say they knew carpentry or chemistry when they knew nothing of the sort.

[115]

Thereby they avoided the first mass extermination and had time to either find or learn a skill that would keep them alive. No job ensured survival, but anything helped. Some, like laundry detail, were valuable mainly to the prisoners who held them. Others, like working in Canada, benefited a wider circle of inmates. And others, as we shall see, were used by the "political" prisoners (members of underground resistance groups) to take a hand in their own fate, to gain a degree of control and thereby save thousands of lives.

The condition of life-in-death forced a terrible paradox upon survivors. They stayed alive by helping to run the camps, and this fact has led to the belief that prisoners identified not with each other but with their oppressors. Survivors are often accused of imitating SS behavior. Bruno Bettelheim has argued that "old prisoners" developed "a personality structure willing and able to accept SS values and behavior as its own" (169). But that needs clarification, for in order to act like an SS man the prisoner had to occupy a position of real power. A cook could lord it over other prisoners, a locksmith could not. Among *Kapos,* block-leaders and other high camp functionaries, there were indeed prisoners who accepted SS standards as their own—this man for instance:

> His specialty was strangling prisoners with the heel of his boot, and he would stand erect in the pose of a Roman gladiator, enjoying the approval of the other Kapos, who would speak admiringly of a "good, clean job" (Donat, 179).

Almost certainly, however, that man had been a killer before he came to the camps. For prisoners like him the camps did not cause brutality so much as simply endorse it. Bettelheim's observations are based on camp conditions in the late 1930's, a time when positions of power were held exclusively by criminals—by men and women who, prior to imprisonment, had been murderers, prostitutes, thieves. The concentration camps had long been a dumping ground for criminals, both in Russia and in Germany, and in the Nazi camps this type was exploited by the SS as the most suitable channel for the delegation of power.

But this is not a case of imitation: such prisoners were like their masters from the start. The Nazis knew their own kind and naturally established an order reflecting SS values. That criminals had so much power was one of the most deadly conditions in the camp world; and only slowly, through years of intrigue, threat, bribery and assassination, were underground resistance groups able to replace the criminal *Kapos* with men of their own. This kind of maneuvering was most successful in Buchenwald, least effective in the Soviet camps. One of the cardinal facts about the camps was that everywhere a battle raged between the "greens" and the "reds"—between those imprisoned for real crimes and those imprisoned for opposition to the regime.

The assumption that survivors imitated SS behavior is misleading because it generalizes a limited phenomenon, but also because it overlooks the duality of behavior in extremity. Eugen Kogon, a member of the Buchenwald underground, points out that "the concentration-camp prisoner knew a whole system of mimicry toward the SS," an "ever-present camouflage" which concealed true feelings and intentions (283). *Strategic* imitation of the SS was enormously important because thereby political prisoners held positions of power which would otherwise have gone to the criminals. In the following instance, a new prisoner, a baker, is attacked by a passing SS guard:

> With purely animal rage, he pulled off the baker's upper garments and tore them to shreds, and then whipped his bare back until the blood oozed. . . . Then the overseer, a Czech-German "political," noticed what was going on. He immediately rushed over and began shouting, "You god-damned Jewish dog! You'll work for the rest of the day without clothes! I'm sick of the trouble you lousy Jews give me!" He made a threatening gesture, and then roared, "Come with me!"
> The SS guard left, confident that the baker was in good hands. Then the overseer took the baker into a

tool-shed where it was warm, dressed him, washed his wounds, and gave him permission to stay in the shed until it was time to quit work (Weinstock, 156-57).

Or take Franz, the *Kapo* of an SS storeroom in Auschwitz. Every day crates of food were "accidentally" dropped and reported as "shipment damage." The contents were then "organized"—for Franz, for his men and others in need. In the "open," however, there was another Franz:

> As we walked . . . past other kapos and SS men he began roaring at us. . . . As he shouted, he swung at us with his club. To the passing SS men he looked and sounded a splendid kapo, heartless, brutal, efficient; yet never once did he hit us (Vrba, 90).

Imitation of SS behavior was a regular feature of life in the camps, and large numbers of prisoners benefited because positions of power were secretly used in ways which assisted the general struggle for life. Even small jobs—working as a locksmith for instance—dovetailed into the larger fabric of resistance:

> We had access to more and better food, and were able to keep ourselves clean; we had sufficient clothing and footwear. In due time we were able to assist other prisoners. . . . We locksmiths had special passes . . . from the camp authorities. With these we were able to go outside the camp and also to visit the other camps at Birkenau. . . . Often enough we merely pretended to work. Many were the good door handles and locks that we unscrewed and screwed up again at the approach of an SS man. If we were to work effectively as contacts between the various resistance groups it was essential that we should be able to hang about in this way, especially when we needed information from other camps or when something unusual was going on (Kraus and Kulka, 2).

The most important jobs were in administration offices. Here is Kogon's description of the "Orderly Room" in Buchenwald:

Its entire personnel was made up of prisoners. It took care of all internal camp administration—files, assignment of barracks, preparation for roll call, ration distribution, etc. It was an institution of great importance to a camp, and for the most part its achievements were constructive. It is no exaggeration to say that in the course of the years the Orderly Room preserved the health and lives of literally thousands of inmates, maneuvering many into positions where they could do effective work on behalf of their fellows (61).

Another "citadel of prisoner power" was the "Labor Records Office," which was a hotbed of vengeance and intrigue, but which also functioned to save the lives of hundreds of prisoners, "either . . . secretly scratched from death shipments, or . . . smuggled into outside labor details when their life was in danger in camp" (Kogon, 62). The "Camp Police" was another branch of administration used to the inmates' advantage. They carried out all orders to the letter, but in subtly subversive ways, and whenever possible with a less than lethal rigor: "thousands of prisoners would have fared infinitely worse . . . had not this prisoner cadre provided an impeccable camouflage of discipline toward the SS" (Kogon, 65).

Of all camp institutions, the one most consistently used to save lives was the camp "hospital." To appreciate the work of prisoners in the medical blocks, it must be understood that the official function of camp hospitals was not at all to save lives. Simply to go in was dangerous, as we have seen, and yet just here the paradox of life-in-death is most clear:

> **In every concentration camp where the political prisoners attained any degree of ascendancy, they turned the prisoner hospital, scene of fearful SS horrors that it was, into a rescue station for countless prisoners. Not only were patients actually cured wherever possible; healthy prisoners, in danger of being killed or shipped to a death camp, were smuggled on the sick list to put them beyond the clutches of the SS. In special cases, where there was no other way out, men in danger were**

nominally permitted to "die," living on under the
names of prisoners who had actually died (Kogon, 141).

Exchanging the living for the dead was a common practice in
Nazi camps. Another tactic was called "submerging": prisoners
singled out for extermination would be hidden, sometimes for
months, in the tuberculosis and typhus wards, which were places
of relative safety because the SS were afraid to enter them. Still
another tactic was to pad the order-list for medicines: after it had
been signed by an SS officer, but before it left for Berlin, "the list
wandered through the typewriter, to emerge with some changes,
allowances having previously been made for spaces" (Poller,
243). And all these practices were carried through, day in and
day out, by men and women who knew they would be shot if
caught.

Arrangements as complex as those just described took a high
degree of coordination and were extensive only in camps where a
political underground had had time to form. Most "maneuvers"
in the medical blocks were simpler. Staff members allowed prisoners extra time to recover from exhaustion or sickness, or deliberately falsified diagnoses for cases which otherwise would
automatically have been sent to the gas chamber. When sickness
was prolonged, or when an individual prisoner was in special
danger, he or she was moved from name to name, ward to ward:

> One morning . . . the *officerine* beat me, . . . shout-
> ing that she was going to send me . . . to my death.
> After she had left, the *blokova* hurried over and took
> me into another ward. She put me in a bunk with the
> light behind me and pinned a new chart at its foot.
> In this way I was able to pass for another patient
> (Maurel, 51).

Tactics like these were successful because with thousands of
prisoners coming and going, all looking alike, the authorities
could not possibly keep track of everything and everyone. In some
cases prisoners were actually able to move from camp to camp, a
situation the political underground regularly exploited to start or

shore up resistance movements elsewhere: "They assigned a lot of dead people to the transports. They never knew who was dead, who was alive. We picked out a few dead ones and changed their numbers for our own. Then we reported to the proper transport" (Weinstock, 169). Prisoners took full advantage of loopholes, death was manipulated in favor of life, and the minimal latitude thus obtained was increased by another small circumstance: a large number of SS men were drunk much of the time. That was another crack through which life seeped. ■

In extremity life depends on solidarity. Nothing can be done or kept going without organizing, and inevitably, when the social basis of existence becomes self-conscious and disciplined, it becomes "political"—political in the elementary human sense, as in the following description by two survivors of Auschwitz:

> **Unlimited egoism and a consuming desire to save their own lives at the expense of their fellows were common phenomena among prisoners who were politically backward, for such people were quite incapable of realizing that in this way they merely strengthened the hand of the SS against the prisoners. . . . Our experience of other concentration camps {prior to Auschwitz} had taught us the vital need to live collectively. Political consciousness and contact with others in the struggle against Nazism were necessary conditions of success; it was this that gave people a sense of purpose in life behind barbed wire and enabled them to hold out** (Kraus and Kulka, 27, 1).

Prisoners were "politically backward" if they did not see that collective action is more effective than individual effort, or if they did not understand that solidarity becomes power in proportion to the degree of disciplined order. Many never understood, and theirs was "the tragedy of all people who live under the illusion that isolation is individualism":

the great "individualists" of our free days, the unorgan-
ized and backward workers, the cynics, not to mention
business men who knew nothing of organized action,
. . . all disintegrated morally. They became witless
tools for the Nazis. They groveled for favours although
their groveling degraded them still further. And they
did not live long in Buchenwald (Weinstock, 125, 95).

Kogon observes that "the lone wolves here were always especially
exposed to danger" (280), and Bettelheim has noted that "non-
political middle class prisoners" were among the first who "disintegrated as autonomous persons" (120-21). Another survivor
sums it up this way: "survival . . . could only be a social
achievement, not an individual accident" (Weinstock, 74).

Human relations in the camps took as many forms as they generally take. The most narrow but intense social unit was the family; beyond that were old friends, and beyond that a sense of
collective identity among those from the same town or area—
bonds reinforced by the earlier ordeal of deportation which all
had suffered together. Another strong basis for solidarity was
nationality. There are endless tales of the toughness of national
groups sticking together, and all survivors recall occasions when
they received help from, or offered help to, a stranger who was a
fellow countryman. The trouble with national allegiance, when it
became a unit of resistance, was that such groups vied among
themselves for control of life-resources. Conflict on the level of
national groups only abated when the political underground,
cutting across national barriers, became strong enough to take
command of resistance activities throughout the camp.

In discussing the achievements of the political prisoners, what
counts is not the different factions or differences in principle, but that as members of the underground they worked together, and that as time went on they achieved greater and greater
power as an organized resistance movement. This was true mainly
in the Nazi camps, however. In Soviet camps there was much "illegal" activity, and over time the rise of organized resistance did

much to improve camp conditions and check at least the worst of abuses by criminal inmates. At the time of Stalin's death, furthermore, open revolt spread throughout GULAG—"strikes" in which whole camp populations refused to work or cooperate—especially in Vorkuta and the camps of Northern Kazakhstan. By contributing to the decay of official power, resistance of this sort saved many, perhaps millions, of lives; yet it cannot be compared to the kind of firmly established underground which operated in places like Dachau and Auschwitz or especially in Buchenwald where, by the end of the war, the political prisoners ran internal camp affairs completely. To speak of a resistance movement in the concentration camps is therefore to speak of a tendency, *a kind of logic or potential inherent in the social foundation of survival struggle.* In different camps this tendency was realized to different degrees. But where it did operate effectively it became the basis of life and was responsible for the survival of thousands of prisoners, including many who knew nothing of its existence. The situation in Ravensbrück was typical:

> The political prisoners displayed great daring and courage. For instance, the list of those who were condemned to the gas chamber occasionally was destroyed. Many prisoners don't know to this day that they were sentenced to death and can thank their political leaders for saving their lives. These political prisoners also risked their own lives and undertook daily to make falsifications on the lists of the food allowances. They canceled out names in the work lists if their comrades happened to be ill. The name of an ill person would be exchanged for the name of a healthy person. When the prisoners were moved to other camps or to the execution places, there political prisoners hid many of them—some were even hidden among the corpses, which were lying in a cellar waiting to be cremated (Gluck, 66).

Unfortunately, political organization did not come into being all at once; nor was it coterminous with the beginnings of the camp system. In Ravensbrück effective resistance did not develop until late in the war. Here, as in all cases, time was the crucial factor. Years were required to create a reliable underground, years of bitter struggle and many deaths. Leaders were usually "political" in the strict sense, men and women imprisoned as early as 1933 for their opposition to the regime. As the war went on, large numbers of partisan fighters and POW's were swept into the camps. Prisoners like these had formed an attitude of resistance *before* imprisonment, and therefore came through the period of initial collapse faster and with less damage. They had no illusions about their predicament, and once they had agreed among themselves that survival was only possible through discipline, they set about their task with a rigor as ruthless as the enemy they opposed. They began by fighting it out with the criminals. At Auschwitz they did it this way:

> **The first tasks assumed by this group were to organize help for their weaker comrades and to exact better treatment from the Kapos. The means adopted for curbing the Kapos soon resulted in improved conditions. . . . The organization would select . . . a particularly vicious Kapo, . . . fall upon him at night, throw his corpse into the camp cesspool and leave him to be found in the morning (Kraus and Kulka, 21).**

The next step was to expand their own ranks by finding men and women already aware of the need for resistance. This was accomplished by screening new arrivals, which in practice became a kind of "favoritism" toward certain prisoners. Thus a survivor of Buchenwald describes his first days:

> **When the boots were issued, I was about to be given a down-at-the-heels pair, when I was asked if I was a political; upon my replying that I was, a better pair of boots was substituted. Only we politicals, too, were asked if we had brought pullovers or woolen jackets with us, and those who had not were given these garments. All other categories of prisoners went without them (Poller, 35).**

In extremity, items like boots and jackets are weapons. They keep the prisoner in better physical and mental shape, and thereby increase his capacity as a fighter. This was not, in other words, a question of favoritism at all, although it was resented as such by prisoners not aware of resistance efforts. The underground was fighting a war as real as any battle on the Western Front; and it was imperative to locate and preserve men and women already prepared to fight. For this reason "it was an unwritten, cast-iron law in the camp that special prisoners were to be protected" (Poller, 95). A prisoner was "special" precisely to the degree that he or she participated in resistance activities. Experienced members had to survive if the underground was to remain organized and effective. In the end everyone in camp would benefit.

Resistance efforts depended "on two essential pre-requisites: power inside the camp, and a well-organized intelligence service" (Kogon, 230). Life depended on getting and spreading vital information, and systems of surveillance and communication sprang up in all the camps. Here is an example from Auschwitz:

> We needed to disseminate war news that would help to bolster the morale of the internees. After solving technical problems of enormous difficulty, our friend, L., thanks to the cooperation of the "Canada," succeeded in constructing a little radio set. The radio was buried. Sometimes late at night a few trusted ones hurried out to listen to an Allied newscast. This news was then broadcast by word of mouth as fast as possible (Lengyel, 155).

Monitoring the progress of the war was also a way to measure the morale of the SS, thus providing a kind of information increasingly valuable as the war neared its end. In order to pass news and messages—information personal as well as political—a system of covert communications spread between different sections of the camps. Locksmiths, electricians and other skilled workers provided this essential service:

The visitor asks for the chief, talks with him about some repairs to electric installations, examines the sockets, moves about here and there looking for a stool, for a ladder. You have to be thoroughly familiar with the camp and its affairs to understand that "repairs" serve mostly as a pretext to enter the women's camp and transact some sort of intimate business. The errand may be a personal one of the "repairman," or it may be for someone else. . . . An uninitiated observer will never notice the imperceptible gesture, lasting perhaps a fraction of a second, which is necessary to perform the mission on which this young man came. He may have brought a woman a letter. . . . He may have called for a letter. . . . He may have brought medicine acquired at the risk of his own life for some seriously sick person (Szmaglewska, 98-99).

The most important positions in the underground intelligence system were filled by prisoners working directly for the SS as messengers, file clerks, typists and the like:

There they were able to observe everything that happened in the ranks of the SS and the prisoners, to obtain information on every personnel shift and policy trend, to overhear every conversation. Everything that seemed of the slightest significance was under constant scrutiny. . . . A prisoner orderly might be unobtrusively sweeping out an office or a hall, apparently minding only his own business, the SS men never dreaming that his attention was focused on anything but the broom in his hand. It is no exaggeration to say that nothing of any importance happened in a concentration camp, including even secret information, that did not come to the attention of the prisoners either immediately or else in a very short time. All reports converged on the underground leaders and the circles around them (Kogon, 230).

Prisoners learned ahead of time about death lists, transports and SS policy shifts, and were thus able to avert or manipulate or at least lessen the destructive impact. Information of this kind was decisive in the last days of the camps, when the intentions of the SS were carefully monitored to forestall mass catastrophe. In Buchenwald the underground made contact with the Allies, resulting in a bombing raid which severely damaged SS sectors of the camp. It was also during this raid (August 24, 1944) that the underground began to arm itself: "Advantage was taken of the general confusion that reigned, and as many rifles, pistols, carbines and hand grenades as possible were removed from the SS divisional replacement depot. The weapons were carefully concealed" (Kogon, 248). Thus the foundation was laid for an eventual uprising, which culminated in the take-over of Buchenwald. The planned extermination of the camp, scheduled by the SS, never took place.

There could be only one uprising, of course, and it could happen only late in the war, when the SS was no longer certain of reinforcements from outside the camp. In general therefore, resistance tactics, while steadily gaining strength for the final fight, were restricted to more humble efforts. Apart from the business of saving particular lives, one of the principal activities of the underground was sabotage, although here too only small deeds could be attempted, since any large-scale damage attributed to the prisoners would have evoked mass reprisal:

> Generally speaking, sabotage had to assume forms that were hard to recognize. The primary possibility was manpower utilization. Naturally the prisoners preferred to assign skilled workers only to plants that were not directly concerned with arms production. The latter were sent mainly unskilled help. Reliable anti-Fascist experts, however, were wormed into positions where they could practice systematic sabotage. . . . As a result it was possible to conduct a comprehensive program of sabotage by means of faulty planning and building, delays in procuring machinery, tools and materials, fostering internal jurisdictional disputes, applying official regulations and test methods to the letter. . . . Such sabotage was by no means confined to the armament plants. It pervaded the whole structure of the concentration camps (Kogon, 243-44).

Another systematic effort on the part of the underground was to keep accurate records of everything, to provide safe hiding places for them, and to arrange escapes so that the rest of the world could know "what deportation really meant." Finally, in almost all the camps, the underground went out of its way to save children. In Buchenwald a Hungarian transport arrived containing four hundred and ten boys. Resistance leaders bargained with the SS and convinced them that if these young prisoners were allowed to live they would make excellent workers. At the same time, members of the underground were assigned to each boy individually, to provide food, clothing, and above all a sense of care: "On the day of liberation every child stood in the yard, alive and healthy. . . . This was Buchenwald's greatest miracle" (Weinstock, 193). ∎

It was all miraculous, or no, it was not. God kept away from the concentration camps, and what was done, miraculous as it might seem, was done by human mind and will—by men and women doing what they could to make life possible. And their victories were never large: "In actual fact, their powers and opportunities were very limited. . . . They could only intervene in a few exceptional cases, and then only at the risk of their own lives" (Poller, 97). The enemy was infinitely more powerful, and the fight to survive was thus a kind of guerrilla warfare—small battles aimed at strengthening centers of defense. Members of the underground, furthermore, were not motivated by sentiment or faith in high causes. They were fighting for life on the principle that only through tight discipline and ruthless tactics was survival, and therefore help, possible. Resistance activities were governed by a "cold, unemotional, devastatingly logical approach to every problem" (Vrba, 193). And what this demanded of individual prisoners was the capacity to face moments of "hard choice." Life was saved by using death strategically, and this involved a moral dilemma which members of the underground simply had to accept and live with, no matter how difficult and cruel, no matter how hurtful to innocence.

In many of the Nazi camps, women who gave birth were automatically sent with their children to the ovens. To save at least *some* of these lives required the following decision by members of the hospital staff in Auschwitz: "One day we decided we had been weak long enough. We must at least save the mothers. To carry out our plan, we would have to make the infants pass for stillborn" (Lengyel, 99). The pain of such decisions was the price which members of the resistance had to pay, just to salvage something rather than nothing in a world where, without this kind of hard choice, all would have died:

> And so, the Germans succeeded in making murderers of even us. To this day the picture of those murdered babies haunts me. . . . The only meager consolation is that by these murders we saved the mothers. Without our intervention they would have endured worse sufferings, for they would have been thrown into the crematory ovens while still alive (Lengyel, 100).

Death was thereby cheated, made less than absolute, which is as much as survivors can hope for. They never win, in a conventional sense, but only lose less than all. And even to accomplish victories so small, so apparently insignificant against defeats so appalling, they must make choices painful often past bearing. Many could not bear it. They chose to die, rather than survive on such terms. The hardness of the survivor's choice, in other words, requires a toughness equal in its way to the forces he or she resists; life goes on by using the methods of the enemy.

Thus when lists were made up of prisoners to be gassed or sent on especially dangerous work details, as many places as possible were filled with criminals, informers or men lost in any case. The underground was forced to make its own "selection" in strategic mimicry of the Nazi procedure, and as one survivor says, "it was the cruelest task that any Underground has ever faced. . . . The Nazi system was so thorough that anti-Nazis, too, had to use death as a tool" (Weinstock, 118). Here is another example: a young man breaks down when told of the death of his family. He decides that in the morning he will commit suicide by attacking an SS officer. Because of the Nazi practice of mass reprisal, his act will cost the lives of all four hundred men in his barracks (remember that the population of Lidice was wiped out because Heydrich, one of the SS high command, was assassinated by a man from that village). All night, therefore, the crazed man's comrades try to talk him back to sanity, but his grief is stronger than their appeals. So two members of the underground must decide:

> "Do you think he'd do it?"
> "I don't know. Maybe not. Maybe he'll calm down."

Maybe. Before roll-call next morning the camp hospital sent for the man, who was not seen again (Weinstock, 150). On the same principle, an informer who "did not shrink from denouncing anyone with whom he had ever had the most trivial dispute" got sick and was "unwise enough to report to the hospital" (Kogon, 229). He too disappeared.

Life was preserved because men and women did not hesitate when moments of hard choice arose. If, as happened at Auschwitz, some members of the resistance got caught, the rest of the organization had to be protected:

> If those men cracked under torture, it would mean more than their deaths, more than fierce reprisals against the rest of us. It would mean that the underground movement . . . would be liquidated. . . . The leaders of the underground were fully aware of the danger and took swift evasive action. They smuggled poison into Block Eleven and within a few hours the men in Block Eleven were dead. Rather than risk revealing the names of their comrades, they had committed suicide (Vrba, 168-69)

As in any war, those who fight cannot afford sentiment. If one's comrade falls, that is that. The battle goes on, as did the smuggling of explosives in Auschwitz:

> A young boy who only a day before had accepted a package from me swung on the gallows. One of my comrades, numb with fright, whispered to me, "Tell me, isn't that the same boy who was in the infirmary yesterday?"
> "No," I replied. "I have never seen him before."
> That was the rule. Whoever fell was forgotten (Lengyel, 156).

Compassion was seldom possible, self-pity never. Emotion not only blurred judgment and undermined decisiveness, it jeopardized the life of everyone in the underground. To oppose their fate in the death camps, survivors had to choose life at the cost of moral injury; they had to sustain spiritual damage and still keep going without losing sight of the difference between strategic compromise and demoralization. Hard choices had to be made and not everyone was equal to the task, no one less than the kind of person whose goodness was most evident, most admired, but least available for action:

> It was the pure in heart who suffered the least damage . . . and . . . their lives shed radiance and beneficence on the rest of us. But on no account could they be placed in situations where they had to take part in making decisions vital to the very existence of the camp. . . . And the more tender one's conscience, the more difficult it was to make such decisions. Since they had to be made, and made swiftly, it was perhaps better that they should have fallen to the more robust spirits, lest all of us became martyrs instead of surviving witnesses (Kogon, 278). ∎

The behavior of the political underground was always strategic. In each case the gain was weighed against the loss in a coldly logical manner: this much life cost that much death. For the majority of survivors, however, behavior was not based on reason and calculation. Most survivors simply found themselves helping each other, as if by instinct, as if in answer to a need. Their experience suggests, in fact, that when conditions become extreme a *need to help* arises; and there is no more terrible, nor more beautiful, instance than the way people helped each other during the days and weeks of the death marches. As the Eastern Front collapsed, camp after camp was evacuated: prisoners were driven into the winter dawn in endless columns, guarded by SS men hysterical with fear and viciousness. Whole camp populations were forced to walk across the frozen wastes of Poland into Germany, sometimes for weeks without food or even shoes. Those who fell behind or stopped for any purpose were shot, and at night many froze to death in their sleep. This last extremity pushed survivors to the limit of endurance, and here if anywhere self-interest made sense, each prisoner determined not to be dragged down now, so close to the end. But just here the testimony of survivors is full of examples of help—men and women giving a vital part of themselves, literally their last reserves, to keep each other going:

> My hand was frozen and the wound on it was endless torture. By now I was completely bent and dragged myself along with my two hands between my thighs. . . . A wearisome drowsiness possessed me; my knees gave way and I collapsed in the snow. . . . Someone was tugging at me and calling my name. "Let me sleep," I murmured. But the woman tugged harder, and through half-closed eyes I recognized Klari. "Please let me sleep, Klari," I begged. But she grabbed my arm and forced me to my feet (Weiss, 212).

That small event occurred innumerable times, and always at the risk of being singled out. Another kind of help, very simple but crucial, was keeping each other awake at night. With bodies so depleted and no place to sleep but in the snow, "sleep means death." And thus they joined in night-long vigilance:

[132]

> "Ilse!" I shook her.
>
> "Leave me alone!" she protested.
>
> "Ilse!" I shouted. "Wake up. You are not going to sleep!"
>
> She was awake now. I rubbed her face, her stiff hands. I called to Suse and Liesel. They responded. We passed the word around not to sleep. . . . We did everything we could think of to keep each other awake and encouraged (Klein, 188).

Staying awake was hard, but it was harder still to give physical support to someone who could no longer walk. A girl faints and falls, someone pulls her up. She regains consciousness and recognizes a member of the kitchen squad from Auschwitz: "She drew me to her still more strongly, and almost staggered under my weight. She herself was slender and quite frail" (Birenbaum, 219). Help reached its limit when survivors began to drag and carry their fallen friends:

> After an hour of indescribable distress, Benzi pleaded with us to drop him and leave him to his fate. We knew only too well that the line of S.S. marching at the rear would riddle his body with bullets once he was helpless. So near the end of our travails, how could we desert Benzi? We drew upon our reserves of strength and dragged him along for the remainder of that never-to-be-forgotten evening (Unsdorfer, 185).

Where such strength comes from, this last expense of energy among men and women themselves nearly dead, is the central mystery of life's resilience. Partly, prisoners on the death march knew the war was almost over and that *one* more effort was possible. Beyond that—and not forgetting that help regularly came from strangers—the need to help was rooted in bonds of friendship and loyalty forged earlier, during the months and years in camp, where by coming to owe each other their lives, survivors now felt the need to stick together no matter what. Having come this far, to repay what one owed seemed not too much, not beyond what those bound life to life are willing to attempt. And to speak of *owing life* is not, in extremity, mere metaphor. Smallest favors saved lives time and again.

Prisoners survived through concrete acts of mutual aid, and over time these many small deeds, like fibers in the shuttle of a clumsy loom, grew into a general fabric of debt and care. At roll-call, for instance, or *Appel,* as it was called in the Nazi camps, prisoners had to form up hours before dawn and stand at attention in thin rags through rain and snow. This occurred again in the evening, and took at least two hours, sometimes three and four, and every survivor remembers roll-calls which lasted all night. Prisoners had to stand there the whole time, caps off, caps on, as SS officers strolled past the ranks. Any irregularity was punished savagely, and irregularities were numerous. Prisoners fainted, collapsed from exhaustion and sickness, simply fell dead on the spot. "Those winter *Appels,*" says a survivor of Buchenwald, "were actually a form of extermination. . . . In addition to those who regularly fell dead during *Appel,* there were every day a number who contracted pneumonia and subsequently died" (Weinstock, 108).

To fall and be noticed by an SS man was to be beaten or shot, and the universal practice among prisoners was to use their own bodies to prop up inmates no longer able to stand. Almost all reports by survivors include moments at roll-call when an individual either gave, or was given, this kind of support: "I was so weakened that during roll call I could scarcely stay on my feet. But the others pressed close on either side and supported me with the weight of their bodies" (Szalet, 69). Or again:

> Turning my face slightly over to the right, I saw the unconscious body of Federweiss propped up straight, squeezed tightly between the bodies of the two men in front and behind him. The man in the rear held him up by his trousers, while the one in front pushed his back on Federweiss's chest to prevent him from dropping. They kept these positions for quite a while—indeed until the S.S. man and the *Blockaeltester* . . . were at a safe distance (Unsdorfer, 104-5).

[134]

Help was forbidden, of course, but there was some safety in numbers, for among so many thousands of prisoners packed together, the SS could view any particular rank only briefly. But despite danger, the need to help persisted, often in elaborate ways. It regularly happened that sick prisoners were carried to roll-call by comrades, who then took turns supporting them. Sometimes this went on for days, and care for the sick did not end with roll-call. Many men and women were nursed back to health by friends who "organized" extra food; who shuffled the sick man back and forth from barracks to barracks; who propped him up at roll-call, and kept him out of sight during "selections" and while he was delirious. In one case a prisoner with typhus was smuggled every day into the "Canada" work detail and hidden in the great piles of clothing where he could rest. This particular rescue involved getting the sick man through a gate guarded by a *Kapo* whose job was to spot sick and feeble prisoners and club them to death. Each day, therefore, two prisoners supported the sick man almost to the gate, and then left him to march through on his own. Once past the guard they propped him up again.

Prisoners in the concentration camps helped each other. That in itself is the significant fact. Sometimes it was help individually given, as in the case of a girl in Birkenau who, "at the risk of being severely beaten if her absence in the potato-peeling room was discovered, every evening . . . brought coffee to the sick. The last time she brought it was on the eve of her own death" (Szmaglewska, 43). Sometimes it took the form of one group helping another, as when a work squad had to carry sacks of cement from the storeroom to a building site:

> I was equal to the job, but working with us were weaker men who grew exhausted after a few trips. The younger of us, myself included, pitched in to help them. We had agreed among our group that we would help one another to whatever extent was possible, rather than surrender to the dog-eat-dog philosophy which poisoned the minds of some prisoners (Weinstock, 154).

And sometimes help came collectively, unplanned and uncalled for, where and when it was needed:

> For example, five women are pushing a conveyor car loaded to the brim with gravel. . . . the car jumps the track. . . . then it gets stuck in the sand. The women stop, completely helpless. Fortunately the chief is not around. All efforts to replace the car on the tracks are fruitless; the heavy-laden car will not budge and the chief may appear at any moment. A clandestine congregating begins. Stealthily, bent figures sneak toward the derailed car from all directions: the women who work on the mound of sand, those who level the gravel, a group just returned from delivering a track. A common exertion of arms and backs raises the car, the spades dig into the sand under the wheels and heave— and the loaded car moves, shivers. Fear gives strength to the workers. With more pushing, one wheel is on the track. A Kapo comes rushing from afar, she has noticed people missing at various points of work. But before she can get there, one more tug, one more push—and the gravel-laden conveyor car proceeds smoothly along the tracks (Szmagelwska, 20-21). ■

The survivor's experience is evidence that the need *to* help is as basic as the need *for* help, a fact which points to the radically social nature of life in extremity and explains an unexpected but very widespread activity among survivors. In the concentration camps a major form of behavior was gift-giving. Inmates were continually giving and sharing little items with each other, and small acts like these were enormously valuable both as morale boosters and often as real aids in the struggle for life. Sometimes the gift was given outright, with no apparent relation between donor and receiver:

> One evening we were served a soup made with semolina. I drank this with all the more relish since I often had to forgo the daily cabbage soup because of my bowels. Just then I noticed a woman, one of the prosti-

tutes, who always kept very much to themselves, approaching my bunk, holding her bowl out to me with both hands.

"Micheline, I think this is a soup you can eat; here, take mine too."

She emptied her bowl into mine and went without food that day (Maurel, 21).

More often gifts came from friends or others in close association:

It was astonishing to see how anxious these hungry men were to share what they had. . . . There was half an orange on all the beds in the room. One of our friends had received a parcel. He had not even been able to wait for our return (Bernard, 90).

On her birthday, a member of the Auschwitz underground received a green apple and "a used toothbrush from which the bristles had been worn off on one end" (Lengyel, 139). Or finally there was just the delight of being *able* to give something, it did not matter what, as long as it was rare and distinctly a gift:

Ilse, who worked on the day shift, came back at noon. . . . She turned away from me so that I could not see what she was doing, and dug into her pocket. "I have brought you a present!" she announced triumphantly. There, on a fresh leaf, was one red, slightly mashed raspberry! (Klein, 175).

Prisoners acquired gift-items by chance and by organizing. In certain camps they received food parcels sent in from outside, and in all the camps things were to be got through the system of barter and exchange. In the following instance a prisoner in Auschwitz was able to get a loaf of bread from an SS man (many were deep in trade with prisoners) in return for a pack of cigarettes:

I was a rich man that night: the proud owner of a whole loaf of bread—not black camp bread, but bread prepared and baked for the elite of the German army. I was glad to share it with my friends on the night shift, but particularly to offer a fair share to Benzi, my friend, who had so often given me part of his bread and soup

**when my hunger was unappeased by my own meager
ration** (Unsdorfer, 159-60).

As the foregoing example suggests, the gift was usually food,
and gift-giving thus became a mode of distribution, a way of
sharing vital wealth, based on the elementary social act of reciprocity or mutual exchange. Most often prisoners shared with
those who shared with them, and this practice was so firmly established that one prisoner had a kind of right to share another's
resources—if, that is, he or she could contribute something of
equal value in return. In a Soviet camp an inmate shared a chunk
of horse meat in the following approved manner:

> I put the meat . . . on the small stove in our room. All
> my neighbors were highly interested. One of them,
> whom I knew only slightly, offered me a bit of salt,
> which I added to the water. When the meat was ready I
> invited him to share it with me. He contributed bread
> to the common repast (Gliksman, 310).

Because they had nothing to exchange, or did not wish to in this
case, the other prisoners did not expect to join in the meal. In the
camp situation, furthermore, salt was rare and valuable, and by
offering it the donor knew he was placing himself in a position
to share the other's food. But of course, the difference between
salt and meat is substantial, and to keep the symmetry of exchange
correct, the second man added bread.

To make the most of their combined wealth, the two prisoners
went through a ritual, understood by all, of "giving, receiving,
repaying." Their act is the concentration-camp version of an elementary social institution which Marcel Mauss has called the
"gift relation" or "gift morality." Mauss observes that in societies of an archaic or segmentary nature, gift-giving becomes a
medium through which people "are constantly embroiled with
and feel themselves in debt to each other" (31). Which is to
say that men and women give in expectation of return, and those
who receive feel bound to repay. Yet the whole of this process is
more instinctive than reasoned upon, and the full power of the

[138]

gift relation depends finally on an absence of conscious calculation. People give and receive, not to bribe or acquire, but to establish relations. Since the gift is identified with the donor, the act of giving creates a personal tie, and Mauss suggests that "the gift itself constitutes an irrevocable link especially when it is a gift of food" (58).

Gift-giving, in other words, creates bonds at once spiritual and concrete, social and economic. It is one of the ties which bind. Exchange brings people together, and makes them conscious of their worth in each other's eyes. Self-interest turns to goodwill, and the gift relation becomes one of the constitutive structures of social being. Through rituals of exchange the dehumanizing effect of xenophobia and mistrust—everything which keeps us apart and at war—is transformed into trust, acquaintance, respect, conditions which bring men together and allow them to function as units distinct yet in concord, each honoring the other's claim to dignity. The gift transforms hostility into allegiance. Even among animals, as ethologists point out, social bonding is achieved through rituals which suppress or transform aggression: "in fact, this bond is the firmer, the more aggressive the particular animal and species is" (Lorenz, 216). If this is true for animals, and for people in primitive societies, how very important for men and women in the concentration camps, where conditions of deprivation and fear intensified the tendency toward mistrust and anger.

Through giving and sharing the state of potential warfare was transcended. In its place sprang up binding moments of frail but real communion:

> There are days when the chief is not here. He bolts the barracks and leaves complete freedom to the locked-in workers. These are wonderful days. A small bribe changes Inga {the *Kapo*} into an angel, graciously open to any further proofs of friendship. From hiding places pots, saucepans, frying pans appear. Someone has potatoes, somebody else a ration of margarine, another has onions and someone else a spoonful of flour for gravy.

. . . On the top of the stove, no larger than twenty square inches, fifty women do their cooking, working in accord and harmony (Szmaglewska, 100).

Whatever form it took, food-sharing was a mode of human interchange through which the survivor's all but defeated humanity could be regained and kept going:

> It became a regular custom in the factory—bearing witness to increased solidarity—that a jug of warm liquid or bread slops passed from hand to hand, among all those at the same work-table. Each woman took a sip, first the sick, then the healthy, by turn. . . . If anyone managed to flavor the water with a pinch of salt acquired somewhere, a scrap of margarine, or clove of garlic, all her comrades without exception enjoyed it. This was a good custom, a humane custom, even though the conditions of our lives were becoming increasingly bestial (Birenbaum, 147).

It was more than a custom; it was, and is, one of the structures of humanness.

"Gift morality," did not, of course, issue in an articulated system of ethics among prisoners. It remained implicit in concrete acts and relations. But in one all-important way a kind of morality did become conscious. In all[11] the camps, Soviet and Nazi alike, there was one law and one law only which all prisoners knew and accepted. This was the "bread law," as it came to be called. And in a definite and clear-cut sense this particular "law" was the foundation and focal point of moral order in the concentration camps. A survivor of Sachsenhausen describes its origin and enforcement:

> thefts occurred continually in the prisoners' barracks, ours as well as others. Hunger tormented us all incessantly and transformed men into irresponsible beasts. Even those who had formerly passed for honorable men stole from their comrades the bits of bread that many had laid by from their evening ration for the next day. By day, all with one voice condemned the theft. By

night, the stealing was repeated, just the same. In our conversation periods we sought counter-measures. We knew that the thieves did not realize the crime they were committing, for hunger had driven them nearly out of their senses. But we knew also that these bits of bread were the life-preserver by which we might keep ourselves afloat until the longed-for moment of freedom. And when we caught a bread thief, we punished him so severely that he lost his taste for stealing (Szalet, 152).

A survivor of the Soviet camps describes the same situation:

The theft of bread among the prisoners themselves was, alas, not altogether rare. Theft from a comrade, no matter in what form, was the most serious crime (next to being an informer) that a prisoner could commit. The punishment meted out by the thief's own comrades was correspondingly harsh (Nork, 56).

It could be harsh indeed, as when a bread thief was caught in an Auschwitz barracks:

"So what happened? Did the others beat him up?"
"They killed him, of course. What's the use of beating up a bastard like that?"
That was the law in Block 18. If a man stole your food, you killed him. If you were not strong enough to carry out the sentence yourself, there were other executioners; it was rough justice, but it was fair because to deprive a man of food was to murder (Vrba, 115).

Hard as such measures seem, an inflexible enforcement of the bread law was necessary, and not just to protect the individual, but to preserve a basis of trust and community on which everyone's life and humanness depended:

I saw people grow pale and collapse when they realized that their piece of bread had been stolen. And it was not only a wrong that had been done to them directly. It was an irreparable wrong that had been done to all of us. For suspicion settled in, and distrust and hate (Semprun, 60).

[141]

The difference between anomie and order, between the sense that nothing mattered and the feeling that even in such places a faintly discerned goodness existed, actually rested on the bread law. It was vital to everyone because theft undermined the significance of giving and receiving, and thereby wrecked the exceedingly frail fabric of social existence as a whole. A survivor of Buchenwald sums it up:

> If hunger so demoralized a man that he stole another's bread, no one reported him to the SS or even to the Block Leader. The room attendants themselves took care of him. . . . If he did not die of the beating, they so incapacitated him that he was fit only for the crematorium. . . . [We] approved of this rule because it actually helped us maintain a certain standard of morale and mutual trust (Weinstock, 120-21). ∎

The assumption that there was no moral or social order in the concentration camps is wrong. Except peripherally and for brief periods similar to the "initial collapse" of individuals, the general condition we call chaos or anomie—what philosophers designate as the "state of nature"—did not exist. Certainly it did not prevail. Through innumerable small acts of humanness, most of them covert but everywhere in evidence, survivors were able to maintain societal structures workable enough to keep themselves alive and morally sane. The "state of nature," it turns out, is not natural. A war of all against all must be imposed by force, and no sooner has it started than those who suffer it begin, spontaneously and without plan, to transcend it.

The "state of nature" is a vacuum which nature itself abhors, an observation made in 1651 by Thomas Hobbes, who defined it as "that condition which is called war, and such a war as is of every man against every man" (106). He goes on to argue that although chaos exists in potential, it does not occur in fact, and for this reason: "nature" provides "laws," knowable through reason, "which tend to nature's preservation" (130). These "laws of nature," in Hobbes' view, are the constituents of existence itself —conditions which must obtain for anything, certainly anything human, to come into being and flourish. If chaos were absolute, there would be neither the time nor the peace necessary for man's fundamental activities:

> no culture of the earth . . . no commodious building . . . no account of time . . . no society; and, which is worst of all, continual fear and danger of violent death; and the life of man solitary, poor, nasty, brutish, and short (107).

Hobbes' aim, in *Leviathan,* was to rationalize force and provide a naturalistic basis for ethics. He wished to define government as a power dedicated to the life and well-being of the community through enforcement of an order based on nature's laws. His principal assumption is that life or nature *protects itself* through forms of necessary behavior which are at once natural and human. Hobbes was thus a forerunner of the Enlightenment in arguing that even the moral law is but a finer version of nature's law. His hope as a social philosopher was to find cause in nature itself for the ethical imperatives on which social harmony and fruitful life depend. He would have agreed that the survivor's behavior is inherently moral, and *must* be, since over time conditions of amoral struggle destroy not only the possibility of human fulfillment, but finally the fabric of existence itself. He was mistaken in one thing only, for like the Enlightenment thinkers to follow him, he assumed that the natural order is a rational order.

Morality and society do not rest on reason, although the critique of them does. But certainly they rest on something, and something too which, in a stricter sense than Hobbes could have known, deserves the name *nature.* The biological sciences confirm the fact that all life depends on systems, that everywhere a tendency to order governs behavior. From cells to men, life-forms possess both internal and external means of bonding and communication. Social behavior among higher animals is very pronounced, having evolved through a process of natural selection to the present range of structures, all of which serve the cause of survival. We are beginning to understand, in other words, that "man comes to sociability not by arrangement, by rational decision, but from the natural primary disposition which he shares with all other higher animals" (Portman, 70). Social organization is a function of life itself, and in man it reaches a pitch of interrelatedness and mutual recognition which in fact constitutes, or is the prior condition for, humanness as we know it.

Hobbes was right in his way. Nature itself—by which I mean the system of living creatures—guards against dissolution and chaos; not through control by government, nor even by rational adherence to "laws of nature," but through the emergence, during times of prolonged crisis, of structures of behavior whose purpose is to maintain the social basis of life. Order emerges. That, as biologists like to observe, is the first and most striking fact about life, since entropy or the tendency to dissolution characterizes all inorganic kinds of organization. For survivors this is crucial. Uprooted and flung into chaos, they do what they must to stay alive, and in that doing achieve enough society to meet the crisis humanly, together. After the period of initial collapse comes reintegration, a process which usually occurs gradually, in accord with the fact that all things human take time. In some cases, however, it can happen remarkably fast, as in the following example from the ordeal of mass deportation:

> Ninety-six persons had been thrust into our car, including many children who were squeezed in among the luggage. . . . As the first hour and then the second passed, we perceived that the simplest details of existence would be extremely complicated. Sanitary disposal was out of the question. . . . As the journey stretched endlessly, the car jerking and jolting, all the forces of nature conspired against us ninety-six. A torrid sun heated the walls until the air became suffocating. . . . The travelers were mostly persons of culture and position from our community. . . . But as

[144]

> the hours slipped away the veneers cracked. Soon there were incidents and, later, serious quarrels. . . . The children cried; the sick groaned; the old people lamented. . . . As night fell we lost all concept of human behavior and the wrangling increased until the car was a bedlam. . . . Finally, the cooler heads prevailed and a semblance of order was restored. A doctor and I were chosen captains-in-charge (Lengyel, 6-7).

The "veneer" of cultivated behavior, which served well enough in normal times, was not equal to such stress. Fear and panic were the initial response, and for a time all was chaos. But then, as necessity bore down and hysteria gave way to realism, a more elementary kind of order, or at least a readiness, began to function. A condition came into being which allowed the "cooler heads" to be heard. Amid this mess they held an election, they came to agree on basic responsibilities, and settled down to face their common plight. This achievement may have been but a "semblance" of past order, but it was sufficient to keep the ninety-six people in that boxcar sane and alive and above the threshold of brutality.

From the last days of the Warsaw Ghetto, when the SS was systematically hunting down everyone, comes another example. Those who remained took refuge in cellars, in attics, behind false walls where they waited:

> The bunker grew increasingly crowded and stuffy. Anyone who went to the water-tap or toilet collided with others or stumbled over their neighbors in the darkness. There was no end to the disputes and squabbles, fights over nothing, insults, name-calling. Exhausted by the want of fresh air and the most elementary facilities, tortured by incessant fear and uncertainty, people began losing their self-control. The bunker became a real hell. . . . Yet, in the midst of this suffering, there grew up a solidarity, a mutual understanding and sympathy. It was no longer necessary to shout for quiet, lest the SS track us down, nor ask too long for neighborly help. People helped one another, even shared the last drops of

> medicine, without caring whether someone was a rela-
> tive or a stranger, a friend or unknown, poor or rich.
> The differences between us disappeared. In the end, our
> mutual and tragic fate had united us into one great
> family (Birenbaum, 71-75).

Civility disintegrates and disorder prevails. Then slowly, in sorrow
and a realism never before faced up to, the mass of flailing people
grow quiet and neighborly, and in the end rest almost peaceful in
primitive communion. In this and other instances,

> the simple, shapeless agglomeration of human beings
> assembled by chance reveals a hidden structure of avail-
> able wills, an astonishing plasticity which takes shape
> according to certain lines of force, reveals plans and
> projects which are perhaps unfeasible but which lend a
> meaning, a coherence to even the most absurd, the most
> desperate of human acts (Semprun, 205).

Order emerges, people turn to one another in "neighborly
help." This pattern was everywhere apparent in the world of the
camps. Giving and receiving were perpetual, and we can only
imagine the intensity of such transactions. When men and women
know they are dying, smallest favors can shake the frail world
of their being with seismic force. The power of such moments is
enormous, and the bonds thus created go far deeper than guilt or
pride or ordinary obligation. And perhaps the most striking thing
about this kind of giving, apart from the extreme gratitude it could
generate, is the fact that pity played no part:

> Yet, how little sometimes suffices to save a perishing
> man: a glance, a word, a gesture. Once I gave a fellow
> prisoner a boiled potato and he never stopped thanking
> me for having saved his life. Another time I helped
> someone to regain his feet after he had fallen during a
> march. He not only reached our destination alive, but
> survived the war; and he maintains that without my
> help that one time he would never have gotten up, he
> would have been killed where he lay. In the camp it
> was easier to get a piece of bread than a kind word.
> Prisoners helped one another as best they could, but

**they shied away from sentiment. Help, yes; compassion,
no** (Donat, 237).

Compassion means to "suffer with." It is an act of imaginative
entrance into the world of another's pain, and is proper on the
part of those who do not themselves bear the same kind or degree
of suffering. Through compassion we close the distance between
one condition and another, and as long as the division between
unearned luck and unearned disaster remains a structure of our
common world, compassion has about it the nature of a moral
imperative. But only for us, whom fate has not tried. For survivors it was different: "Everyone in camp had lost someone and
all bore their grief in silence. Another's tears met with understanding, but not with sympathy: one unhappy man doesn't pity
another, is not moved by another's misfortune" (Donat, 237).
Or as one woman said to another:

> "Why do you cry?" . . . I sobbed even harder. . . .
> "Really, why do you cry? . . . We are all here to-
> gether; we all have it as hard" (Pawlowicz, 113).

The survivor's behavior is not inspired by pity, nor can it be
explained in terms of reason alone. Underground resistance
groups were guided by rational assessment of the situation being
faced, and through time most survivors developed a degree of
political consciousness, an awareness of the common predicament
and of the need to act collectively. But what came first was spontaneous involvement in each other's lives on the immediate level
of giving and receiving. And like the need to bear witness, which
might also be viewed rationally, there was yet an instinctive depth
to the emergence of social order through help and sharing. Human interchange goes on all the time everywhere. But in the concentration camps it was more naked, more urgently pursued.
Judging from the experience of survivors, "gift morality" and a
will to communion are constitutive elements of humanness. In
extremity, behavior of this kind emerges without plan or instruction, simply as the means to life. ∎

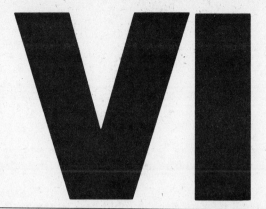

VI

US AND THEM

All around and beneath her she could hear strange sub-merged sounds, groaning, choking and sobbing: many of the people were not dead yet. The whole mass of bodies kept moving slightly as they settled down and were pressed tighter by the movements of the ones who were still alive. . . . Then she heard people walking near her, actually on the bodies . . . , occasionally fir-ing at those which showed signs of life. . . . One SS man . . . shone his torch on her, . . . but she . . . gave no signs of life.

A. KUZNETSOV
Babi Yar

That corpse you planted last year in your garden,
Has it begun to sprout? Will it bloom this year?
Or has the sudden frost disturbed its bed?

T. S. ELIOT
The Waste Land

IN 1959 Stanley M. Elkins put forward his slave-as-sambo thesis in *Slavery*, arguing that the personality of the American slave had been fundamentally regressive and infantile. Elkins does not examine direct evidence; he uses a "comparative" method, and his main comparison is with inmates of the German concentration camps. To identify the Southern plantation with Auschwitz is senseless, of course; but the comparison is still significant, not for what it tells us of either slaves or survivors, but for the assumptions that are made about behavior in extremity. Elkins takes it for granted that in the camps men and women lost their capacity to act as morally responsible adults, and the point of his comparison is to demonstrate that this also happened to American slaves. Specifically, he states that "old prisoners," by which he means the survivors, suffered "deep disintegrative effects" (107); that the "most immediate aspect of the old inmates' behavior . . . was its *childlike* quality" (111); and finally that "all" survivors were "reduced to complete and childish dependence upon their masters" (113). Elkins goes on to say that regression began with the abandonment of previous ethical standards, and to make his point he quotes as representative a brief statement by a survivor of Auschwitz. In Elkins' context, here is her remark:

> One part of the prisoner's being was thus, under sharp stress, brought to the crude realization that he must thenceforth be governed by an entire new set of standards in order to live. Mrs. Lingens-Reiner puts it bluntly: "Will you survive or shall I? As soon as one sensed that this was at stake everyone turned egotist" (109-10).

In extremity, in other words, everyone fights alone; and the "entire new set of standards" comes from the camp system itself. But is there not a contradiction here? Childlike behavior is not the same as rapacious battle in one's best self-interest. The former entails passivity and preference for illusion; the latter demands intelligent calculation and a capacity for quick, objective judgment. All the same, that survivors suffered regression to infantile stages, *and* that they were amoral monsters, are very widespread notions. They constitute nothing less than the prevailing view of survival behavior. Not surprisingly, in *Death in Life* Robert Lifton has used the same quotation—"Will you survive, or shall I?"—as a representative expression of the "competition for survival" which, in his view, lies at the root of the "guilt" survivors are supposed to feel (490). What, then, are we to make of the Lingens-Reiner statement? Is it a fair summation of her own view?

In *Prisoners of Fear* she aims to tell the very worst; and the most striking thing about her testimony is the double vision we have already noted in reports by survivors. The viciousness and horror are certainly there, but also examples of morally intelligent behavior, and many references to resistance and solidarity among camp inmates. There is the moment when the narrator exposes herself by taking action to get another prisoner's name off a death list. She does this, all the time calling herself a fool for taking the risk, because she sees an opportunity: there was a *way* to save someone and that decided her. The incident takes four pages to describe (79-82) and is not an example of "survival egotism" or of "infantile regression." It is one instance among many of men and women acting with courage and intelligence to help others. The following are typical:

> There were girls among them who lived through a typhus attack without staying in bed. Two of their friends would take the sick comrade between them, when she had a temperature of 103° F. and saw everything as a blur, and drag her along with their labour gang; out in the fields they would lay her down under a shrub, and in the evening they would march her back to camp—all to avoid her being sent to the hospital hut and so being exposed to the danger of a selection (122).

The camp doctor would line up all the Jewish patients.
. . . All those who were too ill to get out of bed were
lost from the outset. . . . The rest of the prisoners did
everything in their power to obstruct the doctor and to
save one or other of the victims; I do not think that a
single one among us withheld her help. We would hide
women somewhere in the hut. . . . We would smuggle
them into "Aryan" huts. . . . We would put their
names on the list of patients due for release (76-7).

Under the pressure of a concentration camp you grew
more closely attached to people than you would have
done otherwise in such a short time (162).

The pursuit of self-interest was certainly a determinant of behavior in the camps, but it was everywhere countered by an un-
suppressible urge toward decency and care, a multitude of small
deeds against the grain of one's "best" interest. Prisoners looked
out for themselves first of all, but also for one another when and
however they could. In the whole body of testimony by survivors
there is no better description of this contradiction than in the
book by Lingens-Reiner:

Ena Weiss, our Chief Doctor—one of the most intelligent, gifted and eminent Jewish women in the camp—
once defined her attitude thus, in sarcastic rejection of
fulsome flattery and at the same time with brutal frankness: "How did I keep alive in Auschwitz? My principle is: myself first, second and third. Then nothing.
Then myself again—and then all the others." This formula expressed the only principle which was possible
for Jews who intended—almost insanely intended—to
survive Auschwitz. Yet, because this woman had the icy
wisdom and strength to accept the principle, she kept
for herself a position in which she could do something
for the Jews. Hardly anybody else in the camp did as
much for them and saved so many lives as she did (118).

At least in this instance, Elkins' thesis is not borne out by the
evidence from which he quotes, and if for a time his "sambo"

theory of slave behavior was accepted, that was not because he had offered solid evidence but because by comparing slavery to the camp experience he was able to mobilize the deeply disturbing and largely uncontrolled range of reaction which attends our idea of the concentration camps. Here is how he sums it up:

> Daily life in the camp, with its fear and tensions, taught over and over the lesson of absolute power. It prepared the personality for a drastic shift in standards. It crushed whatever anxieties might have been drawn from prior standards; such standards had become meaningless. It focused the prisoner's attention constantly on the moods, attitudes, and standards of the only man who mattered [the SS guard]. A truly childlike situation was thus created: utter and abject dependency. . . . It is thus no wonder that the prisoners should become "as children." It is no wonder that their obedience became unquestioning, that they did not revolt, that they could not "hate" their masters (122).

Elkins is simply reiterating accepted ideas. But power is never absolute, especially over time, and it is not true that the SS guard was the "one significant other" on whom the prisoners' needs depended. Social bonding among prisoners themselves was a universal phenomenon in the camps. And of course it is not true that survivors were morally crushed, that they lost all sense of prior standards, that moral sanity was meaningless. Certainly it is not true that they did not revolt; to live was to resist, every day, all the time, and in addition to dramatic events like the burning of Treblinka and Sobibor there were many small revolts in which all perished. Prisoners who were capable, furthermore, of organizing an underground and of systematically subverting SS intentions were not behaving "as children." And it is not true, finally, that hatred was absent. Survivors seethed with it, they speak of it often, they describe terrible acts of revenge. In *Prisoners of Fear* the author praises one of her comrades for "the ice-cold self-control by which she hid her abysmal hatred of the German rulers" (123) in order to exploit them. Ella Lingens-Reiner's own rage rings through her prose on every page.

No, most of this was not true, not for many survivors in many camps. Hence these disturbing questions: Why do we insist that prisoners died "like sheep"? Why is it easy to believe, despite the contradiction, that survivors were infantile *and* that they were cunning manipulators using every kind of betrayal and base trick to stay alive? Why, in short, do we insist that survivors did not really survive: that they suffered "death in life" and that if they are alive in body their spirit was destroyed beyond salvaging? Here is how one psychoanalytic commentator summed up the opinions of his colleagues in a symposium on the camp experience: "To one degree or another, they all stifled their true feelings, they all denied the dictates of conscience and social feeling in hope of survival, and they were all warped and distorted as a result" (Hoppe, 83). That word "all"—its assurance, its contempt—must be accounted for. ∎

To date, serious study of the concentration-camp experience has been done almost exclusively from the psychoanalytic point of view. Elkins takes the bulk of his evidence from Elie Cohen and Bruno Bettelheim, both of whom employ the psychoanalytic approach, both of whom offer much valuable insight, but both of whom, in the end, are led by their method to mistaken conclusions. The psychoanalytic approach is misleading because it is essentially a theory of culture and of man in the civilized state. Its analytic power—which is considerable—is maximized when turned upon behavior which is symbolic, mediated, and therefore at a sufficient remove from necessity. To be of use, the psychoanalytic method, which is that of interpretation, must be applied to actions which have more than one meaning *on the level of meaning*. But that is not the case with extremity. When men and women must respond directly to necessity—when defilement occurs at gun-point and the most undelayable of needs determines

[155]

action, or when death itself is the determinant—then behavior has no "meaning" at all in a symbolic or psychological sense.

The purpose of action in extremity is to keep life going; the multiplicity of motive which gives civilized behavior its depth and complexity is lost. We have seen that life in the camps depended on a duality of behavior, but this duality—this layering of behavior —is very different from the kind of layering which psychoanalysis probes. In extremity, action splits into "primary" and "secondary" levels of adjustment, each of which is real and separate in itself. Precisely here the psychoanalytic approach misleads us: in its search for a second meaning on the first or primary level, it overlooks the secondary level. For psychoanalysis, covert behavior is implicit behavior. But for survivors it becomes explicit, actual, necessary in an immediately practical way.

I am assuming, with Freud, that the phenomenon of civilization, no matter how advanced or primitive, is based first of all on processes of sublimation and symbolization. Taken in this broad sense, civilization as a condition can be described as the transcendence of primal needs and crude necessities through systems of technical and symbolic mediation. Thereby a realm of freedom comes into being which is not governed immediately by the necessities which constitute extremity. Prisoners in a concentration camp would eat anything, at any time they could get it, in almost any state of rawness or decay. We, on the other hand, eat the kind of food we choose, when we choose, after it has been transformed aesthetically through cooking, and upon occasions rich in ritual observance. And thus too, the dead in the camps were stacked naked in piles, rammed into ovens, tossed every which way into ditches and pits. But the man or woman who dies in normal circumstances becomes the object of complicated ritual procedures which confer meaning and dignity upon his or her death and thereby humanize it. The primacy of death is denied symbolically; the immediate facts are overlaid with solemn meaning and removed from the center of consciousness. Death is no longer *thought of* as death, just as animal flesh is no longer thought of as animal flesh after it has been transformed by cooking and table rites.

Freedom to mediate facts and instill new significance, to create and multiply meanings, is the essence of civilization. And here the psychoanalytic method correctly assumes that nothing is to be taken at face value. Our actions are invested with memories, wishes and values reaching far beyond the performance itself, and no act is simply and wholly significant in its immediate, con-crete function. Historically, psychoanalysis originated just as the *symboliste* movement was occurring in the arts, and it is tempting to see in both a common pursuit. Both read facts as symbols, both search out the mysteries of an invisible drama, and both take it for granted that in any act or situation there is more than meets the eye. Survivors act as they do because they must— the issue is always life or death—and at every moment the meaning and purpose of their behavior is fully known. We, on the other hand, act for all kinds of reasons, some known and others unconscious, some practical and others governed by an internal will that can only be guessed at. For us behavior requires inter-pretation; indeed, interpretation validates experience, and hence the usefulness of the psychoanalytic approach.

But only for us. Attempts to interpret the survivor's experience —to see it in terms other than its own—have done more harm, than good. The outstanding spokesman, in this respect, has been Bruno Bettelheim, whose application of the psychoanalytic model to survival behavior has been definitive. Bettelheim was in Buchen-wald and Dachau for a year, at a time when prisoners could still hope for release, and before systematic destruction became fixed policy, but he was there and speaks with that authority. His first analysis of the camp experience—"Individual and Mass Behavior in Extreme Situations"—appeared in 1943, adding the weight of precedence to a position which has never been challenged and which has influenced all subsequent study. Even among laymen his ideas are known and accepted. His version is *the* version, and in *The Informed Heart* it takes its final, polemical form. Bettelheim argues that prisoners in the camps exhibited the following general traits: they became "incompetent children"; they identified with the SS, "willing and able to accept SS values and behavior"; they fell into an "anonymous mass," without social base or organization; and they possessed no "autonomy," by which he means the capacity for dramatic acts of self-assertion.

Bettelheim's view differs sharply from that of other survivors—Ernst Wiechert and Ernest Rappaport, for example—who were in Buchenwald at the same time. His claims are not substantiated in the bulk of testimony by survivors, including the comprehensive report by Eugen Kogon, who was a member of the underground and was in Buchenwald from the beginning to the end. Bettelheim's attack on Anne Frank and her family is perhaps the essential expression of his outlook. He suggests that their decision to stay together and go into hiding was stupid—a judgment which disregards the situation in Holland, where the population at large helped many Jews to escape in this way. Rather, he argues, they should have abandoned their commitment to each other: each should have fought alone, each shooting down the Germans as they came. Where the guns were to come from, or how scattered individuals were to succeed when nations failed, he does not say.

Bettelheim develops his argument in terms of a dramatic contrast between the individual, who possesses "autonomy," and the masses, who do not possess "autonomy." In many cases this becomes a contrast between Bettelheim himself and "others":

> they appeared to be pathological liars, were unable to restrain themselves, unable to separate clearly between reality and their wishful or anxious daydreams. So to the old worries, a new one was added, namely, "How could I protect myself from becoming as they are?" (114).

This may refer to prisoners during the stage of initial collapse, but Bettelheim does not say so. He is describing what appears to him to be the general situation, and this contrast between himself and other prisoners is in fact the theme of his book. It is evident not only in the sense of isolation and superiority which attends references to himself, but also in an animus toward other prisoners generally. At one point he attacks camp functionaries by suggesting that inmates with "privileged" positions had "a greater need to justify themselves":

> This they did as members of ruling classes for centuries have done—by pointing to their greater value to society because of their power to influence, their education, their cultural refinement (186).

His specific example is Eugen Kogon:

> Kogon's attitudes are fairly representative. For example, he took pride that in the stillness of the night he enjoyed reading Plato or Galsworthy, while in an adjacent room the air reeked of common prisoners, while they snored unpleasantly. He seemed unable to realize that only his privileged position, based on participation in human experiments, gave him the leisure to enjoy culture, an enjoyment he then used to justify his privileged position (186).

That sounds convincing, but let us look at Kogon's description of the same event:

> In the winter of 1942-43 a succession of bread thefts in Barracks 42 at Buchenwald made it necessary to establish a nightwatch. For months on end I volunteered for this duty, taking the shift from three to six o'clock in the morning. It meant sitting alone in the day room, while the snores of the comrades came from the other end. For once I was free of the ineluctable companionship that usually shackled and stifled every individual activity. What an experience it was to sit quietly by a shaded lamp, delving into the pages of Plato's *Dialogues,* Galsworthy's *Swan Song,* or the works of Heine, Klabund, Mehring! (132).

One of the anomalies of Nazi rule was that books unobtainable in the whole of the Reich were available in the camps. Kogon goes on: "Yes, they could be read illegally in camp. They were among books retrieved from the nation-wide wastepaper collections. The Nazis impounded many libraries of 'enemies of the state,' and turned them over to these collections" (132). There is perhaps a sense of amusement in Kogon's recounting of such details—a *Swan Song* in Buchenwald?—but not a trace of what Bettelheim calls the "need to justify."

Kogon's book, *The Theory and Practice of Hell,* is an extensive record of the achievements of the political underground in Buchenwald, including methods of organization, strategic use of functionary positions, and a detailed account of the take-over of the camp by the prisoners. The episode Bettelheim singles out is, in Kogon's view, just another small example of resistance in action. As a member of the underground, Kogon is simply doing his job. The reason he is there is not to read Plato and Mehring, but to enforce the bread law and thereby help keep a sense of moral order alive among the prisoners. He does not, as Bettelheim says, refer to air which "reeked of common prisoners," but to his "comrades." His private enjoyment is a by-product of responsibility, and if there had been no books Kogon would have volunteered all the same, going without sufficient sleep "for months on end" to do his duty as a man committed to the general struggle.

Bettelheim did not know Kogon in camp, and the incident cited above (one of several he takes from Kogon's report) occurred after his release. Yet this is not a matter of ignorance merely. To reduce Kogon's act to "privilege," and further to declare that it was "based on participation in human experiments," is a grave misrepresentation of basic facts. Bettelheim's obsession with "autonomy," his concept of transcendental selfhood, blinds him to collective action and mutual aid. After reading Kogon's book he remains unaware of organized resistance and of the enormous benefits which the camp population received through covert operations of the underground. He goes on to criticize prisoners who did not, at some point, assert their "autonomy" by openly risking their lives (Kogon's was on the line for seven years but never, if he could help it, openly). Bettelheim tells us that the act he himself performed by talking back to an SS officer, thereby risking his life in a dramatic assertion of self, was the kind of behavior all survivors should have displayed. And that is the heart of the matter. Bettelheim's critique of camp behavior is rooted in the old heroic ethic. Heroism, for him, is an isolated act of defiance through which the individual *as* an individual confronts death. Bettelheim's position is clear from the kind of action he praises:

> Once, a group of naked prisoners about to enter the gas chamber stood lined up in front of it. In some way the commanding SS officer learned that one of the women prisoners had been a dancer. So he ordered her to dance for him. She did, and as she danced, she approached him, seized his gun, and shot him down. She too was immediately shot to death (264-65).

"She was willing to risk her life," Bettelheim concludes, "to achieve autonomy once more" (265). But this is not an example of risking life. The act he celebrates is suicide. It is courageous, beautiful, and under the circumstances the only alternative to passive surrender. It is heroic, but it is still suicide. What can "autonomy" at the cost of personal destruction amount to? How effective would underground activities, or any of the forms of resistance, have been on such a principle? Bettelheim's argument comes down to this: "manhood" requires dramatic self-confirmation, and in the camps this could only be achieved through some moment of open confrontation with death. Insofar as the struggle for life did not become overtly rebellious, prisoners were "childlike."

Bettelheim's polemical objective, in *The Informed Heart*, is to compare the survivor's experience with the predicament of modern man in "mass society," in order to arrive at a critique of the latter. The comparison itself is invalid. No matter how disconcerting conditions become for us, they do not hinge at every moment on the issue of life and death; pain is not constant, options abound, the rule of terror and necessity is far from total. Life for us does not depend on collective action—not directly, that is; nor is death the price of visibility. Bettelheim wishes to rouse us from our sense of victimhood; but by claiming that pressure reduces men and women to children, and by praising a heroism based on death, he tends instead to support what he fears. ■

Whatever his conclusions, Bettelheim's argument for "autonomy" is a defense of human dignity, a call to that principle in man which resists determination by otherness. His fear is not only that human beings can be made helpless, but that prevailing tendencies in modern thinking have accepted the condition of victimhood as final. A primary assumption of his own discipline is that the self is forever in painful bondage to its past. And much of social, economic and political theory—conservative as well as radical—takes it for granted that external forces shape internal being, or finally that the self is constituted by forces it neither controls nor understands but only suffers. Perhaps the case for man-as-victim has been put most strongly by behaviorism, which assumes outright that environment is omnipotent and that the human self is ever and always a unilateral function of the world in which it finds itself. Applied to the concentration camps, the conclusion can only be that monstrosity breeds monstrosity, and therefore that no one survived. Those not killed in body most surely perished in spirit, for men and women could not long endure such inhumanity without themselves becoming inhuman. One sees why B. F. Skinner, in his attack on freedom, also finds it necessary to attack dignity: as long as people persist in their refusal to be determined by forces external to themselves, the belief in freedom will likewise persist as a by-product of this basic recalcitrance.

That the concentration camps were a kind of "experiment" has often been noted. Their aim was to reduce inmates to mindless creatures whose behavior could be predicted and controlled absolutely. The camps have so far been the closest thing on earth to a perfect Skinner Box. They were a closed, completely regulated environment, a "total" world in the strict sense. Pain and death were the "negative reinforcers," food and life the "positive reinforcers," and all these forces were pulling and shoving twenty-four hours a day at the deepest stratum of human need. And yet, survivors are proof that the "experiment" did not succeed.

Their behavior was of course determined by camp conditions, but not in the way behaviorism or current theories of victimhood assume. The distinction overlooked is between responses to necessity which are really unilateral and therefore at one with necessity, and responses which are strategic and therefore provoked by, but opposed to, the same necessity. Facing extreme pressure, human beings either acquiesce or resist or do both. Like the psychoanalytic approach, behaviorism does not take into account the duality of action in extremity. It too fixes attention on the "primary" level of adjustment, precisely on those activities which are informed by, and expressive of, camp logic. On this level it appears that prisoners succumbed to their environment (and life depended on the success of this deception). But on the "secondary" level, as we have seen, prisoners were pushing hard against camp controls. And it is perhaps worth noting, finally, that the behaviorist assumption was held in practice by the SS themselves, who never doubted that force and fear could break anyone, could reduce all behavior to a function of their world.

In a way at first surprising, Bettelheim's idea of heroism dovetails with the view of man as victim—just as psychoanalysis and behaviorism, based on opposite principles, agree in the case of extremity. But in fact, the celebration of man's "indomitable spirit" and our acceptance of victimhood are rooted in the single belief, as old as Western culture, that human bondage can be transcended only in death. Death is at once the entrance to a world of fulfillment unobtainable on earth and the proof of a spirit unvanquished by fear or compromise. Neither is possible to men and women getting by as best they can from day to day; and a life not ready, at any moment, to give itself for something higher is life enchained, life cowed and disgraced by its own gross will to persist. Survival in itself, not dedicated to something *else,* has never been held in high esteem and often has been viewed with contempt. This complex of attitudes is at the heart of the Christian worldview; it had already been expounded in detail by Plato, and before that invested with grandeur by Homer. In the *Iliad,* the progress of a Greek advance is stopped by sudden mist and darkness; whereupon the great Ajax prays aloud for Zeus to send light to continue the battle, even if light should bring death. Many centuries later, in *On the Sublime,* Longinus remarked: "That is the true attitude of an Ajax. He does not pray for life, for such a petition would have ill beseemed a hero" (67).

Just so; when we say of someone that he or she "merely" survives, the word "merely" carries real if muted moral objection. And we say it all the time, as if to be alive, or simply to struggle for life, were not in itself enough. For "meaning" and "significance" we look elsewhere—to ideals and ideologies, to religion and other metaphysical systems; to anything, any *higher* cause or goal which defines life in terms other than its own and thereby justifies existence. Survivors are suspect because they are forced to do openly, without a shred of style or fine language to cover themselves, what the rest of us do by remote control. The bias against "mere survival" runs deep, and derives its force from the fact that all of us think and act in terms of survival, but at a crucial remove and with all the masks and stratagems which cultivated men and women learn to use—of which there would seem to be no end. As Nietzsche observed, man would rather will nothingness than have nothing to will, nothing with which to push life beyond itself. But as Nietzsche implies, the problem with these symbolic superstructures is that they redeem life by negating it.

One of the side-effects of civilization is that life is enhanced by denigrating actual life processes. But is this a side-effect merely? Might it not be the paradox of civilization itself—a direct result of, or even a condition for, the split between mind and body which characterizes the structure of civilized existence as we know it? Surely Descartes was not original when he declared that mind and matter are separate entities, nor was his "I think therefore I am" anything more than the commonplace bias of culture itself. Within the framework of civilization, experience has always been divided into physical and spiritual realms, immediate and mediated modes, concrete and symbolic forms, lower and higher activities. And all things "higher," as we know, are by definition *not* concerned with life itself; not, that is, with life in its physical concreteness.

In *The Presentation of Self in Everyday Life* Erving Goffman has observed that human activities take place either in "front" or in "back" regions. We "present" ourselves (our idealized selves) to ourselves and others in "front regions," while keeping our props, especially those which attend our biological needs, out of sight in "back regions":

> The line dividing front and back regions is illustrated everywhere in our society. As suggested, the bathroom and bedroom . . . are places from which the downstairs audience can be excluded. Bodies that are cleansed, clothed, and made up in these rooms can be presented to friends in others. In the kitchen, of course, there is done to food what in the bathroom and bedroom is done to the human body (123).

Goffman is talking about American society, but the compartmentalization of existence to which he points can be found everywhere, most dramatically at events which have a religious or an official function, places and ceremonies associated with power or the sacred. In all such instances, a division between front and back, higher and lower, is strictly upheld. And as far as ritual and technology permit, everything "lower" is kept out of sight—and thereby out of mind. Mary Douglas has called this "the purity rule":

> According to the rule of distance from physiological origin (or the purity rule) the more the social situation exerts pressure on persons involved in it, the more the

social demand for conformity tends to be expressed by a demand for physical control. Bodily processes are more ignored and more firmly set outside the social discourse, the more the latter is important. A natural way of investing a social occasion with dignity is to hide organic processes (12).

The division between body and mind, between lower and higher, is a structural component of civilization as such. Freud's concept of sublimation is helpful here; it refers to the process through which immediate bodily needs are delayed, set at a distance or denied, and finally transformed into the "higher" accomplishments of mind and culture. That which *is* is negated in pursuit of that which *will* be or *should* be. Taken to its religious extreme, this principle results in the negation of this life in favor of another life, higher, purer, elsewhere. Actual existence is "death," whereas death becomes the entrance to "life," or so St. Paul would have us believe. The meaning of life is found *in* death, and the greatest action an individual can perform is to give his life for some "higher" cause.

The trouble with survivors, in our eyes, is that they do not live by the rules. Their needs cannot be delayed, cannot be transformed or got out of sight. Nor do they seek ideal justification for their struggle. Survivors fight merely to live, certain that what counts is life and the sharing of life. And through this experience of radical de-sublimation they come, as Nadezhda Mandelstam puts it, very "close to earth":

> Our way of life kept us firmly rooted to the ground, and was not conducive to the search for transcendental truths. Whenever I talked of suicide, M. used to say: "Why hurry? The end is the same everywhere, and here they even hasten it for you." Death was so much more real, so much simpler than life, that we all involuntarily tried to prolong our earthly existence, even if only for a brief moment—just in case the next day brought some relief! In war, in the camps and during periods of terror, people think much less about death (let alone sui-

cide) than when they are living normal lives. Whenever
at some point on earth mortal terror and the pressure of
utterly insoluble problems are present in a particularly
intense form, general questions about the nature of being recede into the background. . . . In a strange way,
despite the horror of it, this also gave a certain richness
to our lives. Who knows what happiness is? Perhaps it
is better to talk in more concrete terms of the fullness
or intensity of existence, and in this sense there may
have been something more deeply satisfying in our desperate clinging to life than in what people generally
strive for (261).

For years the Mandelstams lived at life's edge: they saw the
tree in winter outline, barren against a barren land, and saw the
strength of its shape. David Rousset, who passed through several
Nazi camps, likewise insists upon a "positive side" to the experience of survival:

Dynamic awareness of the strength and beauty of the
sheer fact of living, in itself, brutal, entirely stripped of
all superstructures—living through even the worst of
cataclysms and most disastrous setbacks. A cool, sensual
thrill of joy founded on the most complete understanding of the wreckage, and consequently incisiveness in
action and firmness in decisions, in short, a broader and
more intensely creative vigor (171).

Certainly one does not have to survive the concentration camps
in order to arrive at awareness of life's immanent value. It can
come abruptly, with the shock of death-encounter, or gradually
after passing through a period of protracted death-threat, and
sometimes in a moment of character-changing revelation. Dostoevsky is a wonderful example. As a young man he was arrested
for mildly revolutionary activities, condemned to death, and
taken to the place of execution; his sentence was commuted
to imprisonment only after the ritual of execution had been carried up to the actual point of shooting. He genuinely thought
he would die, and later that same day he wrote an extraordinary
letter to his brother:

Brother, I'm not depressed and haven't lost spirit. Life everywhere is life, life is in ourselves and not in the external. . . . This idea has entered into my flesh and blood. Yes, it's true! That head which created, lived by the highest life of art, which acknowledged and had come to know the highest demands of the spirit, that head has been cut from my shoulders. . . . But my heart is left me, and the same flesh and blood which likewise can love and suffer and desire and remember, and this is, after all, life. *On voit le soleil!* (Mochulsky, 141).

His awakening had nothing to do with belief, and in his letter he thanks neither God nor the Tsar. He has simply realized what he did not know before. Life's fundamental goodness is now clear, and he wants his brother to know that through the years in prison this knowledge will be his strength. Using exactly the same details of the letter, Dostoevsky re-described his mock execution nearly twenty years later in *The Idiot*. The Prince is obsessed by two images of man-condemned: one is executed, the other pardoned. Myshkin's desire is to conduct his life in terms of what they, the condemned, know. So too with Father Zosimo, and finally Alyosha and Mitya, in *The Brothers Karamazov*. They know that life justifies ideals and not, as Ivan thinks, the reverse. They know that "life is in ourselves and not in the external."

Survivors develop a faith in life which seems unwarranted to others. Dostoevsky did, and so did Bertrand Russell, to take a final example from *our* world. While in Peking during the winter of 1920-21, Russell came down with double pneumonia. Complications set in and "for a fortnight," as he tells us, "the doctors thought every evening that I should be dead before morning" (180). But with the coming of spring his health returned, and at some point during recovery Russell had an extraordinary experience, which he describes in Volume Two of the *Autobiography:*

Lying in my bed feeling that I was not going to die was surprisingly delightful. I had always imagined until then that I was fundamentally pessimistic and did not

greatly value being alive. I discovered that in this I had been completely mistaken, and that life was infinitely sweet to me. Rain in Peking is rare, but during my convalescence there came heavy rains bringing the delicious smell of damp earth through the windows, and I used to think how dreadful it would have been to have never smelt that smell again. I had the same feeling about the light of the sun, and the sound of the wind. Just outside my windows were some very beautiful acacia trees, which came into blossom at the first moment when I was well enough to enjoy them. I have known ever since that at bottom I am glad to be alive (181-82).

That is the survivor's special grace. He or she is glad to be alive. For camp survivors this affirmation was seldom so joyous or easily won, and often it was made in stubborn bitterness. A survivor of the Nazi camp at Neubrandenberg speaks of having "no right to be unhappy." She goes on to stress the one solid insight which her experience gave birth to, a vision distilled from such masses of suffering as to bear the force of ethical imperative:

Be happy, you who live in fine apartments, in ugly houses or in hovels. Be happy, you who have your loved ones, and you also who sit alone and dream and can weep. Be happy, you who torture yourself over metaphysical problems, and . . . you the sick who are being cared for, and you who care for them, and be happy, oh, how happy, you who die a death as normal as life, in hospital beds or in your homes (Maurel, 140).

To talk like that a person must be very naive or very wise. Coming out of the concentration camps, such words reach the simplest of all knowledge—that life is what counts, life whose internal destiny has had the peace and the time to unfold. This is the wisdom of Lear on the heath, stripped of everything but his pain, who sees at last that ripeness is all. ∎

Merely because they are survivors, the men and women who passed through the camps are suspect in our eyes. But when we consider the specific nature of their identity—not only as survivors, but survivors of *those* places—suspicion deepens to shock and rejection. The concentration-camp experience represents an evil so appalling that we too, when we turn to face it, suffer psychic unbalance. We too flounder in nightmare, in a torment having nothing to do with us yet felt in some strange way to be very much a part of our deepest, most secret being. The terror of the camps is *with* us. Some hideous impression of Auschwitz is in every mind, far removed from conscious thought but *there;* and not only as a repressed perception of historical events but as an image which stirs up the demonic content of our own worst fears and wishes. The image is with us; and anything connected with it, anything which starts it into consciousness, brings with it a horror too large and intensely personal to confront safely. Thus A. Alvarez can say:

> The concentration camps are a dangerous topic to handle. They stir mud from the bottom, clouding the mind, rousing dormant self-destructiveness. In the last few years I personally have known half-a-dozen suicides or near suicides; and each has prefaced his act with a fierce immersion in the literature of the camps. That is why I suggested that these places, these crimes, have an existential meaning beyond politics or shock or pity. They have become symbols of our own inturned nihilism, which their disproportionately vast scale heightens, even justifies, by making individual suffering seem so insignificant (28).

He means that the dark, unspoken passion of fantasy and desire, the whole of life's demonic undertow, has found, at last, its specific image. The concentration camps have given concrete form to the mind's most terrible enactments, such as before had been known mainly from literature, from religion and folktale, from dream and chthonic myth. The camps have justified and made legitimate the imagination's fascination with destruction and pain and mutilation and defilement. By "justified" I mean as history always justifies: not morally but in terms of priority in time, in the weight of real over possible events, in irreversibility. Events, if they are inclusive and compelling, provide imagination with powerful occasions for mythical investment; and we may at least speculate that for an unknown number of years to come, the imaginative deployment of demonic energy will use imagery drawn from the world of the camps. The elegant perversity of de Sade, the demented majesty of Dali and Lautréamont, seem timid and indulgent compared with the forms now at our disposal—imagery as old as the mind's infernal regions but which found its historical basis only after 1945.

The concentration camps are plainly an embodiment of the archetype we call *Hell*. They were "hell on earth," as everybody says, and George Steiner has gone so far as to suggest that they were a deliberate actualization of the demonic tradition in art and literature and theology, the most terrible instance of myth turning into history:

> The camp embodies, often down to minutiae, the images and chronicles of Hell in European art and thought from the twelfth to the eighteenth centuries. It is these representations which gave to the deranged horrors of Belsen a kind of "expected logic." . . . The concentration and death camps of the twentieth century, wherever they exist, under whatever régime, are *Hell made immanent*. They are the transference of Hell from below the earth to its surface. They are the deliberate enactment of a long, precise imagining (53-54).

We must hope that Steiner is wrong, for if the kind of determinism implied in this "transference" is real—if man eventually and necessarily realizes his deep imaginings in fact—then the end will come, the bombs will fall, the myth of the World's End, imagined for millennia, will arrive in actuality. That is possible, but (employing Steiner's model) so is a new Golden Age, another of man's intenser imaginings. The mind of man holds everything, and our common fate may indeed, as Freud came to believe, be bound to the eventual outcome of a battle between conflicting psychic forces.

But finally I want to mark a lesser symmetry between Hell and the camps, simply the comparison itself. We make it all the time, and so do survivors. But for us it is misleading because the archetype informs our perception and we end up seeing the SS as satanic monsters and the prisoners as condemned souls. When we imagine what the survivor's experience must have been, we thus project our own fantasies, our own worst fears and wishes. From our remote vantage point only the horror is visible; the real behavior of survivors goes unobserved because it was covert, undramatic, not at all in accord with our expectations of heroism. And so it happens that we do not see them *as survivors*. They belong to that world, and in Hell there are none but the damned, none but the spiritually maimed unto death. ∎

That mistake is easy to make. The typology of Hell was everywhere evident in the world of the camps. Steiner mentions such conventions as the "whips and hellhounds," the "ovens and stinking air," the "mockery of the damned" (54). And yes, prisoners were mocked while whipped, they were torn to death by dogs, they breathed an air so utterly foul—and this is noted repeatedly by survivors—that nobody ever saw a bird fly over the camps. In its primitive Christian form, Hell is a place of darkness, thick with smoke and flame and stench, in which the damned are tormented by demons with pitchforks. What but Hell could this be?—

> **The burning had reached a peak that night. Every chimney was disgorging flames. Smoke burst from the holes and ditches, swirling, swaying and coiling above our heads. Sparks and cinders blinded us. Through the screened fence of the second crematory we could see figures with pitch forks moving against the background**

of flames. They were men from the special squad turning the corpses in the pits and pouring a special liquid
so that they would burn better. A rancid smell of
scorched flesh choked us. Big trucks passed us trailing a
smell of corpses (Zywulska, 179).

That was Auschwitz in the fall of 1944, when the Jews of
Hungary were being killed so fast and in such numbers that the
usual gas-to-oven process had to be supplemented by pits in
which the victims burned alive. "Yet from those flames," says
Milton in *Paradise Lost*,

> No light, but rather darkness visible
> Serv'd only to discover sights of woe,
> Regions of sorrow, doleful shades, where peace
> And rest can never dwell, hope never comes
> That comes to all. . . .

Milton's Hell is a "universe of death," and his high style should
not deflect us from the fact that Auschwitz might be described in
exactly the same terms (although not in Miltonic diction, which
applied to the camps would generate lunatic irony). But the
camps are there, in Milton's poem and in Dante's, in the under-
realms of Homer and Virgil, in Shakespeare's *Lear*. From the
world's literature we can abstract a set of conditions which make
up the demonic or infernal depths as men have imagined them
always. Northrop Frye has done this, arriving at an archetypal
outline of the "world that desire totally rejects":

> the world of the nightmare and the scapegoat, of bond-
> age and pain and confusion. . . . the world also of per-
> verted or wasted work, ruins and catacombs, instru-
> ments of torture and monuments of folly (147).

Frye is describing an imaginary place, but he could be talking
about a real world where men and women were forced to carry
gigantic rocks back and forth to no purpose; where prisoners
were hung by their hands on trees; where they lay face down in
sewage and mud doing push-ups, and where to this day Dachau

and Auschwitz stand as monuments to an age which is ours. The move from fiction to history argues the prophetic nature of art and perhaps even, as Steiner implies, a kind of cultural determinism. But it is also the special case of a more general relation between contrary realms of experience, between civilization and extremity, which can be formulated this way: what we experience symbolically, in spirit only, survivors must go through in spirit *and* in body. In extremity, states of mind become objective, metaphors tend to actualize, the word becomes flesh.

In *The Great War and Modern Memory,* Paul Fussell has noted the "curious literariness" of experience in the trenches. He observes that "one way of using canonical literature to help suggest the actuality of front-line experience was to literalize what before had been figurative" (165). Thus Shakespeare's metaphor for fallen majesty—Lear saying of his hand, "It smells of mortality"—becomes plain fact in the rank air of a world where corpses of men and horses lay rotting for months. Fussell concludes that "the drift of modern history domesticates the fantastic and normalizes the unspeakable" (74), and that beginning with World War I the perception of extreme events reveals a definite tendency: "The movement was toward myth, toward a revival of the cultic, the mystical, the sacrificial, the prophetic, the sacramental, and the universally significant. In short, toward fiction" (131).

But toward fiction which had actualized; and anyone sensitive to aesthetic form, sometimes called "significant form," is bound to wonder at this odd convergence of art and life. Describing a roundup of hundreds of women in the Soviet prison at Yaroslavl for transport to the camps, Eugenia Ginzburg remembers a small incident which, like a Joycean epiphany, revealed in a moment the shattering of personal life under Stalin. "They made us give up the photographs of our children," she writes, and "I can still see the great pile of them on the stone floor of the yard" (268). That is already an example of significant form: the event in itself embodies and shows forth its larger meaning. But there is more, and Ginzburg goes on to remark:

> If, today, a film director were to show such a heap in
> close-up, he would certainly be accused of striving for a
> forced effect—especially if he were also to show a sol-
> dier's heavy boot trampling on the pile of cards, from
> which little girls in ribbons and boys in short pants
> looked up at their criminal mothers. The critics would
> say, "That's too much." Nevertheless, that is exactly
> what happened. One of the warders had to cross the
> yard and, rather than walk around the pile, stamped
> straight across the faces of our children. I saw his foot
> in close-up, as though it were in a film (268).

Extremity makes bad art because events are too obviously
"symbolic." The structure of experience is so clear and complete that it appears to be deliberately contrived. But the great
majority of books and documents by survivors are not consciously
formal or deliberately shaped. Their testimony is in no way "literary," and yet everywhere great and terrible metaphors are embedded in events described. Hell first of all, and then "spiritual"
states of being like purity and defilement, doom and salvation,
death and rebirth. The following example involves a small mas-
sacre in a German forest:

> Then we were ordered to dig out the soil in the marked
> area. . . . others were told to break off small branches
> and twigs. . . . As evening closed in, the S.S. men de-
> cided that the pit was deep enough. . . . prisoners
> were told to stand in one row facing the forest. . . . I
> watched the dancing rays of the sun glinting through
> the trees. . . . Suddenly terrible screams, accompanied
> by the crackle of rifle fire. . . . There was a stampede
> to the right and to the left. But the women could not
> run far. A few steps and they were riddled with bullets.
> I stood in front of the pit quaking. For a fleeting mo-
> ment, through glazed eyes, I saw my companions in the
> pit. Some of them were still moving convulsively. I
> heard a loud rifle volley, then silence and darkness. . . .
> Is this death? . . . I try to raise my arm but can't. I
> open my eyes but see nothing. . . . I am lying inert in
> the dark. . . . I try to raise myself and I find myself

> sitting up. Fresh branches are brushing my head. It is
> dark and there are stars above me. . . . As conscious-
> ness returns, my mind begins to clear. . . . Trembling
> and weeping I cry out in a faltering voice: "Are any of
> you alive? Come out if you are!" And on the other side
> of the pit sits a dark figure. "It's me," says Charlotte.
> But in the pit itself no one moves. We two are the only
> survivors (Weiss, 74-75).

Bullets did not tear through her, her heart did not stop. But she was certain—her body was certain—that death was coming. She felt that she had died, she lay for hours among the lifeless mass of her comrades, and then got up. Is this the famous valley of death through which souls pass? Is this resurrection? How much is metaphor, how much plain fact? Or is there any longer a difference? Archetypes have actualized in events so exaggerated, so melodramatic and patently symbolic, that no serious novelist, except perhaps in parody, would now attempt to treat them as art.

Man's interior drama, the height and depth of spiritual experience, has been writ large *in the world*. The concentration camps have done what art always does: they have brought us face to face with archetypes, they have invested body with mind and mind with body, they have given visible embodiment to man's spiritual universe, so that the primary states of good and evil are resident in the look and sound and smell of things. The essence of survival is passage through death; this way of speaking may be metaphorical for us, but not for survivors. Of course, a man or woman crawling out of a grave is not thinking of rebirth, may never have thought in such terms. For survivors of those ditches and pits there was only dumb pain. Still, they felt themselves die and then return to life, and the "objective correlative" of their ordeal was not a symbolic representation or a ritual entered imaginatively. It was the world itself, albeit a world such as we know through art and dream only. And here especially we must not be misled by our reliance on metaphor: the survivor is not a metaphor, not an emblem, but *an example*.

[176]

For us the camps are terminal images. They are the realized archetypes of eternal victimhood and of evil forever triumphant. As such they confirm most forcefully our vision of man as monster and victim. And yes, we are monsters. We are victims. But we are also survivors; and once we see the central fact about the survival experience—that these people passed *through* Hell—the archetypes of doom are, if not cancelled, at least less powerful in their authority over our perceptions. Survivors return from the grave, they come through Hell, and some, after descent into darkness and the defiling filth of underground sewers, rise again into the common world of sun and simple life. Existence at its boundary is intrinsically significant. Whatever we make of this fact, we should keep in mind that for survivors the struggle to live—merely surviving—is rooted in, and a manifestation of, the form-conferring potency of life itself. ∎

VII

RADICAL NAKEDNESS

Why, thou wert better in thy grave than to answer with thy uncovered body this extremity of the skies. . . . Unaccommodated man is no more but such a poor, bare, forked animal as thou art.

KING LEAR ON THE HEATH

ONE DIFFERENCE between Nazi and Soviet camps was that in the latter dying was a slower process. There was, though, this exception: during the early years of GULAG, when prisoners were sent into the arctic wastes to construct new slave sites, the ferocity of their ordeal was such, it took so many lives so fast, that later among Soviet inmates it became a sort of legendary standard by which to measure degrees of hardship in different camps. Dumped in the middle of nowhere, men and women had to answer the sky's extremity with, quite literally, nothing but themselves. Here is an "old" prisoner's story of those first days:

> We found only unending forests and marshlands—areas upon which no human foot had ever trod before. For us nothing was prepared in advance. We were brought into the woods and told to build barracks and enclosures, to find water, to cut roads. . . . That was how the northern camps came into being. For months on end we slept in holes dug in the ground. We subsisted on a diet of dry rusks made of black bread and, in the summertime, on wild berries. We were unarmed in the struggle against a harsh nature. The biting cold, the strength-sapping labor, disease—these left alive only a few of the original prisoners here. Even among our guards the death rate was catastrophic. . . . I can recall numerous cases of the "white death"—when a prisoner simply remained alone in the snow, not being able to muster the strength to get up (Gliksman, 266).

That is an image of existence at its limit, the specific case of the worst world possible. From it comes the definition of extremity as a situation in which men and women must live *without accommodation;* and to one degree or another this was true of all the concentration camps. All were places in which the human self was stripped of spiritual as well as physical mediations, until literally nothing was left to persist through pain and time but the body itself.

To pass from civilization to extremity means to be shorn of the elaborate system of relationships—to job, class, tradition and family, to groups and institutions of every kind—which for us provides perhaps ninety percent of what we think we are. In the camps prisoners lost their possessions, their social identity, the whole of the cultural matrix which had previously sustained them. They lost, in other words, the delicate web of symbolic identifications available to men and women in normal times. In Nazi camps they lost even their names and their hair. They were reduced to immediate physical existence through a process of desublimation so abrupt and thorough that—in the plainest, starkest sense—nothing remained of what the self had been:

> You lost the capability of proving to yourself, in a moment of doubt, that you are still the same human being you were when you came here. That being is gone, and only a miserably wretched creature remains in her place. A naked creature deprived of everything and avidly covering her body with someone else's sweat-saturated garments in spite of keen disgust (Szmaglewska, 78).

Or as Viktor Frankl discovered after his first hours in Auschwitz:

> While we were waiting for the shower, our nakedness was brought home to us: we really had nothing now except our bare bodies—even minus hair; all we possessed, literally, was our naked existence (13).

In Soviet camps, new prisoners were regularly robbed of vital possessions, especially warm clothing, by the ubiquitous gangs of *urka*s (criminals). In Nazi camps the reduction to nakedness involved a specialized set of procedures. But in either case the outcome was total loss, and the survival struggle therefore began with a search for minimal items of accommodation, clothing or a blanket or the indispensable cup or bowl. Very often—since new prisoners had not yet learned to "organize"—the things they needed could only be got by trading bread. And once inmates did find some essential item, they had to carry it on their own bodies as the only sure protection against theft: "The picture of a Soviet camp inmate in his torn quilted outfit is incomplete without a rough, rusty tin cup fastened to his belt and dangling at his side" (Gliksman, 239). Survivors did the same in German camps, and even then nothing was secure. At random moments camp officials conducted searches for "illegal" possessions, and anything not hidden was liable to be confiscated:

> They would rush at us, slapping, striking, shouting, emptying our bags, feeling the hems of our dresses and opening them to remove the paper windbreakers, confiscating the mittens and even the belts—those precious pieces of string. They found everything, they stripped us of everything and took it all away, crying sabotage. And we started off again from scratch (Maurel, 16-17).

Starting "from scratch" is in fact the survivor's permanent condition. He or she is always on the line, always being pushed back again and yet again to the outmost edge of existence. In the Nazi camps, a typical method of "thinning out" sick and exhausted prisoners was to force thousands of them to stand undressed for hours in winter weather. Then the survivor's nakedness was radical indeed, nor could he escape the terrible conclusion that in extremity everything depends on the body. All about him stood that "poor, bare, forked animal" which is, as old Lear said, "the thing itself." None of us would wish to depend on something so puny, so frail and easily harmed as the human body. But for survivors there is nothing else. ∎

In civilized circumstances, life unfolds in accord with a fate largely inward, and as it does, the past grows in reality and significance. The growth of a time which is *our* time, the process of chance becoming destiny through an irreversible chain of events, gives us much of the uniqueness we feel about ourselves as individuals. The self comes to feel grounded in its personal past, as indeed it is; and the more our lives are burdened by distress and uncertainty, the more we value what has already been lived. We cling to the past, sometimes in pride, more often in guilt and confusion, but cling all the same. And increasingly as we age we turn in memory to our particular past as to a world in reserve for rest and assurance. Novelists know this especially well. What they seek through their work is a reclamation of the past which will proclaim the reality of human selfhood to its deepest foundations.

But again survivors are different. Their immediate past is collective rather than personal, a past identical for everyone who came through the common catastrophe. Memory and selfhood are rooted, often traumatically, in events which define the individual not as an individual but as a participant in, and the embodiment of, decisive historical experience. Alain Resnais made this point with great tenderness in *Hiroshima Mon Amour,* a film in which the struggle of the lovers to know one another reaches resolution only when each understands and admits that she *is* Nevers, he *is* Hiroshima. No purely private destiny can match their historical fate, no personal agony can equal the war's massive pain. A past of this kind is the basis of the survivor's identity *as* a survivor, and becomes manifest in the act of bearing witness.

In another sense, however, survivors have no past at all—not, that is, while actually going through the camp experience. They have been uprooted from their former life, stripped of connection with it, and forced, finally, to adjust their sense of reality to conditions drastically different from those of that other world. Not even memories remain—partly because fear and pain concentrate awareness on the present, but mainly because survivors cannot *risk* remembering. As a Soviet survivor says: "The experienced Russian camp inmates kept advising us to forget—for our own sakes—our past lives. Otherwise, they maintained, homesickness would soon undermine our resistance" (Gliksman, 278). Which is to say that as long as life depends on ruthless suppression of despair and self-pity, survivors cannot afford to remember.

They cannot drift in and out of the past as we do; not often, in any case, and never for longer than a moment's passing weakness. Those who begin to "live in the past," as we say, inevitably lose their hold on the present. They become less attentive, less disciplined, and in the end they die. To remain strong, therefore, the survivor must cultivate a kind of strategic oblivion:

> From this point of view the perfect prisoner does not exist, but there are men who, after several years behind barbed wire, can control their memories far better than their primitive instincts; a relentless discipline of oblivion has erected an impassable barrier between their past and their present (Herling, 98).

The process of being stripped bare culminates when the past and present are torn apart, as if some actual rending, some intimate severance of the self from prior roots, has occurred:

> There were still naive prisoners among us who asked, to the amusement of the more seasoned ones who were there as helpers, if they could keep a wedding ring, a medal or a good-luck piece. No one could yet grasp the fact that everything would be taken away.
>
> I tried to take one of the old prisoners into my confidence. Approaching him furtively, I pointed to the roll of paper in the inner pocket of my coat and said, "Look, this is the manuscript of a scientific book. I know what you will say; that I should be grateful to escape with my life, that that should be all I can expect of fate. But I cannot help myself. I must keep this manuscript at all costs; it contains my life's work. Do you understand that?"
>
> Yes, he was beginning to understand. A grin spread slowly over his face, first piteous, then more amused, mocking, insulting, until he bellowed one word at me in answer to my question, a word that was ever present in the vocabulary of the camp inmates: "Shit!" At that moment I saw the plain truth and did what marked the culminating point of the first phase of my psychological reaction: I struck out my whole former life (Frankl, 12).

But if the past was struck out, what of time still to come? What of the future with the sense of possibility it gives us, the feeling of life unfolding toward fulfillment which supports so much of personal identity and which, in troubled times, nourishes the will to push on? But of course, in the concentration camps there was no future. At very best, tomorrow meant more of the same. Death might be seconds away, and each day was an agony so endless as never to be got through. Under such circumstances, thinking of the future was even more painful than remembering the past:

> A day begins like every day, so long as not to allow us reasonably to conceive its end, so much cold, so much hunger, so much exhaustion separates us from it: so that it is better to concentrate one's attention and desires on the block of grey bread, which is small but which will certainly be ours in an hour, and which for five minutes, until we have devoured it, will form everything that the law of the place allows us to possess (Levi, 57).

That is a constant theme of survivors: to concentrate on this day, this five minutes, this small need or pleasure. They endure from one day to the next, from one hour to another, "on a short-term basis," as one survivor says—which meant, for example, "eating what one was given without laying aside for the future, since no future was certain" (Berkowitz, 126).

As the war neared its end, prisoners in the German camps were aware of the coming liberation. They also knew that general massacres were scheduled (some of which took place); and once the death marches began, deliverance seemed remote indeed. Some part of the will to live *was* rooted in the hope of ultimate release, however unlikely that possibility might seem at any particular time. Many survivors must surely have drawn upon this faint last hope to carry them through those final days. But almost always this kind of hope was covert, like a repressed desire which affects behavior although it remains unconscious. For Soviet prisoners, the chance of release was even more improbable. Too many inmates, on the day their term was up, were sentenced to another ten or twenty years. At the end of the war, rumors of amnesty were widespread; but here too, the best protection against despair was not to hope:

> Such exaltation was usually followed by deep depression when the imagined zero hour had passed without incident. If, after such a swing from hope to despair, we did not wish to suffer mental instability . . . we had to develop our own technique for preserving our sense of balance. Many became thorough pessimists because of this (Gollwitzer, 81).

To live by looking ahead, as we do, was not possible in the camps. One Soviet prisoner, after serving his sentence of 3,650 days, was told that instead of release his term had been prolonged "indefinitely." That same day he died, for no visible reason. As one of his surviving comrades said, "I can only guess what was happening in his heart, but one thing is certain—that besides despair, pain, and helpless anger, he felt also regret for his thoughtless faith in hope" (Herling, 33). The chances for survival and freedom were so logically improbable that no hope, as we know hope, could be allowed into consciousness. The despair thus generated would be too much to bear. How, standing through the hours of winter roll-call in Auschwitz, could anyone be said to hope or believe in a future?

> It is as if this present moment of existence in camp with the thousands of motionless figures were frozen like the plants at the bottom of a lake, whose surface is covered by a thick layer of ice. And neither your longing eyes nor the efforts of your young arms nor your warmest thoughts can pierce that heavy layer of ice which spreads over your life. No fist, no matter how strong, can crack this barrier with its blow (Szmaglewska, 110).

The temptation to despair was thus compounded by the temptation to hope, in a situation where both were deadly. And as might be expected, April was indeed the cruellest month. The desire to remember, to have one's past self born again, was worst in the spring. The return of growth and fruitfulness, the whole of life's promise implicit in a blade of new grass, suggested a future that in the survivor's case was mockery. In extremity life proceeds by rejecting hope, by refusing to consider the future:

> If you lack the strength to resist the call of the earth awakened by spring. . . . [you] had better grab up a spade, a wheelbarrow, do any task within the camp and glue your eyes on the faded barracks. Not for one moment let yourself forget that you are in a concentration camp. You will be much less unhappy if you do not experience the dreams, and then face the rude awakenings. . . . In order not to become insane from the wonder of life pulsating all around you in newly awakening nature . . . it is better to bury yourself in the camp, as a rock is embedded and cannot move from its place (Szmaglewska, 170).

Prisoners in the camps did struggle, did resist, did plan and carry through revolts. But not, again, with hope as we know it. Sanity depended on always expecting the worst, on the realism of doomed men and women still holding out. This, finally, is the attitude survivors take: they might make it, they probably won't, but they will not stop trying. ∎

Past and future mean little to men and women dying, for whom reality resides in a scrap of string or bread. If survivors thought of things elsewhere, they did it wistfully or with a moment's fierce desire, but without prolonged belief. Everything about the camp experience conspired to reduce them to where they were and what they were—living bodies in a place of death. Gone were the myths and institutions, the symbols and technologies which in normal times allow the self to transcend and lose sight of its actual situation. An apt image of civilization, crude as this may sound, is that of a man sitting on a toilet reading a book. He is there, of course, but in consciousness he is elsewhere. The physical act he performs, and the biological identity it confirms, are neither visible nor in any sense significant. But for men and women in extremity this same event, minus the book, the privacy and the comfort of a clean toilet bowl, becomes an activity requiring tense attention. Survivors are reduced to primal acts and to an awareness circumscribed by primitive needs. They are naked to the roots, radically compressed to their essence as creatures of flesh.

When in ordinary circumstances we discuss the question of basic needs, the most fundamental of all, the need to excrete, is of course never mentioned. There will always, however, be much talk of two others, which for most of us represent man's "animal" side. Hunger and sex, we say, are ineradicable needs; and with hunger there is no doubt. But with sex the case is less clear, despite the belief that sex is as fundamental as hunger. It isn't. One of the striking things about the concentration-camp experience— and there is enormous evidence on this point—is that under conditions of privation and horror the need for sex disappears. It simply is not there, neither in feeling nor in fantasy, neither the desire nor the drive. As one survivor says, "Many of us young men ceased to have any sexual feelings whatever; Karel and I, during all the time we were in Treblinka, and for long afterwards, were men in name only" (Sereny, 237). Or as another puts it, "After two or three weeks of the regime at Maidanek, sex problems disappeared. Women lost their periods; men lost their urge" (Donat, 183). In Buchenwald, according to the report of a doctor imprisoned there, "one hundred per cent of the female prisoners ceased to menstruate at the very beginning of their term of captivity; the function did not reappear until months after their liberation" (Weinstock, 235). And another survivor, this time from Auschwitz, observes that "even in his dreams the prisoner did not seem to concern himself with sex" (Frankl, 31).

The same thing occurred in Soviet camps. As one survivor says: "Oh, how we made fun of ourselves! Someone said that it was a miracle of nature that we had to urinate, . . . otherwise we would forget we had a sex organ" (Gilboa, 236). Another humorous remark, which in time became a camp proverb, was a standard answer to new prisoners when they asked if survival was possible: "Oh, yes, but you won't want to sin with women" (Grossman, 321). The loss of sexual will was a universal phenomenon in the camp world, despite the fact that erotic activity was present in limited degree, more in Soviet than in German camps. And as the following statement suggests, whether or not one was capable of sexual functions depended very much on the degree of hunger, exhaustion and distance from danger:

> **One thing I noticed throughout my experience in these camps for men and women was that sex was not the pervading problem one might have expected. There were always a number of liaisons. Guards and other officials kept a few chosen girls well fed . . . but in general, in the camps I knew, human vitality was at such a low ebb that lust found little place (Fittkau, 204).**

There was more sexual activity in the Soviet camps because there was more opportunity; but also because conditions were less openly horrible. In any of the camps, however, sex was possible mainly for special prisoners. *Kapo*s and cooks, for example—men and women safer and better fed—took advantage of their positions and indulged themselves, often recklessly. Gangs of *urka*s in the Soviet camps were a constant danger to any woman alone; and women in Soviet camps often tried to become pregnant, because bearing a child earned the mother six months of freedom from heavy labor assignments. But still, such instances were not typical. In places like Buchenwald and Auschwitz the SS set up brothels in an attempt to dissipate the growing strength of the political underground. They assumed—incorrectly, it turned out—that powerful prisoners would enjoy themselves at the expense of their comrades. Only criminals went, men in league with the SS and untroubled by the need for solidarity.

The fact would seem to be that when men and women are exhausted and starving, sex is not important, and that it likewise tends to be absent when the threat of death becomes constant. A momentary brush with death may very well intensify sexual desire, but when dread becomes prolonged and seeps to the core of one's being, the capacity for erotic fulfillment is ruined. Perhaps too, disappearance of sexual desire in the camps was a biological phenomenon in service of collective survival. For if a state of nature had prevailed, men and women fighting among themselves for sexual privilege, the kind of community which grew up among prisoners would have been more difficult and open to betrayal. And it would seem, finally, that the most powerful depressors of sexual need are horror and moral disgust. The stationmaster at Treblinka, who directed incoming trains (but who was also a secret agent in the Polish underground), reports that once the killing started, he and his wife could no longer make love: "Of course there was no question of a normal sexual life; we felt we lived in a cemetery; how could one feel joy there?" (Sereny, 155). Sexual joy is one of life's chief blessings, and the biological drive which enforces it is very strong. Even so, eros begins to govern human behavior only after a critical level of safety and well-being has been attained. If this runs counter to Freud's view—that civilized rather than primitive conditions repress erotic need—so be it. Behavior which does not support day-to-day existence tends to vanish in extremity. We may fairly conclude that what remains is indispensable. ■

Survivors act as they do because they have to; and what their predicament reveals is that in extremity life and humanness depend on the same set of activities. This amounts to saying that when external props collapse, survivors fall back on life itself. A survivor of Treblinka speaks for all those like himself when he says:

> I have read more or less everything that has been written about this subject. But somehow no one appears to have understood: it wasn't *ruthlessness* that enabled an individual to survive—it was an intangible quality, not

> particular to educated or sophisticated individuals. Any-
> one might have it. It is perhaps best described as an
> overriding thirst—perhaps, too, a *talent* for life, and a
> faith in life (Sereny, 183).

He is referring to something which enables men and women to act spontaneously and correctly during times of protracted stress and danger. There is no evidence—nor should the above statement be construed—to suggest that this capacity is exclusive to a particular class, race, culture or nation. The survivor just quoted is describing how it felt to him *as experienced;* and for the phrase "talent for life" we might substitute "magic will" or "imperishable power" or "life itself" or any of the other phrases survivors use. The reference is always to something other and greater than the personal ego, a reservoir of strength and resource which in extremity becomes active and is felt as the deeper foundation of selfhood. This is as much as survivors can say of their experience, but in coming to this limit we touch upon a further implication—a view reached precisely at the limit of personal experience. Survivors act as if they were *prepared* for extremity; as if anterior to learning and acculturation there were a deeper knowledge, an elder wisdom, a substratum of vital information biologically instilled and biologically effective.

We may at least speculate that through long periods of extremity, survival depends on life literally—life, that is, as the biologists see it, not as a state or condition but as a set of activities evolved through time in successful response to crisis, the sole purpose of which is to keep going. Life continues, defends itself, expands. It does this by answering environmental challenges with countless behavioral patterns designed to deal with disturbance and threat. Behavior which proves successful for any particular species *over the long run* enters its genotype and becomes "innate." To be sure, this happens by chance, with many failures, and through unimaginably long ages of time. From phylum to phylum, furthermore, the elements of such patterns differ greatly, but each will possess some fixed response to danger, some settled way of meeting major needs, including those of defense and repair. Survival, in this case, depends on a basic fund of "biological wisdom," to use C. H. Waddington's phrase, with which all living creatures are endowed. Stripped of everything but life, what can the survivor fall back upon except some biologically determined "talent" long suppressed by cultural deformation, a bank of knowledge embedded in the body's cells. The key to survival behavior may thus lie in the priority of biological being—which is to say that the properties of life itself may best account for the rather surprising fact that under dehumanizing pressure men and women tend to preserve themselves in ways recognizably human.

To suggest that the survivor's behavior is biologically determined is to assume a number of principles which, from the perspective of the biological sciences, can be considered "facts of life." The first is that almost all behavior in the individual as in the society directly or indirectly serves the general cause of survival. The second is that any particular pattern of behavior is the outcome of millions of years of trial-and-error experience which, once it has crystallized, passes from generation to generation through genetic transmission. The third, which follows from the first two, is that primary forms of behavior are innate, the ingrained inheritance of all life-experience in a particular line of descent. The fourth is that these facts apply as much to man as to other life-forms. The whole of this view is summed up in two broad statements by J. Z. Young: "the capacity to continue is precisely the central characteristic of life" (108); and "the characteristics of human life are the activities by which human continuity is maintained" (8).

There is no question of "vitalism" here, no transcendental life-force or *élan vital* in Bergson's sense. And there is no question of "teleology" either; no grand design, no pre-established harmony tuning up at our expense as Teilhard de Chardin, for example, would have liked us to think. Life has no purpose beyond itself; or rather, having arisen by chance in an alien universe, life is its own ground and purpose, and the entire aim of its vast activity is to establish stable systems and endure. There is nothing especially mysterious about this, although the *feeling* of life—existence experienced subjectively—bears mystical significance and power. Life goes forward through the collision of populations with environments; how fast or slow this happens depends on the interaction of genetic potential and natural selection, "the outcome," as E. O. Wilson puts it, "of the genetic response of populations to ecological pressure" (32).

For any particular life-form, this much is certain: it is what it is, and behaves as it does, as the result of the whole of its past. "Every living being is *also* a fossil," says Jacques Monod:

> Within it, all the way down to the microscopic structure of its proteins, it bears the traces if not the stigmata of its ancestry. This is yet truer of man than of any other animal species by dint of the dual evolution—physical and ideational—that he is heir to (160).

Man's immediate past goes back two million years. The line of hominid descent goes back fifteen to twenty million years. And in the deepest sense, man's inheritance goes back to the appearance of life on earth, some two billion years ago; time enough to acquire the ground-sense necessary to survive in proven ways. And whether we call the configuration of man's biologically determined behavior his "biogram," as Earl W. Count has suggested, or his "biological infrastructure," as Lionel Tiger argues, the basic point is clear: survival behavior reveals a fixed system of activity, biological in origin, which is specific to humanness as such.

It would be strange indeed, with so many millions of years of survival-experience packed into our genes, if at some deep involuntary level we did not possess capacities specially geared to cope with extreme situations. In the beginning there was nothing but extremity, nothing but the random rush of life in a touch-

and-go struggle against extinction. Against the constant threat of oblivion, tendencies had to be developed which would increase the capacity to continue. The process of evolution is thus a perpetual gathering of information, on levels ever more complex, which works to preserve existence not only under normal conditions (which means conditions already adjusted to), but especially in time of disaster. Part of the uniqueness of man is that in addition to normal adaptation, he seems adjusted to *possible* dangers, to threat as a potential condition. At least in its essentials, human behavior may be understood as "a repertoire of possible reactions" (Young, 604) to a range of possible events. The particular response will depend on the situation being faced.

The survivor's experience therefore calls us back to something which Enlightenment rationalism, with its hope of starting over, spent two centuries denying: what N. Tinbergen calls "the innate foundations of behaviour" (6). The biologist's assumption is that like any other animal, man possesses "instinctive" forms of basic behavior. Such deep-seated tendencies are constantly transformed by an endless and often chaotic variety of cultural modes, but they exist all the same, and operate most decisively when life is threatened. What separates man from all other life-forms is of course civilization, although in *Animal Architecture* von Frisch suggests that even in this respect we are not entirely special. Animals also build worlds, modify environments, transform instincts and situations. But they never attain freedom as we know it, never move as we do beyond the immediate dangers and restrictions of physical existence. "Yet, for all his cultural achievements," as S. E. Luria reminds us, "man does not escape biological evolution; he only modifies its effects on himself" (145). Through technical and symbolic means our biological fate has been transcended and denied. But for all that, we are still bodies, and our inescapable condition is that of any other life-form. Each quantum of behavior is another leaf on the barely visible branches of a tree whose trunk never shows as long as civilization works efficiently, but which comes starkly into view as soon as, by some terrible mischance, the leaves and branches fall. ∎

Students of biology are generally agreed that a human "biogram" exists. But one aspect of man's biological make-up—the capacity to modify perceptions and behavior through culture—makes the rest of the biogram difficult to identify. It is there, the sure foundation of everything else. But like any foundation, it lies below-ground and is easy to miss as we marvel at the building it supports. Human behavior, at least in normal times, is always a mix of instinct and learning, of immediate and mediated response; and this distinction, as E. O. Wilson points out, is crucial to further understanding of man as a biological creature:

> One of the key questions, never far from the thinking of anthropologists and biologists who pursue real theory, is to what extent the biogram represents an adaptation to modern cultural life and to what extent it is a phylogenetic vestige. Our civilizations were jerrybuilt around the biogram. How have they been influenced by it? Conversely, how much flexibility is there in the biogram, and in which parameters particularly? Experience with other animals indicates that when organs are hypertrophied, phylogeny is hard to reconstruct. This is the crux of the problem of the evolutionary analysis of human behavior (548).

The problem with man is that his evolution involved a series of "quantum jumps" which radically transformed the use and quality of inherited traits. The relation of human behavior to its own phylogenetic past and to that of other species is therefore unclear. But on one point biologists agree: man is the culmination of a tendency toward social organization which appears everywhere in the biosphere. Certainly there were societies before there were men. The cell itself is a kind of social organization, and any two-cell animal is in fact two animals who long ago worked out a system of mutual support. Primates likewise solved the problem of survival, millions of years before the appearance of man, by evolving social orders which include systems of communication and hierarchy, of mating and care for the young, of food-gathering, territory and defense. The typical primate social group, as Hans Kummer observes, is "an ever-present tool of survival" (36). Man could not have emerged without these prior achievements, and thus Konrad Lorenz argues:

> If it were not for a rich endowment of social instincts, man could never have risen above the animal world. All specifically human faculties, the power of speech, cultural tradition, moral responsibility, could have evolved only in a being which, before the very dawn of conceptual thinking, lived in well-organized communities (246).

Precisely how this occurred is not known: but that human society did emerge from earlier societal forms, and that man is social *by nature,* are aspects of the human condition beyond doubt. I stress this point because thinkers as influential as Rousseau and Freud have insisted that man is anti-social, and that society is held together more by force and fear than by any innate disposition on the part of its members. Precisely this view underlies the mistaken notion that a "state of nature" prevailed in the concentration camps, or that a war of all against all necessarily erupts as soon as constraints are removed. Far otherwise, primary aspects of the camp experience—group formation, "organizing," sharing and the giving of gifts—are evidence amounting to proof that in man social instincts operate with the authority and momentum of life itself, and never more forcefully than when survival is the issue. In *The Social Life of Animals,* W. C. Allee has observed that even among organisms like bacteria and spermatozoa there are signs of "communal activity"; these tiny creatures live more successful *en masse,* and Allee concludes that "a sort of unconscious co-operation or automatic mutualism extends far down among the simpler plants and animals" (88). Animals—

men and women included—tend to survive better in groups, and not only in terms of help and defense, but just by being near each other. One survivor of the Nazi camps describes her struggle in these terms: "As soon as one is alone one thinks: What's the use? Why do it? Why not give up? . . . With others, one keeps going" (Delbo, 116).

To cite striking similarities between animal and human behavior, as ethologists like Lorenz and Tinbergen have done; or to extrapolate a human "biogrammar" from the activities of primates, as Lionel Tiger and Robin Fox have proposed, is not to prove that human existence is governed by biological "laws." From the evidence at hand, however, we may at least speculate on the close relation of basic human acts to similar kinds of behavior in other life-forms. A possible conclusion is that behavior specific to man exists within a continuum of life-activities so fundamental and essential to existence that, in one form or another, they may be found throughout the biological realm. Bernhard Rensch's *Biophilosophy* does indeed approach such conclusions; and although few biologists would care to back him up, the tendency is more and more to expect a "new synthesis," beyond the recent wedding of Darwin and genetics, which might arrive finally at a unified theory of life including man and culture.

Wilson points out that "the rate of change in a particular set of cultural behaviors reflects the rate of change in the environmental features to which the behaviors are keyed" (560). This means that with the fall from civilization into extremity, with that fierce descent to nakedness, significant changes should have appeared in the behavior of survivors—*if,* that is, the basic components of humanness are culturally determined and culturally upheld. But apart from the period of initial collapse, no dramatic change took place. The elementary forms of social being remained active, dignity and care did not disappear. These facts argue an agency stronger than will or conscious decision, stronger even than the kind of practical intelligence which made the need for moral order and collective action obvious. Something innate—let us think of it as a sort of biological gyroscope—keeps men and women steady in their humanness despite inhuman pressure. ∎

The depth and durability of man's social nature may be gauged by the fact that conditions in the concentration camps were designed to turn prisoners against each other; but that in a multitude of ways, men and women persisted in social acts. Fear and privation increased irritability but did not keep inmates from joining in common cause. In fact protracted death-threat is the condition which brings social instincts to their strongest pitch. This is true of animals as well. Group formation in defense against predation is common from insects to primates, and protective strategies often depend on intricate systems of communication and mutual aid. Among many species of birds and other vertebrates, furthermore, the degree of social cohesion is proportionate to the degree of food scarcity or other negative features of the environment. The more pressure from without, the more "solidarity" from within. For animals as for man, return to community is an inborn reaction to danger and prolonged stress. Only under highly favorable conditions can a society tolerate anti-social forms of behavior. We can pretend we owe nothing to anyone, but survivors know they need each other.

Integral to survival at the social level—again in man as in other species—is some form of warning technique, and this is almost certainly the basis of the survivor's obsessive need to "tell the world." The will to bear witness, as we have seen, is an involuntary reaction to extreme situations. Survivors do not so much decide to remember and record, as simply find themselves doing it, guided by the feeling that it *must* be done. Earlier I suggested that this act can be compared to a scream, but perhaps it *is* a scream—a special version of the social animal's call to its group—and thus a signal of warning and appeal which on the human level becomes the process of establishing a record and thereby transmitting information vital for both moral and practical reasons. We learn what to fear, what to call evil and therefore what to call good, by absorbing the costly experience of others. It seems possible that a real connection, biologically encouraged, exists between the survivor's act of witness and the kind of primate behavior described by Washburn and Hamburg in the following instance:

> **In the Nairobi Park there are many groups of baboons that are accustomed to cars. A parasitologist shot two of these baboons from a car and eight months later it was still impossible to approach the group in a car. It is most unlikely that even a majority of the animals saw what happened and the behavior of the group was based on the fear of a few individuals.** *It is highly adaptive for animals to learn what to fear without having to experience events directly themselves* **(DeVore, 619).**

Our strongest instinctive reactions tend to be those provoked by fear and threat, and often the response is most intense—and this may account for the frenzy of political struggle—when the danger is collective. While indirectly of benefit to individuals, behavior concerned with warning and rescue—the whole complex of action surrounding the scream—is geared primarily to survival at the level of the group. "With the alarm call," as Robert Ardrey puts it, "the perception of the first becomes the property of the group"; and this kind of behavior is so widespread that "the alarm signal, in almost all species, becomes the very criterion for society itself" (73-74). E. O. Wilson states that "warning calls seem prima facie to be altruistic" (123), at least insofar as to sight the danger is to be exposed to it, which likewise argues the individual's instinctive concern for the safety of the larger group. Insofar as these facts bear on human behavior, we can appreciate the sense of urgency so apparent when survivors bear witness. For a Jew in Auschwitz, the annihilation of his or her people was *possible*; and in an even broader respect—since not only Jews bear witness—the survivor's scream arises from the deepest fear of all, that mankind, or indeed all life, is now endangered. ∎

Much of the behavior of survivors may thus be traced to the "bio-social" roots of human existence; and not their behavior merely, but also the extraordinary stubbornness of will which character-izes action in extremity—the furious energy of a will impersonal and stronger than hope, which in an accurate, unmetaphorical sense can only be that of life itself. But survivors do more than maintain moral sanity and establish bonds among themselves. They also struggle to preserve dignity as something which cannot be dispensed with. This too may be the specifically human enact-ment of a biological imperative. I say *human* here, because we do not know if anything like a sense of dignity exists for other life-forms. Robinson Jeffers wrote poem after poem celebrating what he called the dignity of lone animals, the puma, the hawk, the wild boar, saying that only animals possess dignity because only they are at all times in complete accord with their essential nature and cannot be corrupted from it. That is exactly the condition sur-vivors struggle to preserve, but with a difference. Animals remain true to their essence because they are not free to betray themselves. Only man has a choice, and only man, furthermore, has a kind of consciousness which transforms the condition of dignity into a sense and a feeling. And here man may truly stand alone. Dig-nity in its human context presupposes self-awareness and a delib-erate resistance to determination by external forces. In this way, as Erving Goffman suggests in *Asylums,* dignity becomes an es-sential element of selfhood:

> The practice of reserving something of oneself from the clutches of an institution is very visible in mental hos-pitals and prisons but can be found in more benign and less totalistic institutions, too. I want to argue that this recalcitrance is not an incidental mechanism of defense but rather an essential constituent of the self (319).

"Recalcitrance" splendidly describes survivors in their stubborn refusal to be completely shaped by their environment. In the camps, dignity was equated with selfhood because it was the only thing left, the one dimension of intimate existence beyond the enemy's reach. As one survivor says: "We had no longer homes to defend. All we had was our human dignity, which was our home, our pride, our only possession—and the moral strength to defend it with" (Perl, 60). Stripped of everything, prisoners maintained moral identity by holding some inward space of self untouchable, and they did it by the way in which the body itself was carried and cared for. The need for dignity and the will to resist are closely related. They may in fact be identical: two ways of warding off capitulation, of saying No, of insisting upon the observance of a boundary between self and world.

Survivors make radical adjustments in order to live; but at the same time, and also in order to live, they strive to keep themselves *fundamentally* unchanged by the pressures to which they respond. In this they are like life itself, which is flexible and conservative at the same time, which is polymorphic in the extreme and yet which exhibits a definite development of greater and greater order, accompanied by a tendency toward irreversibility, on both the individual and the species levels. Life is unlike all other phenomena because it defies entropy. While everything else in the universe is "running down," life is "running up." In some sense this is true of the human self also. It too defies entropy and resists dispersal; it too spends much energy and anguish keeping itself tightly whole—a kind of moral effort we ordinarily refer to as "maintaining integrity"—and works to adjust without losing the continuity of its basic organization. The comparison I am making is pure speculation, of course; it could hardly be otherwise. And yet how apt, in the survivor's case, to take seriously the idea that mankind is life conscious of itself; as if basic biological processes, transformed by consciousness, do indeed reappear as activities specific to selfhood.

Human beings need and desire to be part of a larger whole,

to joint with their fellows and even, in moments of great passion, to lose the sense of self entirely. That is the basis of sex and religion, of politics and society. But just as much, men and women yearn for solitude, they struggle fiercely for an existence apart, for an integrity absolutely unbreachable. That is the basis of dignity, of personality, of the egoism which fuels creation and discovery, and finally of the sense of individual "rights." But throughout the whole of the biosphere a similar duality is evident. From polymers to man, life-forms are perpetually merging, joining, establishing symbiotic and societal modes of relation for mutual benefit. At the same time, however, particular life-forms are differentiating themselves from others, individuation becomes more and more pronounced, a species diverges within itself (even as others converge) until successful breeding no longer occurs. Strangest of all is the tendency of individual organisms to reject tissue from any other organism not "recognized" as "self." This phenomenon, commonly referred to as "immuno-rejection," suggests a tendency toward radical selfhood at the very basis of life. On the human level, this activity of keeping whole and inviolate, this constant resistance to the penetration of otherness, is the essence of dignity. And its organic parallel is striking. "Our theme," says J. Z. Young, "is that living things act as they do because they are so organized as to take actions that prevent their dissolution into the surroundings" (12). ■

What separates man from the rest of the living world, his blessing and his curse, is consciousness. At a fairly recent stage in the evolutionary past, man reached awareness not only of things around him, but of himself and his condition. Once this occurred, characteristics like dignity and conscience could develop, the process of civilization could begin in earnest, because now, for the first time, an animal had become capable of altering its fate. With self-consciousness came the ability to prepare and manipulate, to make changes in basic conditions, and finally to transform or reject the biological foundations of existence. "Biological evolution transcended itself when it gave rise to man," says Theodosius Dobzhansky; and by "transcend" he means "to go beyond the limits of, or to surpass the ordinary, accustomed, previously utilized or well-trodden possibilities of a system" (44-45). Transcendence in exactly this sense is the achievement on which the whole of civilization rests; and we know approximately how and when this process began by two items of anthropological evidence: tools and ritual burial.

Primates use tools—they work food and sometimes defend themselves with rocks and pieces of wood—but no animal except man systematically *makes* tools. As Bernard Campbell says in *Human Evolution*: "An ape cannot conceive the tool without seeing it. He cannot see the stick in the plank or a hand-axe within a piece of rock. This man alone can do" (335). To do that is a sure sign of imagination and forethought, of purpose understood, and of a willingness to tolerate delay in order to proceed with greater efficiency. There is plenty of evidence that at some stage in the pre-dawn of human experience—perhaps two million years in the past—men became aware of themselves sufficiently to start working upon their material condition. The tool is the beginning of technolog process which, once in motion, becomes as inevitable in its development as evolution itself.

But the rise to self-consciousness was decisive for an even more important reason. When men and women became conscious of themselves they became aware of death and of their own vulnerability. And they began to notice, as no other animal can, the frightfulness of infinite spaces opening everywhere around them. As Dobzhansky observes, "death-awareness is a bitter fruit of man's having risen to the level of consciousness" (69). What began a billion years earlier as neurological response to environmental stimuli, with man came to climax in terror. And with it came the need for spiritual defense and preservation: the need for a technology of the emerging soul, for symbols, rituals, myths—all the vehicles of transformation through which death and nothingness vanish and reappear as "higher" life and meaning. Culture and death are profoundly related; and again—this time in René Dubos's words—we have evidence:

> At least a hundred thousand years ago, Neanderthal man buried his dead with offerings in a crouched position oriented from east to west, and in some cases on beds of wildflowers. Some form of ultimate concern may thus be coeval with mankind. The need to symbolize death and the afterlife may constitute one of the attributes that set man completely apart from the animal kingdom (60-61).

Ritual burial is the oldest form of collective symbolic activity, and the fact that the dead were almost always painted with red ocher—a practice reserved for ritualized and sacred objects—implies some rude degree of religious consciousness. We know with fair certainty, moreover, that religion and sacred rites were a central part of the oldest civilizations (those whose artifacts and records still exist); and what these developments imply is that culture—the symbolic machinery of transcendence—began with death-dread. It began, that is, with the will to negate the biological dimension of human existence.

Man as man came into being when the evolution of consciousness forced upon him the knowledge of his own condition. This was simultaneously the birth of civilization—of technology and culture—and from then onward, more and more rapidly, man has been shaped and guided by culture at least as much as by the dictates of physical need. Civilization has long surpassed the immediacy of the survival situation (for those at the top, that is); its ancient roots are hidden, deliberately obscured. The function of technology is to serve physical and economic needs well enough for us to ignore them. The function of culture is to negate the primal facts of nothingness and death. Both aspects of civilization reduce consciousness of our condition as biological creatures. And in the end both breed contempt for life.

The split between mind and body, between man's "higher" and "lower" natures, is not only a consequence but the major goal of this process. The spirit soars, preens, consoles itself in a freedom gained by repressing consciousness of the body and its needs. A short-hand formula for the whole of this endeavor would be (keeping Freud in mind): where body was, there shall spirit be. Western civilization is the negation of biological reality; and unavoidably, since life and death are inextricable, the denial of death comes finally to be a denial of life. At its worst it results in overt hostility to life, as if only by killing, only by administering death with style and majesty, could death itself be mastered. In *Death in the Afternoon,* Hemingway speaks of "the feeling of rebellion against death which comes from its administering":

> Once you accept the rule of death thou shalt not kill is an easily and a naturally obeyed commandment. But when a man is still in rebellion against death he has pleasure in taking to himself one of the Godlike attributes; that of giving it. This is one of the most profound feelings in those men who enjoy killing (233).

Our possible fate is that man's last act will indeed be Godlike. He will lift his finger and destroy all life on earth and thereby—literally—kill death. Already we have machines to make the "final solution" truly final. Just this predicament has given rise to the survivor as a significant human type. Survivors are those who have escaped the murderous circle of our retreat from death, men and women shoved violently back upon a biological wisdom long unheeded. The survivor is the figure of all those who, in Hemingway's words, have had to "accept the rule of death," and for whom "thou shalt not kill" has become a "commandment" *naturally* obeyed. There is terrible irony in this, for whereas awareness of death generates firm care for life, death-denial ends in a fury of destruction. Perhaps the ultimate difference between civilization and extremity—between *us* and *them*—is captured in a single stark comment by Octavio Paz: "Facing death the spirit is life, and facing the latter, death" (52). ∎

The survivor is the man or woman who has passed through the "crisis of civilization" we talk about so much. That some kind of crisis is brewing—that civilization no longer works well even for the few—is evident. The man-made death of one hundred million people in little more than fifty years is proof enough. At the heart of our problems is that nihilism which was all along the destiny of Western culture: a nihilism either unacknowledged even as the bombs fall or else, as with Hitler or Stalin, demonically proclaimed as the new salvation. And it was inevitable; for when mythic structures collapse and symbolism fails, the choice is ourselves or nothing. Nietzsche was the great prophet of this development, and he foresaw the choice we would face. "What is dawning," he wrote in 1886, "is the opposition of the world we revere and the world we live and are. So we can abolish either our reverence or ourselves" (45). So far we have preferred to abolish ourselves, and how easy it has been. Amid high cant and pieties obscenely cynical, whole cities and peoples are wiped out. The value of life has been reduced to zero, to excrement.

This cannot go on for much longer, and the fact that now the whole of life is threatened may be—with luck—a turning point. "As with all evolution's creations," says S. E. Luria, man's "biological fate is to make do, to survive as a species by the skin of his teeth" (120). It seems that for all our achievements and dreams we have not, after all, defeated the body's crude claims. And this, again, is the survivor's special importance. He is the first of civilized men to live beyond the compulsions of culture; beyond a fear of death which can only be assuaged by insisting that life itself is worthless. The survivor is evidence that men and women are now strong enough, mature enough, awake enough, to face death without mediation, and therefore to embrace life without reserve.

Whenever we hear of this or that atrocity, and especially when the revelations of terrorism and modern warfare upset our faith in civilization, we speak with knowing bitterness about the "thin veneer" of culture and about how swiftly man's "real" nature reveals itself under stress. Part of our torment is that we think we know what lies beneath the surface. We look into the darkness of our own hearts and behold every kind of destructiveness —the whole demonic surge of savagery erupting daily in war, torture, genocide, or spilling out imaginatively in so much of modern art and literature. What we have not seen is that our rage stems from nihilism, and that nihilism is the outcome of allegiance to a mind-body split which makes hateful the body and its functions, and storms in spiteful execration against the whole of existence as soon as life is no longer justified by firm belief in "higher" values. And we have altogether missed the fact that beyond our lust for disaster there is another, far deeper stratum of the human psyche, one that is life-affirming and life-sustaining.

A biological wisdom exists, prompting us to know that in life's own needs the spirit can find a home. Not noble or god-approved, not especially dramatic or sublime as in the old days, but rooted in the plain happiness of work and communion with others, and in the small shared universe of physical joy which is our due as creatures of flesh. And also this; that in birth and growth and fruitfulness there is meaning enough to quiet our hunger for high cause—concrete significance, perpetually renewed in the striving and sorrow and brief accomplishment which living demands from day to day. The sun is here, as survivors and condemned men know. Life, the earth in its silence, is all there is. How infinitely sad that Hegel's "secularization of the spirit" reached its first fulfillment in the concentration camps.

Man's kinship with the gods is over. Our Promethean moment was a moment only, and in the wreckage of its aftermath a world far humbler, far less grand and self-assured, begins to emerge. Civilization will either destroy itself, and us with it, or alter its present mode of functioning. And culture—that "life of the mind" as we call it—will of course continue but likewise change. The realm of ideas and symbols will have to be lived closer to the bone, real unmetaphorical bone, bone frail as grass and easily crushed. And as for an ethic based on selfless love, that dream cost two thousand years of misery, and like "faith in humanity" came to its end in Auschwitz, in Hiroshima, in the forests of Vorkuta. What remains to us now is simple care, a care biologically inspired and made active through mutual need.

One thinks of the statues of Classical Greece, the Periclean perfection of their grace and poise, their integral strength meant to symbolize the spirit of man. One thinks of the great painting and sculpture of the Renaissance, the incredible beauty of that faith in a humanness "larger than life." And one thinks now of the survivor, not as an emblem or a symbol, but as he is, in rags and dirt, his face the face of anyone, his eyes just barely bright. His soul lives *in* his flesh, and what his body says is that the human spirit can sink this low, can bear this torment, can suffer defilement and fear and unspeakable hardship and still exist. In our time the fate of man and the fate of life are one, and we would be less than wise to ignore the survivor's voice. Not only his scream, and the horror that provoked it, but his voice in simple talk to others like himself. To new prisoners on their first night in Sachsenhausen, a survivor spoke these words:

> I have not told you of our experiences to harrow you, but to strengthen you. . . . Now you may decide if you are justified in despairing. ∎

BIBLIOGRAPHY

The bibliography is in two parts. The first, Original Testimony, contains the direct testimony of actual survivors. The second part, Secondary Sources, contains all other references. The amount of literature by survivors, or in which survivors are quoted, is truly vast, and only a very small part of it is listed below. No adequate bibliography exists. For an introduction to testimony by survivors in English and English translation, see Janet Ziegler, *World War II: Books in English, 1945-65* (Stanford, Calif.: Hoover Institute, 1971), Section VI, "Social Impact of the War." For a list of bibliographies on the literature of the Jewish catastrophe, see Jacob Robinson and Philip Friedman, *Guide to Jewish History under Nazi Impact* (New York: YIVO Institute for Jewish Research, 1960), Chapter Sixteen, "Collections of Personal Narratives and Anthologies." Survivors of the concentration camps have left records in more than twenty languages, most not in English.

Page references in the text are from the first edition listed.

I ORIGINAL TESTIMONY

Akhmatova, Anna. *Selected Poems,* tr. Richard McKane (London: Oxford University, 1969).

Berg, Mary. *Warsaw Ghetto: A Diary,* tr. Norbert and Sylvia Glass (New York: L. B. Fisher, 1945).

Berkowitz, Sarah Bick. *Where Are My Brothers?* (New York: Helios, 1965).

Bernard, Jean-Jacques. *The Camp of Slow Death,* tr. Edward Owen Marsh (London: Victor Gollancz, 1945).

Bettelheim, Bruno. "Individual and Mass Behavior in Extreme Situations," *Journal of Abnormal and Social Psychology,* Volume 38, No. 4, October 1943, pp. 417-52.

————. *The Informed Heart* (Glencoe, Ill.: Free Press, 1960; London: Thames & Hudson, 1961).

Birenbaum, Halina. *Hope Is the Last To Die,* tr. David Welsh (New York: Twayne, 1971).

Buber-Neumann, Margarete. *Under Two Dictators.* tr. Edward Fitzgerald (New York: Dodd, Mead; London: Victor Gollancz, 1949).

Ciszek, Walter J. *With God in Russia* (New York: McGraw-Hill, 1964).

Cohen, Elie A. *Human Behavior in the Concentration Camp,* tr. M. H. Braaksma (New York: Norton, 1953; London: Jonathan Cape, 1954).

Delbo, Charlotte. *None of Us Will Return,* tr. John Githens (New York: Grove, 1968).

Donat, Alexander. *The Holocaust Kingdom* (New York: Holt, Rinehart and Winston, 1965; London: Corgi, 1967).

Ekart, Antoni. *Vanished Without Trace,* tr. Egerton Sykes and E. S. Virpsha (London: Max Parrish, 1954).

Fittkau, Gerhard A. *My Thirty-Third Year* (New York: Farrar, Straus, 1958).

Frankl, Viktor E. *From Death-Camp to Existentialism,* tr. Ilse Lasch (Boston: Beacon, 1959).

Friedman, Philip. *Martrys and Fighters* (London: Routledge & Kegan Paul, 1954).

Gilboa, Yehoshua A. *Confess! Confess!,* tr. Dov Ben Aba (Boston: Little, Brown, 1968).

Ginzburg, Eugenia Semyonovna. *Journey into the Whirlwind,* tr. Paul Stevenson and Max Hayward (New York: Harcourt, Brace & World, 1967; London: Collins, 1970).

Glatstein, Jacob; Knox, Israel; and Margoshes, Samuel. *Anthology of Holocaust Literature* (New York: Atheneum, 1973).

Gliksman, Jerzy. *Tell the West* (New York: Gresham, 1948).

Gluck, Gemma La Guardia. *My Story* (New York: McKay, 1961).

Goldstein, Bernard. *The Stars Bear Witness,* tr. Leonard Shatzkin (New York: Viking, 1949; London: Victor Gollancz, 1950).

Gollwitzer, Helmut. *Unwilling Journey: A Diary from Russia,* tr. E. M. Delacour (Philadelphia: Muhlenberg; London: SCM Press, 1953).

Grossman, Moshe. *In the Enchanted Land,* tr. I. M. Lask (Tel-Aviv: Rachel, 1960-61).

Hardman, Leslie H. *The Survivors: The Story of the Belsen Remnant* (London: Vallentine, Mitchell, 1958).

Hart, Kitty. *I Am Alive* (London and New York: Abelard-Schuman, 1962).

Heimler, Eugene. *Night of the Mist,* tr. André Ungar (New York: Vanguard; London: Bodley Head, 1959).

Herling, Gustav. *A World Apart,* tr. Joseph Marek (New York: Roy; London' Heinemann, 1951).

Kantor, Alfred. *The Book of Alfred Kantor* (New York: McGraw-Hill, 1971).

Kaplan, Chaim A. *The Warsaw Diary of Chaim A. Kaplan,* tr. Abraham I. Katsh (New York: Collier, 1973). Under the title *Scroll of Agony* (New York: Macmillan, 1965; London: Hamish Hamilton, 1966).

Kessel, Sim. *Hanged at Auschwitz,* tr. Melville and Delight Wallace (New York: Stein & Day, 1972; London: Talmy Franklin, 1973).

Klein, Gerda Weissman. *All But My Life* (New York: Hill & Wang, 1957; London: Elek, 1958).

Knapp, Stefan. *The Square Sun* (London: Museum Press, 1956).

Kogon, Eugen. *The Theory and Practice of Hell,* tr. Heinz Norden (New York: Farrar, Straus, 1953; London: Secker & Warburg, 1950).

Kraus, Ota, and Kulka, Erich. *The Death Factory: Document on Auschwitz,* tr. Stephen Jolly (Oxford: Pergamon, 1966).

Kuznetsov, A. *Babi Yar,* tr. David Floyd (New York: Farrar, Straus & Giroux, 1970; London: MacGibbon & Kee, 1967).

Lengyel, Olga. *Five Chimneys: The Story of Auschwitz,* tr. Paul P. Weiss (Chicago: Ziff-Davis, 1947; London: Mayflower, 1972).

Levi, Primo. *The Reawakening,* tr. Stuart Woolf (Boston: Little, Brown, 1965). Under the title *The Truce* (London: Bodley Head, 1965).

————. *Survival in Auschwitz,* tr. Stuart Woolf (New York: Collier, 1969). Under the title *If This Man Is a Man* (New York: Orion, 1959; London: Orion, 1960).

Lewinska, Pelagia. *Twenty Months at Auschwitz,* tr. Albert Teichner (New York: Lyle Stuart, 1968).

Lingens-Reiner, Ella. *Prisoners of Fear* (London: Victor Gollancz, 1948).

Lipper, Elinor. *Eleven Years in Soviet Prison Camps,* tr. Richard and Clara Winston (London: World Affairs, 1951; Hollis & Carter, 1952).

London, Artur. *The Confession,* tr. Alastair Hamilton (New York: Ballantine, 1971). Under the title *On Trial* (London: Macdonald, 1970).

Mandelstam, Nadezhda. *Hope Against Hope,* tr. Max Hayward (New York: Atheneum, 1970; London: Harvill, 1971).

Maurel, Micheline. *An Ordinary Camp,* tr. Margaret S. Summers (New York: Simon & Schuster, 1958). Under the title *Ravensbruck* (London: Blond, 1958).

Newman, Judith Sternberg. *In the Hell of Auschwitz* (New York: Exposition, 1964).

Nork, Karl. *Hell in Siberia,* tr. E. Brockett (London: Robert Hale, 1957).

Nyiszli, Miklos. *Auschwitz: A Doctor's Eyewitness Account,* tr. Tibere Kremer and Richard Seaver, with "Foreword" by Bruno Bettelheim (New York: Frederick Fell, 1960; London: Panther, 1967).

Pawlowicz, Sala. *I Will Survive* (New York: Norton; London: Muller,

Perl, Gisella. *I Was a Doctor in Auschwitz* (New York: International Universities Press, 1948).

Poller, Walter. *Medical Block, Buchenwald* (London: Souvenir, 1961).

Rappaport, Ernest A. "Beyond Traumatic Neurosis," *International Journal of Psycho-Analysis,* XLIX, Part 4, 1968, pp. 719-31.

————. "Survivor Guilt," *Midstream,* XVII, August-September 1971, pp. 41-47.

Ringelblum, Emmanuel. *Notes from the Warsaw Ghetto,* tr. Jacob Sloan (New York: McGraw-Hill, 1958).

Roeder, Bernhard. *Katorga,* tr. L. Kochan (London: William Heinemann, 1958).

Rousset, David. *The Other Kingdom,* tr. Ramon Guthrie (New York: Reynal and Hitchcock, 1947).

Semprun, Jorge. *The Long Voyage,* tr. Richard Seaver (New York: Grove; London: Weidenfeld & Nicolson, 1964).

Sereny, Gitta. *Into That Darkness* (New York: McGraw-Hill, 1974; London: Deutsch, 1974).

Solomon, Michael. *Magadan* (New York: Auerbach, 1971).

Solzhenitsyn, Alexander. *One Day in the Life of Ivan Denisovich,* tr. Ralph Parker (New York: Dutton; London: Pall Mall, 1963).

————. *The First Circle,* tr. Thomas P. Whitney (New York: Harper & Row; London: Collins, 1968).

————. *The Cancer Ward,* tr. Rebecca Frank (New York: Dial, 1968; London: Bodley Head, 1968-69).

Szalet, Leon. *Experiment "E,"* tr. Catherine Bland Williams (New York: Didier, 1945).

Szmaglewska, Seweryna. *Smoke over Birkenau,* tr. Jadwiga Rynas (New York: Henry Holt, 1947).

Thorne, Leon. *Out of the Ashes* (New York: Rosebern, 1961).

Unsdorfer, S. B. *The Yellow Star* (New York and London: Thomas Yoseloff, 1961).

Vrba, Rudolf. *I Cannot Forgive* (New York: Grove; London: Sidgwick & Jackson, 1964).

Wdowinski, David. *And We Are Not Saved* (New York: Philosophical Library, 1963; London: W. H. Allen, 1964).

Weinstock, Eugene. *Beyond the Last Path,* tr. Clara Ryan (New York: Boni and Gaer, 1947).

Weiss, Reska. *Journey Through Hell* (London: Vallentine, Mitchell, 1961).

Weissberg, Alexander. *The Accused,* tr. Edward Fitzgerald (New York: Simon & Schuster, 1951). Under the title *Conspiracy of Silence* (London: Hamish Hamilton, 1952).

Wells, Leon W. *The Janowska Road* (New York: Macmillan, 1963; London: Jonathan Cape, 1966).

Wiechert, Ernst. *Forest of the Dead,* tr. Ursula Stechow (New York: Greenberg, 1947).

Wiesel, Elie. *Night,* tr. Stella Rodway (New York: Avon, 1969; London: Fontana, 1973).

————. *A Beggar in Jerusalem,* tr. Lily Edelman and Elie Wiesel (London: Weidenfeld and Nicolson, 1970).

————. *One Generation After,* tr. Lily Edelman and Elie Wiesel (New York: Avon, 1972; London: Weidenfeld & Nicolson, 1971).

————. *The Oath,* tr. Marion Wiesel (New York: Random House, 1973).

Wigmans, Johan H. *Ten Years in Russia and Siberia,* tr. Arnout de Waal (London: Darton, Longman and Todd, 1964).

Zywulska, Krystyna. *I Came Back,* tr. Krystyna Cenkalska (London: Dennis Dobson, 1951).

II SECONDARY SOURCES

Allee, W. C. *The Social Life of Animals* (New York: W. W. Norton, 1938; London: Heinemann, 1929).

Alvarez, A. *Beyond All This Fiddle* (New York: Random House, 1969; London: Allen Lane, 1968).

Ardrey, Robert. *The Social Contract* (New York: Atheneum; London: Collins, 1970).

Arendt, Hannah. *Eichmann in Jerusalem* (New York: Viking; London: Faber & Faber, 1963).

Bluhm, Hilde O. "How Did They Survive?" *American Journal for Psychotherapy,* Volume II, No. 1, 1948, pp. 3-32.

Braudel, Fernand. *Capitalism and Material Life 1400-1800,* tr. Miriam Kochan (New York: Harper & Row, 1974).

Campbell, Bernard G. *Human Evolution* (Chicago: Aldine, 1974; London: Heinemann Educational, 1967).

Camus, Albert. *The Plague,* tr. Stuart Gilbert (New York: Random House; London: Hamish Hamilton, 1948).

Count, Earl W. "The Biological Basis of Human Sociality," in *Culture,* ed. M. F. Ashley Montagu (New York: Oxford University, 1968).

DeVore, Irven, ed. *Primate Behavior* (New York and London: Holt, Rinehart and Winston, 1965).

Dobzhansky, Theodosius. *The Biology of Ultimate Concern* (New York: World, 1967; London: Rapp & Whiting, 1969).

Douglas, Mary. *Natural Symbols* (London: Barrie and Jenkins, 1973).

Dubos, René. *A God Within* (New York: Scribner's, 1972; London: Angus & Robertson, 1973).

Elkins, Stanley M. *Slavery* (Chicago: University of Chicago, 1959; 2d ed., Chicago and London: University of Chicago, 1969).

Frisch, Karl von. *Animal Architecture,* tr. Lisbeth Gombrich (New York: Harcourt Brace Jovanovich, 1974).

Frye, Northrop. *Anatomy of Criticism* (Princeton: Princeton University, 1957).

Fussell, Paul. *The Great War and Modern Memory* (New York and London: Oxford University, 1975).

Goffman, Erving. *The Presentation of Self in Everyday Life* (Garden City: Doubleday, Anchor Books 1959; London: Allen Lane, 1969).

———. *Asylums* (Chicago: Aldine, 1962; London: Penguin, 1970).

Hemingway, Ernest. *Death in the Afternoon* (New York: Scribner's, 1960; London: Penguin, 1971).

Hobbes, Thomas. *Leviathan* (New York: Bobbs-Merrill, 1958; London: Dent Everyman's, 1973).

Hoppe, Klaus D. "The Psychodynamics of Concentration Camp Victims," *The Psychoanalytic Forum,* Volume 1, No. 1, 1966, pp. 76-85.

Housepian, Marjorie. "The Unremembered Genocide," *Commentary,* XLII, September 1966, pp. 55-61.

Jaspers, Karl. *The Question of German Guilt,* tr. E. B. Ashton (New York: Dial, 1947).

Kummer, Hans. *Primate Societies* (Chicago: Aldine, 1971).

Lifton, Robert Jay. *Death in Life: Survivors of Hiroshima* (New York: Random House, 1967; London: Weidenfeld & Nicolson, 1968).

———. *History and Human Survival* (New York: Random House, 1970).

———. "Questions of Guilt," *Partisan Review,* XXXIX, Winter 1972, pp. 514-30.

Longinus. "On the Sublime," in *Criticism: The Major Texts,* ed. Walter Jackson Bate (New York: Harcourt Brace Jovanovich, 1970).

Lorenz, Konrad. *On Aggression,* tr. Marjorie Keer Wilson (New York: Harcourt, Brace & World; London: Methuen, 1966).

Luria, S. E. *Life: The Unfinished Experiment* (New York: Scribner's, 1973).

Malamud, Bernard. *The Fixer* (New York: Farrar, Straus & Giroux, 1966; London: Eyre & Spottiswoode, 1967).

Mao Tse-Tung. *Selected Military Writings of Mao Tse-Tung* (Peking: Foreign Languages, 1967).

Mauss, Marcel. *The Gift: Forms and Functions of Exchange in Archaic Societies,* tr. Ian Cunnison (London: Cohen & West, 1954; Routledge, 1969).

Mochulsky, Konstantin. *Dostoevsky: His Life and Work,* tr. Michael A. Minihan (Princeton: Princeton University, 1971).

Monod, Jacques. *Chance and Necessity,* tr. Austryn Wainhouse (New York: Knopf, 1971; London: Collins, 1972).

Moore, Barrington, Jr. *Reflections on the Causes of Human Misery* (Boston: Beacon; London: Allen Lane, 1972).

Nietzsche, Friedrich. *The Will to Power,* tr. Walter Kaufmann and R. J. Hollingdale (New York: Random House, 1967; London: Weidenfeld & Nicolson, 1968).

Paz, Octavio. *Claude Lévi-Strauss: An Introduction,* tr. J. S. Bernstein (Ithaca, N.Y.: Cornell University, 1970; London: Jonathan Cape, 1972).

Portmann, Adolf. *Animals as Social Beings* (New York: Viking; London: Hutchinson, 1961).

Rensch, Bernhard. *Biophilosophy,* tr. C. A. M. Sym (New York: Columbia University, 1971).

Ricœur, Paul. *The Symbolism of Evil,* tr. Emerson Buchanan (New York: Harper & Row, 1967).

Russell, Bertrand. *The Autobiography of Bertrand Russell 1914-1944* (New York: Bantam, 1969; London: Allen & Unwin, 1967-71).

Schopenhauer, Arthur. *On the Basis of Morality,* tr. E. F. J. Payne (New York: Bobbs-Merrill, 1965).

Skinner, B. F. *Beyond Freedom and Dignity* (New York: Knopf, 1971; London: Jonathan Cape, 1972).

Steiner, George. *In Bluebeard's Castle* (New Haven: Yale University; London: Faber & Faber, 1971).

Tiger, Lionel. *Men in Groups* (New York: Random House, 1969; London: Nelson, 1970).

Tiger, Lionel, and Fox, Robin. *The Imperial Animal* (New York: Holt, Rinehart and Winston, 1971; London: Secker & Warburg, 1972).

Tinbergen, N. *The Study of Instinct* (Oxford: Clarendon, 1951).

Waddington, C. H. *The Ethical Animal* (London: Allen & Unwin, 1960).

Wilson, E. O. *Sociobiology: The New Synthesis* (Cambridge: Harvard University, 1975).

Young, J. Z. *An Introduction to the Study of Man* (Oxford: Oxford University, 1971).